STREET FIGHTING YEARS

TARIQ ALI is a writer and filmmaker. He has written more than a dozen books on world history and politics – including *The Clash of Fundamentalisms*, *The Obama Syndrome*, *The Extreme Centre*, *The Dilemmas of Lenin*, and the novels of the Islam Quintet – as well as scripts for the stage and screen. He is an editor of *New Left Review* and lives in London.

STREET FIGHTING YEARS

An Autobiography of the Sixties

TARIQ ALI

VERSO

London • New York

This edition first published by Verso 2024
First published by Verso 2005
Original edition published by William Collins Sons & Co. 1987
Preface to the 2018 edition © Tariq Ali 2018
© Tariq Ali 1987

1 3 5 7 9 10 8 6 4 2

Verso
UK: 6 Meard Street, London W1F 0EG
US: 388 Atlantic Avenue, Brooklyn, NY 11217

versobooks.com

Verso is the imprint of New Left Books

ISBN-13: 978-1-80429-713-1
ISBN-13: 978-1-78663-602-7 (US EBK)
ISBN-13: 978-1-78663-601-0 (UK EBK)

British Library Cataloguing in Publication Data
A catalogue record for this book is available from the British Library

The Library of Congress Has Cataloged the First Edition as Follows:

Ali, Tariq.
    Street fighting years : an autobiography of the sixties / Tariq Ali.
        pages cm
    Rev. ed. of: London : Collins, 1987.
    Includes index.
    ISBN 1-84467-029-5 (pbk. : alk. paper)
1. History, Modern – 1945–1989. 2. Ali, Tariq. I. Title.
    D842.5.A44 2005
    322.4'2'092 – dc22
                    2004029921

Typeset in Bembo by YHT Ltd, London
Printed in the UK by CPI Group (UK) Ltd, Croydon, CR0 4YY

In memory of Ernest Mandel

*who always believed that the real meaning of
life lay in conscious participation in
the making of history*

By the same author

NON-FICTION

Pakistan: Military Rule or People's Power (1970)
1968 and After: Inside the Revolution (1978)
Can Pakistan Survive? (1982)
Revolution From Above: Where Is the Soviet Union Going? (1988)
The Clash of Fundamentalisms (2002)
The Nehrus and the Gandhis (New edition 2005)
The Obama Syndrome: Surrender at Home, War Abroad (2010)
The Extreme Centre: A Second Warning (2018)

FICTION

The Islam Quintet
Shadows of the Pomegranate Tree (1992)
The Book of Saladin (1998)
The Stone Woman (1999)
The Sultan of Palermo (2005)

The Fall-of-Communism Trilogy
Redemption (1991)
Fear of Mirrors (1998)

Contents

Preface to the New Edition

◆

What is it about anniversaries that compels us to mark them in some way? In the case of successful revolutions – English, French, Russian, Chinese, Vietnamese, Cuban – the reasons are obvious. But what of the upheavals that were drowned in blood? The 1857 armed rebellion against British colonial rule in India; the Paris Commune of 1871; the 1916 Easter Rising in Dublin; the Spartacist insurrection in Berlin, 1919; Che Guevara's doomed struggle in Bolivia, 1967. These events are often remembered for the remarkable form of struggle that emerged. Furthermore they have become invaluable in educating future generations to avoid repeating the same mistakes.

Where should we place the year 1968, or the period 1967–1975, within this constellation? There are no easy analogies. What distinguishes this period is its astonishing global scope. Every continent was affected, far beyond the well-rehearsed narratives of uprisings in Europe and the United States. In retrospect, it is clear to see that the most blood was, in fact, spilt in Vietnam, Mexico and Pakistan.

In the last of those examples, the military dictatorship was toppled after an escalating three-month struggle led by students, workers and other social strata. At that time, democracy was the pill that the military and civilian elite could not swallow, with inevitable results. A vicious civil war, unleashed by the military, saw the implosion of the Pakistani state. In the ensuing conflict, tens of thousands of Bengalis were butchered by their Muslim brethren from Western Pakistan. This forced a majority of the population to decamp and set up a new nation, Bangladesh.

The Tet Offensive, launched by the Vietnamese in January 1968, marked the beginning of the end of the American war in Vietnam. In April 1975 the US accepted defeat and withdrew their armies and close collaborators.

Ten days before the opening of the 1968 Olympics in Mexico City, the country exploded. Hundreds of thousands of Mexican students and workers marched against the regime. The image we remember is that of two African-American US athletes giving the clenched fist salute in solidarity on the podium after receiving gold and silver medals. Between four and five hundred people were shot dead by the military in the Plaza de las Tres Culturas in the Tlatelolco district of Mexico City. All the universities were occupied by the army. Graffiti proclaimed: 'The Mexican Army is the best educated in the world. It never leaves the University.'

There was to be no success in Europe, East or West. The closest a European country came to a situation of dual power was Portugal in 1974–75. But here Portuguese social democrats promised the masses radical socialism plus democracy. This was how they outwitted and defeated forces to their left – the Communist Party and far-left currents – who offered people who had already suffered seventy years of a right-wing dictatorship another variety in the shape of the 'dictatorship of the proletariat'. It was a strategic error that led to their marginalization. The social democrats, heavily funded by the Ebert Foundation, restored stability. To imagine, as the Portuguese Communists and the far-left groups did, that a revolution could happen without its features being specified was short-sighted. As if the invasion of Prague in August 1968 to crush 'socialism with a human face' had never happened.

Elsewhere, radical and anti-imperialist politics helped create the women's and gay liberation movements. The ideas of Lenin, Mao, Che and others spread through African-American youth, leading to, among other things, the formation of the Black Panther Party in the United States.

The most lasting impact has been that of the movements for sexual liberation, though the backlash refuses to disappear. Here, too, some of the demands of the gay movement have been incorporated by capitalist states: same-sex marriage, for instance, has become a prerequisite for adherence to the values of the neo-liberal elites in most of Europe and North America.

The once dominant socialist–feminist current of the women's movement is barely perceptible today, except during emergencies such as when defending truncated abortion rights in Poland and demanding a referendum on the subject in Ireland. In the United States of 2016 many older feminists saw their principal task to be propelling Hillary

Clinton into the White House; a case of identity subsuming politics. The younger generation of women were more steadfast in backing Sanders and not shy of stating why.

Black Lives Matter was much more in tune with black radicalism of the last century. Its activists made no secret of their hostility to the layer of corrupt black politicians fully incorporated into the Democratic Party and busy making money like most of their peers. In 2016, former presidential candidate Jesse Jackson was heckled off the stage in Ferguson when he tried to hustle for money for some dodgy project or other. These are signs of hope.

Nor has the attempt to resuscitate a radical left completely failed in Europe. Progress is uneven. Anti-capitalist politics, even at its most radical, has no alternative plan for a vision beyond contemporary capitalism. A revival of a left variant of social democracy has seen the rise of Corbyn in Britain, Mélenchon in France, and Iglesias in Spain, each with their own strengths and weaknesses, but posing a challenge to neo-liberal capitalism. A victory for any of these candidates could open up a new space for discussion and action beyond the present.

Serious and sustained intellectual work is a necessity to understand the world in which we live and to formulate an alternative that can win over a majority in every country and continent. As the late Edward Thompson wrote in reply to a militant in 1974 (a time when Britain was engulfed in a serious proletarian upheaval led by the miners): 'There is nothing more "real" about the shop-floor than the library. Both are points of production. Both can become unreal in different ways ... the socialist movement every five years puts out to sea bravely in rotten boats whose planks haven't been caulked for fifty years, sinks within sight of the shore and struggles back to find some more rotten hulls.'

This book was first written for the publisher William Collins in 1987; it was subsequently reprinted by Verso with a new introduction in 2005. This edition has been reprinted for the fiftieth anniversary of 1968. Whether it is of any use is not for me to say. Of the dreams we had when we were young, all I can say is that though I sometimes forget, I rarely regret.

Tariq Ali,
London, November 2017

Introduction

◆

Chronicles from Now and Then

oh unfortunate generation
you'll weep, but lifeless tears
because perhaps you won't even know how to return to
what, not having had, you couldn't even lose;
poor Calvinist generation as at the bourgeoisie's origins
adolescently pragmatic, childishly active
you sought salvation in organisation
(which can't produce anything but more organisation)
and you've spent the days of your youth
speaking the jargon of bureaucratic democracy
never departing from the repetition of formulas,
for organising can be signified not through words
but through formulas, yes,
you'll find yourself using the same paternal authority,
at the mercy of that ineffable power that willed you against power,
unfortunate generation!
Growing old, I saw your heads filled with grief
where a confused idea swirled, an absolute certainty,
an assumption of heroes destined not to die –
oh unfortunate young people, who've seen within reach
a marvellous victory that didn't exist!

Pier Paolo Pasolini, born in Bologna in 1922, the year Mussolini's fascists took power, wrote this poem in 1970. Slightly unfair to my generation and the many comrades who have not abandoned hope, but prescient.

Iraq Is Arabic For Vietnam

History rarely repeats itself, either as tragedy or farce, but it echoes. On 15 February 2003, crowds chanted in city squares and climbed atop monuments. Hoarse, eloquent school students furiously denounced the President of the United States and his British poodle for threatening conflict in Iraq. All over the world and in every major capital there were heated and spirited meetings to denounce the unjust and immoral war that lay ahead. The demonstrators failed to stop the war but they had revived memories of another period. The echoes were ever present.

Some months later, after Baghdad had just been occupied, pro-war politicians and toadying journalists, who had repeatedly lied to the public, were celebrating what they thought had been an easy victory. They were busy manufacturing images that portrayed the invasion of a sovereign state as liberation. Then the resistance in Iraq began to strike back and the bogus argument used to justify the war fell apart like lumps of dried cow-dung. The echoes became noisier and in New York the anti-war people produced an anticipatory bumper sticker: *Iraq Is Arabic For Vietnam*. It wasn't exactly true, but a nice thought nonetheless.

I hear more echoes in the fall of 2004 while visiting the United States on a pre-election lecture tour. In Madison, after an anti-war meeting, there was a small get-together at the apartment of my host, Allen Ruff, the founding-father of Rainbow, one of the best independent bookstores in the mid-West. Prior to the meeting, the sound engineer, a bearded Mexican-American, came up to me and whispered proudly that his son, a twenty-five-year-old Marine, had just returned from a tour of duty in the besieged Iraqi city of Fallujah and might show up. He didn't come to the meeting, but joined us later with a civilian friend. He could see the room was packed with anti-war, anti-Bush activists. Wisconsin was a 'swing state' and in one corner a fierce debate was raging as to whether or not it was kosher to vote Kerry. His own friend was voting against Bush.

The young, crew-cut Marine, G, with bristling muscles, spoke in a calm, staccato voice, like a tocsin attempting to rouse us with his tales of duty and valour. I asked what had made him join the Marine Corps? He became slightly tense but was confident in his response: 'There was no choice for people like me. If I had stayed here I would have been killed on the streets or ended up in the penitentiary serving life. The Marine Corps saved my life. They trained me, looked after me, and changed me completely. If I died in Iraq, at least it would be the enemy that killed me. In Fallujah all I could think of was how to make sure that the men under my command were kept safe. That's all. Most of the kids demonstrating for peace have no problems here. They go to college, they demonstrate and soon they forget it all as they move into well-paid jobs. Not so easy for people like me. I think there should be a draft. Why should poor kids be the only ones out there. Out of all the Marines I work with, perhaps four or five percent are gung-ho flag-wavers. The rest of us are doing a job, we do it well and hope we get out without being KIA [killed in action] or wounded.' He surprised his father when he added that if Bush were re-elected he might re-enlist and go back for a second tour of duty. When his father protested he suggested they save the argument for later.

We talked for nearly an hour as he consumed water by the jarfuls. I was impressed but chilled by the ease with which he appeared to have imbibed the Marine code, and yet I could not help feeling that he and his comrades were having another experience, seething with unknown currents of which his anti-war father and the rest of us were unaware.

Later, G sat on a sofa between two older men, with whom I had been speaking prior to his arrival. If he didn't know who they were, he soon found out. They were both ex-soldiers. Their ideas had been defined and refined in the wars they had fought and had given them the civic courage needed to take on the task of educating their peers back at home, men and women whose lack of knowledge of the outside world – an indictment of both primary education facilities and the media – they found frightening.

Sitting on the left of the young Marine was Will Williams. Now sixty years old, he came out of central Mississippi and enlisted in the army in 1962 when he was seventeen – his mother signed the papers.

Like G, he too had been a rebellious youth. He was convinced that if he had not left Mississippi when he did the Ku Klux Klan or some other racist gang would have killed him. He, too, claimed that the military 'saved my life'. Following a stint in Germany, he was sent to Vietnam and ended up doing two tours of duty. He volunteered to return after his first tour, having been alienated by the anti-war movement on his return home. Wounded in action, he received a Purple Heart and two bronze stars as well as the highest decoration awarded by the puppet regime in South Vietnam. While still there he began his 'turn around', following a rebellion by black troops at Camranh Bay protesting racism within the US Army. Today he says that it was Daniel Ellsberg and the release of the 'Pentagon Papers' – which revealed the lies they tell to drag young men to war – was instrumental in his transformation. Following a period of difficulty 'readjusting', Williams went through a lengthy self-education project. An autodidact, he read deeply in politics and history. Realizing that 'we were being lied to again', he and his life-long companion of over forty-three years, his wife Dot, decided they could not remain silent in their opposition to the war on Iraq. They joined the anti-war movement at its inception, bringing their Gospel choir voices to rallies and demonstrations, including the meeting which I had just addressed. Active in the Madison chapter of Vets for Peace, Will Williams has become well known as an articulate and respected anti-war voice, able to stand up as a Vietnam combat vet and an African-American before audiences who would normally be hostile to the average 'peacenik'.

On G's right there was seated Clarence Kailin, ninety years old last summer and one of the few remaining survivors of the Abraham Lincoln Brigade that had fought on the Republican side in the Spanish Civil War. He, too, has been active in the movement against the war in Iraq. 'In mid-January, 1937, six of us from my home state of Wisconsin decided to go help defend the Republic. Our passports were stamped "not valid for travel in Spain". So, fearing arrest, our trip was made in considerable secrecy – even from our families. I was a truck driver, then an infantry man and for a short time a stretcher-bearer. I saw the brutality of war up close. Of the five Wisconsinites who came to Spain with me, two were killed.'

A voracious reader to this day, Kailin is now almost totally deaf, but obstinately resists the hearing aid – which gives him a natural advantage. Unable to hear anyone else, he dominates every conversation. Despite everything he has experienced, Clarence believes that there is an innate goodness in people, which is why so many can break with unworthy pasts. As the men were speaking, I watched from a distance and wondered what G. made of the two veterans.

100,000 Funerals

The first scientific study of the human cost of the Iraq war suggests that at least 100,000 Iraqis have lost their lives since their country was invaded in March 2003.

More than half of those who died were women and children killed in air strikes, researchers say. Previous estimates have put the Iraqi death toll at around 10,000 – ten times the 1,000 members of the British, American and multi-national forces who have died so far. But the study, published in *The Lancet*, suggested that Iraqi casualties could be as much as 100 times the coalition losses. It was also savagely critical of the failure by coalition forces to count Iraqi casualties ...

Les Roberts of the Bloomberg School of Public Health at Johns Hopkins University in Baltimore, Maryland, said: 'Making conservative assumptions, we think that about 100,000 excess deaths or more have happened since the 2003 invasion of Iraq. Violence accounted for most of the excess deaths, and air strikes from coalition forces accounted for most violent deaths.' The Lancet, which published the research in its online edition yesterday, said it was 'a remarkable piece of work by a courageous team of scientists', which had been completed under testing circumstances.

Jeremy Laurance and Colin Brown in the *Independent*
London, 29 October 2004

Previous to *The Lancet* report, the highest figure for civilian casualties was 36,000, and when I had mentioned it in an article for the *Guardian* it had been challenged. Now we know. When the World Health Organization claimed that that the sanctions against Iraq had cost the lives of at least half a million children, the then US Secretary of State, Madeleine Albright, told CBS that it was a price worth paying. No doubt the debased politicians and even more debased apologists in the media think the same of the hundred thousand killed in 2003–4. Nice of them to be so generous with Iraqi lives.

Heroes/Villains

Why do the 1960s still arouse so much suspicion and hatred? Why do politicians, prelates, pundits and professors rubbish an epoch that means little to the new generations? Could it be that the events of that time still trigger unsettling memories – political, sexual, social, cultural – that challenge the conformism of today? Do they fear that a new generation might go beyond that past and threaten the new order with 'marvellous victories'? Whatever the reason, the sixties refuse to recede. At the first sign of 'trouble' – students demonstrating against loans, trade unionists defending the social welfare state, anti-war demonstrators protesting the occupation in Iraq and Palestine – a lazy journalist reaches for the sixties' file.

I am often at the receiving end of the same boring question. How does it compare to the sixties? Well, it doesn't. Each generation is unique. What they say and how they act is determined by the time in which they live. During the sixties there were heroes and villains for both sides of the divide. The heroes of today are largely anonymous – peasants, workers, unemployed slum-dwellers on every continent whose anger sometimes explodes to remind us that all the old problems remain. The villains remain the same and rule most of the world.

And yet there are other reasons for the interest as well. There is nostalgia, which is both unproductive and distorted, reducing the sixties to lifestyle and ignoring the politics. Many young people are drawn to the period for another reason. They want the truth which they rarely get at school or in the mainstream media. Who were the Black Panthers and were they really wiped out by state repression? And the Weather Underground. Was it real? The Tupamaros in Uruguay, the student insurrectionaries in Paris and Lahore, the massacre in Mexico City . . . The history textbooks are silent.

Vulture Capitalism

During the last two decades of the 20th century the world was turned upside down again. As each alternative to its rule crumbled into dust, Capital and its worshippers celebrated a victory that seemed definitive. For the left it was a defeat of historic proportions. Utopia was erased from the map of the world. In its place there emerged a Washington Consensus, embodying a neo-liberal dystopia: The new world order was presented as something that was both pure and perfect. Privatization, deregulation, the forced entry of capital into the hitherto sacred precincts of health, education, housing and public service broadcasting have become an unchallengeable norm. Rationality can only be individual rationality. The language of neo-liberalism infiltrated virtually every institution and affected the thinking of many who oppose the new order. The realm of freedom is now necessarily linked to rampant, unadulterated capitalism. In this brave new world official politics is little more than concentrated economics. War a continuation of both.

The fall of communism has been written about and discussed at length, but the collapse of European social democracy is less frequently addressed. Its leaders, men of moderate cast, have promoted neo-liberal policies with the fervour of new converts, the British variant boasting openly that New Labour would go further than Thatcherism and then justifying the boast. The redistribution of wealth, once a time-honoured social-democratic goal, is now regarded as unacceptable. The state is either a market-state or it must not exist.

The differences between centre-right and centre-left political parties in Europe and elsewhere are now confined to rhetoric. In terms of policy there is no basic difference. A tax on profits made by pure speculation? Unthinkable. Restrictions on the mobility of capital (a mobility that wreaked havoc in large swathes of Europe, Latin America, Asia and Africa)? Forbidden by new laws and policed by multilateral institutions. The Multilateral Agreement on Investment (MAI) has been designed exclusively to defend global corporate interests from national governments, thus further reducing the democratic and social rights of citizens. In this world of vulture capitalism it is a case of the survival of the fittest, that is, of those who have the firepower to enforce these new rules. Pierre Bourdieu, deeply hostile to the new dispensation and whose death in 2002 deprived the new social movements of one of their most gifted defenders, described the process well:

> In this way, a Darwinian world emerges – it is the struggle of all against all at all levels of the hierarchy, which finds support through everyone clinging to their job and organization under conditions of insecurity, suffering, and stress. Without a doubt, the practical establishment of this world of struggle would not succeed so completely without the complicity of all of the *precarious arrangements* that produce insecurity and of the existence of a *reserve army of employees rendered docile by these social processes that make their situations precarious*, as well as by the permanent threat of unemployment. This reserve army exists at all levels of the hierarchy, even at the higher levels, especially among managers. The ultimate foundation of this entire economic order placed under the sign of freedom is in effect the *structural violence* of unemployment, of the insecurity of job tenure and the menace of layoff that it implies. The condition of the 'harmonious' functioning of the individualist microeconomic model is a mass phenomenon, the existence of a reserve army of the unemployed.

Perhaps it is this that explains why the epoch of the sixties continues to loom large. It marked the climax of a revolt against authority and tradition, which the Russian Revolution had initiated. Its originality lay in the fact that it marked an entire generation and every continent – it was the first truly global movement from below. In retrospect it is easy to see that the revolt had its limitations. There were too many flourishes, too few serious calls to arms, but despite this the ideas advanced by the movements and political parties of that time were audacious, the causes espoused both utopian and real: proletarian power in France and Italy, socialist democracy in Czechoslovakia and Poland; national liberation in Vietnam, Angola, Mozambique, Guinea, South Africa and Palestine; democratic revolutions in Portugal and Pakistan; armed struggles inspired by Fidel Castro and Che Guevara throughout Latin America; newer social movements that demanded equal rights for women, sexual freedom for all and the repeal of the archaic judicial codes that buttressed a repressive social and sexual order. A new cinema resulting from the turbulence: Godard, Pasolini, Fassbinder, Pontecorvo and Costa-Gavras, Agnes Varda, Mrinal Sen, Glauber Rocha, Ken Loach, amongst others.

It was this political culture that formed the attitudes of both defenders and detractors. The sixties (1967–75) saw few political victories – the Vietnamese triumph against the might of the American Empire, and the toppling of dictatorships in Pakistan and Portugal, marked the high-tide of the movement. To these must be added the gains achieved by women and gay people in North America and Western Europe. But already by the end of the seventies the tide had begun to recede. Just as it is not possible for even the best long-distance sea swimmer to separate himself from the waves, so it is difficult to make progress in a world dominated by vulture capitalism. Against strong winds and treacherous currents it is only possible to cover short stretches. Some who go with the tide disappear completely. Others end up as flotsam and jetsam on a safe beach.

And so it happened that some, who were once the defenders of sixties' political culture (and, incidentally, amongst its worst 'offenders'), are now establishment politicians in Western Europe, North and South America and in Brazil, Pakistan, Sri Lanka, India, Japan, etc. Others occupy important positions in the media. They beached safely. The worst of them in the West rarely miss an opportunity to urinate on their past, blaming 'social problems' and other failures on attitudes and social policies formed and implemented in the 'sixties'. The period that appeals to them is the sixties of the nineteenth century, when imperialism reigned abroad, hypocrisy and corruption at home.

The decades that followed the sixties saw a renewal of the cold war that ended with the collapse and break-up of the Soviet Union and the restoration of capitalism in Eastern Europe and China. The social cost of all this for the less privileged sections of society was high. In virtually every case former bureaucrats or their children became the new capitalists and eagerly embraced the Washington Consensus. Poland, Bulgaria and the Ukraine – genetically doomed to satellite status – loyally supplied contingents for the war in Iraq as they once had to invade Czechoslovakia in August 1968. Another echo.

On one occasion (it was either in Australia or the US) I was saying something to this effect when an angry questioner denounced me for never mentioning the evolution of various former members of the editorial committee of the *New Left Review*. 'Your lot weren't that pure either.' To which I reply that nobody is pure except the religious believer, and s/he too is often a hypocrite. We all have our contradictions. As the capitalist flood tides engulfed the world and new ethnic/religious solidarities arose, how could the *NLR* remain unaffected? Former editors went in different directions. But what is more important than any individual is the institution. Some of us did not panic. We kept the magazine afloat in bad times, opposed the 'humanitarian wars', defended the Palestinians, denounced the sanctions against Iraq, and thus prepared our readers for the recent invasion. Unlike others, they were not too surprised by the emergence of a resistance against the US occupation. Of that, too, we are proud.

Homage I

Between 1984 and 1998 much of my time was spent producing documentaries and films for Channel 4 television and writing a few novels. Regarded then as Europe's most innovative TV station, Channel 4 had been set up in 1982 via a parliamentary remit that insisted the new channel cater for minority tastes in politics and culture. Originally nurtured by old Labour (Philip Whitehead and

Anthony Smith were important influences), it was Thatcher's Deputy Prime Minister, William Whitelaw, who pushed the project through Parliament. Would the deadly New Labour trio of Blair, Mandelson and Campbell have done the same? I doubt it.

The first Chief Executive, Jeremy Isaacs, was one of the most gifted broadcasters of his generation, not easily intimidated by corporate managers or government. It was his conviction that the creative experience would be enriching and rewarding for the viewer only if producers and directors were not interfered with too much. I remember being summoned to see him just before *Bandung File*, a weekly current affairs show for which Darcus Howe and I were responsible. Isaacs was blunt: 'I know you will make trouble. I want you to make trouble. But if you are producing a show that could get us into trouble legally, you must warn the Channel in advance so that our lawyers can help you. That's all.' And when we exposed the corruption at the heart of the BCCI (Bank of Credit and Commerce International) the Channel 4 lawyers backed us all the way.

It was usually like that, but once Isaac's successor, Michael Grade, decided that the channel should started selling its own advertising, the marketing men and the schedulers moved in, marking the beginning of the end of creative commissioning. Grade was strong enough to resist them, but his successor, Michael Jackson, was the Peter Mandelson of broadcasting, in love with himself and the market, though not necessarily in that order. The speed with which Channel 4 moved downhill, becoming exploitative and reactionary, took its viewers by surprise. To this day when I show young people videos from the early period of Channel 4, the response is amazement: 'God, you could show that on television?' One reason why Michael Moore's documentaries are so successful is because of what has happened to television. In the eighties, both *Bowling for Columbine* and a film like *Fahrenheit 9/11* would have been commissioned and shown on Channel 4.

As late as 1992, a few commissioning editors were still independent-minded enough to be interested in slightly wacky ideas. Not all of them had become the grasping, meddlesome timeservers and opportunists of today. I was reminded of all this in October 2000 as I was driving through southern England and sighted a once-familiar signpost. Dungeness, its nuclear reactor and the Kent coast were only a few miles away. For a moment I was tempted. It was a miserable, autumnal afternoon. The rain had been constant that whole day. Nature defeated sentimentality. I was anxious to reach London, but all the way back I was thinking of a summer's day many years ago, when I had driven to Dungeness to see the filmmaker, artist and gardener, Derek Jarman.

When I proposed to Gwyn Pritchard, then in charge of education programming, that a quartet on philosophy might be timely, he was excited by the idea. Over lunch the following week I suggested four chamber epics constructed around the lives and ideas of Socrates, Spinoza, Locke and Wittgenstein. He agreed to four scripts, insisted that I write Spinoza myself, alerted me to the fact that his budgets were small and warned me not to exceed £200,000 per film. We did the deal.

By the time all the other scripts were written (Howard Brenton/ *Socrates*, David Edgar/*Locke*, Terry Eagleton/*Wittgenstein*) and approved, we had already completed filming *Spinoza* with Henry Goodman in the title role. Gwyn Pritchard had left Channel 4. His successor was enthusiastic, but, unable to assert her authority intellectually, she did so bureaucratically by dumping the old Greek. The only reason poor old Socrates was discarded was a change in management in the education department. This made it necessary to ensure that what remained was really good. But who would direct *Wittgenstein*? Chris Spencer had filmed Spinoza beautifully but the style was naturalistic. Wittgenstein needed to be different – edgy and slightly surreal.

On an impulse I rang Derek Jarman. I had never met him before, but greatly admired two of his films – *Caravaggio* and *Edward II*. After speaking to him that morning I went out and bought a copy of *Modern Nature*. I read it in the office for the rest of the day and finished it the next morning. I enjoyed it enormously. He was much more than a filmmaker or a gay saint. He was interested in ideas.

I made the call, according to Jarman's diary, on 19 May 1992. His enthusiasm reassured me. I was on the right track. He confided that he had always wanted to make a film on the philosopher, but had never got beyond the title – 'Loony Ludwig'. I sent him Terry Eagleton's script, which was definitely not 'Loony Ludwig', but very witty and full of ideas. He read it and rang back the next day. He wanted to make the film. A week later I drove to Dungeness and found Prospect Cottage by the sea. The garden was, as every visitor had claimed, a work of art, but my enjoyment was marred by the knowledge that we were permanently overlooked by a giant nuclear reactor. It was then that his illness really hit me. Nobody else I know would deliberately choose to live so close to a nuclear reactor. Derek no longer cared. AIDS would carry him off sooner rather than later and he enjoyed living life on the edge. He grinned as he told me that it was so lovely to swim on a deserted beach. 'In the summer I often run out of the cottage naked and straight into the sea. It's radioactive all right. Friends have tested it with Geiger counters. Sometimes the reactor OD's and the whole place lights up. It's really sensational. You know what I mean?' I did.

We spent most of the day discussing Wittgenstein. He knew exactly what he wanted. No Merchant–Ivory nonsense. No English Heritage atrocities. Leaving aside our aesthetic sensibilities, we simply did not have the money to make a chocolate-box movie. The film, like the philosophy, had to be austere. Wittgenstein would record his life in front of black drapes straight to the camera. As Derek notes in *Smiling in Slow Motion*: '... the visualisation must mirror the work – no competition from objects'. He was sure he would make it work. He asked which of his films I had seen and liked. I named them. He laughed. After a pause I confessed that *Sebastianne* had not succeeded in keeping me awake. It was sweet lemonade. *Caravaggio* and *Edward II* were much stronger stuff.

'Why did you make *Sebastianne*?' I asked him. The reply was instant. 'There was only one real reason. I wanted to be the first to show a hard-on on the screen. Do you know what I mean?' We discussed the production of *Wittgenstein*. It was the only time he mentioned his illness. 'You better put an extra Director in the budget. The insurers will insist on it. His name is Ken Butler. He shot the best two scenes in *Edward II* when I had to go into hospital.' He looked so well that day that it was difficult to imagine him in hospital. As I was about to leave I suggested to him that *Wittgenstein* should really shock his fans. 'What do you mean? What do you mean?' 'Not a single bum or willie. Let the audiences suffer from withdrawal symptoms.' He threw his head back and laughed. 'It's a deal. It'll make a change.'

It did. And so it came about that the only sex in *Wittgenstein* is a single chaste kiss on the lips exchanged between Wittgenstein and Johnnie. Today the ratings-driven controllers of our TV channels, were they ever to take such an idea seriously, would insist on maximum bum/willie exposure.

We talked on the phone over the next few days and then I returned to Dungeness, this time by train. We went, as he records in his last diaries, to have lunch in the pub at Lydd and talked about everything. There was no God. There were no ghosts. He was prepared for blindness and death. It did not frighten him. He said something that has always stayed with me: 'If you want nothing, hope for nothing and fear nothing, you can never be an artist.' He hated the monarchy and savaged the honours system. He was livid with Ian McKellen for accepting a knighthood and entering No. 10 Downing Street. I was amused, but not in the least surprised to note the following entry in his diary. This is the voice I remember so well: 'Vivienne Westwood accepts an OBE, dipsy bitch. The silly season's with us: our punk friends accept their little medals of betrayal, sit in their vacuous salons and destroy the creative – like the woodworm in my dresser, which I will paint with insecticide tomorrow. I would love to place a man-sized insectocutor, lit with royal-blue, to burn up this clothes-moth and her like.'

I had seen a reference in *Modern Nature* to a trip he made to Pakistan and questioned him on it. It emerged that his father had been a senior airforce officer in India and had been seconded to help establish the Pakistan Air Force after independence in 1947. Throughout the fifties, Derek had spent part of the summer holidays in the Himalayan foothills in Northern Pakistan. The Air Force had a special holiday resort in Kalabagh, two miles north of Nathiagali where my family spent every summer to escape the heat of the plains. Those were idyllic months. As teenagers we climbed mountains went for twenty-mile walks, played tennis, mooned constantly over the girls, trying desperately to draw them into our fantasies. There was a freedom in the mountains untouched in those days by urban inhibitions. The thought that a young Jarman had been only a few miles away amused both of us. He had not discovered his sexuality at the time and roared when I told him that homosexuality in that part of Pakistan was very pronounced. The more snobby locals traced it back to the Greek Generals and soldiers left behind after Alexander's conquests. 'If you had shown the slightest interest, Derek,' I told him, 'there would have been a queue outside your cottage.'

As we began preparations to film *Wittgenstein* he moved into the Bandung offices in Kentish Town, with Ken Butler at his side. Scripts were rewritten. Actors were auditioned. Most of them were people he'd worked with before and there was always a very special place in his heart for Tilda Swinton. 'If only she'd been a boy', he would mutter wistfully. Those were joyous days. We were short of money. The BFI helped out, but not enough. Derek was enraged. 'They've just given X a million. A million to make crap and we can't even get a few hundred thousand.' He asked me to ring a Japanese producer who was 'always good for fifty thousands or so.' Takashi did not let us down. Still there wasn't enough to make a film that could be shown on the big screen. In order to make it happen people worked for Derek virtually for free, including Sandy Powell who designed the stunning costumes.

During the actual filming we were all amazed. His energy was staggering. He drew on all his reserves and worked twelve-hour days for two whole weeks. Ken Butler was never needed though his presence cheered us all. Throughout this period, Arif, Bandung's in-house cameraman, recorded Jarman at work. There are fifteen hours of tape. I watched some of them for the first time recently to refresh my own memory. It was as I had remembered. The zest for life dominates each tape. We are in the pre-production stages of *Wittgenstein*, but he's been captured on tape ringing New York to discuss a new film, set in the Deep South. Then he sees the camera and laughs. He's been caught out.

After the film was finished we stayed in touch. I went to the preview of *Blue*, laughing to myself as sundry celebrities whispered to each other in bewilderment. They couldn't believe that all they would ever see was a blue screen with a stunning soundtrack. The idea had occurred to him when he was temporarily blinded in hospital. It was the colour he saw when eye-drops were put in his eyes. It was the Yves Klein blue. Another film idea was born and executed. He wrote: 'The key to *Blue* was to do away with the images altogether, and to integrate the personal by integrating diary entries into the script.' It worked.

Still he refused to stop working. Early one morning he rang me in a state of great excitement. An idea had occurred to him. Later that day, over lunch in a greasy-spoon Chinese in Soho's Lisle Street, we discussed *The Raft of the Medusa*. He wanted a film based on the Gericault painting. It would be a film about death. The people on the raft would be AIDS victims. He wanted me to get a commission immediately. The following morning I rang George Faber, Head of Drama at the BBC. To his enormous credit he commissioned a script the following day. Work began. We used to meet and talk. I was somewhat apprehensive of a whole film devoted to death. A new biography of J. Edgar Hoover had just appeared which revealed that he had always been a homosexual and a secret transvestite. We laughed and laughed. I suggested that the *Raft* might take a surreal turn. A limo surrounded by G-men enters the studio. Out steps Hoover in a stunning red dress and orders his cops to arrest the Director. I suggested it might lighten the mood. This excited him enormously. 'You're right. You're right. Let's do it. A *hommage* to Buñuel. Know what I mean?'

Some months later I got a letter from the St. Petersburg Film Festival. They wanted to show *Wittgenstein* and were inviting Derek and me to introduce the film. I informed them that he was dead and I did not wish to travel alone.

The New Missionaries

The fall of the Berlin Wall did not usher in a new era of peace dividends and social-democratic bliss. Vulture capitalism was on the march and new wars soon began. In terms of lives and dislocation, the citizens of Rwanda, Chechnya and the former Yugoslavia paid the highest price. The austerity programmes imposed on the latter by the IMF created the objective conditions for the rise of an ugly nationalism in Serbia and Croatia, exploited by the dominant EU powers for their own purposes. The break-up of the country affected every nationality adversely. The Bosnians became the target of Serb and Croat revanchism as competing armies fought each other and the Muslims.

The Serb and Croat armies and the irregulars attached to them committed atrocities (Srebrenica and Mostar), but the Western powers, for their own reasons, chose to highlight those of the Serbs alone. Since Croatia was considered an ally, the Bosnian Muslims were pressured into an alliance with Zagreb. Simultaneously the United States entered the conflict, first indirectly by flying in Wahhabi war veterans from Kabul to shore-up the Bosnian army militarily and ideologically, and subsequently by despatching its own soldiery. The partition of the country was sealed by the establishment of Bosnia as a UN/US Protectorate occupied by foreign troops. Wrecked by a civil war not of their own making, the secular Muslims of Bosnia watched the social fabric of their region destroyed. Will Sarajevo ever be the same again?

I have always felt that the break-up of Yugoslavia was an avoidable tragedy. It was not simply the rogue quality of Milošević and Tudjman that led to disaster. A marginally more thoughtful European Union could have intervened with massive aid and conditional entry to the EU. This might well have averted an ugly civil conflict. Others, members of the cult that worships accomplished facts, saw the disintegration exclusively as the result of national oppression by the Serbs. And the Croats were merely demanding the right to national self-determination. According to this view, the EU and US were disinterested parties acting purely out of humanitarian motives. In which case, as some asked at the time, why was there no intervention in Rwanda where an actual genocide was taking place in contrast to an ugly civil war marked by ethnic cleansings. These reminded me of the Partition of India in 1947 when nearly two million innocents died in the movement of populations and carefully orchestrated killings by both sides: one of the least recalled episodes of the 20th century. Strange that nobody refers to it as genocide.

In reality the motives of Western intervention in Yugoslavia became clearer in the case of Kosovo. The Serbian leadership had agreed to the deal being suggested at Rambouillet that would have led to the withdrawal of every single Yugoslav soldier from Kosovo, but Clinton wanted a war to justify the expansion of NATO and establish a quiescent regime in Belgrade, an aim that was achieved after the bombing of Yugoslav cities and with Russian collaboration. Kosovo became a new UN/US Protectorate and Serbia was now open to corporate capital investments. In return for Russian support in the Balkans, first Yeltsin and subsequently Putin were left alone to get on with the task of pacifying Chechnya. Its capital Groszny was virtually razed to the ground and nearly 100,000 Chechens have been killed. The total casualties in Kosovo were under 3000. Some humans do not qualify for 'humanitarian interventions'.

In the days of the old European Empires, the churches and kirks played their part in helping to cement Western domination in Asia, Africa and Latin America. The missionaries of modern imperialism are the NGO brigades. Like their predecessors they try to soften the impact of the new order. The new Archbishops are Professors of Human Rights on US campuses. The sacred is now the secular. Civil society is the new *Regnum Dei* (the Kingdom of God). Different times, different people, different needs, similar processes.

Empire Loyalism

9/11. Exactly one year before the hijackers hit the Pentagon, Chalmers Johnson, a distinguished American academic, one-time senior analyst for the CIA, and staunch supporter of the US during the wars in Korea and Vietnam, tried to alert his fellow-citizens to the dangers that now lay ahead. In his book *Blowback: The Costs and Consequences of American Empire* he offered a trenchant critique of his country's post-cold war imperial policies: 'Blowback', he prophesied, 'is shorthand for saying that a nation reaps what it sows, even if it does not fully know or understand what it has sown. Given its wealth and power, the United States will be a prime recipient in the foreseeable future of all of the more expectable forms of blowback, particularly terrorist attacks against Americans in and out of the armed forces anywhere on earth, including within the United States.'

Whereas Johnson utilized his past – as a senior state-intellectual from within the heart of the American establishment – to warn us of the dangers inherent in the imperial pursuit of economic and military domination, a few former critics of imperialism found themselves trapped by the debris of September 11. I am not, in this instance, referring to the *belligerati* – Salman Rushdie, Martin Amis and chums – ever-present in the liberal press on both sides of the Atlantic. They might well shift again. Rushdie's decision to pose for the cover of a French magazine draped in the Stars and Stripes could be a temporary aberration. What concerns me more is another layer: men and women who were once intensely involved in left-wing activities. It has been a short march for some of them: from the outer fringes of radical politics to the antechambers of the State Department. Like many converts, they display an aggressive self-confidence. Having honed their polemical and ideological skills within the left, they now deploy them against their old friends. This is why they have become the useful idiots of the Empire. They will be used and dumped. A few, no doubt, hope to travel further and occupy the space vacated by Chalmers Johnson, but they should be warned: there is already a very long queue. Others still dream of becoming the Somali, Pakistani, Iraqi or Persian equivalents of the Afghan puppet, Hamid Karzai. They, too, might be disappointed. Transcontinental transplants are expensive. Operations can go wrong and, more to the point, the disaster in Iraq has had a sobering effect globally.

What unites the new Empire loyalists is an underlying belief that, despite certain flaws, the military and economic power of the United States represents the only emancipatory project and, for that reason, has to be supported against all those who challenge its power. A few prefer Clinton-as-Caesar rather than Bush, but recognize this as a trivial self-indulgence. Deep down they know the Empire always stands above its leaders.

What they forget is that Empires always act in their own self-interest. The British Empire cleverly exploited the anti-slavery campaigns to colonize Africa, just as Washington uses the humanitarian hand-wringing of NGOs and the *bien pensants* to fight its new wars today. September 11 has been blatantly used by the American Empire to re-map the world. European pieties irritate Cheney, Rumsfeld, Rice and Wolfowitz. They laugh in Washington when they hear European politicians talk of revitalising the United Nations. There are 187 member-states of the UN. In 141 of these there is now a US military presence. Imperial power is buttressed by creating satrapies that accept its economic priorities and strategic control. Neo-liberal economics, imposed by the IMF mullahs, have reduced countries in every continent to penury and brought their populations to the edge of despair. The social democracy that appeared as an attractive option during the cold war no longer exists. The powerlessness of democratic parliaments and the politicians who inhabit them to change anything has begun to discredit democracy and institutionalise apathy. When in the British general election of 2000 voter participation fell to its lowest ever, a New Labour leader (Gordon Brown) and the Editor of the *Times Literary Supplement* (Ferdinand Mount) both opined that the reason for this was that people were happy with the existing order.

At a time when much of the world is beginning to tire of being 'emancipated' by the United States, too many liberals have been numbed into silence. One of the most attractive aspects of the United States has always been the layers of dissent that have flourished underneath the surface. I never tire of explaining to some of Osama's sympathisers why the Generals in the Pentagon suffered a far greater blow (than 9/11) in the '70s, when tens of thousands of serving and former GIs demonstrated in front of the building in their uniforms and medals, opposed the war and publicly declared their hope that the Vietnamese would win. The new Empire loyalists, currently helping to snuff out this honourable tradition, are only creating the conditions for more blowbacks.

Homage II

Edward Said (1935–2003) was a longstanding friend and comrade. We first met in 1972, at a seminar in New York. Even in those turbulent times, one of the features that distinguished him from the rest of us was his immaculate dress sense: everything was meticulously chosen, down to the socks. It is almost impossible to visualize him any other way. At a conference in his honour in Beirut in 1997, Edward insisted on accompanying Elias Khoury and myself for a swim. As he walked out in his swimming trunks, I asked why the towel did not match. 'When in Rome', he replied, airily; but that evening, as he read an extract from the Arabic manuscript of his memoir *Out of Place,* his attire was faultless. It remained so till the end, throughout his long battle with leukaemia.

Over the last eleven years one had become so used to his illness – the regular hospital stays, the willingness to undergo trials with the latest drugs, the refusal to accept defeat – that one began to think him indestructible. In 2002, purely by chance, I met Said's doctor in New York. In response to my questions, he replied that there was no medical explanation for Edward's survival. It was his indomitable spirit as a fighter, his will to live, that had preserved him for so long. Said travelled everywhere. He spoke, as always, of Palestine, but also of the unifying capacities of the three cultures, which he would insist had a great deal in common. The monster was devouring his insides but those who came to hear him could not see the process, and we who knew preferred to forget. When the cursed cancer finally took him the shock was intense.

His quarrel with the political and cultural establishments of the West and the official Arab world is the most important feature of Said's biography. It was the Six Day War of 1967 that changed his life – prior to that event, he had not been politically engaged. His teenage years in Cairo were lonely, dominated by a Victorian father – in whose eyes the boy required permanent disciplining – and an after-school existence devoid of friends. Novels became a substitute – Defoe, Scott, Kipling, Dickens, Mann. He had been named Edward after the Prince of Wales but, despite his father's monarchism, was dispatched for his education not to Britain but to the United States, in 1951. Said would later write of hating his 'puritanical and hypocritical' New England boarding school: it was 'shattering and disorienting'. Until then, he thought he knew exactly who he was, 'moral and physical flaws' and all. In the United States he had to remake himself 'into something the system required'.

Nevertheless, he flourished in the Ivy League environment, first at Princeton and then Harvard where, as he later said, he had the privilege to be trained in the German philological tradition of comparative literature. Said began teaching at Columbia in 1963; his first book, on Conrad, was published three years later. When I asked him about it in New York in 1994, in a conversation filmed for Channel 4 television in Britain (the programme was recorded in his Riverside Drive apartment, on a day so humid that Said removed his jacket and tie as the cameras began to roll – creating much merriment in the household), he described his early years at Columbia between 1963 and 1967 as a 'Dorian Gray period':

TA: So one of you was the Comp Lit professor, going about his business, giving his lectures, working with Trilling and the others, yet at the same time, another character was building up inside you – but you kept the two apart?

ES: I had to. There was no place for that other character to be. I had effectively severed my connection with Egypt. Palestine no longer existed. My family lived partly in Egypt and partly in Lebanon. I was a foreigner in both places. I had no interest in the family business, so I was here. Until 1967, I really didn't think about myself as anything other than a person going about his work. I had taken in a few things along the way. I was obsessed with the fact that many of my cultural heroes – Edmund Wilson, Isaiah Berlin, Reinhold Niebuhr – were fanatical Zionists. Not just pro-Israeli: they said the most awful things about the Arabs, in print. But all I could do was note it. Politically, there was no place for me to go. I was in New York when the Six Day War broke out; and was completely shattered. The world as I had understood it ended at that moment. I had been in the States for years but it was only now that I began to be in touch with other Arabs. By 1970 I was completely immersed in politics and the Palestinian resistance movement.

His 1975 work *Beginnings* – an epic engagement with the problems posed by the 'point of departure', which synthesized the insights of Auerbach, Vico and Freud with a striking reading of the modernist novel – and, above all, *Orientalism*, were the products of this conjuncture. Published in 1978, when Said was already a member of the Palestinian National Council, *Orientalism* combines the polemical vigor of the activist with the passion of the cultural critic. Like all great polemics, it eschews balance. I once told him that, for many South Asians, the problem with the early orientalist British scholars was not their imperialist ideology but, on the contrary, the fact that they were far too politically correct: overawed by the Sanskrit texts they were translating. Said laughed, and insisted that the book was essentially an attempt to undercut the more fundamental assumptions of the West in relation to the Arab East. The 'discourse' – Foucault was, alas, an important influence – of the Orient, constructed in France and Britain during the two centuries that followed Napoleon's conquest of Egypt, had served both as an instrument of rule and to shore up a European cultural identity, by setting it off against the Arab world. Thus Lord Cromer, British Consul-General in Egypt for some quarter of a century after 1881: 'The European is a close reasoner; his statements of fact are devoid of any ambiguity; he is a natural logician ... The mind of the Oriental, on the other hand, like his picturesque streets, is eminently wanting in symmetry ... He will often break down under the mildest process of cross-examination' (*Orientalism*, p. 38).

He had deliberately concentrated on the exoticization, vulgarization and distortions of the Middle East and its culture for that reason. To portray imperialist suppositions as a universal truth was a lie, based on skewed and instrumentalist observations that were used in the service of Western domination. I thought about that while debating Niall Ferguson in Minneapolis in 2004.

Orientalism spawned a vast academic following. While Said was undoubtedly touched and flattered by the book's success, he was well aware of how it was misused and would often disclaim responsibility for its more monstrous offspring: 'How can anyone accuse me of denouncing "dead white males"? Everyone knows I love Conrad.' He would then go through a list of postmodernist critics, savaging each of them in turn for their stress on identity and hostility to narrative. 'Write it all down', I once told him. 'Why don't you?' came the reply. What we recorded was more restrained:

TA: The 1967 war radicalized you, pushed you in the direction of becoming a Palestinian spokesperson?

ES: Arab, at first, before Palestinian.

TA: And *Orientalism* grew out of that new commitment.

ES: I started to read, methodically, what was being written about the Middle East. It did not correspond to my experience. By the early seventies I began to realize that the distortions and misrepresentations were systematic, part of a much larger system of thought that was endemic to the West's whole enterprise of dealing with the Arab world. It confirmed my sense that the study of literature was essentially a historical task, not just an aesthetic one. I still believe in the role of the aesthetic; but the 'kingdom of literature' – 'for its own sake' – is simply wrong. A serious historical investigation must begin from the fact that culture is hopelessly involved in politics. My interest has been in the great canonical literature of the West—read, not as masterpieces that have to be venerated, but as works that have to be grasped in their historical density, so they can resonate. But I also don't think you can do that without liking them; without caring about the books themselves.

Culture and Imperialism, published in 1993, extended the core arguments of *Orientalism* to describe a more general pattern of relationships between the metropolitan West and its overseas territories, beyond that of Europe and the Middle East. Written in a different political period, it attracted some vituperative attacks. There was a celebrated exchange in the *Times Literary Supplement* with Ernest Gellner – who thought Said should give 'at least some expression of gratitude' for imperialism's role as vehicle of modernity – in which neither side took prisoners. Later, when Gellner attempted a reconciliation of sorts, Said was unforgiving; hatred must be pure to be effective and, here as elsewhere, he always gave as good as he got.

But by now, debates on culture had been overshadowed by events in Palestine. When I asked if the year 1917 meant anything to him, he replied without hesitation: 'Yes, the Balfour Declaration.' Said's writings on Palestine have a completely different flavour from anything else he wrote, passionate and biblical in their simplicity. This was his cause. In *The End of the Peace Process*, *Blaming the Victims* and some half-dozen other books, in his *al-Ahram* columns and his essays in the *New Left Review* and the *London Review of Books*, the flame that had been ignited in 1967 burned ever brighter. He had helped a generation to understand the real history of Palestine and it was this position, as the true chronicler of his people and their occupied homeland, that won him respect and admiration throughout the world. The Palestinians had become the indirect victims of the European Judeocide of the Second World War; but few politicians in the West seemed to care. Said pricked their collective conscience and they did not like him for it.

Two close friends whose advice he had often sought – Ibrahim Abu-Lughod and Eqbal Ahmad – had died within a few years of each other, in 1999 and 2001. Said missed them greatly, but their absence only made him more determined to continue his literary onslaught against the enemy. Though he had served for fourteen years as an independent member on the Palestinian National Council, and helped to polish and redraft Arafat's address to the UN General Assembly in 1984, he became increasingly critical of the lack of strategic vision that typified most of the Palestinian leadership. Writing in the immediate aftermath of what he termed the 'fashion-show vulgarities' of Arafat and Rabin's handshake on the White House lawn, Said described the Oslo Accords – imposed on the vanquished by the United States and Israel after the Gulf War of 1991 – as 'an instrument of surrender, a Palestinian Versailles'.

Arafat's lieutenant, Nabil Shaath, echoing *Orientalism*'s more reactionary critics, responded: 'He should stick to literary criticism. After all, Arafat would not deign to discuss Shakespeare'. History has vindicated Said's analysis. One of his most scorching attacks on Arafat's leadership, published in the *New Left Review* and *al-Ahram*, denounced Oslo as a mere repackaging of the occupation, 'offering a token 18 per cent of the lands seized in 1967 to the corrupt, Vichy-like authority of Arafat, whose mandate was essentially to police and tax his people on Israel's behalf':

> The Palestinian people deserve better. We have to say clearly that with Arafat and company in command, there is no hope ... What the Palestinians need are leaders who are really with and of their people, who are actually doing the resisting on the ground, not fat cigar-chomping bureaucrats bent on preserving their business deals and renewing their VIP passes, who have lost all trace of decency or credibility ... We need a united leadership capable of thinking, planning and taking decisions, rather than grovelling before the Pope or George Bush while the Israelis kill his people with impunity ... The struggle for liberation from Israeli occupation is where every Palestinian worth anything now stands.

Could Hamas provide a serious alternative? 'This is a protest movement against the occupation', Said told me:

In my opinion, their ideas about an Islamic state are completely inchoate, unconvincing to anybody who lives there. Nobody takes that aspect of their programme seriously. When you question them, as I have, both on the West Bank and elsewhere: 'What are your economic policies? What are your ideas about power stations, or housing?', they reply: 'Oh, we're thinking about that.' There is no social programme that could be labelled 'Islamic'. I see them as creatures of the moment, for whom Islam is an opportunity to protest against the current stalemate, the mediocrity and bankruptcy of the ruling party. The Palestinian Authority is now hopelessly damaged and lacking in credibility – like the Saudis and Egyptians, a client state for the US.

Behind the reiterated Israeli demands that the Authority crack down on Hamas and Islamic Jihad, he detected 'the hope that there will be something resembling a Palestinian civil war, a gleam in the eyes of the Israeli military'. Yet in the final months of his life he could still celebrate the Palestinians' stubborn refusal to accept that they were, as the Israeli Chief of Staff had described them, 'a defeated people', and saw signs for a more creative Palestinian politics in the National Political Initiative led by Mostapha Barghuti: 'The vision here is not a manufactured provisional state on 40 per cent of the land, with the refugees abandoned and Jerusalem kept by Israel, but a sovereign territory liberated from military occupation by mass action involving Arabs and Jews wherever possible.'

With his death, the Palestinian nation lost its most articulate voice in the Northern hemisphere, a world where, by and large, the continuous suffering of the Palestinians is ignored. For official Israelis, they are *untermenschen*; for official Americans, they are all terrorists; for the venal Arab regimes they are a continuing embarrassment. In his last writings, Said vigorously denounced the war on Iraq and its many apologists. He argued for freedom, from violence and from lies. He knew that the dual occupation of Palestine and Iraq had made peace in the region even more remote. His voice is irreplaceable, but his legacy will endure. He has many lives ahead of him. On the first anniversary of his death there were commemorations at the Barbican in London (the

Diwan orchestra of young Palestinian and Israeli musicians was conducted by Daniel Barenboim) and a more traditional academic conference on his legacy at the Bibliothèque National in Paris and more informal gatherings in many other cities of the world.

Zionism, Anti-Semitism, and Palestine

'The New Testament words, "He who is not for me is against me", lay bare the heart of anti-Semitism down the centuries,' wrote Adorno in *Minima Moralia* and suggested that 'it is a basic feature of domination that everyone who does not identify with it is consigned for mere difference to the enemy camp'. He argued that the German fascists and the authoritarian legal philosophers of the period such as Carl Schmitt had 'defined the very essence of politics by the categories of friend and enemy'. Adorno rejected such a primal approach, insisting that genuine freedom entailed the right to reject all prescribed choices.

After 11 September 2001, the US President declared that those who were not with the United States were with the terrorists: Bush or Bin Laden? The bulk of the world's politicians and mediacrats accepted the choice and backed Bush. Some of us rejected it: neither the Empire nor al-Qaeda. I have explained my reasons for this at length in *The Clash of Fundamentalisms*, but a few related questions have arisen concerning the use of the words 'fascism' and 'anti-Semitism'.

During the '60s and '70s the word 'fascist' was used lightly and light-mindedly on the left to describe a political opponent as, say, 'an old fascist'. In most cases this was not intended as a serious accusation. In the years that followed the end of the cold war, the dominant culture reduced history to a set of unrelated episodes in which the heroic struggle of the West against fascism appeared much larger than it actually was during the Second World War. Needless to say the role of the Soviet Union was virtually forgotten. Western leaders began to refer to all opponents as reincarnations of Hitler. This fashion had begun with the Anglo-French-Israeli assault on nationalist Egypt in 1956. The British Prime Minister of the time referred to Gamal Abdel Nasser as the 'Hitler on the Nile'. Later, the Serbian leader, Slobodan

Milošević, became the Hitler on the Danube and, of course, Saddam Hussein the Hitler on the Tigris. Then came 9/11, and Francis Fukuyama coined the appellation 'Islamo-fascism', which was eagerly adopted by supporters of the 'war against terror'.

The Zionist leaders of Israel and their apologists abroad had no problems with any of this, but when pro-Palestinian demonstrators added Ariel Sharon to the list they were denounced as 'anti-Semites'. France, in particular, has become the site of a peculiar and somewhat belated hysteria. Leading figures of the liberal left, such as Alain Finkielkraut, Pierre-André Taguieff (see, for example, his latest book *Prêcheurs de la haine: traversée de la judéophobie planétaire*), Alexandre Adler and André Glucksmann have become ever more virulent in their denunciations of a supposed new 'judeophobia' quite distinct from the traditional anti-Semitism of the racist and fascist right or the Catholic fundamentalists. According to these intellectuals, the new hatred of Jews, hidden in the form of anti-Zionism or even simply concern for the treatment of the Palestinians, is being mobilized by young Arabs in the *banlieues*, by the anti-imperialist and Palestine solidarity movements, by the far left and its 'Islamo-leftist' wing, as well as by the *altermondialistes*, who had the temerity to invite a figure like Tariq Ramadan to the Paris ESF in 2003. In this way, all forms of hostility to Israeli policies, whether expressed in the crude form of burning the Israeli flag on a demonstration or in careful analyses of the pathologies of a religious exclusivist state and arguments for a bi-national solution, are labelled as manifestations of a new, hidden but far more pernicious, form of anti-Semitism (linked, of course, with 'knee-jerk anti-Americanism'). Perhaps the paroxysmic moment of the equation of anti-Zionism and anti-Semitism came recently when Jean-Christophe Rufin, novelist and winner of the 2001 Goncourt Prize and former Vice-President of *Médecins sans Frontières,* proposed in his official report on the struggle against anti-Semitism and racism to the government that 'radical anti-Zionism' (which, in his eyes, is merely 'anti-Semitism by proxy') become a punishable offence on a par with racist or Holocaust revisionist statements: 'Such a (legislative) text would allow the punishment of those who make unfounded claims of racism against groups, institutions or states and who, with regard to the latter, make unjustified comparisons with apartheid or Nazism.'

Ariel Sharon is an authoritarian and a brutal war criminal and he should be tried for his crimes. He is no more a fascist than Saddam Hussein or Milošević, leave alone Nasser; but if the word 'fascist' is loosely applied to enemies of the West why complain when the same language is used against Western allies. To label hostility to the Zionist project that Sharon defends so vigorously as a new rise of anti-Semitism is a form of political blackmail by Israel and its supporters designed to mute criticism of the daily crimes being committed against the Palestinian people. Occasionally, Israelis themselves have used the fascist analogy. For instance, the Israeli Colonel who, before the assault on Jenin, calmly informed *Ma'ariv* that if they were ordered to crush the Palestinians they would have to use the tactics deployed by the Germans in the Warsaw Ghetto. The Colonel could certainly hear some echoes from the past.

Then came satire: a text published in the daily *Ma'ariv* on 10 October 2003 as part of Yehuda Nuriel's lively weekly column 'Midbar Yehuda' (The Yehuda Desert). It was popular and taken up in weekly papers as well. Angered by the ferocious attacks on the Israeli pilots who had refused to bomb Palestinian cities and refugee camps, stating that they had joined the Israeli Air Force and not a mafia intent on revenge killings, Nuriel published 'A brave and moving response to the refusenik pilots. A must read.' The must read was signed by A. Schicklgruber (Hitler's real name). It consisted exclusively of quotations from *Mein Kampf* and Hitler's speeches:

Those who want to live, let them fight, and those who do not want to fight in this world of eternal struggle do not deserve to live.

What we must fight for is to safeguard the existence of our people, the sustenance of our children and the freedom and independence of the fatherland, so that our people may mature for the fulfilment of the mission allotted it by the creator. The world has no reason for fighting in our defense, and as a matter of principle God does not make cowardly nations free.

Our nation wants peace because of its fundamental convictions. We want peace also owing to the realization of the simple primitive fact that no war would be likely essentially to alter the distress in our region. The principal effect of every war is to destroy the flower of a nation. We need peace and desire peace!

The war against our enemies cannot be conducted in a knightly fashion. This struggle is one of ideologies and will have to be conducted with unprecedented, unmerciful and unrelenting harshness. Man has become great through struggle. Whatever goal man has reached is due to his originality plus his brutality. If you do not fight, life will never be won. The man who has no sense of history is like a man who has no ears or eyes. It must be thoroughly understood that the lost land will never be won back by solemn appeals to God, nor by hopes in any United Nations, but only by the force of arms.

A single blow must destroy the enemy, without regard of losses. A gigantic all-destroying blow. Success is the sole earthly judge of right and wrong.

There is a road to freedom. Its milestones are Obedience, Endeavour, Honesty, Order, Cleanliness, Sobriety, Truthfulness, Sacrifice, and love of the Homeland. Universal education is the most corroding and disintegrating poison that 'liberalism' has ever invented for its own destruction. One of the worst symptoms of decay was the increasing cowardice in the face of responsibility, as well as the resultant self-hatred in all things.

In actual fact the pacifistic-humane idea is perfectly all right perhaps when one law rules the world. Therefore, first struggle and then perhaps pacifism. Pacifism as the idea of the State, international law instead of power - all are means to unman the people. They hold India up to us as a model and what is called 'passive resistance'. True, they want to make an India of us, a folk of dreams which turns away its face from realities, in order that they can oppress it for all eternity.

What food did our press dish out to the people before the violent events? Was it not the worst poison that can even be imagined? Wasn't the worst kind of pacifism injected into the heart of our people at a time when the rest of the world was preparing to throttle us, slowly but surely? Even in peacetime didn't the press inspire the minds of the people with doubt in the right of their own state? Was it not the press which knew how to make the absurdity of 'democracy'?

The best means of defense is attack.

Ours is not a warlike nation. It is a soldierly one, which means it does not want a war, but does not fear it. It loves peace but also loves its honour and freedom. We will never allow anyone to divide this people once more into camps, each fighting the other. The world will not help, the people must help themselves. Its own strength is the source of life. That strength the Almighty has given us to use; that in it and through it, we may wage the battle of our life. May God Almighty give our work His blessing, strengthen our purpose, and endow us with wisdom and the trust of our people. Lord God, let us never hesitate or play the coward.

If we are forced to send the flowers of the nation into the hell of war without the smallest fear, then surely we have the right to remove millions of another race that breeds like vermin. For we are fighting not for ourselves but for the whole country.

A. Schicklgruber

Learning of the 'trick', *Ma'ariv*'s editor-in-chief, Amnon Dankner, sacked Nuriel, and gave the following explanation: 'This is an extremely repulsive satire, which means that anyone who opposes Sarbanut [Conscientious Objection] is Hitler, quasi-Hitler, or about to become

Hitler. In my view, as an editor of a Jewish newspaper in Israel, it is a horrible act which can not be forgiven, and can not be protected by the right to free speech.' But how could an Israeli print such a text in the first place? The content was clearly acceptable. And had it not been for the alert editors of *Harper's* in New York we might never have known about this incident.

A few years earlier, in September 2001, the Israeli journalist Uri Blau conducted a set of interviews with Israeli soldiers (identified with pseudonyms) that were published in the Jerusalem weekly, *Kol Ha'Ir*. The extracts below are instructive on several levels:

Uri Blau: What is the first thing that comes to mind when you hear the word 'territories'?

Roi [*nineteen, paratrooper, serving in Hebron for the past six months*]: The first thing that comes to my mind is children throwing Molotov cocktails. Basically, you should shoot them in the legs and you don't.

Tzvi [*twenty, serving in the Gaza Strip*]: My first memory is of security patrol. You see unbelievable things there: people sitting under the bulldozers, begging us not to demolish their houses. There's a guy who lives in a tent where his house stood once, and now this tent is on ground that has been annexed by the settlement. But there are stories much worse than this. Real pogroms. Angry settlers coming out with sticks and pitchforks and burning down houses. Just like that.

Roi: In Hebron there's basically a settlers' mafia. No supervision. They can do anything they want. The police are terrified of them. When you go to arrest settlers in Hebron who've made a little pogrom, it's much more complicated than arresting an Arab fugitive. Little children throwing rocks at old Arab ladies, that's a common sight, and diapers – they throw their shit out the windows.

Erez [*twenty, serving in the Nahal brigade*]: My first memory is when all the riots started and we were ordered to some hilltop. Around us were

Arabs, and there were five trailers there, and we were a whole company on that hill. The settlers took it for granted that we were there, a whole company, defending a few trailers.

Tzvi: They wrap the whole world around their little finger in order to serve their ideology.

Blau : Do you feel that something has changed in you while serving in the territories? When you go back home, do you see things differently?

Dubi [*twenty-one, Golani infantry brigade, served in Samaria, about to finish his tour of duty*]: You get to a point where you're just sick of it all. They fire at us, we get there, fire on whoever fired on us, hope it'll be over. You don't even know who supports whom, who collaborates and who doesn't. So you have to stand at that checkpoint and stop them all and make them wait for hours.

Yaron: One thing I learned in the army is that no matter how funny it sounds, it's a game. As an IDF soldier, you have to represent this country. You also have to look as good as you can. If you look like a jerk and do your job like a jerk, the Palestinians on the other side will see that, and people who are out to hurt you eventually will. When you stand at that checkpoint, you have to be mean, even if you feel shitty about it. You have to show them who's in charge. You can't afford to look soft. I've become an actor. I can go to the Habimah National Theater and show them my résumé.

Blau: How does being on checkpoint duty change your outlook on life?

Erez: These checkpoints, and the fact that you can treat people this way, all of this makes a guy more confident. I mean in general, not me personally. I really didn't like treating them that way, taking part in that game, as Yaron put it.

Yaron: You think that way because no one close to you has been hurt. You'll have that experience, and then you'll believe me.

Erez: I understand this attitude, but personally I have a really hard time with it. I'm in a calm area; they're actually good people, and most of them are stoned. They don't care. People want to work, to bring home some money. They don't want trouble. When there's a closure they go crazy. They have nothing. They can't work anywhere. When I'm on checkpoint duty, I almost always bring the Border Police. Those guys start screwing them up, slapping them around, etc.

Blau: Did any of you ever shoot someone?

Roi: When I first got to Hebron I wouldn't open fire on little children. And I was sure that if I ever killed or hurt anyone, I'd go so crazy that I'd leave the army. But finally I did shoot someone, and nothing happened to me. In Hebron I shot the legs off of two kids, and I was sure I wouldn't be able to sleep anymore at night, but nothing happened. Two weeks ago I hurt a Palestinian policeman, and that didn't affect me either. You become so apathetic you don't care at all. Shooting is the IDF soldier's way of meditating. It's like shooting is your way of letting go of all your anger when you're in the army. In Hebron there's this order they call 'punitive shooting': just open fire on whatever you like. I opened fire not on any sources of fire but on windows where there was just wash hanging to dry. I knew that there were people who would be hit. But at that moment it was just shoot, shoot, shoot.

Erez: What do you mean 'punitive shooting'? A reaction to something?

Roi: Reaction to their shooting. In Hebron there's punitive fire. Shoot at everything you see. Cars, things, anything that moves. It's like taking out your anger on everything. Shooting relaxes you, like meditation.

Tzvi: I find what Roi said a bit sick, that shooting people is therapy.

Roi: Don't you release stress when you shoot?

Tzvi: No, not at all. I don't even have the energy for that anymore. I'm totally apathetic. I've had occasion – I believe everyone here has – to shoot people.

Roi: We had a five-day operation in the territories on firing grounds, and basically Bedouins are not allowed to be there. The officer stops the vehicle and asks, 'Who's ready?' I step out, another guy steps out, and then about 300 yards from us we see a poor Bedouin shepherd walking out on the grass at the firing ground. The officer says, 'Okay, go ahead.' We lie down, one bullet to the left of the herd, one bullet to the right of the herd ...

Blau: Why?

Roi: Because shooting live ammo has become so fluid, so trivial.

Tzvi: You can live with having shot at an old man grazing his sheep? Just like that? If my officer were to tell me to open fire on a shepherd who's obviously not endangering anyone, I would beat my officer up.

Roi: Officially you don't open fire just like that. On the ground our guys would do it for the hell of it, as though they were returning fire. For them, shooting in Hebron is simply a video game.

Erez: If anyone were to tell me, 'You have to open fire on a seven-year-old girl', I'd shoot without hesitation.

Blau: Really?

Erez : Yes. Because that's what you have to do. If that's what I'm ordered to do.

Blau : Don't you use your own judgment?

Erez: I'll make my own judgment later. It is a crime, but listen, it depends on the actual case, all right? Seven-year-old girls are not shot at just like that. I don't believe that whoever shot a seven-year-old girl did it just like that.

Blau: In the Givati brigade someone shot a fourteen-year-old boy just like that.

Blau : Does anyone here feel differently?

Yosef: Most of the orders I've ever received have made sense and were absolutely sane and correct. As hard as it is to shoot a person, even if that person holds a gun and opens fire at you, I have no doubt that it is absolutely justified.

Roi: There was this case where Nahal guys shot an old man who didn't stop when they tried to arrest him. There was no reason to shoot him. Looking back on it now, when you're not in the army you say it's impossible. But when I think of that soldier, it seems fine. There's nothing you can do about it. In my first months in Hebron, I wouldn't shoot even rubber-coated bullets at kids. I was so much against it I often went to see the unit shrink. I had to open live fire on someone at the beginning, and I missed on purpose.

Blau: Are you proud to be combat soldiers in the IDF?

Dubi: Obviously it's shit to be a combat soldier, but what can you do? I mean, you go back home, see all your desk-job buddies who have no idea what's going on in this country – they just go home every day, fuck their girlfriends, and see you around. And you, you get fucked even more.

Tzvi: I'm proud to serve my country, even if there are things I do contrary to my beliefs. Even if this country doesn't act exactly [???] the way I think it should, it's still my country. I try to do what I have to do.

Roi: I hate it. Especially the paratroopers. It's the most disgusting unit.

Dubi: Why did you choose a combat unit?

Roi: I was so close to getting out of the army as psychologically unsuitable, but in the end I stayed out of some feeling of commitment. I don't feel any obligation toward the state or anyone – I don't give a shit. The only reason is that my parents live here, and when I was a kid in third grade someone else defended me, so now it's my turn to do this. No other reason, nothing political or Zionist. Just that others defended me in the past, and now it's my turn.

Erez: I'm not at all proud either. I don't know, I don't feel any commitment to this country. I didn't even want to enlist, it was a mistake. But I stayed because of the guys on my crew. I was in a good crew, had a good time, and now I'm stuck.

Blau: Whether you like it or not, you've given quite a lot of yourselves. Had you been born on the other side, where would you be now?

Tzvi: I have no doubt that if I were on the other side I'd join one of the factions, just as I'd have joined one of the underground organizations if I'd lived here fifty-five years ago, because that's how it is. And I believe that eventually everyone did sign up to defend their country and didn't end up in a combat unit by accident.

Ariel [*twenty-one, paratrooper, yeshiva student, served in Hebron and Ramallah and returned to the yeshiva three months ago*]: This is a religious matter, and I'm religious. For them, it's not just the fact that their life is fucked up now; they have religion, these guys. My religion, like theirs, is something that leads me. I follow, and I would do anything it tells me to do. If it's to go to war, then there are no borders and you shoot everyone. If I feel that for myself and for this life, and in the name of my religion, I have to do it, then I do it. But by the same token, just as I'd refuse an order if my company commander told me to shoot a seven-year-old girl, if I were in the Tanzim and I was told to shoot a soldier who wasn't doing anything, just standing there eating pizza, I'd refuse no matter what. But if my religion said that I had to shoot for the sake of my people and my religion, I'd do it. That's the problem here.

Ran [*twenty, serving in a special armor-corps unit in Samaria*]: I can't – no matter how hard I try – I can't picture myself in their place. But I think that if I were in their shoes I might have joined one of their factions. Look, all those people who do join them are really in distress.

Blau: It seems that, unlike in previous wars, this time the IDF soldiers don't feel that absolute justice is on their side.

Erez: Of course it's not right. But there's no choice. That's the whole point here. You have no other choice. No other solution's been found.

Roi: I feel I'm a bit different from everyone here. Our attitude toward the Arabs – hate, love, pity – depends on the soldier's mood. If it's a day when I'll be going home and I'm happy and everything's cool, or if it's a day when I don't go home and don't want to be in the army, then that day we'll take it out on them.

Yosef: I don't hate the Arabs. I just think there's really no choice.

It is possible to publish all this in Israel, but not in the mainstream press of France or the United States. Here it will be denounced hysterically as 'anti-Semitism'. It is this blackmail that prompted a reflection.

Anti-Semitism is a racist ideology directed against the Jews. It has old roots. In his classic work, *The Jewish Question: A Marxist*

Interpretation, published posthumously in France in 1946, the Belgian Marxist, Abram Leon (active in the resistance during the Second World War, he was captured and executed by the Gestapo in 1944), invented the category of a 'people-class' for the role of the Jews who managed to preserve their linguistic, ethnic and religious characteristics through many centuries without becoming assimilated. This was not unique to the Jews, but could apply just as strongly to many ethnic minorities: diaspora Armenians, Copts, Chinese merchants in South-East Asia, Muslims in China, etc. The defining characteristic common to these groups is that they became middlemen in a pre-capitalist world, resented alike by rich and poor.

Twentieth-century anti-Semitism, usually instigated from above by priests (Russia, Poland), politicians/intellectuals (Germany, France and, after 1938, Italy), big business (USA, Britain), played on the fears and insecurity of a deprived population. Hence August Bebel's reference to anti-Semitism as 'the socialism of fools'. The roots of anti-Semitism, like other forms of racism, are social, political, ideological and economic. The judeocide of the Second World War, carried out by the political–military–industrial complex of German imperialism, was one of the worst crimes of the twentieth century, but not the only one. The Belgian massacres in the Congo had led to between 10–12 million deaths before the First World War. The uniqueness of the judeocide was that it took place in Europe (the heart of Christian civilization) and was carried out systematically – by Germans, Poles, Ukrainians, Lithuanians, French and Italians – as if it was the most normal thing in the world, 'the banality of evil' in Hannah Arendt's phrase. Since the end of the Second World War popular anti-Semitism of the old variety declined in Western Europe, restricted largely to remnants of fascist or neo-fascist organizations.

In the Arab world there were well-integrated Jewish minorities in Cairo, Baghdad and Damascus. They did not suffer at the time of the European judeocide. Historically, Muslims and Jews have been much closer to each other than either to Christianity. Even after 1948, when tensions rose between the two communities throughout the Arab east, it was largely Zionist provocations, such as the bombing of Jewish cafés in Baghdad, that helped to drive Arab Jews out of their native countries into Israel.

Non-Jewish Zionism has an old pedigree and permeates European culture. It dates back to the birth of Christian fundamentalist sects of the 16th and 17th centuries who took the Old Testament literally. They included Oliver Cromwell and John Milton. Later, for other reasons, Rousseau, Locke and Pascal joined the Zionist bandwagon. There is no such thing as the 'historical rights' of Jews to Palestine. This grotesque myth ignores real history (already in the 17th century, Baruch Spinoza referred to the Old Testament as 'a collection of fairy-tales', denounced the prophets and was excommunicated by the Amsterdam synagogue as a result). Long before the Roman conquest of Judea in 70 AD, a large majority of the Jewish population lived outside Palestine. The native Jews were gradually assimilated into neighbouring groups such as the Phoenicians, Philistines, etc. Palestinians are, in most cases, descended from the old Hebrew tribes and genetic science has recently confirmed this, much to the annoyance of Zionists.

Later, and for vile reasons, the Third Reich too supported a Jewish homeland. The introduction to the Nuremburg Laws of 15 September 1935 state:

> If the Jews had a state of their own in which the bulk of the people were at home, the Jewish question could already be considered solved today, even for the Jews themselves. The ardent Zionists of all people have objected least to the basic ideas of the Nuremberg Laws, because they know that these laws are the only correct solution for the Jewish people.

Many years later, Haim Cohen, a former judge of the Supreme Court of Israel stated:

> The bitter irony of fate decreed that the same biological and racist argument extended by the Nazis, and which inspired the inflammatory laws of Nuremberg, serve as the basis for the official definition of

Jewishness in the bosom of the state of Israel. (Quoted in Joseph Badi,
Fundamental Laws of the State of Israel, 1960, p. 156.)

Modern Zionism is the ideology of secular Jewish nationalism. It has
little to do with Judaism as a religion and many orthodox Jews to this
day have remained hostile to Zionism, like the Hassidic sect which
joined a Palestinian march in Washington in April 2002 carrying
placards which said: 'ZIONISM SUCKS' and 'SHARON: PALES-
TINIAN BLOOD IS NOT WATER'.

Zionism was born in the 19th century as a direct response to the
vicious anti-Semitism that pervaded Austria. The first Jewish immi-
grants to Palestine arrived in 1882 and many of them were interested
only in maintaining a cultural presence. Israel was created in 1948 by
the British Empire and sustained by its American successor. It was a
European settler-state. Its early leaders proclaimed the myth of a 'A
Land without People for a People without Land', thus denying the
presence of the Palestinians. Last February, the Zionist historian Benny
Morris, in a chilling interview with *Haaretz* (reprinted as a document
in English in the *New Left Review*, March/April 2004), admitted the
whole truth: 700,000 Palestinians had been driven out of their villages
by the Zionist army in 1948. There were numerous incidents of rape,
etc. He described it accurately as 'ethnic cleansing' not genocide and
went on to defend ethnic cleansing if carried out by a superior civilization, comparing it to the killing of native Americans by the European settlers in North America. That too, for Morris, was justified.
Anti-Semites and Zionists shared one thing in common: the view that
Jews were a special race that could not be integrated in European
societies and needed its own large ghetto or homeland. The fact that
this is false is proved by the realities of today. The majority of the
world's Jews do not live in Israel, but in Western Europe and North
America.

Anti-Zionism was a struggle that began against the Zionist colo-
nization project, intellectuals of Jewish origin played an important part
in this campaign and do so to this day inside Israel itself. Most of my
knowledge of Zionism and anti-Zionism comes from the writings and

speeches of anti-Zionist jews: Akiva Orr, Moshe Machover, Haim Hanegbi, Isaac Deutscher, Ygael Gluckstein (Tony Cliff), Ernest Mandel, Maxime Rodinson, Nathan Weinstock, Michel Warshawsky, Yitzhak Laor, Gaby Piterburg, to name but a few. They argued that Zionism and the structures of the Jewish state offered no real future to the Jewish people settled in Israel, except one of infinite war.

The campaign against the new 'anti-Semitism' in Europe today is essentially a cynical ploy on the part of the Israeli Government to seal off the Zionist state from any criticism of its regular and consistent brutality against the Palestinians. The daily hits carried out by the IDF have wrecked the towns and villages of Palestine and killed thousands of civilians (especially children); and European citizens are aware of this fact. Criticism of Israel cannot and should not be equated with anti-Semitism. The fact is that Israel is not a weak, defenceless state. It is the strongest state in the region. It possesses real, not imaginary, weapons of mass destruction. It possesses more tanks and bomber jets and pilots than the rest of the Arab world put together. To argue that any Arab country militarily threatens Israel is pure demagogy. It is the occupation that creates the conditions which produce suicide bombers. Even a few staunch Zionists are beginning to realize this fact. That is why we should understand that as long as Palestine remains oppressed there will be no peace in the region.

The daily suffering of the Palestinians (the deaths in Gaza and elsewhere always include young boys) does not excite the liberal conscience of Europe, guilt-ridden (and for good reason) by its past inability to defend the Jews of central Europe against extinction. But the judeocide of the Second World War should not be used as a cover to tolerate crimes against the Palestinian people. European and American voices need to be heard loud and clear on this question. To be intimidated by Zionist blackmail is to become an accomplice of war crimes. To remain silent is not helpful to those Israelis who are ashamed by the misdeeds of successive governments.

The Bugler and the General

Exactly a year before they invaded Iraq, the United States green-lighted an attempted coup in Venezuela, where the elected President, Hugo Chavez, was regarded as disloyal to US interests in the region. Venezuela is also the largest oil-producer in South America. The oligarchs were thrilled. A former President of the Chamber of Commerce, dilapidated even by Venezuelan standards, was dressed up for the job. A few tame Generals then ordered the arrest of Hugo Chavez and he was taken to a military base. So far, so bad. As the news spread, anger grew in the *favelas* that surround the city and the poor decided to march to the Miraflores Palace. Simultaneously another event, equally important, was taking place in the palace. With the Western media ready and waiting to introduce the bent President to the world as the saviour of Venezuelan democracy (the *New York Times* had defended the coup for 'enhancing democracy') a General came out of the palace and spoke to the military band. He informed them that a new President was about to come out and they should play the national anthem as per usual. The soldiers questioned his orders. Angered by the disobedience, the General turned to the young bugler, an eighteen-year-old soldier, and instructed him to blow the bugle as he saw the new President. 'Excuse me General, but which President do you speak of? We know of only one. Hugo Chavez.' The furious General told the bugler to obey orders. At this point the bugler handed his instrument to the General and said: 'You seem to be very keen on playing the bugle. Here it is. You play it.' This was a soldier who can proudly tell his children: 'I did not obey orders.' The combination of a popular upsurge and the threat of a soldiers' mutiny saw the triumphal return of Chavez.

The oligarchs and their backers refused to give up. They demanded a referendum. When it happened in August 2004, the turnout was huge. 60.9 percent of the electorate voted in the recall referendum. Venezuela, under its new Constitution, permitted the right of the citizens to recall a President before s/he had completed their term of office. No Western democracy (excepting Switzerland) enshrines this right in a written or unwritten constitution. Chavez's victory will have repercussions beyond the borders of Venezuela. It is a triumph of the poor against the rich and it is a lesson that Lula in Brazil and Kirchner in Argentina should study closely. It was Fidel Castro's, not Jimmy Carter's, advice to go ahead with the referendum that was crucial. Chavez put his trust in the people by empowering them and they responded generously. The opposition will only discredit itself further by challenging the results.

The Venezuelan oligarchs and their parties, who had opposed this Constitution in a referendum (having earlier failed to topple Chavez via a US-backed coup and an oil strike led by a corrupt union bureaucracy), now utilized it to try to get rid of the man who had enhanced Venezuelan democracy. They failed. However loud their cries of anguish (and those of their media apologists at home and abroad), in reality the whole country knows what happened. Chavez defeated his opponents democratically and for the fourth time in a row. Democracy in Venezuela, under the banner of the Bolivarian revolutionaries, has broken through the corrupt two-party system favoured by the oligarchy and its friends in the West. And this has happened despite the total hostility of the privately owned media: the two daily newspapers, *Universal* and *Nacional*, as well as Gustavo Cisneros' TV channels and CNN, made no attempt to mask their crude support for the opposition. Some foreign correspondents in Caracas have convinced themselves that Chavez is an oppressive caudillo and, desperate to translate their own fantasies into reality, their reports border on science fiction: Phil Gunson (*The Economist* and *Miami Herald)* and Andrew Webb-Vidal (*Financial Times)* were two of the worst offenders, embedded deep in the posterior of the oligarchy. They provide no evidence of political prisoners, leave alone Guantanamo-style detentions or Abu Graib-style tortures or the removal of TV executives and newspaper editors (which happened without too much of a fuss in Blair's Britain).

In Caracas, a few weeks prior to the referendum, I had a lengthy discussion with Chavez ranging from Iraq to the most detailed minutiae of Venezuelan history and politics and the Bolivarian programme. It became clear to me that what Chavez is attempting is nothing more or less than the creation of a radical social democracy in Venezuela that seeks to empower the lowest strata of society. In these times of deregulation, privatization and the Anglo-Saxon model of wealth subsuming politics, Chavez's aims are regarded as revolutionary, even though the measures proposed are no different to those of the postwar Attlee government in Britain.

Some of the oil wealth is being spent to educate and heal the poor. Just under a million children from the shanty-towns and the poorest villages now obtain a free education; 1.2 million illiterate adults have been taught to read and write; secondary education has been made available to 250,000 children whose social status excluded them from this privilege during the *ancien régime*; three new university campuses were functioning by 2003 and six more are due to be completed by 2006. As far as healthcare is concerned, the 10,000 Cuban doctors who were sent to help the country have transformed the situation in the poor districts, where 11,000 neighbourhood clinics have been established and the health budget has tripled. Add to this the financial support provided to small businesses, the new homes being built for the poor, and an Agrarian Reform Law that was enacted and pushed through despite the resistance, legal and violent, of the landlords. By the end of last year 2,262,467 hectares had been distributed to 116,899 families.

The reasons for Chavez's popularity become obvious. No previous regime had even noticed the plight of the poor. And one can't help but notice that it is not simply a division between the wealthy and the poor, but also one of skin-colour. The Chavistas tend to be dark-skinned, reflecting their slave and native ancestry. The opposition is light-skinned and some of its more disgusting supporters denounce Chavez as a black monkey. A puppet show to this effect with a monkey playing Chavez was even organized at the US Embassy in Caracas. But Colin Powell was not amused and the Ambassador was compelled to issue an apology.

The bizarre argument advanced in a hostile editorial in *The Economist* during the week of the referendum, namely that that all this was done to win votes, is extraordinary. The opposite is the case. If Chavez had become a creature of the oligarchy, he would have easily been elected and re-elected and with the support of the global financial press. The Bolivarians wanted power so that real reforms could be implemented. All the oligarchs have to offer is more of the past and the removal of Chavez.

It is ridiculous to suggest that Venezuela is on the brink of a totalitarian tragedy. It is the opposition that has attempted to take the country in that direction. The Bolivarians have been incredibly restrained. When I asked Chavez to explain his own philosophy, he replied:

> I don't believe in the dogmatic postulates of Marxist revolution. I don't accept that we are living in a period of proletarian revolutions. All that must be revised. Reality is telling us that every day. Are we aiming in Venezuela today for the abolition of private property or a classless society? I don't think so. But if I'm told that because of that reality you can't do anything to help the poor, the people who have made this country rich through their labour – and never forget that some of it was slave labour – then I say 'We part company'. I will never accept that there can be no redistribution of wealth in society. Our upper classes don't even like paying taxes. That's one reason they hate me. We said 'You must pay your taxes.' I believe it's better to die in battle, rather than hold aloft a very revolutionary and very pure banner, and do nothing ... That position often strikes me as very convenient, a good excuse ... Try and make your revolution, go into combat, advance a little, even if it's only a millimetre, in the right direction, instead of dreaming about utopias.

And that's why he won.

Homage III

I was still in Caracas when bad news came. Three cold, impersonal e-mails: Paul Foot is dead. My impulsive, self-assured, audacious and

witty friend had gone forever. An odd rhyme formed and kept
repeating itself in my head. Do not weep that he is dead/Remember
him and smile instead. But the smile would not come. The sense of loss
was too overwhelming. And not simply on a personal level. He was
one of the finest investigative journalists in Britain, respected by many
who disagreed with his or any brand of radical socialism. His departure
left a giant vacuum in British political culture. 'There are hardly any
journalists with the guts or the passion to stick around for long in the
vast, uncharted areas of irresponsible power'. That was Foot in the
London Review of Books on Peter Taylor's exposé of the tobacco
industry in July 1984. His own guts and passion had become legendary
in a media world – dominated by cronyism, obsessed with celebrity,
peopled by dull and deferential columnists and news presenters – that
regarded both as old-fashioned vices.

I tried to remember the exact moment we had first met, but
memory failed. It's often the way with people one has known a very
long time. He had been a friend and a comrade over so many decades
that many things had become jumbled. Over the years we had spoken
together on many platforms, traded gossip – personal, political and
malicious – and had once quarrelled and not spoken to each other for
months. During that period I ran into him unexpectedly at the home
of mutual friends who had invited us both to dinner – they had no idea
we were not speaking to each other and were bewildered by the
tension. Foot, eyes smiling, extended his hand with a greeting: 'Hello,
comrade.' I responded with a stern face: 'Hello, citizen.' The cause of
the conflict was totally trivial as we both admitted several weeks later
when we made up over a luxurious lunch at the Gay Hussar and
laughed at ourselves. He said: 'I never thought "citizen" was such an
insult till I heard you said it with so much venom.' A discussion on the
relative merits and demerits of the Committee of Public Safety and the
Bolshevik Central Committee followed, over a bottle of Bull's Blood.
Or perhaps it was two.

Slowly the first memory came back. It was autumn 1965 when I
first met him. The connection was not left-wing politics, but *Private
Eye*. I had already met Richard Ingrams and William Rushton while I

was at Oxford. They had invited me to the *Eye* offices in 22 Greek Street to discuss a 'Letter from Pakistan'. Later, we trooped off to lunch at the neighbouring Coach and Horses. And I think that's when I first saw him. Peter Jay was present on that occasion which was enlivened by the Keynes versus Marx banter between him and Foot. Nobody present, as far as I can recall, mentioned Hayek, not even Peter Cook, who was more knowledgeable on these matters than is generally assumed.

At Oxford, the Ingrams/Foot duo collectively edited *Parson's Pleasure*, handed to them by Adrian Berry of the *Telegraph* clan. The mag did not last long. It was closed down as a result of legal action by a non-parson who did not wish to see his pleasures recorded in public. Foot went on to edit *Isis* which, as Ingrams reminded us in an affecting speech at the funeral, was temporarily banned by the proctors because of a radical innovation: publishing regular reviews of lectures and reducing a female don to a breakdown. What Ingrams forgot to mention was the name of the offending reviewer. It was John Davis, currently Warden of All Souls.

There was a sense of real camaraderie at the *Eye* of those days, due partially to the fact that three key figures (Ingrams/Foot/Rushton) had all been chums at Shrewsbury. The combination of the Shrewsbury mafia and Peter Cook produced a potent (enemies might say poisonous) brew, a *Private Eye* that mercilessly lambasted the political and cultural establishment of the day, sparing nobody, not even personal friends. Cook's hatred of a pompous and hypocritical establishment was legendary. Ingrams' relaxed, bumbling and low-key approach concealed (as it was designed to) a fearless and uncompromising Editor, often granite-hard in his choice of covers for the magazine.

Paul Foot's journalism flourished in this climate. Politicians and businessmen alike feared his meticulously researched investigations. Judges and barristers, too, read him closely as he exposed numerous miscarriages of justice. He never wrote to please or flatter, but was thrilled when his targets crumbled, as they often did. Of late he had begun to complain that too many good stories were being spiked. In one of the last conversations I had with him he was amazed by the naivety and spinelessness of a colleague who had written a flattering letter to Tony Blair and received a spin-doctored, but handwritten response. The colleague was stupid enough to boast about this to Foot. That's what surprised him. 'Why me?' he said. 'Did he think I would be impressed by a note from Downing Street?'

Richard Ingrams remained a close friend for the rest of his life, even after Foot left the *Eye* in 1972 to edit *Socialist Worker*, the weekly organ of the SWP. The pretext for his departure was the cover planned to commemorate Bernadette Devlin's pregnancy. She was unmarried at the time. The proposed cover had a photograph of her with Harold Wilson. The bubble captions went like this: HW: 'What are you going to call the little bastard?' BD: 'Harold, after you.' Foot's rare display of anger, on behalf of the Irish MP, led to the cover being dumped, even though Devlin, when told, thought it was very funny. Foot left nonetheless. The revolution needed him. The strike wave had led some to believe that a British revolution was on the agenda. They weren't the only deluded ones. Insider reports from Buckingham Palace indicated the nervousness of the monarch.

PF and I belonged to different sets of initials on the far-left, often stupidly sectarian towards each other, but it never affected our friendship. After Mrs Thatcher came to power, and it was obvious that the radical wave had receded, I found it difficult to stomach the absurd factionalism within the group to which I belonged. In 1980, I left, but with a public explanation in the *Guardian*. The day it was published, the phone rang. 'Footie here. What are you doing?' It emerged that we were both engaged in childcare duties. We met at Golder's Hill Park, and became immersed in a lengthy political discussion. He was really worried that I might move to the right. I thought it unlikely. He confessed that he was tempted whenever he saw the Labour Party Conference on television (this was then). He knew he could do so much better than most of the idiots on the platform, but despite Benn, Dalyell and others, the thought of becoming a Labour MP was a nightmare. The SWP was an important anchor and he feared where the tide might take him without them. As we were talking, Rose Foot appeared on the scene and asked where the children might be. We looked around. They had disappeared. 'Typical,' she yelled, 'two bloody men talking politics while their children are lost.' It was a temporary panic. They soon reappeared. And young Tom (now almost as tall as his father) and his brothers Matt and John moved us all by they way they spoke at their dad's funeral, and by their own love of books. Bibliophilia now appears firmly embedded in the Foot genes. The books Paul collected all his life and the purchase of which sometimes took precedence over more pressing household needs, will remain in the family.

The fact was that despite his radical, non-conformist family – the Feet were staunch West Country liberals, and then there was Michael – Footie did not want to end up like them, though he admired and loved them greatly. The roots of his radicalism, it's true, were embedded in English history from the 1640 Revolution onwards, a lineage that extended from Winstanley down to Paine, Cobbett, Shelley, the Chartists, Orwell, E.P. Thompson, CND and the Glasgow shop-stewards movement. All this was already there when he met Ygael Gluckstein (Tony Cliff), the Palestinian Trotskyist, who recruited him to the International Socialists over four decades ago and introduced him to another world.

Five years ago, Paul was felled by a giant stroke and lay unconscious/semi-conscious for weeks. We would take turns to go and talk to him in this semi-inert state, give him the news (Belgrade was being bombed), read something from *Private Eye* or a letter to the *Guardian* or something by Shelley, and crack desperate jokes in the hope that some of it would trickle through to his subconscious. We feared the worst, but he survived. Prompt medical attention, loving care and a fierce will to live had resulted in a recovery. The doctor testing his memory was amazed to hear lengthy recitations from Shelley and Shakespeare (a tribute to his old schoolteacher, Frank McEachrane, who had always encouraged his love of poetry). He had lost movement in one leg, but his brain was fine, though his energy was beginning to flag. He would often talk of death and the book he wanted to complete before it struck him down. He succeeded. When the end came at Stansted Airport he was with his companion Claire Fermont and their ten-year-old daughter Kate, she who has inherited her father's eyes and his piercing gaze. For Paul himself it was sudden and quick. No pain. It is those left behind who will suffer and recall the words of his favourite poet Shelley:

> You are not here! The quaint witch Memory sees
> In vacant chairs your absent images,
> And points where once you sat, and now should be
> But are not.

'We want electricity in our homes not up the arse.'

Most legends contain a small grain of truth, but none is to be found in the fraudulent images being presented each day by the BBC (and the US networks) at home and abroad. The print media is not much better. Official propaganda is constantly repeated in sentences like: 'On June 28, the United States and its coalition partners transferred sovereign control of Iraq to an interim government headed by Prime Minister Ayad Allawi. The transfer of sovereignty ended more than a year of American-led occupation', etc. Meanwhile US intelligence agencies admit that the size of the resistance increases every day. The assault on Fallujah, far from crushing the resistance has strengthened its resolve. The reporting of the US assault on this town, however, was a disgrace.

The craven capitulation of the BBC since the removal of its defiant Director-General and Chairman has been in evidence ever since the Hutton whitewash. This is not self-censorship. Soon after he took over as D-G, Mark Thomson told a small meeting senior managers and news executives that he thought the news was too critical and 'left-wing'. He must be really happy now.

The notion that Iraq today is a sovereign state, governed by Iraqis, is a grotesque fiction. Every Iraqi citizen, regardless of political views or religious affiliation, is aware of the actual status of the country. And if the BBC carries on in this fashion, its credibility, already at an all-time low, could disappear altogether. In a public statement some months ago, the imperial princess, Condoleezza Rice, declared: 'We want to change the Iraqi mind.' But the US-funded Arab TV channel called 'Truth' (or 'Pravda' in Russian) has proved a dismal failure. And now to prevent any alternative images from reaching Iraqis and the rest of the world, a plucky puppet at the 'Ministry of Information' has banned *al-Jazeera* TV from reporting out of Iraq – a traditional and simplistic recipe from an oppressive cookbook.

The 'handover' designed largely to convince US citizens that they could now relax and re-elect Bush was also an invitation to the Western media to downgrade its coverage of Iraq, which it dutifully did. As Paul Krugman noted in the *New York Times* (6 August 2004): 'Iraq stories moved to the inside pages of newspapers, and largely off TV screens. Many people got the impression that things had improved. Even journalists were taken in: a number of newspaper stories asserted that the rate of U.S. losses there fell after the handoff. (Actual figures: 42 American soldiers died in June, and 54 in July.)'

Like previous confections to justify the war, this one is not working either. Of the two Iraqis plucked from primitive obscurity to be the front men for the occupation, 'President' Yawar is a relatively harmless telecoms manager from Saudi Arabia. He was perfectly happy to don tribal gear for official functions and photo-ops with Rumsfeld and the boys. 'Prime Minister' Allawi was a low-grade intelligence employee for Saddam, reporting on dissident Iraqis in London. Subsequently, Anglo-American intelligence outfits recruited him. After the First Gulf War he was sent to destabilize the regime. His hirelings bombed a cinema and a school bus carrying children. Before the war he invented the 45-minute WMD delivery systems warning for the dodgy dossier men in Downing Street. After the recent occupation he was rewarded and put on the 'Governing Council'. He hired a lobbying firm (Theros and Theros), which spent $370,000 campaigning in Washington for him to be made Prime Minister and also got him a column in the *Washington Post*.

As 'Prime Minister' he cultivates a thuggish image. On 17 July 2004 in a remarkable despatch from Baghdad, Paul McGeough, the respected Australian foreign correspondent (and former Editor of the *Sydney Morning Herald*) alleged that:

Iyad Allawi, the new Prime Minister of Iraq, pulled a pistol and executed as many as six suspected insurgents at a Baghdad police station,
just days before Washington handed control of the country to his
interim government, according to two people who allege they witnessed the killings.

They say the prisoners – handcuffed and blindfolded – were lined up
against a wall in a courtyard adjacent to the maximum-security cell
block in which they were held at the Al-Amariyah security centre, in
the city's south-western suburbs.

They say Dr Allawi told onlookers the victims had each killed as many
as 50 Iraqis and they 'deserved worse than death'.

The Prime Minister's office has denied the entirety of the witness
accounts in a written statement to the Herald, saying Dr Allawi had
never visited the centre and he did not carry a gun.

But the informants told the Herald that Dr Allawi shot each young man
in the head as about a dozen Iraqi policemen and four Americans from
the Prime Minister's personal security team watched in stunned silence.

McGeough appears regularly on Australian TV and radio to defend his
story, which refuses to go away. Astonishingly, it was not picked up by
any British newspaper. The fact is that Iraq is in a much bigger mess
today than it was in the years that preceded the war. The situation was
summed up by a former inmate of Abu Ghreib prison: 'We want
electricity in our homes not up the arse.'
   The citizens of the warmonger states can see this for themselves and
regardless of the media will, one hopes, punish their leaders for taking
them to war. And this regardless of the fact that the alternatives on
offer in most cases are weak. In the United States, Senator Kerry, for all
his pathetic militaristic displays prior to the November 2004 election,
was a weak and unconvincing politician. Unlike some of his liberal
apologists he does not like to portray the Democrats as the consistently

less aggressive of the two parties. It was, after all, Democratic not Republican Presidents who launched the American wars in Korea and Vietnam. Eisenhower's electoral appeal in 1952 was based on being the more peaceful of the two candidates. Vice-versa, in 1960, Kennedy attacked the Republicans for the 'missile gap', denouncing their weakness before the Soviet threat and demanding greater military spending. Carter, not Reagan, launched the second cold war. As recently as 1992, Clinton was thundering against Bush Sr's weakness on Cuba and China. In the current conjuncture, Bush Jr has clearly outpaced any Democratic rival in accelerated militarism. It is enough to remember that on the eve of 9/11, Hillary Clinton and Lieberman organized a collective letter, signed by virtually every Democratic Senator, denouncing Bush's policies on the Middle East as too weak. They wanted more support for Israel. They got it with a vengeance.

Homage IV

Abdelrahman Munif died, after a protracted illness, in his Damascus exile in January 2004. He was one of the most gifted Arab novelists of the 20th century. His last work was a set of three epic novels set in Iraq, complementing his *Cities of Salt*. Together with Naguib Mahfouz, he succeeded in transforming the literary landscape of the Arab world by making the novel central to its cultural and political concerns just as it had been in Europe during most of the 19th century. The day after his death, in a unique tribute to his integrity, he was denounced in the Saudi-owned Arab language media, particularly in the newspaper on *Al-Hayat* and *Al-Arabyia* television – a cable channel launched to compete with *al-Jazeera*. As a consequence, Munif's widow, Suad Qwadri, defied convention and refused to receive the Saudi Ambassador who had come to offer his condolences.

Born in Amman in 1933 to a Saudi trader and an Iraqi mother, Munif spent his first decade in that city. Despite the defeat of the Ottoman Empire, this was still a world dominated by cities, a world where frontiers were porous and Arab families and trade moved comfortably from Jerusalem to Cairo to Baghdad to Damascus and beyond. All these territories (with the exceptions of Damascus and Beirut) were under the control of the British Empire. The lines had been drawn in the sand but no barbed-wire or armed guards policed them. Abdelrahman Munif went to primary school in Amman, a secondary school in Baghdad and the university in Cairo.

Throughout his teenage years he would spend the summer holidays in the Peninsula with his Saudi family. It was here that he heard the stories and spoke with the Bedouins and the oil merchants and the nouveau riche Emirs who would later populate his fictions. Like the bulk of his generation he was shattered by the Palestinian catastrophe of 1948 and became a staunch Arab nationalist. The rise of Nasser in Egypt and the revolutionary wave that swept the Arab world as a result did not pass him by and he became a secular socialist militant. For his political opposition to the royal family he was stripped of his Saudi nationality in 1963 and fled to Baghdad. Here he obtained work as an economist in the petroleum industry and understood the importance of the liquid gold that lay underneath the sands of Arabia and Meso-potamia. His knowledge of the commodity and the industry was used with devastating effect in his novels.

He started writing fiction in the seventies, almost a decade after resigning from the Ba'ath Party leadership in Baghdad and moving to neighbouring Damascus. His active political life was now at an end. Henceforth his mind was fully concentrated on his fictions. He wrote a total of fifteen novels, but it was *Cities of Salt* – a quintet based on the transformation of the Arab peninsula from ancient Bedouin homeland to a hybrid tribal kleptocracy floating on oil – that established his reputation in the Arab world. He depicted the surprise, fear, uneasiness and tension that gripped Saudi Arabia after the discovery of oil, and his portraits of the country's rulers were thinly disguised, causing a great deal of merriment in the Arab street and the odd palace.

The two M's – Mahfouz and Munif – became the patriarchs of Arab literature. Mahfouz's Balzacian reconstruction of family life in Cairo, from the beginning of the twentieth century to the rise of Nasser, won him the Nobel.

Many Arab critics (though not Munif himself) felt that it was the

Saudi who merited the award, but his savage and surreal satires of the Royal family, their entourage and the oilmen had made him contraband within official culture. He wrote of the oasis towns, small and coquettish in character, that were lost in the tidal wave of oil and replaced with tall symmetrical buildings that bore little relationship to the region or the environment. Munif depicted how the al-Saud dynasty, with the help of the British Empire, possessed the Peninsula as sole proprietor and arbiter. Their voice and their interests drowned all else: contrary opinions were disallowed, literature discouraged. But the world of ideas (nationalism, communism, revolution) was stirring elsewhere in the Arab world and these could not be stopped at the border. They entered the minds of many citizens, Munif included, and even infected a young prince or two.

All his books were banned in Saudi Arabia and elsewhere in the Gulf. But they travelled nonetheless and were read secretly by many a Peninsula potentate. Munif's genius lay in his ability to impose the intellectual and the popular on characters that were neither. He penetrated the internal lives of his fellow-citizens, rich and poor. Three novels of the Saudi quintet were translated into English by Peter Theroux – *Cities of Salt*, *The Trench* and *Variations on Night and Day* – and published by Knopf in New York. But the American critics did not like them and John Updike famously denounced the books for not being the fiction he was used to reading. When I told Munif this he chuckled and his hands gestured in despair. Despite his enormous popularity with ordinary Arab readers and literary critics (Edward Said was one of his biggest fans) he was not feted and celebrated by officialdom. He was proud of this fact.

I met him in the flesh only once, when he came on a rare visit to London in the mid-'90s to be interviewed for a TV documentary I was producing. He was a soft-spoken and modest individual, genuinely bemused by the thought that a film was being made about his work. In that sense he was the polar opposite of his over-hyped counterparts in the West. Why, I asked him, had he chose the title *Cities of Salt* for his master work:

Cities of salt means cities that offer no sustainable existence. When the waters come in, the first waves will dissolve the salt and reduce these great glass cities to dust. In antiquity, as you know, many cities simply disappeared. It is possible to foresee the downfall of cities that are inhuman. With no means of livelihood they won't survive. Look at us now and see how the West sees us.

The 20th century is almost over, but when the West looks at us, all they see is oil and petrodollars.

Saudi Arabia is still without a constitution; the people are deprived of elementary rights. Women are treated like third-class citizens. Such a situation produces a desperate citizenry, without a sense of dignity or belonging ...

He was not in the least surprised that the majority of the 9/11 hijackers were Saudi citizens. After all, he had been warning us of what might happen for the previous four decades. His most recent work was a set of essays on Iraq. He had despised Saddam Hussein and written of the need for social democracy throughout the Arab world, but he was angered by the war and occupation. His son, Yasir, who I met in the states a few months ago, told me that the re-colonization of Iraq had reignited his old father's radicalism, and this is obvious in his last essays. The new situation had forced him to put his fiction aside and wield his pen as a weapon against local dictators and imperial warmongers alike.

But it is as a novelist that he will be missed the most. He was a storyteller without compare, who enriched the culture of the Arab world as a whole. He was a strong and independent-minded intellectual who refused to bend the knee before Prince or Colonel. His work and his example inspired younger writers, both men and women, throughout the Maghreb and the Mashreq and, for that reason, I am almost sure we will see his like again.

Reading Sappho in Ohio

Too many deaths. Too many defeats. In Iraq a resistance against the Empire continues; in the United States a homophobic victory for the Christian Caesar. Needed optimism of will and intellect. Goethe a good example in this regard:

> Who shall achieve it?—Gloomy question
> To which destiny wears a mask
> When on the day of great misfortune,
> Bleeding, all mankind falls dumb.
> But revive yourselves with new songs,
> Stay no longer deeply bowed:
> For earth engenders them again
> Just as always it has done

A Klee painting named *Angelus Novus* shows an angel looking as though he is about to move away from something he is fixedly contemplating. His eyes are staring, his mouth is open, his wings are spread. This is how one pictures the angel of history. His face is turned towards the past. Where we perceive a chain of events, he sees one single catastrophe which keeps piling wreckage upon wreckage and hurls it in front of his feet. The angel would like to stay, awaken the dead, and make whole what has been smashed. But a storm is blowing from paradise. It has got caught in his wings with such violence that the angel can no longer close them. This storm irresistibly propels him into the future to which his back is turned, while the pile of debris before him grows skyward. This storm is what we call progress.

Walter Benjamin, *Illuminations*

Chapter One

Preludes

When the finger points at the moon,
the idiot looks at the finger.

Chinese Proverb

1949

The news from Peking that October had not come like a thunderbolt from a clear blue sky. Edgar Snow's *Red Star Over China* had been a subcontinental classic for almost a decade, as a result of which expectations had built up over the last few years. At a May Day rally earlier that year, I had heard strange-sounding Chinese names – Mao Zedong, Chu Teh, Chou en Lai, Ho Lung. I forgot everything else about that meeting (I was only five and a half at the time), but the strange-sounding Chinese names refused to go away. For me, and no doubt for many others growing up in the subcontinent at the time, the drama of the Chinese Revolution eclipsed everything else.

There could not have been a better antidote to the recently concluded war, which had claimed a total of eighty million lives. In the photographs and newsreels, which depicted the horror of Hitler's concentration camps, anyone could see the fragility of Western civilization. The emaciated bodies of those who survived the Holocaust symbolized the traumas of the Second World War. The mushroom clouds over Japan, which ended the war, were manifestations of a new form of barbarism. The first victims of atomic weapons were the defenceless citizens of Hiroshima and Nagasaki. Their burnt bodies were testimony, if any were needed, that savagery and genocide were not the monopoly of the German state. In this context the victory of China's communist-led peasant armies was seen by the rural and urban poor throughout Asia as a triumph without parallel. China was, after all, the largest country in the world.

The centre of the town was swathed in red flags. It was my first demonstration and one that I remember to this day. The city was Lahore, which for many centuries had been a much envied metropolis in Northern India. Then the last conquerors had departed, leaving behind a divided subcontinent. The old town had become part of a new country – Pakistan. The founder of this state, Mohammed Ali Jinnah, an agnostic, had cynically used religion to create a 'Muslim nation'. Jinnah had expressed the hope that Pakistan would, despite everything, remain a secular state, but the logic of history had proved fatal. All the Hindu and Sikh families in Lahore had fled across confessional frontiers. Little 'Lahores' had sprung up in Delhi.

For my parents, most of whose friends suddenly vanished, Lahore in the fifties was like a ghost town. The pain of Partition has been sensitively depicted in a number of short stories by the Urdu writer, Saadat Hasan Manto, and by poets like Faiz Ahmed Faiz and Sahir Ludhianvi. I had been three and a half years old in 1947. Pre-Partition Lahore, for me, existed only in numerous overheard conversations. The recent past became a subject for discussions, sometimes heated, but more often sad, and these could be heard in every quarter of the city. They frequently centred on the vibrancy of the town. During the twenties, thirties and forties, it had been an important cultural centre, a home for poets and painters, a city that was proud of its cosmopolitanism. Nineteen forty-seven had changed all that for ever. The old coffee houses and teashops were still in place, but the Hindu and Sikh faces had disappeared, never to return. This fact was soon accepted; political gossip and poetry reasserted their old primacy under new conditions.

The red flags were held aloft by the proletarian vanguard of Lahore: its railway workers. I cannot now remember the occasion of the demonstration, but the mood was one of great excitement and one slogan dominated that march: *We shall take the Chinese road, brothers! The Chinese road!* The railway workers' leader was a communist in his late thirties, but already regarded and treated as a veteran. Mirza Ibrahim had worked on the railways for many years. He had been imprisoned, intimidated, offered management positions and straight-forward financial bribes, but he had held firm and organized a strong union. I think his popularity derived more from his incorruptibility than his political affiliations, but perhaps I am wrong. It is true that later that year, when, as a communist, he contested an important by-election against a nonentity backed by the regional strongman of the Muslim League, he won. Or rather he should have won. What happened was that several hundreds of votes cast for him by the railway workers were disallowed by the Deputy Commissioner in charge of supervising the polls. His reason? The ballot-papers were dirt-stained! The Deputy Commissioner went on to become a senior, and rich, civil servant. Mirza Ibrahim's supporters merely demanded that in future soap should be distributed to the poor before every election.

Prior to its success, the Chinese Revolution had been ignored by the superpowers. After 1949, the United States became obsessed with the triumph of Mao's partisans and determined to prevent the spread of the virus. Asia was to become engulfed in a series of wars. Europe on the other hand was relatively lucky. Its future had been agreed on pieces of paper by Stalin, Churchill and Roosevelt. The continent, by common agreement at the Crimean seaside resort of Yalta, had been bifurcated into what was euphemistically referred to as 'spheres of influence'. Accord at the top had been considered vital to contain popular discontent from below. Stalin was permitted a free hand between the Elbe and the Oder, in return for which he pledged support for the status quo in France, Italy and Greece. The fate of Germany remained unsettled. The West did well out of Yalta. They preserved the capitalist order in Italy and Greece, where Stalin's coercive powers and Moscow's ideological straitjacket helped ensure that the partisans were effectively disarmed both militarily and politically. The agreement was breached in Yugoslavia. Stalin and Churchill had agreed that there would be '50–50 influence', whatever that may have meant in the circumstances. The leader of the Yugoslav partisans, Tito, refused to accept Stalin's advice and restore the monarchy, and confident of popular support in his own country, the Yugoslav leader broke first with capitalism and subsequently with Stalin.

The fifties may have been bleak years in Europe, but despite all the insults, the war remained cold. Internal conditions deteriorated in both the USA and the USSR, where the executioners of the soul were hard at work. McCarthy in Washington and Zhdanov in Moscow produced some real horrors. But there was no war.

We were not so lucky in Asia. A rash of hot wars had disfigured our continent. We were to be punished for the success of the Chinese, who were perceived at the time as the willing and conscious tools of Moscow's subversion. The forward march of the Asian revolution had to be challenged, stopped and militarily defeated. The Peninsular Wars of Korea and Indochina became centres of global conflict. It was argued by the US Secretary of State, Dean Acheson, that the Red victories which had been inaugurated by the Chinese October could 'paralyse the defence of Europe'.

The Korean War was an unnecessary conflict and attempts to portray it as a 'defence of democracy' were never very convincing. The regime defended by the US Proconsul in Occupied Japan, General Douglas MacArthur, was corrupt to the core and the South Korean strongman, Syngman Rhee, was loathed by the citizens of his country. One reason, amongst many others, was that when, prior to 1945, Korea had been occupied by the Japanese, Rhee had collaborated with Tokyo. Later, he did so just as happily with the United States who, in an attempt to reverse the gains of the Chinese Revolution, had revived a quisling administration. The local opposition to Rhee had not been dominated by Southern supporters of Kim-il-Sung. In fact, Kim was widely regarded by Korean communists as a talentless usurper transplanted in Northern Korea by Soviet tanks. He later paid his detractors back. Most of them were liquidated when they fled to the North to avoid Rhee's repression in the South.

The Korean War was, from the very start, enshrouded in a web of legal mystifications. Who fired the first shot? Who crossed the 38th Parallel (the dividing line between North and South Korea) first? In reality, the war was an attempt by the United States, backed by the Labour Government of Clement Attlee, to turn the tide in China. General MacArthur was not the sort of war-hero addicted to diplomacy. He did not attempt to conceal that what he was after were the scalps of the Reds in Peking. He stated that he would, if necessary, cross the Yalu river and occupy Manchuria. On 30 November 1950, President Truman told a press conference that if the United Nations sanctioned military intervention in China, he would have no inhibitions in authorizing MacArthur to use atomic bombs. This created a panic in Western Europe. The Labour Prime Minister, backed by Churchill, was despatched to the White House to argue against their use in China. What was probably more decisive, however, were rifts within the American High Command. MacArthur was not universally popular and there were many who found the General's thinly-disguised Bonapartist aspirations repulsive. The hot war in Asia did not, therefore, become nuclear-powered.

The fright had been enough to make us aware of the precarious nature of world politics. In Lahore, a rhymester from the Progressive Writers' Association was seconded to teach some of us an anti-nuclear weapons hymn. This lesson never got very far, since the versifier insisted on pronouncing 'bomb' as 'bum'. Since the word dominated the chorus in Urdu, the only result was to encourage a wave of irrepressible laughter. What else could we do when he sang: 'Enemy of life, Enemy of Human, Enemy of Pakistan, This Dread Accursed Atom BUM'? He was persistent, but so were we and after a week the attempt collapsed amidst bitter recriminations. The Progressive Writers abandoned the attempt to encourage a children's choir. Instead we recited the odd poem before the assembled throng, which for many years met outside our garage in the evenings. I was made to learn Pushkin's 'The Hanging Chains of Siberia', which was recited to popular acclaim. Of all the poems I read, enjoyed and often learnt as a child, this is the only one I have totally forgotten. Only its title remains.

1953

My mother wept on the day that Stalin died. It was outside Fazal Din's, the chemists along the Lower Mall in Lahore. We had been shopping and she must have caught a glimpse of the headlines in the evening papers. I was waiting for her in the car. When she got in, her face was drawn and tense. At first she did not say anything. She did not cry aloud or uncontrollably. I just saw a few tears trickling down her face. She saw that I was worried and explained in a quiet voice: 'Stalin's dead!' I was upset, but more for her sake than the dead Stalin. I remember feeling that perhaps I, too, should cry, but I found myself unable to do so.

My mother was twenty-seven years old at the time. She had been an active communist and had joined the Party in 1943, the year that I was born. (My maternal grandmother, whose sympathies lay elsewhere, had nonetheless knitted me a white sweater with a red hammer and sickle.) My mother and large numbers of communists elsewhere in the world wept when they heard of Stalin's death. Why did they cry? There is no single answer to this question nor could there be, but, whatever the reasons, it was surely not because they thought that the world revolution would now be leaderless or that there was nobody capable of presiding over the next set of purges. It was because Stalinism had organized itself as a religion, albeit a primitive one, with its special symbols and a Living God. When he died it must have seemed to many loyal communists that all their certainties had died with him. For over two decades, formative years for many communist parties in the colonies and semi-colonies, Stalin had dominated their world and now they wondered whether political life was possible after his death.

J. V. Stalin's *Collected Works* were given pride of place in my father's study. His busts and portraits were also visible, though my mother's sensibilities prevented any vulgar displays in the living room. Happily, in this case, aesthetics prevailed over politics. This addiction to Stalinism had an interesting side-effect. The whims of the cultural commissars in Moscow were faithfully reproduced in numerous homes around the world. I doubt whether, as a child, I would have ever heard Paul Robeson singing Negro spirituals had it not been for the fact that one of the greatest voices of black America was a tireless fellow-traveller on the political front. Other treats were also in store. Our house contained tons of Russian literature. Stalin was not known for his kindness to the talented generation of post-revolutionary poets and writers and in most cases they were savagely repressed. Many committed suicide. Others perished in the camps. Some stayed silent. A few became time-servers. Interestingly enough, however, none of the classics of Russian literature were banned in Stalin's Russia. Pushkin, Gogol, Turgenev, Chekhov, Tolstoy and Dostoevsky were available everywhere, despite the fact that in a number of cases the merciless lampooning of Tsarist tyranny could have been construed as subversion. Nonetheless, millions of copies were printed and translated into other languages, including English. These books took me into another world. Tsarism had created the conditions for the birth of an amazingly alive and interventionist literary tradition, whose style and quality was very different to the output of Dickens or even Zola.

There were other books as well, but most of these were the literary versions of Stalinist realism and some verged on the grotesque. I did manage to read Makarenko's trilogy *Road to Life*, however, a moral extravaganza designed for the Young Pioneers. There were also numerous film-shows, as my father had always been a home-movies buff. His 16mm Kodak projector was often used to show the latest Soviet newsreels to the comrades and their progeny. The comrades, naturally, watched a Ukrainian harvest with a praiseworthy stoicism. We children would moan the minute a tractor appeared on the screen and some one or other would say, 'Oh no! Not another tractor' or 'Oh no, not another giant crane'. It was a closed world in many ways, but what made it different from anything else was that it was a world. It was a deformed internationalism because it was based on the blind worship of the USSR and its infallible Leader. Neither could be wrong. Mistakes were sometimes committed, but the Leader in his wisdom would ensure that they were soon corrected. For three whole decades being a communist anywhere in the world meant becoming a Great-Russian nationalist. With such a world view it is hardly surprising that the first response of many communists to Stalin's death was to cry.

In Eastern Europe, the dictator's death was greeted with relief. East German workers and students, including many communists, celebrated the event by a spontaneous uprising against their own bureaucratic regime. Their main demand was for the institutionalization of democratic rights for all. The movement was crushed by Soviet tanks, which led the Marxist German playwright and poet, Bertolt Brecht, to pen an open missive to the Central Committee entitled 'The Solution':

> After the uprising of the 17th June
> The Secretary of the Writers' Union
> Had leaflets distributed in the Stalinallee
> Stating that the people
> Had forfeited the confidence of the government
> And could win it back only
> By redoubled efforts. Would it not be easier
> In that case for the government
> To dissolve the people
> And elect another?

The Korean War ended and an armistice was signed on 27 June 1953. The US administration had mercifully rejected Syngman Rhee's thoughtful request that they use nuclear weapons against Moscow and Peking. The United States and its supporters had lost over a million lives as had the North Koreans and the Chinese. The total of those who died was well over three million.

1954

Two names emerged in this year. One short man and one small town: Vo Nguyen Giap and Dienbienphu. The Vietnamese communists had waged a continuous guerrilla war against the Japanese occupiers who had replaced the French, but the postwar settlement was to bring them no joy, even though the Viet Minh controlled the whole country in August 1945. British troops under General Gracey (who was the first Commander-in-Chief of the Pakistan Army in 1947) occupied Saigon and held it till the French could reoccupy the country. The Viet Minh foolishly (some might say criminally) did not resist during the early stages. This was undoubtedly due to their reluctance to take on the British who were, after all, still allies of the Soviet Union. It was to prove a costly mistake. The Second Indochinese War lasted nine years (1945–54). It was brought to an end by the crushing defeat of the French, who had arrogantly dismissed Giap as a 'bush-General', at the Battle of Dienbienphu. The French General Navarre, under strong American pressure to expedite a plan for victory, decided to parachute 20,000 of his best troops into the valley town of Dienbienphu. The Viet Minh controlled the surrounding countryside and Navarre intended to use the town and wipe out the Vietnamese partisans in the region. The tactic was referred to as a 'hedgehog' position. The 'bush-General' decided to go for the kill. Giap's troops surrounded the 'hedgehog' and subjected the French fortress to a continuing barrage of artillery fire from the hills that overlooked the town. This was daytime warfare. At night, the Vietnamese began to dig a series of zig-zag trenches that took them ever closer to the French. It soon became apparent that the master-strategist's encirclement could not be broken.

The men in Washington watched the situation with growing unease. The US Secretary of State, John Foster Dulles, an unashamed defender of the theory of permanent counter-revolution, sent the French a message. Were they, by any chance, interested in the use of nuclear weapons to burn the red termites off the hills around Dienbienphu? The offer was politely rejected. Apart from all other considerations, the termite armies had now penetrated the perimeters of Dienbienphu and nuclear weapons would have wiped out the French forces as well. Instead they decided to surrender to the 'bush-General'.

The battle marked the end of French colonial rule in Indochina. When the news reached the French capital in that week of May, the ruling classes were traumatized. Jean-Paul Sartre and Simone de Beauvoir, however, walked out into the sunshine of the Paris streets and found it difficult to contain their joy. At home we, too, were delighted, though there were no official celebrations since the Pakistan Government had been strongly pro-French. But in neighbouring India, the Prime Minister, Jawaharlal Nehru spoke for the whole subcontinent when he congratulated the Vietnamese on their epic victory and publicly celebrated yet another defeat for European imperialism. General Giap became a teenage hero.

A conference was rapidly convened in Geneva to deal with the crisis. The Americans, Russians, Chinese, Indians and the Viet Minh sent delegations. The Vietnamese were offered a truce: they could have Northern Vietnam since they already controlled the region, but the South, where there were immense complications, would have elections within two years to determine the future. The Vietnamese were unhappy as total victory lay within easy grasp, but against their better judgement they bowed to pressure from Moscow and Peking; the struggle would not be pursued in the South. More than a decade later, as Hanoi was being bombed day and night, the North Vietnamese Prime Minister, Pham van Dong, would tell me that 'it was the unhappiest phase in our history and, as you see, we are paying the price for our mistake'.

The Geneva Conference had also been the first public meeting of American and Chinese leaders. John Foster Dulles had stared hard at Chou en Lai. The Chinese had already begun to replace the Russians in the more bizarre cold-war productions from Hollywood. When the Chinese Prime Minister had walked towards Dulles and extended his hand, the American had simply turned his back and walked away. Asia's outrage was articulated by Nehru, who set into motion the convocation of a special Afro-Asian Conference at Bandung in Indonesia in 1955, which would assert the sovereignty of the newly-independent states of two continents.

1956

Growing up in a newly independent country should have provided at least a tiny bit of inspiration, excitement or stimulation. Pakistan, alas, was a state without a history. Its ideologues, on the few occasions when they were coherent, could only think in terms of comparing and counterposing everything, big or small, to neighbouring India. Pakistan's rulers suffered from a gigantic inferiority complex. This created problems on many levels, but for those of us at school in the fifties it created a terrible vacuum. Nationalism in Pakistan did not mean keeping a self-respecting distance from the former colonial power, but crude anti-Indian chauvinism. It was not totally illogical. The Congress in India had waged a two-pronged struggle against British imperialism. The Muslim League had been created by the British to organize the Muslim gentry. Even in the years prior to 1947, the Muslim League had essentially fought, not the British, but the Congress. In secret, I admired Nehru, but to have said so publicly would have led to too many fist-fights at school.

The bureaucrats who really governed Pakistan from 1947 to 1958 were totally committed to the West. Successive prime ministers had gone to Washington to kiss hands in the White House. It was therefore with some relief that I read about the rise of an Arab nationalist – Gamal Abdel Nasser. Here was someone who could be defended in public. When Nasser nationalized the Suez Canal and told cheering crowds that the 'imperialists could choke in their rage', we felt excitement mingled with pride. Nasser became a hero throughout the subcontinent. He was especially popular amongst the people in Pakistan. The only unsurprising feature of the whole affair was that while Indian leaders pledged him their complete support, in 'Muslim' Pakistan the governing circles sided with his enemies till a wave of popular discontent compelled them to step backwards and keep silent.

My father was at that time the editor of the *Pakistan Times*, the country's largest circulation daily and part of a chain of left-wing newspapers, which had been launched on the eve of Independence by a socialist politician and close family friend, Mian Iftikharudin. Pakistan, deprived of a viable left after the migration of Hindu and Sikh communists following Partition, gained a set of radical mass-circulation daily papers and journals which had no equal in neighbouring India or elsewhere in the continent.

The news that Egypt had been invaded by an Anglo-French expeditionary force supported by Israel reached us in the evening. My father had returned with the proofs of an editorial he had crafted. It contained a savage condemnation of the whole affair and marked the beginning of a campaign which totally isolated the government. The next morning at school there was no other subject for conversation. Our school was run by Irish missionary Catholic Brothers, a bunch of bigots who discouraged any topical discussions in or out of the classroom. The atmosphere was heavily apolitical. The morning after the Suez invasion, however, these restrictions simply could not be enforced.

Later that day, the university students went on strike against the war and marched to the British consulate via the schools, most of which closed down in sympathy. News of this had spread and we were eagerly awaiting their arrival, when a dilapidated looking Mr Walters came and told us that the Brothers wanted the Junior Cadet Corps to get on to the school roof and point its rifles at the university students, whose chants could already be heard. This suggestion was greeted with obscene gestures and abuse by the older boys, but before the matter could go any further our school was occupied by angry students demanding that it be closed down. The Principal, Reverend Brother Xavier Henderson, refused to meet a delegation. He was then unceremoniously, but gently, dragged out of his office and taken before the demonstrators, who were chanting anti-imperialist slogans. The sight of Brother Henderson, the only white face present, inevitably raised the temperature. Hendy realized that he would have to close the school down and decided to do so in style, and on his own terms. He climbed on a chair and addressed the crowd, explaining that he was not British, but Irish. This only partially silenced the students since the colonial educational system had not fully explained the historical divide between Britain and Ireland. Suddenly Hendy held up his deformed right hand. We had always wondered how this had happened, and there were, needless to say, a number of theories, most of them the product of schoolboy fantasies in which 'priests' holes' played a major part. Now the Reverend Brother Henderson informed the angry young men of the city that his fingers had been permanently disabled when he had participated in the campaigns of the Irish Republican Army against British imperialism in the late twenties and thirties. There was silence as he spoke about the Irish struggle, ending with a marvellously fake peroration which announced that he had decided to close the school in protest against the invasion of Egypt. There was loud applause and even a few chants of 'Henderson Zindabad' ('Long Live Henderson'), which emphasized the comic aspect of the affair. Some of us joined the demo to the British consulate. It was my first parentless participation in a political event.

Nineteen fifty-six was one of those years that leave their mark on an entire generation. The Suez débâcle had symbolized the end of an era. Britain, once the imperialist power *par excellence*, could not undertake any independent initiatives. Prior approval and permission from the United States was a necessary prerequisite for all actions East or West of Suez. Nasser's political success made neutralism a potent force in the colonial world. Nasser, Nehru and Tito became the three kings of non-alignment. The contrast with the supine attitude of the Pakistan Government could not be ignored. Nasser's actions had delivered a body blow to Pakistan's ruling parties. Pakistan's bureaucrats and generals prevented a general election from taking place.

The rise of a new Third-World nationalism seemed the most exciting development that year, at least to schoolboys and girls in their early teens. Our household, however, was much more shaken by the strange news that was beginning to seep through from Moscow, where Nikita Khrushchev had been addressing the 20th Party Congress of the Communist Party of the Soviet Union. The uprising in East Berlin had frightened the men in the Kremlin. Stalin had suppressed all opposition via a series of cold-blooded and systematic purges both in his own party and elsewhere in Eastern Europe. His successors were beginning to realize that they could not carry on in the same old way. The spectre of East Berlin had to be exorcized. Khrushchev, more than any other bureaucrat, realized that it was time to lift the curtain of fear. He decided to go as far as possible without actually destroying the structures of bureaucratic domination. His speech to the 20th Party Congress was an audacious move insofar that he was appealing to the delegates over the heads of the Politburo, in which he remained in the minority. But it was carefully planned and the wily Ukrainian restrained his more ardent supporters (such as Anastas Mikoyan) from going too far. His denunciation of Stalin was, of course, sensational and created a major storm within the old Stalinist family. Till that time a critique of Stalinism from the left had largely been the work of tiny bands of Trotskyists. For making many of the same points as Khrushchev, twenty-five years previously, they had been denounced as agents of Hitler (except during the period of the Stalin–Hitler Pact), of Churchill (but not during the years of the Great Alliance) and the CIA. How would loyal Stalinists square the circle?

In the West the communist parties lost an important layer of intellectuals and fellow-travellers. The defection was most pronounced in Britain, where the Party lost several thousand members, including its most distinguished historians. Many of these resigned from the Party because the apparatus refused to permit any serious internal discussion of the issues at stake. In Asia, the Chinese leaders published a pamphlet entitled 'On the Question of Stalin', which was a crude and simplistic defence of the dictator motivated largely by a factional hostility to Khrushchev on other important matters. Thus 1956 also marked the official beginnings of the Sino-Soviet dispute which would later be conducted with a rare ferocity.

In our house there were many perplexed discussions, but ultimately Khrushchev prevailed. Ironically enough, Khrushchev's victory was the result of a politico-psychological refusal of the comrades in many parts of the subcontinent to admit that Moscow could be wrong. The changes in our small world were dramatic. Overnight the busts of Stalin disappeared, first to the attic and then as presents to the rag-and-bone men. Many years later I used to wonder whether one of these discarded statuettes, suitably aged, with the head and nose partially destroyed, would turn up in some middle-class drawing-room and the proud hostess would introduce it as a rare find from the Harappa mounds in Sind, anywhere between 400–300 BC. *The Collected Works* of J. V. Stalin also disappeared to some storeroom where they languished for many years, gathering dust and feeding moths.

Having accepted de-Stalinization, the local comrades were somewhat bewildered when Khrushchev sent the tanks into Hungary in order to crush an anti-Stalinist uprising headed by members of the

Hungarian Communist Party. Suez had overshadowed Budapest in our world. There was very little information about what had actually taken place. Nasser was much closer to us in terms of both geography and politics. The English-speaking magazines which arrived regularly from London were the *New Statesman* and *Labour Monthly* and the latter provided a steady pole of reference. RPD's crisply written 'Notes of the Month' were reproduced in different forms throughout India and Pakistan.* It was not until I came to Europe that I really understood the importance of what had happened in Hungary that year.

Nineteen fifty-six had shown that the two camps were divided within themselves. This helped to loosen the rigid ideological categories imposed by the exigencies of the post-1948 freeze. The carefully-constructed certainties of the cold warriors had begun to crumble. The edifices were shaky. Both sides had, it was true, put their houses together again, but how strong were the new foundations? Such questions were never publicly posed in Lahore.

The closing down of our school because of Suez had already made this an eventful year. Now something else was about to happen, which would overshadow even Nasser's triumph. The leaders of revolutionary China were due in Pakistan on a state visit. Lahore was on their itinerary. This would have been exciting enough on its own but, much to everyone's surprise, the government had permitted the Chinese to accept an invitation to a private lunch which was being hosted by the socialist politician Mian Iftikharudin. It was a large party and as a local wit commented, 'much larger than *the* Party in Pakistan'. The city's left intelligentsia, the bulk of whom were employed as journalists on the Progressive Papers Ltd, were present, as were a few dignitaries, such as the portly Governor of the province. Protocol brooked no interference on these occasions. I was introduced to both Chou en Lai and Marshal

---

* RPD were the initials of Rajani Palme Dutt (of mixed Swedish and Indian origin), a leading theoretician of British communists, whose immense talents were grotesquely squandered by the advent of Stalinism. The price of Dutt's loyalty to Moscow was a self-imposed mental discipline. Despite this, it is unlikely that Dutt himself would have survived the purges had he been resident in Moscow durng the late 1930s.

Ho Lung. A new language was entered in my tatty autograph book, which jostled uneasily with the likes of Hanif Mohammed and the three W's of West Indian cricket (Worrell, Weekes and Walcott).

Chou en Lai was urbane and gracious, and smilingly answered all questions. Everyone was disappointed and turned to Marshal Ho Lung, a veteran of the civil war who had once been a bandit warlord, but who had been won over to the revolution. At least that is what his Chinese interpreter told Sohail Iftikhar and myself as we stared at him in awe. I do not recall the Marshal speaking a single word that day. He went up in our estimation even more as a result. His mute exterior seemed to emphasize his strength of character, or so it seemed at the time. In the years that followed I would scour many a volume on Chinese history to find references to Ho Lung. Though he was often mentioned in revolutionary despatches, he had clearly not been in the habit of writing war diaries or making memorable speeches. This could have been another explanation for his silence on that day.

1957

The events of 1956 must have had some effect on me. I think they gave me a self-confidence about politics, which, in preceding years, had been confined to accompanying one or the other of my parents to political happenings of one sort of another.

Sometime during this year, I read a tiny news item in the news-paper, which shocked me profoundly. A black American, Jimmy Wilson, had been sentenced to death for stealing a dollar in some backwood hell-hole in the Southern United States. I had been lis-tening to Paul Robeson singing virtually from infancy. The American magazine *Masses and Mainstream*, which also arrived regularly, had carried a great deal of material on the condition of blacks in the United States. But the sentence on Wilson surpassed everything. I went to school in a rage, discussed the issue with some friends, most of whom were apolitical, but shocked nonetheless by the scale of the atrocity that was about to be perpetrated. Something had to be done and I decided that we should organize a school student demonstration to the US Consulate on Empress Road.

There was some enthusiasm for the idea and we agreed to hold the demonstration on the following Saturday, which was a half-day at school. We did not get permission from anybody, but distributed leaflets and made a few placards. I had thought that we might get about a hundred schoolboys on the streets. Others were more circumspect. Nonetheless we hoped that at least fifty would attend, particularly as we had obtained pledges from over three dozen friends. On the day, however, only six stayed behind after school. The others had not been able to override parental disapproval. The small turnout raised new dilemmas. Should we march at all or simply hire a *tonga* (horse and cart), pile in and discreetly deliver our protest note? The majority (four of us) decided that since the placards had been made, the march would take place. So we began. As we marched on to the streets our protest attracted both genuine interest, but also a great deal of ribald mirth. At a critical stage, when even I was beginning to get depressed and was entertaining the thought that we might, after all, have to get a *tonga*, a gang of street urchins came to our rescue. A few dozen grabbed some of our placards. Then one of them said: 'Why exactly are we demonstrating today?' 'Because of Jimmy Wilson', I explained. I had foolishly imagined that the case was already a cause célèbre. The urchins nodded sagely. Then, just as we were about to cross the town's main thoroughfare, opposite the provincial legislature, they erupted into a cacophony of slogans. The bystanders had been on the verge of taking us seriously (or so we thought), but the loud cries from our ranks created a tiny furore on the pavements. Even the street-vendors looked up to see what was happening. We, the initiators of the march, were paralysed with terror. The urchins were chanting: 'Jimmy Wilson, Murabad!' ('Death to Jimmy Wilson!'). Had we been infiltrated? I stopped the procession in the middle of the road, explained to our street-warriors that Jimmy Wilson was on our side and that we were marching to save his life. They outnumbered us six to one and the situation could have become tense. Fortunately they realized their error, corrected it publicly by shouting 'Jimmy Wilson, Zindabad!' and we moved forward. At the Consulate, the urchins were not allowed to enter the compound, but a friend and myself were permitted to hand in our letter of protest to the Consul-General, a dour mid-Westerner called Spengler. He accepted our letter, said we were being duped by communist propaganda, insisted that Wilson had been tried and found guilty by a jury and that was all he had to say to us. He then took our names, said he would write to the Principal of our school and register a formal complaint. The following Monday we discovered that this had not been an idle threat. It was my first real experience of American democracy.

Our overall balance-sheet of the event was that we had averted a total disaster, largely because of the additional support we had mobilized *en route*. After that day, and for the next few years, whenever I ran into any of those who had so graciously swelled our ranks, he would whisper with a grin, 'Jimmy Wilson, Zindabad, eh?'

1958

The year of the Generals. In France, General De Gaulle, backed by the French Army, took power and ended the political instability that had characterized the Fourth Republic. He declared a Fifth Republic and arrogated for himself the powers and privileges of 'the President'. As the strongman of the new Republic he constructed a political party, which was able to reflect the concerns and interests of the French ruling classes. In Pakistan, too, General Ayub Khan abrogated the Constitution and declared Martial Law. His aim was to prevent the country's first ever general election, scheduled for spring '59, from taking place. At his very first cabinet meeting, dominated by Generals and a few hand-picked civilians, Ayub laid down strict guidelines as to the political perimeters of his government. Many years later, one of the civilians, Zulfiqar Ali Bhutto, told me that when asked about the country's foreign policy, Ayub had replied: 'As far as we are concerned there is only one important embassy and that is the American embassy.' There were, as a result, few doubts as to the strongly conservative orientation of the military dictatorship at home and abroad. One of my paternal aunts was, at the time, married to one of the three Generals flanking Ayub. Her husband was the new Minister for Interior. 'The new regime', she told us one day over lunch, 'is fiercely anti-communist.' We already knew.

After the coup the majority of the country's newspapers had greeted the General as a saviour. The single exception was the collage of newspapers and magazines published by Progressive Papers Ltd, as the military regime had imposed a strict censorship. No criticism of Martial Law was permitted. The Progressive Papers had always been an anomaly in Pakistan, where the bulk of the post-Partition intelligentsia was not merely conformist, but engaged in a project to rewrite the history of the struggle for Indian independence in order to provide the new state with a *raison d'être*. Mian Iftikharudin, the proprietor of the papers, as a radical Member of Parliament, had been a powerful and consistent critic of successive governments and the all-powerful United States embassy. The latter genuinely found it very odd that the largest newspaper chain in a country umbilically tied to the United States could be so uniformly hostile to American interests in the region. With the Ayub dictatorship in place the offending thorn could now be painlessly extracted.

In both France and Pakistan, the politicians had lost the will to resist the Generals. Paris had, it is true, witnessed a demonstration of a quarter of a million men and women in support of democracy. This turned out to be the funeral procession of the Fourth Republic. The Socialist leader, Guy Mollet, a staunch supporter of the war in Vietnam, the occupation of Algeria and the ill-fated Suez expedition, wrote a private letter to De Gaulle urging a takeover of the country. But there was no general strike against the emasculation of democracy in either France or Pakistan. The rise and fall of successive parliamentary governments, an outcome of the continuous shift in parliamentary loyalties, had become a national pastime in both countries. This legislative variant of musical chairs had increased the alienation of many people towards traditional bourgeois politics. The sight of a strong man on a white charger appeared to offer some hope to sections of the demoralized populace. The French Communist and Radical parties did attempt to resist the tide, but they failed to mobilize much support. The French Socialists had, in reality, paved the way for De Gaulle by their disgraceful attitude towards the colonial wars in which France was involved.

The reaction to the victory of De Gaulle in Britain was predictable. The right-wing press was delighted; the Labour Party National Executive was acquiescent. Labour leftists of that period condemned the dissolution of the Fourth Republic. Aneurin Bevan was eloquent in his denunciations and Michael Foot, his loyal lieutenant, condemned the pusillanimity of French politicians. For this act he was expelled from France. Richard Crossman defended De Gaulle in the pages of the *Daily Mirror*, portraying the General as the only leader who could prevent a slide into fascism. The same Richard Crossman attacked the French Communists in the columns of the *New Statesman* for not having resisted De Gaulle with all their strength. Interestingly enough the *New Statesman* would soon defend General Ayub Khan's regime as a benign and gentlemanly interregnum in the country's history. This was written while Kingsley Martin was still at the magazine's helm.

Generals De Gaulle and Ayub Khan had both seized power in the same year. A decade later both men would be confronted by the rise of new and powerful mass movements.

1959

In January, a small island in the Caribbean, situated just off the shores of the North American continent, made itself known throughout the world. As the US-backed dictator, Batista, fled from Cuba to Miami, the rebel units of the 26th July Movement, with Fidel Castro at their head, entered Havana. The entire city turned out to greet the heroes of the revolutionary war. The Batista regime, which had been marked by a combination of sadism and corruption, had made Havana a mafia haven. The fighters in the Sierra Maestra had always been heavily outnumbered by the troops supporting the dictatorship, but the struggle waged by the guerrillas had won the hearts and minds of the poor peasants and the workers in the towns. The poor, as is usually the case in most parts of the world, constituted an overwhelming majority of the country's population. For them Fidel Castro, in 1959, was a giant. Marx had written that 'Men make their own history, but not just as they please. They do not choose circumstances for themselves, but have to work on circumstances as they find them, have to fashion the material handed down from the past.' In the early days it seemed that Castro was making history just as he pleased. The series of episodes and encounters that constituted the revolutionary war were a remarkable catalogue of courage and daring. Some years later the best-known European chronicler of the Cuban Revolution, Régis Debray, would describe Fidel Castro, Che Guevara and their comrades as people who 'risked everything to win everything' and conclude that 'at the end they deserved to get everything'. For an entire generation in Latin America and Western Europe this revolution would prove to be a formative experience. It would teach them that it was possible to challenge oppression, fight and win. The success in Cuba radicalized millions in Latin America and tens of thousands in Europe.

It would be nice to record that from Lahore I had been faithfully following the progress of the war; that the valleys, gorges and impenetrable jungles of the Sierra Maestra were deeply embedded in my consciousness and that when Havana was liberated, transformed in one stroke from a brothel for the mafiosi into a furnace for the continental revolution, my heart, too, was set alight. It would be nice, but totally false. The fall of Batista was certainly recorded in the Pakistan press, but a confusion prevailed, not entirely dissimilar to the disarray prevalent in Washington. Who was Fidel Castro? He had never been a communist or leftist. This gave Washington hope and made the old left, wedded to Muscovite conceptions, suspicious and nervous. Peking and Hanoi had fallen to the forces of traditional communism. Where would Castro take Cuba? Would he become a national-populist like Peron, or a simple nationalist like Arbenz in Guatemala and be overthrown by a US-instigated coup in a few years? Or would he permanently alter the map of Latin America by breaking completely with the American companies who dominated his country's economy?

In Pakistan we got very little news from Cuba. There was no Cuban embassy and hence no Cuban literature landed on my father's desk. In fact, the only material which seemed to arrive regularly in those days was the daily communication from the official censor, a big envelope containing editorials and/or newsstories that had been clumsily mangled. It was both a hazardous and nerve-wracking exercise to produce oppositional papers under a Martial Law regime, but I'm sure that our side would not have made any strategic or tactical mistakes. The Generals, alas, found it equally irksome to deal every day with a set of recalcitrant newspapers, especially when all other newspapers and magazines were effortlessly toeing the line. At a highly confidential cabinet meeting the Generals agreed a plan to solve the problem. A bogus case was manufactured accusing Mian Iftikharudin of being the recipient of 'Moscow gold'. This was used as a pretext to seize the papers. Mian attempted to force the uniformed brigands to try him in a civilian court; he failed and died broken-hearted some years later.

I, too, was deeply affected by the episode. Early one April morning the pre-breakfast calm of our house was disturbed by the sound of a car horn, gates being opened and a great deal of unexpected activity. I looked out of my bedroom window to see a government limousine flying the state flag. As I was the only member of the family who was dressed in preparation for school, I rushed out just in time to see a solitary cabinet minister alight from the car and greet me with a smile. It was Zulfiqar Ali Bhutto, then one of Ayub's civilian favourites. He demanded to see my father immediately. I showed him to the study and left. Much to my annoyance I was not permitted to await the outcome, but packed off to school. I instinctively realized that whatever it was that Bhutto had come about, it must be serious and bad news. I did not concentrate at all that day.

When I got back home there were grim faces everywhere. My mother told me in a very calm, uncharacteristic voice that the army had taken over the papers, that armed police had surrounded the building, that my father had resigned on the spot and had gone to collect his personal belongings and that I shouldn't worry. Why, I remember asking her, had Bhutto arrived that morning? It emerged that it was a gesture of courtesy designed to warn my father that his offices were under military occupation and simultaneously plead with him to stay on as Chief Editor of all the publications in order to ensure that standards were preserved. My father had explained that the 'standards' were determined by the political stance of the newspapers and that any real independence from or criticism of the regime was now impossible. The Minister then reminded the Editor that since he was now, technically speaking, a state employee, the Essential Services Maintenance Ordnance could be deployed to keep him in place. The Editor smiled sadly and told the Minister that if such a mechanism was utilized they would have to arrest him since he was not prepared to stay on for a single day. Ultimately Bhutto agreed. The issue of the *Pakistan Times* which announced its takeover by the army also reported the resignation of its editor. The rest of the press which had chafed at the competition which the Progressive Papers represented now thanked the government editorially for expelling 'the strangers in the house'. *Time* magazine, incidentally, noted that the military regime had taken over 'Asia's best-edited daily'. In the years that followed, the Pakistani press became increasingly more servile and catered to the tastes of every successive leader. The country's journalists were often compared to prostitutes. This was unfair. The women concerned only sold their bodies. The journalists had sold their souls.

1961

When I got to the University of Lahore, the military regime had been in power for nearly four years. General Ayub had promoted himself and now carried a Field Marshal's baton, but his change in status had not helped halt the decline of his administration. Oppositional talk was increasingly hard in the students' unions and cafeterias. Politics remained stifled. Political parties and trade union activities were still banned; demonstrations were illegal and any breach of certain Martial Law regulations was technically a capital offence. Nonetheless, the temperature was beginning to rise on the campuses. In a country where a dictatorship muffles all dissent and does not permit free assemblies, the universities become the main centre of political organization. This is especially true of Third World countries where the bulk of the population still lives in the countryside. In Pakistan, in 1961, the peasants constituted over 80 per cent of the population.

I was a student of Government College. Established in 1864 in a neo-Gothic structure, this institution had, in the days of the Raj, trained countless civil servants and lawyers, but had also become a meeting place for the leaders of the cultural opposition to imperialism. In other words, the campus had developed a tradition of academic and cultural freedom, to which lip-service was regularly paid by professors and lecturers, who were all, it should be remembered, employees of the state and often at the mercy of unscrupulous civil servants. The Principal, Dr Nazir Ahmed, was a scientist, though his unkempt appearance and long hair were more reminiscent of a hippy guru. He was unpretentious and extremely intelligent. He despised those of his colleagues who found it difficult to take controversial decisions without consulting the Ministry of Education. They, foolishly, were deceived by his appearance and underestimated his brainpower. He was a lover of poetry and one of the top experts on the Sufi poets of the Punjab, who had espoused a popular existentialism and galvanized the common people during the 15th, 16th and 17th centuries.

The good Doctor was extremely hostile to the Martial Law regime and its votaries. We were to discover this when listening to one of his addresses to a college assembly. With a slightly absent-minded look on his face he had made some references to the situation in the country. He then combed his hair with both his hands and gestured as if to say that it was futile to talk too much. Suddenly he changed metaphors. 'Freak storms,' he muttered, 'do not go on for ever. The weather always returns to normal.' As this was said on a normal hot, summer's day when outside temperatures were reaching 110 degrees Fahrenheit, it did not take us long to get the message. After the initial surprise, there had been a burst of loud applause and laughter. The Doctor had laughed and appealed for quiet. He then told us that we should take advantage of the shelter provided by his college administration to set up study-circles and analyse what the freak storms meant and why they occurred. He promised that there would be no repression on the campus.

When we decided to observe Algeria Day and honour the resistance in that country as well as raise funds for the guerrillas, the Ministry of Education stepped in and prohibited any activity on the subject. Pakistan was then supporting France. Both countries had collaborated with each other in common defence organizations set up by the United States. We did hold a meeting nonetheless, where militant speeches were made, but the college authorities took no action. The doctor went up yet further in our estimation.

In February there was a new addition to the scroll of Third World martyrs: Patrice Lumumba, the elected leader of Free Congo had been deposed and foully murdered. The killers were indigenous mercenaries in the pay of the departing colonial tyrant – Belgium, which received support from the UN and the USA. Fearful of Belgian machinations, Lumumba had naively invited the UN to send a peace-keeping force and supervise the departure of the Belgians. The bulk of UN officials were undoubtedly deeply hostile to Lumumba. Their prejudices were widespread in the West at the time. Thus the *Guardian* correspondent, Clyde Sanger, was notorious for his hostility to the Congolese leader. His report on the Independence Day celebrations had criticized Lumumba's indictment of colonial rule as 'offensive' and the newspaper had shamelessly headlined the despatch as 'Congo Festivities Marred'. It is a futile exercise to compare one colonialism with another, but Belgian rule in the Congo was the nadir of European colonialism. It was marked by sadism, systematic torture and mass murder bordering on genocide and institutionalized brutality.

The West was later to feign surprise at the cruelty of post-colonial Congo. They forget the century-old lesson they had provided every day in butchery. Lumumba was 'offensive' because he refused to mouth inanities and pinned the convict's badge firmly, but politely, on the lapel of the Belgian King Baudouin, whose grandfather had inaugurated a spate of political perversions in Africa. One of the few Westerners to sympathize with the plight of the Congolese was an Irish UN official named Conor Cruise O'Brien, who had denounced UN complicity in the overthrow of Lumumba and had proceeded to describe Belgian rule in the Congo as 'a form of exploitation of human and other resources unparalleled in colonial annals for murderous and destructive greed'.

Lumumba's murder gave us the courage to defy the military regime's blanket ban on street marches. We were shocked at the news from the Congo. As the elected Chair of the undergraduate wing of the students' union, I convened a meeting of our executive on the same day that his death was announced. Much to my surprise, there was no dissension. Even the most apolitical representative was horrified by the speed with which the West had removed Lumumba from the scene. Then we discussed whether or not to demonstrate. Divisions inevitably emerged. The country was under Martial Law. The costs could be high. Should we let the crime go unnoticed in our country? We talked for a long time. Ultimately, those of us arguing for immediate action won the day. To say that we were nervous would be an understatement. We were all scared, but determined to act. Leaflets and posters were hurriedly prepared and distributed amongst the students. The speed of our activity took everyone by surprise. Within an hour of the decision, nearly 500 students had assembled and marched quietly out of the college. We did not realize it fully at the time, but we were the advance guard of a movement that would one day topple the Field Marshal. On the streets we denounced US complicity in the murder and marched to the American Consulate. We were wearing black armbands to mourn Lumumba and outside the Consulate we approved a resolution which described the murder as 'one of the more cold-blooded and inexcusable crimes in recent history'. We appealed to the newly independent nations of Afro-Asia to punish the murderers. As we made our way to Government House to hold a rally, a familiar figure was sighted on a bicycle, moving towards us like a fury, his long hair blowing in the wind. It was our much-loved Dr Nazir Ahmed. We cheered him as he dismounted and walked towards the head of the march. 'Please,' he pleaded, looking straight at me, 'come back immediately. I can't defend you here.' We declined. Never a man to threaten, he offered inducements. We were promised free Cokes and *samosas*. A demonstrator shouted: 'Shame on you, doctor. It's Coca-Cola that we're marching against today.' He laughed and offered us fruit juices instead, but we persuaded him to return, which he did, shaking his head ruefully.

On our march back to the college we were greatly encouraged by the sympathy on offer from the street-population. Our demonstration, illegal to the core, gained in confidence every minute. Intoxicated by our own success, we started chanting anti-Ayub and anti-Martial Law slogans and demanding a democratic order in Pakistan. Many bystanders applauded, which increased the intensity of our chants. There were no recriminations from the college, but the police had arrived at the American Consulate and taken the names of the orga- nizers, myself included. The next day the papers reported the demonstration, but did not mention the anti-dictatorship slogans. The District Magistrate of the city of Lahore did, however, intervene and the *Civil & Military Gazette*, then still in existence, wrote: 'Meetings and processions have been banned in Lahore District following student demonstrations on Monday against the murder of the late Congo Premier, Mr Lumumba. The ban was imposed under Section 144 Cr. P.C. by Agha Ahmed Raza, District Magistrate, who prohibited assembly of five or more persons within the limits of Lahore District. The District Magistrate said that the ban had been imposed as more demonstrations were feared in view of the Congo situation.' The District Magistrate did not explain how students had managed to defy Martial Law regulations or why the Congolese crisis threatened peace in Lahore. The District Magistrate also failed to mention that the anti- regime slogans had seriously alarmed the authorities. The success of the march in honour of Lumumba was not lost on the country's student population.

1962

Our world in Pakistan began to appear very small this year. It was not that we had become passive, in fact the tempo and temper of student mobilizations against the dictatorship were on the increase. One large demonstration had run into serious trouble. The police, unable to prevent us from marching, attempted to draw a line (in the most literal sense of the word) before we reached Government House. They painted a white line across the road and warned us that if we crossed it they would drive us back with tear gas. Three rows behind the frontline was our mechanized cavalry in the shape of a hundred-strong scooter contingent. At a given signal they revved, we moved aside and they charged across the white line, taking the police completely by surprise. We began to run and within minutes the police frontline had collapsed and we were on our way. More police arrived and baton-charged us, but without success. Escalation now seemed inevitable. First the tear gas came, but it was fired inefficiently and the wind changed course leaving a number of policemen coughing and choking. Then came the bullets, fired over our heads. We fell flat on the road. Suddenly there was a loud cry. A student had been shot dead. The next day virtually the entire student population joined the funeral march and trouble spread to other cities, notably Karachi, where the left was much stronger on the campuses. Dozens of students were arrested; some were tortured.

Earlier in the year a well-known communist, Hassan Nasir, had been tortured to death in the Lahore Fort. We had been incredibly moved by the speech his old mother, who had come from India for the burial, had made at the graveside. 'He died for a good cause,' she had said as the tears poured down her face, 'but I know I have many more sons who will carry on the fight for which Hassan Nasir gave up his life.'

We had few illusions as to the brutal methods used by the police. The reports of torture emanating from Karachi were frightening and succeeded in halting the protests for some months. Then the government decided to start externing troublesome students. A number of student leaders in Karachi had been asked to leave the city. They did so and came to Lahore where we got, for the first time, detailed and accurate reports on what had taken place. Soon after, I was served with an externment order to leave Lahore for one year. I was defended by the inimitable Doctor and there was also a great deal of manoeuvring behind the scenes by members of my family. These illicit pressures resulted in the externment order being withdrawn much to my embarrassment. Instead I was instructed in writing by the Governor of the province to refrain from contesting any union elections in college, and from participating in any political debates. If I defied this injunction externment would follow.

We devised methods to circumvent some of these restrictions, a popular one being Aesopian debates. A subject would be chosen that was superficially non-political and I became adept at searching for sentences which had a double meaning. Thus in a debate, the subject of which was that '*Lasee* (butter-milk − a staple drink of the Punjabi peasants since time immemorial) is better than Coca-Cola', we did not bother to discuss the ingredients of the drinks in question, but rather world politics.

It was the Cuban missile crisis that had made me think about Cuba seriously for the first time. If the USA and the USSR were on the verge of a nuclear war over a small island, it followed that what Fidel Castro had done must be important. Opinions on the confrontation were divided. When the Soviet leader, Khrushchev, decided to unilaterally withdraw the missiles we heaved a special sigh of relief. An American spy-plane, the U2, had used a US military base in Peshawar to fly over the Soviet Union. The pilot, Gary Powers, had parachuted to safety and been captured by the Russians. The Americans had denied that the flight had taken place. Then Khrushchev had produced the pilot. He had done more. He had threatened the Pakistani dictatorship with retaliation if the episode was repeated and stated that Peshawar was encircled with a red pencil. So we knew that if there was war, our cities would suffer.

This was not, however, the main preoccupation of those days. It was the actual confrontation that became the subject of heated debates. A friend, who was very hostile to the regime at home, turned out to be pro-American in this instance. 'Why', he kept asking in a manner both irritating and offensive, 'did they try and take the missiles there in the first place?' 'Because', I would respond, 'the Americans have bases in Turkey, Iran and Pakistan and two of these satrapies have borders with the Soviet Union. Why shouldn't the Russians respond in kind?' 'In which case,' someone else would say, 'why did Khrushchev retreat?' This seemed an easy one. 'To save world peace', was my response. And so the arguments would continue. Then one day I read a Chinese statement on the affair, which was characteristic in those early years of the Sino-Soviet dispute. The Chinese attacked Khrushchev as an 'adventurist' for sending in the missiles and as an 'opportunist and capitulationist' for taking them out under US pressure. The statement appealed to me since it showed that one could both preserve and eat a cake at the same time, but more importantly it established a new rule: there could be differences within the movement.

Coincidentally, in the same year, my parents had visited Britain and returned with a copy of a magazine I had neither seen nor heard of before. It was the January–April 1962 double issue of the *New Left Review*. Most of the articles were on Britain and seemed extremely dull. I gave them a miss, but there were two subjects which interested me: Claude Bourdet on the Algerian war and its consequences for internal politics in France, which revealed the strength of proto-fascist currents in that country, and an internal document of the Italian Communist Party, which was discussing all sorts of problems. There was an introduction to this text by a Perry Anderson, who described one of its main demands thus: 'Freedom of expression and the right to disagreement are principles which must be as valid and relevant for relationships inside the communist parties as between them. The main target here is the concept of *monolithism*.'

All this helped me to see the war of words between Moscow and Peking as something that was both necessary and healthy. It is worth recalling that the main thrust of the Chinese assault on the Russians was that the latter had gone soft on the Americans and were preparing to sell-out the revolutionary movements of the three continents on the altar of peaceful coexistence. The Chinese issued a series of popular pamphlets to explain their position. The imagery used by the scribes in Peking was designed to appeal to Third World militants. It did, and we exulted over 'Imperialism and All Reactionaries are Paper Tigers', 'Commemorate the Victory Over German Fascism! Carry the Struggle

Against US Imperialism Through To The End!', and much more in similar vein. The level of argument tended to be rhetorical, but the message was easily comprehensible: 'Imperialism and its lackeys in all countries are like the setting sun in the western sky, while socialism and the national revolutionary movements which have its support are like the rising sun in the eastern sky. This is the characteristic of our times.' Simple and direct. That is why the Chinese had an impact. The Soviet responses tended to be uninspiring, dull, packed with out-of-context quotations from Lenin and utterly lifeless.

Towards the end of the year we were informed that a cabinet minister wanted to address a closed meeting of students. The minister, Zulfiqar Ali Bhutto, was the youngest and most intelligent member of the dictator's entourage. He had got permission from Ayub to start a dialogue with selected students. The delegation from our college was left to the discretion of the students' union. We went to a heavily guarded hall in the old university buildings and met up with students from other colleges, some of whom were political acquaintances. Bhutto walked in smartly attired, but slightly nervous. He clearly thought that he would warm us up with a carefully chosen diatribe against India. He demanded that the Indians permit the people of Kashmir to determine their own future and decide whether or not they wanted to stay in India or join Pakistan. 'There has to be a plebiscite in Kashmir', he thundered, expecting a round of applause. There was none. Unable to contain myself I shouted from the back: 'What about a plebiscite in Pakistan first?' He was so shocked at my effrontery that, uncharacteristically, he was silent for a few seconds as he frowned at me. This was taken as a signal and heckling began on a massive scale. 'Why are you in a military government?' 'Are you scared to contest free elections?' 'Death to Ayub Khan!' Bhutto refused to answer these questions, but kept insisting that he was there to talk on a different subject. We said we weren't interested in that topic, but wanted to discuss Pakistan. He refused. The heckling began to look menacing and we refused to hear the speech. He promised as he left: 'I know who the ringleaders are, but I give you my word that there will be no CID investigation.' We were fairly amazed. Amidst our sudden silence he flounced out, sweating profusely. At one stage during the proceedings he had taken off his jacket and challenged any one of us to a boxing duel. We had roared with laughter. That night, at the Park Luxury Hotel, he smashed a few whisky glasses and cursed us the whole evening. Yet the incidents of that day left their mark on the man. He was to remind me of the whole business several years later as we were sipping coffee at the Dorchester in London. He had by then been sacked by Ayub. He kept his word as far as the CID was concerned. There were no arrests and no interrogations, though my CID file had begun to mount.

One of my mother's brothers, a friendly and jovial man, was not particularly amused when he got reports of my activities in his capacity as head of military intelligence. He was more concerned than angry, however, and recommended privately that I should be encouraged to leave the country as soon as possible. He was extremely helpful in ensuring that I was issued with a passport, not an easy thing in those days for people on a blacklist.

The thought of leaving Lahore permanently had never entered my head. I was not all that keen on coming to Oxford since I felt that politics in Pakistan were destined to reach an explosive climax sooner than anyone else realized. I suppose what was pretty decisive was that the father of a young lady-friend had just been transferred to the Pakistan High Commission in London and in these circumstances a few years abroad didn't seem such a long time.

Chapter Two

First Thoughts on Britain: 1963–65

I know thy works, that thou art neither cold nor hot; I would thou wert cold or hot. So then because thou art lukewarm, and neither cold nor hot, I will spue thee out of my mouth.

Revelations, iii, 15–17

I had not thought a great deal about Britain prior to my arrival here in October 1963. I was aware, of course, that the Tories had been in power for over a decade and that the postwar economic boom had generated full employment and rising living standards coupled with a strong welfare state. The Tory message to the predominantly working-class electorate of the fifties was expressed in the catchy slogan 'You've never had it so good'. This was certainly true, except for the fact that those who coined the phrase had always been much better off than those whose votes they needed to stay in power. A series of sex-scandals connected to men in high places had damaged the Tory Party, but not beyond repair. The Profumo affair had, curiously enough, become a cause célèbre in our part of the world as well. The reasons in this case were purely nationalistic. It had been widely reported that Field Marshal Ayub Khan had shared a swimming pool with Christine Keeler. Both had been house guests at Cliveden and Keeler was reputed to have commented favourably on certain attributes of the Field Marshal. This event, alas, did not bring the dictator down. In fact, if anything, it enhanced his prestige at home. Was he not, after all, the equal of (some said better than) a member of the British Government.

As a regular reader of the *New Statesman*, I also knew that in their

long postwar reign the British Tories had shed three leaders. Churchill
had been toppled by senility, Eden was brought down by Suez and
Macmillan, probably the sharpest of all three, had retired after the
Profumo affair. All this was clear. What I did not understand was how
Alec Douglas-Home, a 14th Earl and veteran of many a discredited
Tory escapade (he accompanied Neville Chamberlain to Munich)
could ever have succeeded Macmillan to lead a party which still
possessed Butler and Macleod. This remained an unsolved mystery
when I landed on these shores, for what I assumed would be a short
three-year visit.

I was much better placed to understand the workings of the British
Labour Party. Harold Laski had always been held in great esteem in our
household and it was his books which first gave me some idea of
working-class politics in Britain. He was joined on the shelves by
G. D. H. Cole, John Strachey, Tawney and Nye Bevan, amongst
many others. Then, at regular intervals, *Labour Monthly* would arrive
and the inimitable rhetoric of R. P. Dutt would inform us that yet
another of these veteran socialists had abandoned his beliefs and
become a renegade. Strachey's final act of treachery, I recall, created a
great deal of anger. As a minister in the Attlee Government he was
photographed in Malaya with a colleague, standing triumphantly,
while at his feet lay the decapitated heads of executed communist
guerrillas. It was a sorry epitaph for one of the great popularizers of
socialism during the thirties. Bevan had never moved that far to the
right, but then he did have a shorter distance to travel. Hounded and
vilified by the British press during the late forties and early fifties, he
became a tame mascot after he renounced unilateral nuclear disarma-
ment. His reward was the Deputy Leadership of the Labour Party, but
he died soon afterwards, mythologized by all sides in the inner-party
disputes.

Bevan's long-time opponent and Leader, Hugh Gaitskell, survived
him by only a few years. The man who succeeded both was Harold
Wilson. Claimed by the left, Wilson was elected Leader by the votes
of the right and centre, which dominated the Parliamentary Labour
Party. He attempted to create a new synthesis that would transcend

both Gaitskell and Bevan, unite the party and pave the way for elec-toral victory.

When I joined the Oxford University Labour Club in the autumn of 1963, there were no signs of any unity. The factions were still at war. The Gaitskellite remnants of the Campaign for Democratic Socialism effectively controlled the Club. The combination of Fabian politics and Stalinist organization norms (Stabianism) had always been the chosen strategy of the right in the Labour Party. At the Oxford Labour Club I was to see it in action regularly. Of the group which ran the Club, a key figure is now a leader of one of the most right-wing Labour councils in the country, somewhere in the North-East. Three of his colleagues became founding members of the Social Democratic Party. This is hardly surprising since the two cult figures of the Oxford right after Gaitskell's death were William Rodgers and Brian Walden, who regularly addressed the Club and kept their followers supplied with anti-Wilson gossip.

The Left opposition – a rainbow coalition – met separately as the Socialist Group inside the Labour Club. It was a motley collection of left-socialists, Communist Party fellow-travellers and a handful of Trotskyists. Speakers invited to address this group were an accurate reflection of its political composition: Michael Foot, Konni Zilliacus, Ian Mikardo, as well as various luminaries from the Communist Party and the International Socialist (then organized in the Labour Party, with a regular newssheet, *Labour Worker*, which advanced their views on a whole series of questions). I attended many of these meetings, sympathized a great deal with much of what was stated, but was never entirely convinced by the strategies that underlay the speeches. My central concerns at that time were far removed from the minutiae of British politics. It was not that I was uninterested. It was simply that compared to what was going on elsewhere in the world, the pre-occupations of the Oxford Labour Club seemed utterly parochial and irrelevant.

The gang that ran the Club was repulsively straightforward. They were unashamed careerists, permanently inspired by the vision of a very high ladder which had to be scaled, step by step. Nothing that obstructed the slow climb could be tolerated. Similar groups existed throughout the country. Their main function was to supply the Parliamentary Labour Party with reliable and sturdy foot-soldiers. To argue with them about socialism was a total waste of time. There were no shared premises, except, of course, that we were all in favour of a Labour victory. On every other question there was a gigantic gulf. We wanted fundamental changes; they celebrated the status quo. The Labour Club, for most of them, was simply a launching pad for their future. As a result they enjoyed their self-imposed claustrophobia.

The slogan which, I must confess, had given me the greatest pleasure when I first reached Oxford was not directly related to politics. If there was a greater enemy than Marxism in Pakistan it was atheism. Both were banned from the public domain, but we could, at least, talk about Marxism and socialism at college or in the cafes. Religion had to be questioned in whispers and even then one had to be careful. I had never believed in supernatural deities, not even as a child, but had learnt not to broadcast the fact. At college the lecturers and fellow-students with whom one could share one's atheism were, in many ways, much closer personal friends than those who were on a similar wavelength politically, but had not abandoned old superstitions. When I first saw a pimpled youth, wearing a tattered crimson corduroy jacket, standing on a chair in front of a stand at the Freshers' Fair and shouting at the top of his voice, 'Down with God', I was both excited and moved. In fact I was a trifle incredulous, which must have explained the fact that I just stood there and stared. Finally, a bit embarrassed, the man in the corduroy jacket stepped down and recruited me to the Oxford University Humanist Group. I was to discover, much to my surprise, that debates and discussions here were far more stimulating than those conducted within the careerist confines of the Labour Club. Nor were they restricted to religion, despite odd ahistorical excesses such as an OUHG debate on the motion, 'Jesus Christ Should Have Been Crucified', which was designed to shock more than educate.

The only arena for arguing against the other side on national and international politics at that time was the Oxford Union. The warriors of the Oxford left were active participants, especially after 1962 when women were permitted to become full members in their own right after a long and often bitter struggle. The main function of the left was to challenge existing orthodoxies from every quarter and, when possible, to scandalize the opposition by ferocious assaults on national totems.

One such occasion arose on the death of Winston Churchill. The elected officers of the Union proposed, as was customary, that the Union express its condolences by rising to its collective feet and observing a minute's silence in memory of the departed leader. In normal circumstances this would have been a formality, but to everyone's surprise, the motion was opposed by Richard Kirkwood, an active member of both the International Socialists and the Oxford Union. I had first seen Kirkwood in action at one of Isaiah Berlin's lectures, where he effectively punctured the pomposity and arrogance of one of the more celebrated academic knights of the university. This was far more serious. Kirkwood's audacity created a minor sensation. He was greeted with familiar abuse from the Tories, who suggested that he needed a bath and the birch. But rules were rules. Kirkwood had to be heard. He went straight to the point, challenging the mythologies that surrounded Churchill, without denying his status as one of the most effective leaders of the British ruling classes. *They* had every right to mourn his passing, but the Labour Movement should be more circumspect. Kirkwood pointed out to a stunned audience that Churchill had been decisively rejected by the British working class in 1945, after his biggest triumphs. He then went through a list of what he described casually as the more notorious of 'Churchill's crimes'. The catalogue, it must be admitted, was impressive. It was Churchill who had been the most vociferous proponent of armed intervention against the Russian Revolution of 1917; it was he who had justified the use of troops against the Welsh miners at Tonypandy; led the siege of Sidney Street in East London against a couple of anarchists; played the provocateur during the General Strike of 1926; backed the Greek far-right against the Resistance in 1944; and opposed the independence of India. It was for his consistent and long record of

vindictiveness and hostility towards workers throughout the world that
he was being mourned. For these reasons alone, shouted Kirkwood
above the growing din, he, for one, would not stand and observe even
a second's silence. He sat down to a chorus of boos, with some of his
opponents literally frothing at the mouth. Kirkwood, however, was
unmoved. As over 400 people stood up to observe the formalities,
about twenty-five of us remained seated and were counted. Kirkwood
was delighted. After all, he had separated the Bolsheviks from the
Mensheviks.

Meanwhile, on the stage of national politics, what appeared to
unseasoned observers such as myself to be an unequal political duel had
already begun. The 14th Earl was defending 'thirteen wasted years'
against plain Harold Wilson. It was inconceivable that Labour could
lose. Wilson exuded self-confidence and appeared superior in every
way. His speeches were incisive, concise, witty, skilful and radical in
both tone and content. The central theme was the necessity for
modernizing Britain. Wilson, a former history don at Oxford, could
deploy his knowledge of the past, when it suited him, to score points
against his antediluvian rival. At one of the meetings I attended in the
London borough of Putney, Wilson reminded his audience of the
famous Putney Heath debates of the 17th century, when Levellers
inside the New Model Army had advanced radical concepts of
democracy against Oliver Cromwell. Wilson had delighted us by
arguing that some of these demands retained their relevance and had
then proceeded to expose the democratic pretensions of a political
party whose secret cabals were adept at imposing new leaders on the
electorate. In reality Wilson could not have been more pleased that the
Conservative magic circle had decided on Douglas-Home. He knew
that Butler or MacLeod would have been formidable opponents.
Douglas-Home became a useful symbol for Wilson and an ideal foil for
Labour's sword of modernization. In a speech delivered during the last
months of 1963, Wilson made four references to the Tory leader's
antecedents in one sentence alone: 'For the commanding heights of
British industry to be controlled today by men whose only claim is
their aristocratic connections or the power of inherited wealth or

speculative finance is as irrelevant to the 20th century as would be the continued purchase of Commissions in the armed forces by lordly amateurs.'

The 'lordly amateur' then ensconced in 10 Downing Street did not deem it fit or necessary to reply in the same tone. He was confident that the status and respect awarded to the British aristocracy by the common people who really mattered would be sufficient to keep the Labour upstart at bay. It was not a totally foolish assessment. The following description of a pre-election TV confrontation by one of the more astute political commentators resident in Britain captures well one aspect of the reverence and conformism that undoubtedly existed at the time. Wrote Tom Nairn in the pages of the *New Left Review*:

> The plan was obvious. The Rt. Hon. Sir Alec Douglas-Home, Knight of the Thistle and starkest of aristocrats, was due to arrive for an interview in the BBC's Panorama studio on the evening of Monday, February 17 [1964]. For high mystagogue Richard Dimbleby, this occasion was too pregnant for commonplace procedures. Symbolism was imperative. No sooner had the symbolic Panorama globe finished, therefore, than the viewers saw Sir Alec sidling symbolically round a screen and into the studio, trailed at the proper distance by interviewer Robin Day. The aristocrats allow people to wander casually into their homes and sometimes even shake hands with them, do they not? – here was an aristocrat being shown into the Dimbleby demesne, in a neat reversal of roles manifestly intended to show we are all upper-class, nowadays. It was all to be so cunningly natural. Sir Alec stalked sleekly forward and extended a limp hand to the owner. 'Good evening, Sir ...' began Dimbleby, as he took it with determined ease. Alas, the laboriously constructed symbol exploded before our eyes, as the contact turned his hand at once into the cloven hoof of the mere bourgeois. The illusion of a thousand evenings, the striving of centuries of English bourgeois gentilshommes, all evaporated in a flash. A vulgar technician stood quaking in his double-breasted suit, being polite to his superior.

Dimbleby's *Panorama* may have been a bastion of servility, but it would be wrong to describe the BBC of the time as an outpost of scared conformists. A programme which was both more representative of the time and had a much larger following than *Panorama*, was the weekly satirical show, *That Was The Week That Was* (*TW₃*). The Tory Prime Minister and his cabinet were the main targets of the BBC humorists. Satire and ridicule were used with devastating effect during those last months of Douglas-Home's stewardship. *TW₃*'s relentless caricatures of the ultra-reactionary Tory Home Secretary of the period, Henry Brooke, made him a laughing stock throughout the country. It also dented the credibility of a cabinet still reeling from the effects of the sex-scandals and Macmillan's departure. The very success of *TW₃* ensured its demise. Effective lampooning was, soon afterwards, banished permanently from the small screen. Governments, whatever their shade, simply did not feel safe. Nothing like *TW₃* has ever been seen since and the brilliantly-constructed puppets of *Spitting Image* only serve to emphasize this fact. The crude cudgel is no match for the deft rapier.

As election fever grew, so did the pace of our canvassing. It was a dreary task, made even more cumbersome by the knowledge that Labour's prospective parliamentary candidate for Oxford was a colourless time-server. The politics he espoused were marginally to the right of the local Conservative MP, C. M. Woodhouse. We discovered, much to our relief, that the Oxford electorate was far more interested in Harold Wilson than the Party specimen we had on display. What surprised me a great deal then was the support enjoyed by Douglas-Home from within the ranks of older working-class voters. Time and again one would encounter an expression of genuine affection for the Tory leader from those who were, in any conceivable sense, his polar opposites. The phrase used most often in his favour was that he was a 'gent' and had 'been at it a long time'. Here was an indication that *TW₃* did not prevail over *Panorama* in every sphere.

It soon became obvious that Labour would not win Oxford, but we did not let this demoralize us too much. Oxford, after all, was hardly representative of the country as a whole. We stayed up watching the results of the October 1964 contest and realized that a large Labour majority was not on the agenda. The 'lordly amateur' from Scotland had come very close to retaining power. Labour's victory was based on a tiny majority of three – a narrow margin that became an alibi for the consensual conservatism that characterized the Wilson Government. Labour activists had felt suffocated and stifled for thirteen years. They wanted the changes promised by Wilson in the pre-election campaigns. Few had expected Wilson to implement any socialist policies, but to ditch all the promises of radical innovations and modernization so soon? That fuelled anger and despair.

As Leader of the Opposition and Shadow Foreign Secretary, Wilson has promised to abandon the independent nuclear deterrent. In fact the promise to do so was contained in the Party's election manifesto. Wilson had attacked the Tories as late as May 1964 for kowtowing to the United States in Indochina and had been explicit as far as his own views were concerned: 'It was right to issue a warning to the Government not to go any farther in the subordination of British policies to the United States. I believe at the moment the danger to a negotiated settlement in Asia is provided by a lunatic fringe in the American Senate. Asia, like other parts of the world, is in revolution, and what we have to learn today in this country is to march on the side of peoples in that revolution and not on the side of their oppressors.'

Polaris, however, was retained. Labour's electoral victory coincided with increasing US involvement in Vietnam. On 24 March 1965, Wilson as Prime Minister stated: 'I have said a number of times in the House, and my Right Honourable friend [The Foreign Secretary] repeated it yesterday, that we fully support the action of the United States in resisting aggression in Vietnam.'

Similar turnabouts on the domestic front led *The Economist* to summarize the Labour Government's record after their first year in office as: 'Bomb the communists in Vietnam, keep blacks out of Britain and bash the unions.' When Michael Foot and Ian Mikardo came to speak to the Socialist Group of the Labour Club in 1965, they were greeted by a near-unanimous revolt. Even sections of the Labour right were amazed at the illiberality of government policies. Foot explained it all by the small size of the parliamentary majority. 'Surely,'

I remember asking, 'if right-wing MPs like Wyatt and Donelly can stop the renationalization of steel by threatening to vote against the Government, why can't the left do the same on Vietnam. Why not let him be seen to sustain a Tory foreign policy with Tory votes?' Michael Foot made no attempt to defend the Government's record. He instead advised us to wait until there were new elections and Labour had a larger majority. 'With a majority of fifty seats,' he declaimed, 'we shall see socialism.' This remark was greeted with jeers, which caused Foot to shout, 'Harold Wilson is the most left-wing Prime Minister this country's ever had or likely to have.' We laughed then in horror, but in retrospect I have often wondered whether this was Michael Foot's way of educating one on the limits of British democracy.

At the university itself we were receiving more effective lessons. In June 1964, the Oxford Tories had invited the South African Ambassador, Carel de Wet, to enlighten them on the virtues of exterminating communism in South Africa. Nelson Mandela had just been sentenced and the Sharpeville massacres were still fresh in our minds. The local Anti-Apartheid group backed by the Labour Party had called for a picket of the meeting, which was in Northgate Hall, just opposite the Oxford Union buildings. A crowd of 500, mainly university students, had assembled as had veteran Labour councillors, Olive Gibbs and Roger Dudman. Nothing much happened apart from a scuffle between demonstrators and police when the Ambassador came out of the meeting. He drove off in his car, which was forced to stop in St Clement's with a flat tyre. At this stage a group of unknown undergraduates surrounded the car and thumped hard on the roof. As the police arrived, the undergraduates departed. The main chants had been in favour of Nelson Mandela's release. The police regarded the affair as relatively minor, but the University Proctors, a disciplinary institution dating back to the Middle Ages, decided that the demonstration had 'brought the good name of the university into disrepute'. Six of us were summoned to appear before the Proctors. We were informed that our actions had been in violation of university norms. Consequently we were fined £10 each (a great deal of money in those days) and asked to leave Oxford by midnight. There was no right of appeal.

Furthermore, the particularly nasty Mr McGuinness informed us that when we returned at the beginning of October that year, we would be gated for a number of weeks. I was gated for half a term. The letter from the University Marshal or Chief Bulldog was explicit: 'The period of gating will run from 9pm on Sunday 11 October to 6am on Sunday 8 November. During this period you are required to stay in your house of residence in Oxford between the hours of 9pm and 6am unless you have the written authorities of the proctors ... I am to inform you that your keeping of this gate will be subject to the usual supervision.' I was also ordered not to take part in any demonstrations in Oxford for a whole year. When I addressed a local May Day rally organized by the Oxford Trades Council, I was reprimanded and fined.

On the eve of the gating a 'freedom party' was organized in my lodgings. A great deal of wine was imbibed and the guests flowed out on the streets, marched to the Clarendon Buildings, where the Proctors held their meetings and burnt an effigy of a Proctor. During the 14th century Proctors were sometimes lynched and burned by rebellious hoards of students. Our generation was relatively moderate.

The Proctors graciously agreed that I could leave my rooms every Thursday evening in order to attend Union debates. This was a small concession, but welcome nevertheless as it was on one of these evenings that I met the black American leader, Malcolm X. He had been invited to speak in favour of the motion that 'Extremism in the defence of liberty is no vice, moderation in the pursuit of justice is no virtue'. It was a speechwriter's phrase which had been made famous by right-wing American Senator Barry Goldwater of Arizona, the scourge of American liberalism. Malcolm X had been approached to speak in its favour and had not hesitated for a minute. I had, of course, read about Malcolm X, but this had been when he was a follower of Elijah Mohammed and the American sect known as the Black Muslims. Even though one's sympathies were instinctively on the side of black America – from Martin Luther King leftwards – the Black Muslims had always struck me as a sinister outfit. It was not just the religious fundamentalism, which was bad enough, but a feeling that they were not even sincere in their beliefs. At times I thought that the whole business was a gigantic public relations swindle designed to raise money from gullible Arab regimes; on other occasions I suspected that the FBI had invented the group to create mayhem inside the black ghettoes of America.

Malcolm X had been the most inspired orator of the Black Muslims and I was deeply suspicious of him that evening, even though I knew he had broken with Elijah Mohammed. Prior to joining the Black Muslims, Malcolm X had been at various times a gangster, a drug pedlar and a pimp. In 1964 he was one of the most feared black men in the United States. When we were introduced he smiled at my name and said in a soft voice, 'A fellow Muslim?' I shook his hand firmly and whispered in his ear, 'In name only.' He laughed aloud. That evening we sat together in the debating chamber. He looked around at the audience and said he'd never addressed so many well-dressed whites. His speech was, by common agreement, the most brilliant to have been heard in that hall for many decades. The entire audience was spellbound by his use of words, his imagery and, surprisingly, his total lack of demagogy. The opposing guest debater, Humphrey Berkely (then a radical Tory, subsequently a conservative Labourist and later a nondescript Liberal) had raised a few laughs by mocking Malcolm's chosen name 'X'. 'Why X?' Berkely had joked, 'Why not Malcolm A or C or even Z. Surely Malcolm Z sounds even better!' Malcolm had stiffened slightly, but kept his cool. Later when it was his turn to close the debate he had allowed his voice to rise a bit and the repressed anger had been felt throughout the hall. He explained why he refused to continue bearing the name of a slave-owner and demonstrated how slavery had degraded the whites and oppressed the blacks. He reminded the Oxford Union that Britain had played a leading part in the slave-trade and many of the so-called nobility had grown rich by trading in black human beings. The hands of the British ruling class were stained with the blood of blacks who died of disease in the crammed quarters of the slave-ships or were worked to an early grave in the New World. After he had finished, Malcolm looked at Berkely and said: 'It is for these reasons Mr Berkely that I decided to call myself

X.' There was a momentary silence and then he was applauded for a long time. At the end of his speech, which had evoked the struggles of black America and the three continents, Malcolm X received an emotional standing ovation. Few who heard that speech could have forgotten its impact.

After the formalities in the Union had been concluded (a photograph still hangs on one of the Union walls which shows the Union's officers and committee members with Malcolm X seated at the centre as the guest of honour) we retired to his hotel. We talked for many hours while he consumed his tea and I sipped my brandy. I explained why religion could never be a solution to anyone's problems in a collective sense. Islam was no better or worse than Judaism or Christianity. Many crimes had been committed on behalf of all three faiths. He listened quite attentively, only venturing an opinion when I gave him a chance. 'Suppose', I asked him aggressively at one point, 'you lived in Saudi Arabia or Pakistan or some other Muslim paradise. How would you define yourself? To say that you're a Muslim doesn't mean a thing. Everyone's a Muslim. How are you different from the King of Saudi Arabia?' He had been smiling a lot while I was talking and I stopped, waiting to receive a devastating rebuke. 'It's good hearing you talk like that', he said, much to my amazement. 'I'm beginning to ask myself many of the same questions.' I then told him what I thought about the Black Muslims. He did not rebut me, but explained the conditions which helped them to recruit young blacks. He said that he did not trust them either and had established his own group called the Organization for Afro-American Unity. He did not believe in non-violence. On this he was firm, unrepentant and refused to compromise. 'Martin Luther King plays into their hands', he said. 'The Klan lynches blacks, terrorizes and kills white kids who go to the South for registration drives. The cops are part of the Klan system. King tells people to turn the other cheek. You can't deal with bullies like that ... I know that's why the white liberal establishment loves King and denounces me. I have to tell the truth. I tell them that their system is corrupt and based on the oppression of blacks in America and elsewhere. Blacks are a powder keg. King wants to spray the keg with water. I think we have to light the fuse. It's the only way to teach them to respect us.'

Malcolm X was a great admirer of Cuba and Vietnam. He spoke with affection of Fidel Castro and Che Guevara for 'having done it right under Washington's nose'. He reminisced about Castro's decision to stay in Harlem when he visited New York to address the United Nations and insisted that black Americans would remember the gesture for a long time to come. His real anger was reserved for what America was doing to Vietnam. It was 'a horrible expression of the American nightmare', but he was convinced that his country would be humiliated 'just like the French'.

At 2am I realized that I was in breach of Proctorial regulations and explained the whys and wherefores to Malcolm. He was truly amazed and laughed aloud. As I was getting ready to leave I shook hands and expressed the hope that we would meet again before too long. He smiled and, without any trace of emotion, said: 'I don't think so. By this time next year, I'll be dead.' I froze, staring at him in disbelief. We sat down again. He explained that as long as he had been a Black Muslim they had just about tolerated him. But since his break with the Nation of Islam, he had been moving in other directions. He had realized that race alone could never be a sufficient criterion for achieving social change. He had dropped his opposition to black–white intermarriages. He had allied openly with the enemies of Washington in Havana, Hanoi and Algiers. These facts meant that 'they have already ordered my execution. They don't like uppity niggers. Never have. They'll kill me. I'm sure.' Who were 'they'? He shrugged his shoulders, as if to say that the question was too foolish to merit a reply. We embraced warmly and I walked away from the Randolph Hotel in a slight daze, wondering whether to believe him or not, but finding it difficult to dismiss the whole business as either bravado or paranoia or a form of posturing. I found it very hard to sleep that night. The images and sounds of Malcolm X refused to vacate my head.

Some months later, in February 1965, Malcolm X was addressing an assembly at the Audubon Ballroom in New York, on the south side of West 166th Street. He had always refused to allow people coming to his meetings to be searched and argued that if he wasn't safe amongst his own people his entire political project was worthless. A few minutes after he rose to speak, three black men in the front row stood up, took out their guns and fired at him simultaneously. Malcolm was dead when he reached the hospital. A woman who had been present at the meeting told the press, 'It looked just like a firing squad'. The night I heard the news I sat down and reminded myself of Malcolm by transcribing all that I could recall of our brief encounter and conversation in a notebook. After his death there were numerous requests to the Oxford Union for a tape-copy of his speech. All Union debates were recorded. The tape-recorder, I was told by the Steward, had not functioned properly that evening. Nothing of the event had been recorded. The explanation may have been perfectly true, but none of the numerous callers from the United States, who badly wanted the tape, could believe that its non-existence was an accident. And, who knows, perhaps they were correct.

At roughly the same time I first met Enoch Powell, then a leading member of the Tory Shadow Cabinet. His strong espousal of the principle of free and collective wage bargaining meant that he spoke on the same side as the local left when it came to attacking the notion of an incomes policy, which the Labour Government had decided to impose on the trade unions. Powell had not yet decided to play the black card. After the debate he came up to me and spoke in Hindustani. I was a bit taken aback, until he told me of his colonial record (he had been an officer in India) and how much he missed the subcontinent. I smiled politely, the way one is meant to on such occasions. He then embarked on a discussion of what my name meant, which indicated that he understood more of the language than I had suspected. 'Interesting that your name means "history"', he remarked, or words to that effect. 'History is *tareekh*,' I corrected, 'with the emphasis on the *kh* which is a totally different sound.' He thought hard and accepted this, but then asked what my name did mean. I was flummoxed. The question had never entered my head before and what was worse I did not have an answer. In such circumstances improvisation is often the only solution. 'I know you're not going to like this,' I told

him with a smile of fake triumph, 'but what it really means is "progress". Tariq is a simple derivation of *taraqqi*. Progress!' He laughed and
accepted this version, which was one way of knowing that his command of Persian was much more limited than his knowledge of Latin
and Greek.

I cannot recall what other paths the conversation took that evening.
There was no reason for me, then or later, to scribble my reflections on
the encounter in some notebook. Powell did strike me, however, as an
extremely capable and intelligent Conservative politician. There was
no fanatical gleam in his eyes, though I do remember feeling that his
attitude to India was slightly strange. I could not place it at the time; it
was neither jingoism nor simply nostalgia, but nor was it the scholarly
interest of a historian or the detached reflections of a logician. Many
years later when I was reading Paul Scott's opus on the British in India,
I suddenly remembered Powell. One of the major characters in Scott's
novels reminded me of him. It was Ronald Merrick, whose ambiguous
class background in Britain ultimately exploded in colonial India. This
was a reflection of something that ran very deep in many middle- and
lower-middle-class Englishmen and women who had served as colonial administrators or officers in India. It was this that had made me
sense something odd in Powell's recollections of life in India that
evening in 1965, but what he said had not been sufficiently articulated
to alert me either to his repressed traumas or the political bombshells
that he was to explode in 1968.

Harold Wilson's Labour Government had decided on a single
priority: everything had to be subordinated to the task of defending
and reviving British capitalism. Since Wilson had come to power at a
time when the postwar economic boom was already over, it was clear
that drastic measures were needed. Wilson's decision not to devalue
the pound had been taken under heavy pressure from the United
States, which feared that any such measure would have an adverse
effect on the dollar. Instead, Wilson decided to borrow money and, in
the process, incurred a very large foreign debt. He was aware of the
risks entailed in this operation and had been refreshingly blunt while
addressing the TUC on the eve of the 1964 elections: 'You can get

into pawn, but don't then talk of an independent foreign policy, or an independent defence policy . . .' By 1965 Wilson had pawned Labour's manifesto pledges and Washington was an extremely stern pawn-broker. Thus Wilson became an abject apologist for US foreign policy, telling Parliament that 'we fully support the action of the United States in resisting aggression in Vietnam'. A few months later he angrily denied that this turnabout had been the result of Labour's economic dependence on the international banking system and contradicted his own statement to the TUC: 'I am surprised that this question can even be put. At no time – and I say this categorically – has there been any attempt to link economic co-operation with any aspect of foreign policy.' The facts, alas, spoke for themselves.

In Vietnam itself, the United States was preparing a massive esca-lation by increasing the number of troops from under 100,000 to 400,000. At a time when the Swedish leader, Olaf Palme, was in the forefront of opposition to America's war, British Labour leaders were being economical with the truth and acting like tame poodles of the White House. We had set up a Vietnam Committee in Oxford and organized one of the first demonstrations outside the US embassy in Grosvenor Square in February 1965. We carried a banner which read: 'Where has Harold Wilson gone? Crawling to the Pentagon!' Some of us had also collectively written new words to the tune of 'Where have All the Flowers Gone?' This ditty was, much to our pleasure, com-municated to the French President, De Gaulle, by his biographer Alexander Werth, who reported that the General had chuckled and remarked that the song seemed apt. De Gaulle, who understood the tenacity of the Vietnamese better than most, was opposed to US intervention in Indochina, a view that put him well to the left of the British Labour Government.

The war in Vietnam had by this stage become an obsession as far as I was concerned. It dominated my thoughts and severely disrupted the stifling routines of academic life. What made matters worse was the complete sense of powerlessness that one felt in the face of the two-pronged assault launched by the United States. The situation of Spain during the thirties was strongly rooted in my consciousness and I felt that Vietnam should not be allowed to become isolated simply because it was an Asian country thousands of miles away from Europe. I often thought about the possibilities of organizing international brigades from Europe, America and South Asia, which would enable some of us to fight side by side with the Vietnamese and the idea only left me when I was actually in Vietnam discussing this very question with the country's Prime Minister.

On the TV screens we caught glimpses of the battles taking place in the Mekong Delta. We saw the use of indiscriminate firepower and US troops in action, but it was the other side which scored the victories – a side which was invisible on British TV screens, but which, nonetheless, determined the course of the war. The world's most powerful industrialized nation was pitted against a poor, predominantly peasant country, whose people had been fighting against oppression for almost three decades. It was a war of West against East, North against South and, above all, imperialism against revolution. Conflict on such a scale necessitated a war of words. As the marines went into battle against the enemy in Indochina, their civilian backers unleashed an ideological offensive, which utilized cold war images and a brutal language to justify the genocidal proportions of the real war.

Inside the United States itself the grotesque distortions and outright lies of the propaganda machine began to be challenged by American journalists on the ground in Vietnam. *Time* magazine, hardly a repository of liberal sentiments, began to censor and mangle beyond recognition the despatches of Charles Mohr, its distinguished war correspondent. They had described a reality that was out of tune with the music being supplied by the Pentagon and the State Department. Mohr resigned from the magazine in disgust. David Halberstam of the *New York Times* spent fifteen months in southern Vietnam and sent back some of the most powerful reports to be penned by a journalist during wartime. His material was not censored, though the family running South Vietnam for the Americans – the notorious Nhus – were outraged. Madame Nhu demanded that Halberstam 'be barbecued' and herself offered 'to supply the fluid and the match'. It was Halberstam who won that particular duel. His reports on the large-scale corruption and CIA bungles led to the despatch of Henry Cabot Lodge as US Proconsul to Saigon. This scion of an aristocratic Republican dynasty had an impeccable cold war record. He was given the authority to remove the Nhu family from the seat of power, which he did by orchestrating a quick *coup d'etat*.

Even as far as TV was concerned, Morley Safer's reports for CBS were far more informative than much of the coverage on British television. In France the authoritative *Le Monde* published daily reports from its correspondents in Washington, Saigon and Hanoi, which savaged US policy and contradicted the version supplied by the US Government on virtually every detail. The British press was, by contrast, tame and conformist to the point of servility. The two liberal newspapers, the *Guardian* and the *Observer* were classic examples of the extent to which the cold war had infected the mandarins of Fleet Street. Both papers gave the United States an easy ride, published a great deal of US propaganda handouts and editorially supported the general aims of US policy.★ Of course they were for 'peace' in Vietnam, but the real obstacle to such a 'peace' was Vietnamese intransigence. This was true, because the 'peace' which Harold Wilson and the two editors of the great liberal newspapers of Britain wished to impose on the Vietnamese was the peace of the graveyard.

One Sunday morning in the spring of 1965, I was so outraged by the *Observer* that I sat down and typed out an angry paragraph in the form of a letter to the editor. A friend who was having breakfast with me that day was cajoled into co-signing the missive. It was published the following week with a reply, which was predictable and pathetic. There the matter might have rested, except that a few days later I received a letter in the post from Wales. It was from 'The Earl Russell, O.M. F.R.S.', and the two lines read: 'I should like to congratulate you on your just and excellent letter to today's *Observer*. The *Observer*'s reply to it sickens me. Yours sincerely, Bertrand Russell.' I was thrilled

---

★ The *Guardian*'s policy was not uniform. The editorials drafted by Frank Edmead from Manchester were hostile to the United States. Edmead, a Quaker, was very knowledgeable on Asian realities.

beyond belief. Bertrand Russell had been known to me through some of his books a long time ago. He was a legendary figure somewhere up in the mists and to receive a letter from him completely out of the blue was both a shock and an inspiration. I soon established contact with the Bertrand Russell Peace Foundation and went to meet its director, an American called Ralph Schoenman, at its offices in Shavers Place, just off Piccadilly in the heart of London. Schoenman was extremely friendly, courteous and very encouraging. He, too, was obsessed by Vietnam and especially by the horrors being practised on that country by his own government. His face became contorted with anger and hatred as he described the use of napalm and defoliants and went into the most gory details of the effect these weapons had on the victims. Schoenman's abrasiveness was well-known to the British left. Radical Americans of his type were a rare breed in those days and Schoenman's hatred of the United States' actions shocked some of the gentler souls of liberal England. At many a dinner party when the topic reverted to Schoenman and his activities, someone would invariably wonder, aloud of course, whether Schoenman could be an *agent provocateur* sent here to disrupt the peace movement. This was always a vile slander. Schoenman undoubtedly had many defects but what some people regarded as blemishes appealed to my particular sensibilities. He was no respecter of persons, was ruthless in his approach to achieve whatever goal he had decided upon and did not refrain from speaking home truths, sometimes with a venom that he found it difficult to conceal.

Schoenman was of Hungarian-Jewish stock. His father, as a fifteen-year-old schoolboy in post-imperial Hungary, had supported the Bela Kun revolution of 1918 and had been made a member of one of the revolutionary committees as a representative of the school students. Several months later, when the counter-revolution triumphed, Schoenman senior, along with thousands of others, fled the country to escape a bloodbath. He worked as a meat-packer in Latin America and finally ended up in the United States. He was proud of young Ralph's early radicalism and saw him enter Yale, where he was widely regarded as a talented student. Schoenman came to Britain as a post-graduate student, became active in the old CND and was one of the original members of the direct-action oriented Committee of Hundred, where he met Bertrand Russell. The veteran campaigner was impressed by the young American's energy and intelligence and took him on as his secretary. The establishment of the Peace Foundation was one of Schoenman's first ideas.

On that day in April 1965, I heard him talk with an amazing intensity about the world. He was emotional, which I found a refreshing quality; encountering someone like him in Britain came as a pleasant surprise. He told me of an idea that had occurred to him one day after reading reports of the scale of the US bombings in Vietnam. He wanted to set up a Nuremberg-style tribunal to arraign the United States for war crimes against the people of Vietnam and humanity. We talked for hours about the various possibilities and I suggested that a leading liberal, Mahmud Ali Kasuri, a civil liberties lawyer in Pakistan, should be invited to be amongst the judges. Kasuri was a meticulous barrister whose knowledge of international law would help such a tribunal. I returned to Oxford that night in a state of exhilaration, both because at last one could do something useful for Vietnam, but also because Schoenman had suggested a meeting with Russell prior to the launching of the tribunal. I found it difficult to conceal my excitement at the very thought.

I had been elected President of the Oxford Union that summer term after a contest which had become (as such things are not meant to do) polarized by two sharply opposed political ideologies. My opponent had been Douglas Hogg, a leading figure of the Oxford University Conservative Association, and on polling day a number of Union Life Members who were also members of the Conservative Shadow Cabinet had been seen casting their votes. Neither Hogg nor myself made any attempt to conceal our political beliefs and the turnout had been the largest recorded in the history of the Union. The vote was close, but I had won. This fact was decisive in my being approached by two young dons, David Caute from All Souls and Steven Lukes from Nuffield, to become part of a three-person committee and organize an Oxford teach-in on Vietnam.

The idea of a teach-in had originated on the Berkeley campus in

California. The purpose was to invite both sides to debate the war as thoroughly as possible. The teach-ins had spread like a rash across campuses throughout the United States and played an important role in helping to generate the student radicalization that led to the formation of the Students for a Democratic Society (SDS) the following year, 1966. Many liberal academics in the United States had come out against the war. Lukes and Caute felt that we should repeat the experiment in Britain. I agreed and some of the better-known Oxford academicians consented to act as sponsors, including the two knights, Isaiah Berlin and William Hayter. Oxford dons were divided on the war, but Caute ensured that both sides were equally represented. The anti-war sponsors included Christopher Hill, Alan Montefiore and A. J. Ayer. The voice of America was Max Beloff. Because of the sponsorship, the Foreign Office agreed to send the Labour Foreign Secretary, Michael Stewart, an undistinguished and grey Gaitskellite, who was despised by many Labour Party members, to defend American policies. We had been pestering the US embassy to send the Ambassador, but they remained non-committal until they heard that Stewart would be speaking. We were rung up one day and told that the US Proconsul to Saigon, Henry Cabot Lodge, would fly over from Massachusetts to address the teach-in. BBC Radio's 'Third Programme' already had permission to broadcast the entire proceedings. Cabot Lodge's presence resulted in BBC TV deciding on 'live' coverage as well, on *Gallery*, with a TV journalist named Ian Trethowan acting as a linkman from the Union. The Vietnamese remained unrepresented. The unofficial representatives in London had no authority to speak and the Home Office could not guarantee the issue of visas to the Vietnamese in Paris, even if they could find someone who spoke English.

The teach-in coincided with a state visit to Britain by Pakistani dictator Ayub Khan. He was accompanied by his Foreign Minister, Zulfiqar Ali Bhutto, who was known for his hostility to the American adventure in Vietnam. I left messages at the Pakistan High Commission asking Bhutto to speak at the teach-in. He rang and apologized, pleading more pressing engagements. A few years later he admitted to me that he had argued desperately with Ayub, but the Field Marshal had forbade him from speaking that day.

The teach-in was attended by several hundred students. I had warned Cabot Lodge that convincing this audience would not be as easy as organizing a coup in Saigon. This advice had been reinforced in a slightly unorthodox fashion by 'Big Joe' Richards, a shop steward from the Cowley car plant. As I was escorting Lodge to the debating chamber, Big Joe walked up to him and shouted, 'Fucking mass murderer'. Lodge kept on walking, and the incident did not alert him to change his prepared script. He assumed that his audience would be on a similar wavelength to the Daughters of the American Revolution. It was a foolish error. He was consistently heckled and when he referred to Vietnamese peasants under US rule as 'laughing and happy people enjoying their bananas' the bulk of the audience collapsed with uncontrollable laughter.

The State Department case was more effectively put forward that day by the Labour Foreign Secretary. He, too, was heckled but refused to be disconcerted and continued with his speech, prepared by a Foreign Office mandarin well-trained in cold-war phraseology. The speech was demolished by Professors Ralph Miliband and Bill Wedderburn from the London School of Economics, both of whom received some of the warmest applause of the day. When the seven and a half hour teach-in came to an end the verdict of those who attended was overwhelmingly against the American presence in Asia. This was also the reaction of those who heard the 'Third Programme' broadcast during the afternoon and who wrote to us and the BBC about the television coverage. By the time Ian Trethowan went on air later that evening, however, the entire event had become transformed. Neither Miliband nor Wedderburn were shown (not even a token thirty-second clip to maintain some pretence of impartiality); instead Michael Stewart was presented as a Daniel who had survived the lion's den. Letters of complaint were sent to the BBC by the organizers but had nil effect. Ian Trethowan's verdict was that the 'British left had received a drubbing'. The viewers were not permitted to judge for themselves.

Cabot Lodge was defended by three letter-writers in the *Daily Telegraph* a day later. From the depths of Surrey and Sussex, they apologized to the distinguished visitor for the 'disgraceful, offensive' behaviour of the 'unruly students' and bemoaned the fact that 'a large proportion of undergraduates at Oxford appeared to be from other lands'. Interestingly enough, none of the letter-writers made any reference to Vietnam.

The Oxford teach-in had not been restricted to members of the university. It had been an open meeting and many people had come from other towns. Soon afterwards another teach-in was organized at Central Hall, Westminster, where, unsurprisingly, Michael Stewart and Henry Cabot Lodge declined to appear. It was at these two events that I met, for the first time, some of the radical figures active in CND, among them Peggy Duff, a brilliant organizer who chain-smoked with the result that her infectious laughter often merged with a ghastly cough; Malcolm Caldwell, from the School of African and Oriental Studies; Richard Gott, Dick Gilbert and John Gittings (the three G's) and many others who would later resurface as activists in the Vietnam movement. Soon after the teach-ins, I received a letter from the British Peace Committee asking whether I would like to join the delegation from Britain to attend the Peace Conferences at Helsinki during the summer vacation. When it emerged that Peggy Duff and Malcolm Caldwell had also been invited, we decided to accept.

The Peace Conferences had been one of Moscow's responses to the cold war. They served a variety of purposes. The first was to orchestrate Moscow's propaganda offensives; another was to bring together pro-Moscow party members from all over the world and make sure they understood the latest tactical nuances being perfected by the Kremlin. It was also an opportunity to line up fellow-travellers and notables from the West and parade them before the assembled delegates. As such, the conferences were lifeless affairs where one pair of lips after another paid tribute to peace, justice, brotherhood (*sic*) and where awkward issues were never discussed. Thus the uprisings in East Germany and Hungary, the mass mobilizations in Poland or other 'family differences' within the 'socialist camp' became the great unmentionables. To even raise such an issue – and the delegates were carefully hand-picked to prevent any such calamity – was akin to being a member or under the influence of Western intelligence agencies and their ideological networks. Either delegates were a hundred per cent for the 'socialist camp', and ipso facto for all the crimes that were committed *against* socialism, or they were on the side of the enemy.

I decided to attend the Helsinki Peace Conference in 1965 for one very simple reason. The dispute between the Soviet Union and China was reaching a climax and it was clear that the Chinese would not tolerate a tame assembly this time, but would attempt to put forward their arguments. Delegates were also expected from Vietnam and Indonesia, which had the largest Communist Party outside China and the USSR. I did not wish to miss the debates or forego the chance of meeting the Vietnamese.

We were flown from London to Moscow, which gave me my first glimpse of the Soviet capital. We were put up in an architectural monstrosity, which reminded me of Milan railway station, but the schedule was tight and there was not time to explore or see the old city. The same night we were taken to the railway station, where a special 'peace train' was waiting to transport us to Helsinki via Leningrad. It was an old train, beautifully preserved, with samovars in every carriage, together with an attendant who made sure we were kept supplied with tea. Malcolm Caldwell and I shared a wagon-lit and before lights out we were joined by Peggy Duff and some veterans of the British CP. The combination was designed to spark off a few fireworks. Nor were they long in coming. Peggy had expressed the hope that this conference, at least, would be lively. G., a communist in his early fifties, was horrified at such a thought. He was aware that there were people coming whose sole aim was to wreck everything, but he hoped that the delegation from Britain would see its main task as being that of helping to further Anglo-Soviet amity. Malcolm did not like the reference to the Chinese as 'wreckers' and enquired politely why they were being invited if their only purpose was to destroy. Looks were exchanged, but no reply was forthcoming. I asked why the three of us were in the delegation if what they really wanted

was propaganda carriers. No reply. Peggy then lightened the atmosphere by suggesting that for the sort of conferences G. wanted they
should not even bother with wasting time and money transporting
delegates. All they needed was a vast gathering of pigeons, which could
carry the happy news back to various capital cities in the West.
Malcolm did not think this would be all that cheap to organize. Labour
was expensive in Helsinki and the pigeon-droppings would have to be
cleared by the organizers. Some of the others did laugh at the frivo-
lities, but not G. He embarked on a tirade and said that he did not
know why people like us were on a 'peace train'. He would raise the
matter with the Peace Committee on his return. A great deal of vodka
had by now been imbibed and some of G.'s more enlightened comrades ended the discussion by dragging him away.

Later that night, Malcolm and I were woken by loud and incoherent renderings of 'The Red Flag' just outside our door. This was
followed by heavy, physical sounds of two people grappling with each
other and then a loud thud as a body hit the floor. A murder on the
'peace train'? It was my turn to go out and look. I did so and found G.
and the Russian attendant in a deep and passionate embrace on the
floor, oblivious to the world. I came back, choking with silent laughter
and told my fellow-traveller. He refused to believe me until he had
peeped out into the corridor and observed it for himself. He, too,
returned giggling uncontrollably. The next morning we told Peggy.
She chuckled as she lit her pre-breakfast cigarette. A few hours later,
when a red-eyed G. passed the compartment where we were playing
bridge, Peggy shouted that he should come and make friends. As he
entered Malcolm and I started laughing, while Peggy, completely
straight-faced, asked: 'How long did you cement Anglo-Soviet relations for last night?' G. went crimson and stalked out, but not before
Malcolm had warned him that he should be more careful lest the poor
Soviet worker lose his job. (Homosexuality was frowned upon as a
disease in those days.) After this episode G. neither spoke to nor came
near us for the next ten days.

Meanwhile, as the train speeded along to Leningrad we realized
why we were being taken to Helsinki in such a relaxed, friendly and

comfortable style. Normally we would have been out on an old
Aeroflot and transported to the Finnish capital without ceremony. The
train contained many other delegations, including the heavy brigade
from the Soviet Union. Intense canvassing was in progress throughout
the journey. In the bar I stumbled into Faiz Ahmed Faiz, the much-
celebrated Urdu poet, who was representing the Pakistan Peace
Committee. We hugged and embraced and he gave me all the news
from home. He then tried in his most avuncular fashion to pressure me
into withdrawing from the British delegation and joining his one-man
group. 'The problem is', he said slowly, 'that I am a member of the
Presidium and we won't be represented on the conference floor. You
should be there in order to speak and show our colours.' I was quite
prepared to shift delegations, but I thought it was only fair to warn him
that my sympathies were not with the bland, 'peaceful co-existence at
all costs' approach of the Soviet delegates. Faiz understood immediately and without ceasing to be affectionate (our families were old
friends and I had known him since childhood) withdrew his invitation,
which solved my dilemma. Later that afternoon as we were sipping tea
and playing cards there was a knock and a couple of Soviet delegates
entered. They introduced themselves and welcomed us on behalf of
the Soviet Peace Committee. I don't think G. had warned them that
we three were, in a manner of speaking, dissidents and, therefore, best
left alone. The Russians showed us the draft resolution for the conference and hoped that our support would be forthcoming. They were
both men, in their mid-fifties. One of them introduced himself as a
delegate from the *Komsomol* (the Communist Youth League of the
USSR), causing Peggy Duff, then of a similar age, to remark that she
might apply to join the Young Communist League on her return to
Britain. On a more serious note we told them that we could not decide
without seeing what resolutions were being tabled by other delegations
especially the Chinese, Vietnamese and Indonesians. The two men
looked at each other, smiled politely and withdrew.

At Leningrad station there was a festive atmosphere. Red flags,
young pioneers, music and many toasts were exchanged by the leaders
of the various delegations and the Leningrad Peace Committee. We

watched the proceedings from the window as Peggy Duff began to
recognize some of the other delegation leaders in her inimitable
fashion. 'O my god! That hack from France is here ... I thought she
was dead ... There's so-and-so. I thought he'd been expelled from the
party ...' and so on till the train moved on for the last lap to Helsinki.

At the conference centre in Helsinki, there was a great deal of
tension and excitement. Even the bureaucrats appeared to be in a state
of agitation. Finally, news trickled down to the likes of us. In order to
avoid a public debate, the Soviet delegation had proposed that the
plenary session be limited to a few speeches from some of the better-
known fellow-travellers and then the conference should break into
smaller workshops, where matters could be discussed in greater detail.
The manoeuvre lacked subtlety, but an amended variant was pushed
through the relevant committee, only to be challenged at the plenary
by the Indonesians, who informed the delegates that their plane was
waiting at Helsinki airport to take them back that very day if the
proceedings were going to be manipulated into a farce. The irony
here, of course, was that all the dissident delegations, especially the
Chinese and the Indonesians, ran their own conferences in exactly the
same fashion. Nothing was ever left to chance. Even the speeches of
individual delegates were carefully plotted. Because they understood
the system, they were more irate at being deprived of a voice. On the
same day a familiar figure had suddenly arrived at the conference and
been taken straight to the Presidium. It was Ralph Schoenman from
the Bertrand Russell Peace Foundation. He had a message from Bertie
for the big public meeting in the town that evening. Schoenman had
hardly been there a few minutes, when he entered the fray. He was
recognized and strode angrily to the podium from where he demanded
the right of free speech for the Chinese and the others. Ultimately, a
compromise formula was agreed and a number of speeches attacking
the Soviet view of peaceful co-existence were heard by everyone.

The central point made by those of us who were sympathetic to the
Chinese position at the time was that with Vietnam being bombarded
daily and its people North and South being subjected to torture and
terror on a grand scale by the United States and its allies, to talk about

'peaceful co-existence' was somewhat obscene. I argued this position forcefully at the workshop where Vietnam was discussed and found myself being warmly embraced afterwards by Pham van Chuong and Dinh Ba Thi, the two Vietnamese from the National Liberation Front (NLF) in the South. After that we used to meet virtually every day and discuss the war.

I was sharing a room with a veteran peacenik from Britain. One evening, a rotund and loquacious Englishman entered our room. We introduced each other. He was Geoffrey Bing, a one-time left Labour MP who had been an active supporter of African independence during the late forties and fifties. Subsequently, after Gold Coast became independent and changed its name to Ghana, Bing had been invited by his close friend Nkrumah to help ease transition from colonialism to independence. He had become a close adviser and later had been appointed Attorney-General of the newly freed state. Kwame Nkrumah was undoubtedly one of the great nationalist leaders of the African continent, but he surrounded himself with sycophants who failed to challenge him and fed his egomaniacal illusions such as accepting the title of 'Redeemer'. Not surprisingly, an opposition had developed. Given the fact that Nkrumah's foreign policy was one of strict non-alignment, coupled with a bold defence of many countries fighting against US domination or control such as Vietnam and Cuba, it is not inconceivable that the CIA was involved in stoking up hostility to the new regime. This was used as a catch-all to denounce and imprison anyone who dared raise their voice against obvious errors and mistakes. Bing as Attorney-General became the retributive arm of the Ghanaian state. As such he was loathed by many who were not intrinsically unsympathetic to Nkrumah, but were appalled by his failure to pierce the cocoon carefully constructed by the time-servers who ran his office.

In Helsinki late that night, after the requisite number of whisky and sodas, Bing was boasting how he had been instrumental in persuading Nkrumah to lead a Peace Mission to Hanoi and how Harold Wilson had congratulated him for the initiative, but wanted Britain involved as well. I was enraged by the self-congratulatory tones of the man.

'Surely', I ventured, 'the place to take the Commonwealth Peace Mission is Washington. That's where the matter could be resolved very rapidly.' This was a mild enough comment or so I thought. Bing was furious. What did people like me know about statecraft and diplomacy and how wars are brought to an end? I admitted that my knowledge of these matters was limited since I had not served as an adviser to a Head of State. I told him, however, that the operation he had been describing so proudly smacked more of pimping than statesmanship. Bing went purple. 'Why', I asked, 'are you playing the part of a broker and boasting about your links with Wilson. He's implicated in this bloody war. He backs the Americans. How can he or his wretched Foreign Secretary be part of any genuine Peace Mission?' Bing denounced me with a ferocity which gave me an insight as to why Nkrumah had appointed him the State Prosecutor. He was good. Finally it was my tired roommate who ended the discussion by pleading for time to sleep. I wished Bing a friendly goodnight, but he did not respond as he stumbled out of the room.

The footnote to this tale, alas, is not very edifying: Nkrumah did embark on his abortive mission some months later. While he was in mid-flight the news was brought to him that a military coup had taken place in Ghana and some of his closest colleagues were in prison. The man who wanted to be an African Garibaldi would spend the rest of his life in exile in Conakry, Guinea. Nkrumah, to his credit, did draw some lessons from his fall. The result was a set of perceptive essays and interviews on the future of his continent. The same, unfortunately, cannot be said of Geoffrey Bing, who returned to Britain and died a few years later.

One of the largest delegations from the non-communist world was the contingent from India. This included members of the Congress and Communist Parties, together with a sprinkling of professional fellow-travellers – veterans of many a conference. They had seemed the most embarrassed by the political debates. It was almost as if a nice pantomime had been ruined by some ill-behaved children. Nonetheless, it was nice meeting Mulk Raj Anand, the Indian novelist, and Dr Z. Ahmed – both had many friends in Pakistan – and we spent a whole afternoon walking by the lake and discussing the pain which the Partition had caused to Northern India. It was one of history's ironies that the first Indians I met after 1947 were either at Oxford or in Helsinki. Travel restrictions from Pakistan to India and vice versa were extremely strict in those days.

Another writer who was much in evidence at the conference was the Soviet novelist Ilya Ehrenburg. Both Anand and Ehrenburg had produced socialist-realist novels. The latter under compulsion and the Indian out of affection for the Revolution. The unsurprising result was a literary disaster in both cases, as Ehrenburg had partially acknowledged in his memoirs. At Helsinki, however, Ehrenburg was very much the doyen of the pro-Soviet intelligentsia. On the last day of the conference, which had ended without any real agreements and only approved compromise resolutions of the most banal sort, there was a giant public rally in the town. The person chosen to preside over this great peace meeting was Ehrenburg. What, in normal circumstances, would have been an event designed to boost the morale of the faithful, ended, like the conference, in total confusion. One of the speakers, due to read his message from Bertrand Russell, was Schoenman. 'What's Bertie's message like today, Ralph?' Peggy Duff had enquired innocently in the foyer outside the big meeting hall. 'Fairly average. A bit low-key and not as good as some', had been Schoenman's somewhat muted response. 'Come now, Ralph,' Peggy had retorted with a twinkle in her eye, 'it's not like you to be so modest.' We had all roared with laughter, including the philosopher's secretary, who had little idea of what lay ahead.

The public meeting began with the usual tributes to the heroism of the Vietnamese and other global struggles. A desultory opening speech from Ehrenburg established the mood for the occasion. It threatened to be a heavy evening. A few other speeches followed as clichés and homilies jostled competitively to see which could dominate. Then it was time for Lord Russell's message. Schoenman's tone was aggressive from the very beginning. His speaking style matched the language. His lips curled in a sneer, which gradually enveloped his entire face. The audience, unprepared for surprises, woke up and the hitherto dead hall came to life as the tension spread from the platform to the hall. Bertie's 'low-key' message turned out to be a savage assault on Moscow's 'peaceful co-existence'. The US President was compared to Hitler. Peggy Duff, sitting next to me, wondered in a whisper how this open defiance of bureaucratic norms would end. We did not have to wait long. Ilya Ehrenburg, outraged and angry, told Schoenman to stop as his time was up. Schoenman refused to heed the red-faced novelist and carried on speaking. He was not unused to such tactics. Suddenly Ehrenburg stood up, walked round the edge of the table and, and with his back to the audience, attempted to grab Schoenman's microphone, but the American was clutching it too tightly for a simple wrench to deprive him of the instrument. An undignified, but highly entertaining tug of war ensued with the audience evenly divided. Ultimately, some thick-set stewards arrived and we shouted to Schoenman to accept defeat and step down. This he did to a mixture of applause and boos. As he walked towards us he was waylaid by two Albanians, who hugged and kissed him demonstratively on both cheeks and invited him to visit their country. This was one of the few invitations which I think the Peace Foundation did not accept. Its director was probably aware that any attempt to challenge monolithism in the tiny Stalinist republic might lead to more drastic punishment than simply being deprived of a microphone.

As I flew out of Helsinki I had a strong feeling that this would be the last Peace Conference to be attended by the Chinese and the parties which supported the Peking line. A turning point had been reached in the Sino-Soviet dispute. The ideological disputes would soon be transcended as both states, breathing chauvinist and ultra-nationalist nonsense, would soon confront each other militarily on the Ussuri River. Those who were then most saddened by this division were the Vietnamese. In private they did not conceal their anger. They were worried and with good reason, for they knew that the reapers of this bitter harvest would be the men in Washington.

Chapter Three

———————◆———————

Revolution and Counter-Revolution: 1965–67

'Order reigns in Warsaw!' 'Order reigns in Paris!' 'Order reigns in Berlin!'
This is how the reports of the guardians of 'order' read, every half-century, from
one centre of the world historical struggle to another. And the exulting 'victors'
fail to notice that an 'order' that must be maintained with periodic bloody
slaughters is irresistibly approaching its historical destiny, its downfall . . . 'Order
reigns in Berlin!' You stupid lackeys! Your 'order' is built on sand. Tomorrow
the revolution will rear its head once again, and, to your horror, will proclaim,
with trumpets blazing:
   I was, I am, I will be!

Rosa Luxemburg, *Collected Works*, 1919

The conversations with the Vietnamese in Helsinki had convinced me that there was one overriding priority for radicals, socialists and democrats in the West. We had to do everything in our power – if necessary turn the world upside down – to help the Vietnamese drive the Americans out of their country. I had thrown myself whole-heartedly into political activities related to the Vietnam War on my return to Britain. I had accepted invitations to speak to Young Communists, CND, Quaker groups, a few Labour clubs and various other organizations.

At one such meeting in Croydon I had met Carl Oglesby, a leading member of the American SDS, who had shared a platform and described the growth of the peace movement in the United States. The campuses were beginning to assume the role of organizing centres against the war, helped in their task by singers like Pete Seeger, Joan Baez and Bob Dylan. From what Oglesby reported to that tiny assembly in a suburban English town it was obvious that the times were beginning to change and the new generation was not prepared to let the needs of the cold war determine the future of humanity. The simultaneous growth of the civil rights campaigns and the beginnings of anti-war radicalism gave grounds for hope. If America itself could change, then anything was possible.

This optimistic train of thought was interrupted in October 1965 by the news that was seeping out of Indonesia. A holocaust was in progress. Its victims were the members and supporters of the PKI (the Indonesian Communist Party) and affiliated trade unions. The *Sunday Times* had published reports of the white terror, which depressed me greatly. I had met several Indonesians at Helsinki, and argued with them about their uncritical support for Sukarno, but they had assured Malcolm Caldwell and myself that everything was under control. One of them had hinted that Sukarno had agreed to pave the way for a PKI victory. Then a mysterious coup led by a nonentity called Untung had, in the name of the country's strongman, Sukarno, attempted to decapitate the leadership of the Indonesian Army. Two Generals, Nasution and Suharto, had escaped, organized their forces and hit back. Sukarno had disavowed the coup, but some PKI involvement was undeniable, though no decision as such had been taken by the Party. Without ceremony, the military junta had ordered the arrest and execution of D. N. Aidit, the Secretary-General of the PKI, and other leaders. This was the signal for a generalized bloodbath. The PKI claimed a membership of three million and more than ten million sympathizers in various front organizations. Even if these figures were exaggerated, it was well established that the PKI did command the allegiance of millions of poor Indonesians in town and country. The reports in the European press were horrific. The *Frankfurter Allgemeine Zeitung* published an account from a special correspondent on the island of Bali. This tropical paradise was also a stronghold of the PKI. The newspaper reported that the roads were strewn with dead bodies; that streams were full of corpses and half-burnt bodies were piled high in freshly dug pits in the countryside. Within weeks, even the most conservative estimates spoke of the liquidation of a quarter of a million people. Sukarno did not suffer, but the PKI, which the dictator had used as one important pillar of his Bonapartist project, was physically and politically eliminated by Generals closely identified with the Pentagon. Nasution had in the old days collaborated with the Dutch colonialists and had helped the post-independence massacre of communists in 1948, but, in comparison to the terror of 1965–66, that had been a relatively small affair.

The killers in Jakarta alleged that the PKI was preparing to launch an insurrection in order to 'Vietnamize' the islands. If that had been true, it would not have been possible to wipe out the Party so easily. Insurrection implies armed struggle and a party preparing a rebellion does, in most cases, arm and prepare its supporters. If only that allegation had been true, the Generals might not have succeeded. The tragedy of the PKI lay in its almost total dependence on Sukarno and the state. It had failed to take even the most elementary precautions. There were, after all, PKI members of Sukarno's government. They drove in cars with flags and were saluted by the Generals at airports. On the eve of his execution by the Indonesian Army, the deputy Chairman of the PKI, Njoto, told two Japanese journalists that the PKI refused to build its own army because it had enormous confidence in the Indonesian Army, which was 'not the same as armies in the imperialist countries or as in India now'. It was a truly 'national army'. He also reconfirmed the PKI's undying support for Sukarno as 'the great leader of the revolution'. The next day Njoto was shot dead, without a word of protest from the 'great leader'. Sukarno's powers were clipped, but he was permitted to live in a style for which he became notorious throughout the world.

Why had the PKI, a party of millions, placed all their trust in the ability of this clever demagogue to preserve indefinitely only a stalemated status quo? If only they had reserved some of this trust for their own supporters.

I suppose what made me angry was the fact, irrelevant to all but myself, that I had never found Sukarno to be a particularly inspiring political leader. His rhetoric was stale, his vision severely limited and his achievements few. Nehru had fathered the concept of nonalignment, Nasser had nationalized the Suez Canal, Nkrumah had dreamt of African unity, Mao Zedong and Fidel Castro had led successful revolutions and Ho Chi Minh was in the process of completing another. But what had the degenerate mystagogue of Jakarta ever achieved, apart from a futile and thoughtless confrontation with Malaysia, which had ended in a disaster? More to the point it had strengthened the most revanchist elements in the army: the very men who had presided over 150,000 deaths in Bali alone. I remembered a state visit by Sukarno to Pakistan a few months before I left for Britain. He had been received by Field Marshal Ayub with full honours. He had then embarked on a visit to Dhaka, which was then the capital of what was still East Pakistan. Prior to leaving Dhaka for Lahore, accompanied by the country's Foreign Minister, Zulfikar Ali Bhutto, the Indonesian leader had been presented with a special 'guard of honour'. The host country's airline had lined up a dozen of its more 'presentable' air stewardesses and asked the visiting dignitary to choose the pair he would most like to fly with that day. Sukarno had done so with a broad grin. The plane had been over an hour late in landing at Lahore. The 'great leader' had been hard at work and the Pakistani Foreign Minister had evidently instructed the pilot not to land until the President's lust had been fully exhausted. The instruction had been obeyed, but the circumstances of the late arrival could not be kept secret. Bhutto himself remarked that Sukarno could 'never come on time'.

For months afterwards I was dejected by the news from Indonesia. It had raised the first real doubts in my mind about Chinese policies. The PKI had been extremely close to Peking. The advice they had received from Peng Chen and other Chinese leaders was that the alliance with Sukarno must be the cornerstone of their policy because of Sukarno's anti-imperialist stance. The pro-Moscow parties were not too embarrassed by the turn of events since it was an opportunity to criticize the supposedly 'leftist errors' of the PKI, which the East German daily *Neues Deutschland* did in its issue of 24 October 1965, while extending the fullest possible support to Sukarno. The Chinese leaders had been denouncing Moscow repeatedly for advancing the 'absurd and revisionist thesis' that it was possible to have a state that was neither fish nor fowl, neither socialist nor bourgeois. They had heaped scorn and abuse on Soviet analysts for even suggesting that in the Third World it was perfectly permissible for local communists to enter into alliances with their rulers, provided the latter were anti-imperialist. The PKI leaders had been guilty of all these errors and the mass murders of at least 250,000 communists was the clearest indication of the linkages between theory and practice. The political blunders of the PKI had led to the loss of lives on a sensational scale. What would be Peking's response? We waited anxiously and eagerly for some clarification, but Peking remained silent. No explanations. No analyses. No criticisms. The defeat in Indonesia had many similarities with Chiang Kai-shek's purge of Chinese communists in Shanghai in 1927. Peking opted to remain quiet since any real discussion of the débâcle would have meant spotlighting its own role. China's leaders had been fully aware of, and had enthusiastically supported, the orientation of the PKI. As far back as September 1963, the Indonesian Communist leader, D. N. Aidit, had outlined his theses to the School of Advanced Studies of the Central Committee of the Chinese Communist Party in Peking. He had not attempted to cover up the truth, but had explained how the Indonesian 'national bourgeoisie starts to return to the side of the revolution'. He had confessed proudly to his Chinese comrades that:

> We have now collaborated with the Indonesian bourgeoisie for nearly ten years, and the revolutionary forces have continually developed rather than grown fewer during this time, whereas the reactionary forces have experienced failure after failure ... President Sukarno has played an important role in the struggle against Communophobia and for national unity.

At the time they had raised no objections. After the massacres they preferred to forget the nightmare.

The silence in the West was in many ways far more oppressive. The failure of liberals, humanists, traditional defenders of human rights and their friends to respond to the terror of the Suharto regime was an unmistakeable manifestation of the double standards that prevail on such issues. Chiang Kai-shek's bloodbath of communists in Shanghai in 1927 had produced one of Malraux's most powerful pieces of writing in the shape of a novel, *Man's Estate*. The news from the killing fields in Sumatra and Java revealed that the scale of butchery was on a much larger scale than Shanghai in 1927, but nothing moved in the capital cities of the West. The Generals in Indonesia had, you see, succeeded in wiping out the communists. If their actions had unleashed a civil war and the PKI had been in control of central Java and Bali, if guerrilla war had been raging in Sumatra, then there would have been a lot of noise and condemnation of both sides. But the success was applauded in secret and many Pentagon strategists asked in public why what was possible in Jakarta appeared difficult in Saigon. In reality, and the Vietnamese communists understood this well, the defeat in Indonesia made victory in Vietnam even more important.

Towards the end of 1965, I received a letter from the American TV network CBS, enquiring whether I would be prepared to take part in an Oxford versus Harvard debate on Vietnam. The intention was to set up a TV confrontation via Early Bird satellite (this was a novelty in those days). The BBC would organize a studio for Oxford students at their Shepherds Bush TV centre and CBS would organize our counterparts at Harvard. Both of us would have teams of three. Harvard would defend US policies and we would oppose. There was one stipulation: both teams were to include a senior member of the university or a distinguished alumni. I agreed immediately and suggested Stephen Marks as my seconder and Michael Foot as the 'senior member'. We were also invited to take fifty students from the university to the studios, for whom transport and refreshments would be provided.

On 21 December 1965, we all arrived and were warmly welcomed by Sir Hugh Greene, the Director-General, who turned out to be an extremely liberal, witty and cultured human being. Very different, I might add, from Ian Trethowan, the only other BBC person with whom I had dealt at that time. Greene expressed the hope that we would trounce Harvard and I had a distinct impression that this was not mindless chauvinism. He was manifestly very hostile to the American war effort. Foot, Marks and myself had a fairly clear idea of what we intended to propose that night. The only mystery was our opponents. This was solved when we exchanged introductions courtesy of the satellite. The two students were campus Democrats and the 'senior member' from Harvard was a don called Henry Kissinger.

The debate began and ended fairly predictably. None of us were impressed with Kissinger, whose performance was dull and mediocre. What was more interesting was the fact that a number of the Harvard students in the audience agreed with us. When Kissinger repeated a well-worn fiction blaming the Vietnamese for refusing peace by not agreeing to negotiate, I responded by referring to this remark as obscene and asked whether the United States would have negotiated with the Japanese a few months after the attack on Pearl Harbor. Some of the Harvard people had applauded, while Kissinger had stared across the screen at me in horror. I suppose that in a highly protected ideological environment, equations of the sort I had made were too wild even to gain admittance.

There was universal agreement at our end that we had won the debate, which was seen live throughout the United States but was never screened in Britain. That was certainly the view of the BBC bosses who were present and Michael Foot concurred. Since it was a fairly ordinary, old, debate, I soon forgot about the whole affair. A few weeks later, after the Christmas break, I was amazed to receive hundreds of letters from the United States. Some of these included press clippings reviewing the debate, most of which were favourable to our side. An overwhelming majority of the letters supported the stance I had taken. The correspondence came from every corner of the United States. I even had a fan letter from Dallas. The bulk of the mail was from school and university students, who wrote to express their amazing (or so it seemed at the time) hostility to their own government's war in Asia. This was the first concrete sign, as far as I was concerned, that something was changing in the United States. In later years I often wondered how many of the fourteen–sixteen year olds who had written to me and to whom I had replied at length had graduated to join SDS or the mushrooming Committees to End the War in Vietnam.

Politics in Britain had continued to be dominated by Labour's quick march rightwards. While newspaper and magazine editors began to discover the discreet charm of Harold Wilson, revulsion against his domestic and foreign policies grew rapidly within the Labour Party and especially amongst students who had initially been excited at the prospect of a Labour Government. The major reason for the rapid disillusionment was that Wilson had failed to deliver any of the promises of radical change. His policies, as he was later to confess, were dictated by the City and international bankers. In January 1966, there was a by-election in a marginal Labour-held seat in Hull. It was felt by a number of us that an independent candidate should challenge Labour and make Vietnam a central issue in the campaign. A small meeting was held in London, which was attended by a variety of CND activists, some of whom had played an active part in floating the idea of single-issue candidates in favour of CND standing against right-wing Labour MPs. The gathering was small and unrepresentative, a fact which nobody attempted to either deny or confront. A central role was played by one Michael Craft, a dynamic dentist and longtime CND activist. He pledged to organize support and raise funds for the campaign.

The candidate selected for the task of embarrassing Wilson was Richard Gott, a red-bearded journalist from the *Guardian*, who was an active participant in the wave of teach-ins and meetings on Vietnam. (If Gott had refused, the most likely choice would have been Pat Arrowsmith, poetess and veteran of the Committee of Hundred.) It was agreed to call our strange outfit Radical Alliance, though Rainbow would have been a more appropriate title. As time was short, we decided that the candidature should be announced immediately and an appeal for canvassers and volunteers to come to Hull with their sleeping-bags launched as soon as possible. The day Richard Gott went public a bucketful of criticism was hurled at us from within the left. Some of it was friendly, some hostile, some perplexed. Friends rang

Richard Gott to dissuade him from this quixotic venture, but it was decided to go ahead. Vietnam had to be made a central issue in British politics in order to force Wilson and Labour to change their appalling policies. At roughly this time Wilson's parliamentary factotum, a Welsh MP called Harold Davies, had just returned from Hanoi where he had been reluctantly received by the Vietnamese. Davies had refused to visit the bombed areas of the city or nearby towns on the grounds that he did not wish to become part of the Vietnamese propaganda machine. The Labour candidate in Hull, Kevin MacNamara, was a fairly typical Wilsonite loyalist, which made the task of justifying our decision easier, but many left notables declined to back Gott's campaign. In this they were at one with Gott's own newspaper, which was critical of his decision.

I rang up Bertrand Russell and he agreed to see Richard Gott and myself the following day. Ralph Schoenman was opposed to the campaign, but did not try to dissuade us from seeing the old man or, more to the point, vice versa. We arrived on the doorstep of Russell's flat in Chelsea promptly at 11am the next day. The veteran dissenter, one of the few living embodiments of the old radical tradition in British politics, was a regular target of Fleet Street's most vicious snipers. Because of his political opinions he was always being dismissed as a senile fool, whose best days were over. The contrast with the recently dead Churchill, whose senility had been real, could not have been more pronounced.

Russell opened the door to let us in, greeted us warmly and made us sit, while he went and put the kettle on for some tea. The suggestion that one of us take over on this front was greeted with disdain. We told him why we had come. He congratulated Gott on his decision, which he thought a good one, even though he did not believe that we would get very far. He had only recently renounced his Labour Party affiliations after many decades of membership. The reason? Labour's support for the Americans in Vietnam. He had known every single leader of the Labour Party from Keir Hardie onwards. I asked whether he regarded them all in the same light or was there a particular one he disliked more than the others. He chuckled as he relit his pipe. 'I really do think very little of Wilson, you know. He is a contemptible man. I was invited to meet Nkrumah at the Ghanaian High Commission a few days ago. As he was escorting me back to my car I saw Wilson coming in, presumably to discuss this so-called Peace Mission to Hanoi. He saw me and came forward with outstretched hand and said "Oh hullo, Lord Russell" as if we were close acquaintances. I could not bring myself to shake hands with this man, so I put my hand firmly behind my back, ignored the fellow, said goodbye to Nkrumah and got into my car.' He stopped to see how we reacted since he was obviously delighted with what he had done. 'So,' I began, 'Wilson is the worst of the bunch?' He appeared deep in reflection. Then he shook his head. 'Wilson is a small and petty man, but he is not the worst. I suppose if one has to make a choice I would say that Ramsay MacDonald was very dreadful, I can still hear his awful voice telling us that socialism would be built "brick by brick". Dreadful man. Some say that a party gets the leader it deserves. I don't think the Labour Party deserved either MacDonald or Wilson.'

The issue which agitated him the most that day was the Sino-Soviet dispute. He regarded the Russians as the villains, particularly as they were simply not doing enough to help the Vietnamese. Russell had written one of his famous public letters to the Soviet Prime Minister, Kosygin, asking why the Soviet Air Force could not be sent to North Vietnam to defend a friendly, fraternal state against foreign attack. Kosygin had sent a reply claiming, probably accurately, that the Vietnamese themselves had not made such a request. Russell was angry. 'Obviously the Vietnamese are cautious in their dealings with Moscow and Peking. They have to be, but we don't. I rather tend towards the Chinese view of the world on these matters, don't you?' We did admit that on a number of questions the Chinese positions were more militant, but I added that Indonesia had made me careful. He did not respond, but nodded. The Chinese had invited him to visit Peking, but it was a long journey and if he went anywhere it would be Hanoi. Richard Gott asked if he would send a message of support to the campaign in Hull and he assented happily. I asked what he thought the chances were of the War Crimes Tribunal which bore his name being a success. He said that the very fact that it was being organized was a success. 'We are doing it in the face of universal hostility. Even the Russians are not in favour, but it has to be organized and the United States has to be tried for genocide. There is no other way.'

The war in Indochina had revived the passionate side of Bertrand Russell's character. His political activities had spanned two world wars and he was to spend the last years of his life completely immersed in the battles that were being fought in Vietnam. He used the enormous authority that his name enjoyed throughout the world to aid the Vietnamese cause. The staggering fact was that he was still in total command of all his senses. His body appeared frail as he was by now ninety-three years old, but he spoke lucidly and the clarity of his thoughts was the most powerful rebuttal of the obloquies hurled at his head by the mercenary scribes who slandered him mercilessly. His position in British society was virtually unique. Unlike France, the country of Russell's birth had studiously avoided encouraging the growth of an intelligentsia that was not dependent, in some way or the other, on the state. Writers and philosophers have usually been treated with far less respect in these islands than in Europe. Russell towered above everyone else, both through the strength of his intellect and, of course, the fact that he had outlived most of his peers. His writings had given him an international audience and he was respected in every continent (though not by everyone) as a deeply humane and rational person. I had been drawn to his essays after reading his book on the dangers of a nuclear conflict and his exchange of letters with Kennedy, Khrushchev and Nehru during the Cuban missile crisis. It is a fact that in many parts of the Third World where Wilson was reviled as a toady of the White House, it was Russell's uncompromising tones that enabled one to explain that there were other voices in Britain. Richard Gott and I made our farewells and as we came out into the cold we stood for a while on the pavement marvelling at the stamina of this remarkable old man.

The Hull campaign got under way. Gott spoke at various meetings but failed in his attempt to get the Labour candidate to debate us on Vietnam. The campaign was not short of debates, but these were mainly with those who agreed with us on Vietnam, but disagreed on our decision to oppose Labour. We did win some support. A farmer who was a CND supporter promised to drop our leaflets on the city from his private plane! Many students from Hull University joined our canvassing parties, which were usually bleak expeditions to the housing estates. Some voters were sympathetic, many of them said that they did not think Labour should be supporting the Americans, but they would vote Labour nevertheless. They could not afford to let the Tories win and 'your lot have no chance of winning'.

One major achievement of our campaign was to divide the Saville family. John Saville was a senior professor at the university, but he was much more than that to all of us. He had resigned from the Communist Party in 1956 after Hungary and had helped to establish *The New Reasoner*, which he had co-edited with E. P. Thompson during its short life before it merged with the *Universities and Left Review* to become the *New Left Review*. Under the editorship of Saville and Thompson, *The New Reasoner* had become a lively and stimulating mix of British and European politics. The quality and breadth of its cultural coverage has yet to be equalled by the left in Britain. In 1964, Saville had teamed up with a fellow new-reasoner, Ralph Miliband, to establish an annual, *The Socialist Register*, which was intended as a socialist version of the political registers of yore. I write all this to establish the fact that John Saville had impeccable credentials on most counts. He had even served as a 'mole' in the service of the crown during the Second World War. As a soldier in the British Army he had been posted to India, where he had not wasted any time before he established contact with the Indian communists, whom he had helped in a number of ways.

The Saville household was our natural headquarters for the campaign. John Saville's companion, Constance, and his youngest son, Richard, were staunch supporters of the Gott candidature, but the veteran Leninist was unshakeable. In vain did we argue the merits of our candidate. He refused to even enter the debate on such a petty level. He was not opposed to breaking Labour's monopoly of working-class representation in Parliament, but he did not believe that

Radical Alliance was the requisite instrument. The divisions inside the house were only too visible from the outside. The rooms on the top floors displayed 'Vote Gott' posters, while the ground floor proclaimed a more traditional allegiance. The electorate agreed with John Saville and returned Kevin MacNamara to Parliament. I won the sweepstake by coming closest to the number of votes that we finally obtained. Slightly under 300 worthy citizens of Hull were prepared to rock the Labourist boat on that occasion. The British electorate, alas, does not usually favour protest votes.

There was another general election that year and Labour received a huge vote of confidence. It had a majority of seventy in the new Parliament and could have attempted to implement the party's manifesto. Michael Foot, among others, made the point well:

> There was an excuse for governing from hand to mouth between 1964 and 1966 because the government had to design matters in order to win a majority, and they did that successfully. But they comforted themselves that they could continue with that kind of consensus policy, and indeed the whole consensus idea had become even more deeply ingrained within them than it was before. It was between March 1966 and June 1966 that the government eventually collapsed into accepting the full deflationary policy. This was an acknowledgment of defeat. Then when they accepted the July measures, they accepted international financial doctrine. All the efforts they had made to get beyond orthodoxy were abandoned. The great opportunity of this government was lost when they got the majority of 100 in 1966. That was the moment when the government should have taken steps to show who was master in its own house and instead of doing that it travelled in the opposite direction.

The 1966 election campaign had been a relatively tame affair. In contrast to 1964 there was no talk of an 'alternative philosophy' to the Tories 'who identify the national interest with the interest of the money-makers, not with the interest of the wage-earners, with the speculators and not the producers'. In 1964 Wilson had pledged to build a society whose priority 'will no longer be private profit and the accumulation of personal wealth'. In 1966, all this was forgotten as Wilson basked in the praise of *The Economist*. In Oxford we went out to canvass again and found that most people wanted to give Labour a bigger majority. Richard Crossman had come to speak at a big Labour election rally in Oxford. Some of us had challenged him on a number of issues, especially Labour's appalling record on race and immigration. Crossman's reply to me was symbolic of the entire campaign. He did not attempt to conceal the reactionary character of Labour's stance, which would have shocked Gaitskell, but his excuse charted new ground: 'There was massive pressure from Labour voters in the Midlands,' he had argued, 'you can say that they're wrong and racist, but we cannot afford to ignore that pressure.' It was a dangerous logic for it implied a politics where, in order to stay in power, the lowest common denominator became the sole criterion. It was also short-sighted. The Tories were natural masters of this process and could always outflank and outmanoeuvre the Labour Party. Not that this prevented the local Tory, Monty Woodhouse from embarrassing me on more than one occasion. He used to stop me in the street and say: 'I am to the left of the local Labour candidate on immigration, on Vietnam, on Rhodesia and probably also on economic measures. But you and your friends will be voting, I take it, for him?' To which I replied that we were voting for parties and not individuals and moved off rapidly before getting involved in a debate on the political positions of the Labour candidate, who, incidentally, after being elected in 1966, became a junior Foreign Office spokesman and later helped to found the Social Democratic Party.

There was no Chinese wall separating domestic conservatism from a radical foreign policy. Each was inextricably linked to the other. Harold Wilson had few illusions on this score. Nor did the artist Gerald Scarfe. In his own fashion he, too, was conscious of the realities of power. In one of his most savage caricatures he depicted a servile Wilson on his knees clutching at the falling trousers of the American President, Lyndon Johnson, whose half-bare posterior he is attempting to penetrate with his long, forked tongue. Scarfe labelled his masterpiece, 'Special Relationship'. Rejected by the *Sunday Times* for its 'breach of taste', the cartoon found its way to Soho and became a cover of *Private Eye*. It could be seen on kitchen walls and campus billboards for many years afterwards.

Harold Wilson had won the parliamentary majority he needed to challenge existing orthodoxies. Instead he chose to suffocate Labour's natural supporters by accepting and justifying every single constraint imposed on his government by financial and ideological establishments at home and abroad. The result was only too predictable. The failures of right-wing Labourism in the crucially important post-1966 years paved the way for a new-style Tory regime. Margaret Thatcher, unlike Wilson, refused to treat the postwar consensus as sacrosanct and made a virtue of shattering shibboleths.

I had finished my time at Oxford and was faced with a number of dilemmas. Should I complete my bar exams at Gray's Inn, where I had already gone through the bizarre process of eating the requisite number of 'dinners' – one of the many medieval rituals that should have been swept aside by a modernizing Labour Government – or participate in the opening of 'new fronts' against the United States. The thought of spending the next few years leafing through immensely boring legal tomes was not an enticing prospect. A phone call and a letter, not linked to each other, helped to make the choice easier.

The phone call had come as a complete surprise. An American woman had rung, saying that she was Marlon Brando's secretary and was ringing to invite me to have dinner with him as soon as it was convenient for me. She claimed that Brando was in London for a fortnight. My first response was to treat the affair as a practical joke. I replied that I was far too busy since I had prior engagements to eat with Henry Fonda and Laurence Olivier. I then put the phone down. My second response, when she returned the call an hour later, was to be more friendly and pleaded with her to tell me which of my friends had put her up to this jape. She was puzzled and amused, but kept assuring me that it was a genuine invitation. The third time she said, 'Don't hang up, I have someone who wishes to speak to you himself.' I was intrigued. To my utter astonishment the voice was unmistakeably that of Brando. I had seen *On the Waterfront* and *Viva Zapata* too many times and this was no cheap mimic, but the real thing. I apologized. He laughed. This allowed me to recover my composure. I thanked him for his invitation to supper and we agreed a time and date. I then asked why he was inviting *me*. 'I saw you on CBS debating Harvard on Vietnam,' he replied, 'and you did well. I'd like to meet.'

The following week I arrived at his rented accommodation somewhere in Chelsea and was greeted by the much-amused secretary, a Ms Sanchez, who introduced me to my host. We sat down and talked about Vietnam. Brando was deeply hostile to the war and it was he who told me that Kissinger was not an insipid nonentity, but a man desperate to become a grey eminence to the powerful and the mighty. He asked whether I thought the United States could win the war. I gave him three reasons why they could never win a permanent victory and would be forced to leave sooner or later. He nodded in agreement. Then I asked him whether his position would be the same if he thought that his country could win the battle. I explained that many Americans were despondent because they thought the situation was hopeless and not because they were on principle opposed to the intervention. He grinned and assured me that he did not belong in that category: 'You said on TV that in your opinion US intervention in Vietnam was as immoral as that of Nazi Germany and Fascist Italy in Spain during the thirties. Well I'd go along with that...'

There were two small tables beautifully laid out for supper and soon other guests arrived, somewhat less punctually than myself. Kenneth and Kathleen Tynan and Eleanor Bron were assigned the same table as me, while sundry starlets and Ursula Andress, attired in an amazingly low-cut outfit, were seated on the other table a few feet away. Brando was the perfect host, dividing his attention equally between us and his other guests. Tynan insisted that before we started eating we all took turns to explain what each of us was doing there that evening. It emerged that Eleanor Bron, too, had initially regarded the invitation as a jape. She had been glimpsed by the master on a satirical programme on the BBC. Tynan was given no particular reason except that his company would be greatly appreciated, which it certainly was by us that evening as he regaled us with one tale after another. Dinner was followed by dancing and later Brando kindly offered to put me up for the night, but the Tynans, who had left early, had insisted I spend the rest of the night at their flat in Mayfair. This seemed a more relaxed option.

Over brunch the next day Tynan was indignant at the thought of my becoming a lawyer. 'Why do you want to stop living?' I remember his saying, and since it was not an unimportant question I thought about it a great deal. In fact the only reason for getting the qualification had been that when I returned home, it would enable me to be independent. However since I had got immersed in anti-dictatorship activities in this country and had written a four-page diatribe against Ayub in *Isis*, I had been advised not to return for a holiday since my passport might be confiscated. Gray's Inn began to recede considerably in my consciousness, but I might still have been driven to the Bar had it not been for a letter that was waiting for me when I returned to Oxford.

It was another invitation to London, but this time from Julian Critchley, who had just been appointed Editor of *Town* magazine (a British attempt to recreate *Esquire*). He wondered whether I was interested in working for the magazine. I rang immediately to fix an appointment and was on the train to London the next day. After an amiable chat, Critchley asked what I wanted to do on the magazine. I suggested that I would happily review plays, since I had long been interested in the theatre. My editor-to-be concurred, but thought that I should take responsibility for the books and films as well. I agreed, was appointed Reviews Editor and taken to meet the proprietor and publisher, a Michael Heseltine, Esquire. He was equally affable and asked how much I wanted to be paid. On hearing my response – 'An NUJ wage' – he grunted agreement, but warned me in the friendliest possible fashion against any attempts to unionize the outfit. Thus for one whole year I became an employee of the Haymarket Press. It was, I have to admit, a pleasant way to spend the day. Critchley was not an overbearing editor. In fact he was one of nature's liberals and he permitted me a fair amount of space in every sense of the word. It was also perfectly possible to commission odd articles for the non-reviews section of the magazine; one of my favourites was an 'Opinion' piece by Paul Foot in December 1966 in which he penned a devastating profile of the new breed of young MPs who had entered the House of Commons. Foot described the Hattersley/Walden influx as follows:

The young reformer comes from far away in the North somewhere, and his father was a staunch trade-unionist in the red old days, who flirted with the ILP [Independent Labour Party] and even with the Communists. The young reformer went to a good school and even better university, and notched a chairmanship or two in university politics. He learnt a little law, and little less economics, but above all he studied language; the right language; the sort of language which really means something in this harsh, realistic, modern world. And, because he watches the telly a lot the young reformer learnt to speak the language correctly: that is, in the jerky, didactic tones of Ian Trethowan and Alan Whicker.

Nothing serves the young reformer better than this knowledge of the right language. He has learnt how to express opposition to 'restrictive practices on *both* sides of industry', which he takes to mean keeping Frank Cousins firmly under control. He has learnt, too, the up-to-date epithets to replace the crude, outdated nonsense of the thirties.

Instead of 'equality' he talks of 'increased productivity'; instead of 'brotherhood', 'a more efficient technology'; and instead of 'God', 'growth'.

The young reformer does not normally read books; though he has read *The Making of the President* (1960 and 1964) by Theodore White, twice each. He encourages his wife to go to work because he believes in female emancipation and because it leaves him freer for his duties. He sent his two children to the local comprehensive school, after they failed the Common Entrance. He likes his Wates-built house, within easy reach of Charing Cross, and enthuses about the 'common facilities' in his housing estate, though secretly he prays for a high-walled garden, separated from the neighbours. He goes once a year to the opera, and tells two dirty jokes a year when judging a beauty contest in his constituency.

The young reformer is happy as long as there is work to do; a meeting to attend; a local paper to read; a division to vote in. He is thoroughly bored by his family, his friends and his leisure time, and does his best to exclude them all as far as it is politically possible.

His politics are his life. And his politics are always the politics of his party.

Oh, yes, of *course*, he is a member of a political party. But he cannot for the moment recollect which one.

It was a mark of those times, I suppose, that the politico-cultural mix that made up each issue of *Town* in 1966–67 was fairly radical. The issues edited by Critchley, if analysed carefully today, would make the Conservative MP for Aldershot too left-wing to be considered as a member of the Communist Party journal, *Marxism Today*, which celebrates everyday bourgeois existence far more forcefully than *Town* ever did. My chosen profession, alas, was beginning to depress me a great deal. I often wondered why I had ever asked to be a theatre critic. What had once seemed an interesting way of passing the time had, in reality, become a ghastly chore. Attending theatrical first nights was like visits to the cemetery in the company of corpses attired in black. An average of three evenings a week spent in the company of dead souls, watching events which had nil artistic or any other significance, was enough to deaden my senses. In the prevailing atmosphere it was hardly surprising that Tom Stoppard's clever, though frothy, word-plays appeared to some as a welcome break.

The one director, apart from Joan Littlewood, who I admired a great deal was Peter Brook. I had travelled from Oxford to see his production of Peter Weiss' *Marat/Sade*. It had been a revelatory experience. I think it was one of the few occasions that I left a theatre feeling both moved and excited. *The Persecution and Assassination of Marat as performed by the inmates of the asylum of Charenton under the direction of the Marquis de Sade* – the full title of the play – was Weiss paying his tribute to Brecht. The combination of the playwright's unalloyed Marxism and Brook's direction electrified the audiences. The play with its perfect marriage of form and content was an artistic triumph, acclaimed even by those who disagreed strongly with its message. The dialogue and songs had been translated into English by Adrian Mitchell and he gave them a vigour which ensured the play's success. Weiss spoke to his audiences through the character of the revolutionary French priest, Jacques Roux, the voice of the *sans-culottes*, but for British audiences the most contemporary note was struck by Marat, who in one of his speeches made a direct reference to the Tory election slogan of 'You've Never Had It So Good'. This was before the election of Harold Wilson and the following lines never failed to evoke a response from the audience:

> Don't be deceived
> when our Revolution has been finally stamped
> out
> and they tell you
> things are better now
> Even if there's not poverty to be seen
> because the poverty's been hidden
> even if you ever got more wages
> and could afford to buy
> more of these new and useless goods
> which these new industries foist on you
> and even if it seems to you
> that you never had so much
> that is only the slogan of those
> who still have much more than you
> Don't be taken in
> when they pat you paternally on the shoulder
> and say
> that there's no inequality worth speaking of
> and no more reason
> for fighting
> Because if you believe them

[*turns towards audience*]
they will be completely in charge
in their marble homes and granite banks
from which they rob the people of the world
under the pretence of bringing them culture.
Watch out
for as soon as it pleases them
they'll send you out
to protect their gold
in wars
whose weapons rapidly developed
by servile scientists
will become more and more deadly
until they can with a flick of the finger
tear a million of you to pieces.

The success of Brook's *Marat/Sade* had led those of us who wanted a new type of theatre to hope that his next production a few years later, *US*, would repeat and transcend the previous success. The title was an intended pun since the play was about Vietnam. *US* was both the US and *US*. This time I had gone to the play as a critic. The very fact that Brook had thought it important to produce a play on Vietnam was a startling innovation for a mainstream theatrical company like the RSC. The play had been denounced in advance by the right as being anti-American and, as a result, my own sympathies even before I entered the auditorium were entirely on the side of Brook and his cast. Yet the play was a total disappointment. It had left me cold, unmoved and feeling extremely embarrassed for the actresses and actors who took part. At the end of the first act the performers, heads covered in paper bags, crawled off the stage in simulated agony. This was a test. Would the audience guide them to the exits. In the event no one moved. Brook denounced the audience as 'callous', but this was far from the truth. The fact was that the unevenness of the performance was a result of a script which had been worked on by too many people and did not succeed in conveying anything coherent. The contrast with Weiss' skilful and carefully filleted episodes from the French Revolution could not have been demonstrated in a more painful fashion. As I wrote at the time, the structural weaknesses of the play were, in essence, political:

> And the reason why US does not succeed is because Mr Brook refuses to take sides. This lack of commitment is so irritating that there are times when one wishes that he had consistently supported the LBJ/ Wilson/Ky position: it would have made the show that much more provocative. For what is the point of having a Theatre of Commitment if you refuse to commit yourself and try to disguise the fact by playing with our emotions. If Mr Brook's sole purpose was to make us angry, then he has succeeded. We are very angry with him for wasting an excellent opportunity. That all wars are bad is an axiom which has been repeated often enough and we did not need mere reaffirmation of this ... We expected something more and are sad to be disappointed.

Some months later, I ran into Brook at an event in Hyde Park. One of his cohorts introduced us and, to my surprise, he was extremely friendly. It was he who mentioned the review (no other critic had attacked it from a similar position), smiled and said 'it was interesting'. I did not prolong the discussion, but moved on. The real reason for dwelling on this episode is not to revive memories of my days as a dramaturg. It is because the publication of this particular review led to my receiving another phone call from a man I did not know. It was Clive Goodwin, who introduced himself as a 'literary agent', said he had greatly enjoyed my review 'only because I agreed with everything you said' and suggested that we meet for lunch. I was due to leave for an assignment in Prague, but Clive insisted that it had to be before my departure. We had lunch the very next day at Biaggi's, just off the Edgware Road, very close to the offices of *Town*.

He did not tell me all that much about himself on that occasion, but he talked a lot about Vietnam, and the state of the theatre and television, which was his main interest. He believed that it was far easier to get radical plays performed on TV than on the stage and he reeled off a number of names, which meant nothing to me at the time. These included Denis Potter, Trevor Griffiths, Jim Allen, John McGrath and Troy Kennedy Martin. 'What about David Mercer?' I asked, since I had seen *Morgan: A Suitable Case for Treatment* three times already that month. He stared at me as if I had uncovered an Achilles heel. 'No,' he said in a very definite way. 'I agree he is very good, but he's not one of mine. Margaret Ramsay's got him.'

The real reason for the lunchtime summit, however, had nothing to do with these matters. Clive was convinced that we needed to start a new paper, which would be wholly committed to the left. He asked what I thought about such a prospect. I concurred with great enthusiasm. He said that he would organize a gathering at his flat in Cromwell Road to discuss the matter further after I returned from Prague. It had emerged during the conversation that he was a great friend of the Tynans, who had told him all about the evening with Marlon Brando. I took to Clive instinctively. He was extremely open, very witty and thoroughly unpretentious. Both of us felt that the growing disillusionment with the Labour Government's policies was creating a space on the left and a newspaper or magazine that could fill the vacuum was badly needed.

The day before I left for Prague I was summoned to the offices of the Bertrand Russell Peace Foundation. There Ralph Schoenman told me that I was needed to form part of an investigating team to visit Kampuchea and Northern Vietnam for the War Crimes Tribunal. I might have to fly out directly from the Czech capital and I would be away for several weeks. I rapidly cleared this with Julian Critchley, who was totally sympathetic, but said I must do a long report for the magazine. He promised to forward expenses for the Vietnam trip to me in Prague.

Chapter Four

From Prague to Hanoi: Jan–Feb 1967

But these are tainted years, ours; the blood of men far away tumbles again in the foam, the waves stain us, the moon is spattered. These faraway agonies are our agonies and the struggle for the oppressed is a hard vein in my nature.

Perhaps this war will pass like the others which divided us, leaving us dead, killing us along with the killers but the shame of this time puts its burning fingers to our faces. Who will erase the ruthlessness hidden in innocent blood?

Pablo Neruda, *The Water Song Ends*, 1967

We were flying to Prague after changing aircraft in Brussels. The tiny Sabena plane carrying us was a contraption with propellers. The photographer accompanying me, Clive Arrowsmith, was the only other passenger on the flight, a fact celebrated by the two stewardesses with champagne, which they served throughout. We flew over vast tracts of snow. As we hovered above the Czech capital everything appeared frozen, except the spires, which gave it a magical quality.

The first glimpse of Prague from the ground confirmed the splendours I have visualized from above. This was a city for all seasons. It was unspoilt architecturally and, in contrast to most of the big capitals of Western Europe, was not cursed with an excessive flow of traffic and pollution. We were to stay at the Europa on Wenceslas Square in the heart of the town. The hotel was not a new-fangled five-star monstrosity, but an Art Deco construction built in the early years of the 20th century. The rooms were large and the dining hall was a spectacular throwback to the *belle époque*, complete with balconies. Over the next few days I saw the old Prague and the new. It was an unbelievable aesthetic treat. I fell in love with the old, narrow streets, the walk in the snow over Charles Bridge, the incredibly well-pre-served baroque houses and palaces as well as the cultural vitality that existed just below the bureaucratic facade. I have revisited Prague a number of times since then and it has changed over the last two decades, but it still remains my favourite European city.

Prague excited the senses at a time when my mind would often wander away from the frozen Vltava to the battlefields of Indochina and the smells of Asia. For that is where I was headed next. Despite wartime preoccupations, I was distracted by the splendours of this city. And its inhabitants? Unfortunately I did not meet any of the activists who would come to the fore during the heady days of the Prague spring. One reason for this was that few of them were at that time aware of what lay ahead or the roles that history has assigned them. Within the upper reaches of the ruling Czech Communist Party there was some discussion of reforms, but everything was still at a very primitive stage.

One evening in the tavern made famous by Hasek in *The Good Soldier Svejk*, I was drinking beer with some socialist students from West Berlin. I told them that I was on my way to Vietnam for the Russell Tribunal. To my surprise, they knew all about the initiative and were wholly supportive. I then realized that my Vietnam obsession was nothing exceptional. Here were these Germans, like me in their early twenties, and they too, could think about nothing else but the war. We talked long into the night and discovered that despite our varied political and cultural backgrounds we were affected in a very similar fashion by the same events. As we were leaving the *U kalicha*, one of the Berliners suddenly launched into a diatribe against the Czech students. They were only interested in Western pop music and clothes and unconcerned about Vietnam. The political passivity he encountered had shocked him greatly.

My brief from *Town* was to provide a cultural profile of Prague and we had been provided with interpreters and transport by the ministry concerned, whose bureaucrats provided us with the necessary help. I knew the people I wanted to meet and politely, but firmly, rejected suggestions as to who I should interview. I think one important factor which alienated me from the bureaucrat assigned to help us was that she was completely devoid of humour. She had even frowned slightly when I had insisted on meeting the theatre director Otto Krecma, a Czech Peter Brook whose experimental innovations were tolerated by the regime, but adored by the masses. In Czechoslovakia, as in much of Eastern Europe and the USSR, all culture is popular. The higher its quality, the greater its popularity. The hint of a scowl on the brow of the woman bureaucrat coupled with her grim visage was deceptive. One of the names she suggested in order to help us evaluate the Czech cinema, past and present, was Milan Kundera. I had turned down the offer.

The same woman had told me that there was nothing to see as far as the Mime Theatre was concerned. She was adamant on this question. I had pleaded with her to let us at least photograph and interview the legendary mime artist, Ladislav Fialka, but she had said it was simply not possible. One morning she rang to inform me in a severe voice, designed to conceal her own bureaucratic embarrassment, that we could see Fialka perform that afternoon. When we arrived we realized why this had become possible. An American was in town and was interested in the Czech Mime Theatre touring the United States. And when the dollar raised its voice, everything suddenly became possible. I thanked the dollar-man that day as Fialka performed for over an hour before an audience of under a dozen people. Whatever he may or may not have felt at being exposed in this fashion, his genius was over-powering. His facial and body movements expressed love and happiness, anger and finally sorrow and despair. I can still see the hauntingly sad look on his face as his one-man performance drew to a close. It was a face that returned to me when I thought about the agony of Prague in the summer of 1968.

The last two days were spent in the company of Jiri Mucha, the writer and son of the famous Art Nouveau painter, Alphonse Mucha, whose Sarah Bernhardt appeared on many posters of the sixties. Jiri Mucha lived in a beautiful old house in Hradcany, just opposite the palace where the decaying President Novotny lived in conscious iso-lation. Mucha's house was full of amazing art objects as well a fine collection of books on the history of art and cinema, novels in English, German and Czech and a host of memorabilia collected by Mucha *père* during the course of his travels through Europe. The father's paintings adorned the sitting room and were the indispensable backcloth of his son's existence.

Jiri Mucha had long grey hair and wore a black polo neck sweater and black trousers. Garbed in his satyr's uniform he played host to the denizens of the film world in grand style. His house was the venue of small all-night parties called at short notice to celebrate some event or happening. Politics was not discussed on the first occasion I stayed with him, but when I passed through in 1972, even Mucha had been sobered by the re-establishment of 'order' and discussed the past with a sense of loss. On this my first trip he played the part of a bohemian to perfection, taking particular delight in pointing out which of the actresses present would reach the top of their profession. They were all talented, but that wasn't enough, not even in Czechoslovakia. Mucha's theory of the triple gauntlet was explained thus: 'In Hollywood, you see, a starlet has only to sleep with the director or casting director, depending on the scale of her ambition. Here it is the director, the producer and, most important of all, the bureaucrat in charge of the ministry.' Those present would complain that this was a slander, but it was obvious that Mucha's joke was deadly serious.

On the morning of 9 January I received a cable informing me that I was expected in Phnom Penh within the next three days. My ticket arrived the following day as did some money from *Town*, courtesy Julian Critchley. I sat down the night before my departure, typed up my interviews and report on the cultural underworld of Prague and handed it to a bleary-eyed Clive Arrowsmith at the first sign of daylight. He had just returned from an all-night party and was not pleased, but accepted the package, gave me a hug and muttered something about making sure I focused properly. He had given me some useful hints on taking photographs and had helped me buy a second-hand Pentax in order to prepare me for my tasks in Indochina. I boarded a Czech airlines flight to Phnom Penh a few hours later and did not think about Prague again till the spring of 1968.

It was a strange sensation to be actually flying to the war zone. I had thought about Vietnam so continuously and to the virtual exclusion of everything else that the flight seemed unreal. The war had affected me to such an extent that I had written about it in every single examination paper in my finals at Oxford. Some of this had been easy since in Politics and Moral Philosophy, the war, as far as I was concerned, had a natural place. Economics had proved more difficult, but I had found a way. In answer to a question which asked the examinees to detail the cheapest form of public transport in the world I had cited the American contribution in Vietnam and described the non-stop helicopter service from Saigon and other cities on the hour and every hour to the forest interiors of the country. The only problem here was that replacement costs for helicopters lost in 'accidents' was becoming prohibitive and therefore the US taxpayers might soon stop the subsidies. The chief examiner that year, John Vaizey, had not been amused at all and had suggested that I not be given a degree, but the others had overruled him and awarded me a Third, without even the courtesy of a viva voce – a terrible disappointment since I was looking forward to a debate with Vaizey.

I slept most of the journey, but woke up at Rangoon to disembark and breathe the air. A few hours later I was in the Cambodian capital, where I was received by a protocol person from the Ministry of Foreign Affairs who swept me through all the barriers at amazing speed and drove me straight to the Hotel Royale. The rest of the team had arrived and were awaiting my arrival anxiously since we were meant to travel inside Cambodia the following day. Prince Sihanouk had decided that the War Crimes Tribunal was to be given total support and we were accordingly treated as honoured guests. Sihanouk had insisted that we travel and see for ourselves the so-called Ho Chi Minh Trail, question the people in the villages and ascertain whether or not the North Vietnamese were using it to supply the guerrilla armies in the South. At that time Sihanouk was the Cambodian state. He was Head of State, Head of Government, the country's top composer of music and its best-known film director. The Prince was undoubtedly eccentric and zany, but he did not wish Cambodia to get involved in the war. This was a perfectly comprehensible desire and I have little doubt that Cambodian neutrality could have been preserved had not the pro-United States elements inside the Cambodian state machine organized a coup some years later.

At the hotel, I bathed, ate and went into a special room for our delegation, where we were to be briefed regarding our travel plans. Our team-leader was Lawrence Daly, the Scottish mineworkers' leader, a man with a powerful sense of humour and a strong record of involvement in British left politics. In 1959, Daly had set up the Fife Socialist League and challenged the official Labour candidate. He had saved his deposit and obtained some thousands of votes, a rather different experience to that of the ill-fated Radical Alliance in Hull. Moreover, Daly was a passionate reader of books, an avid reciter of poetry and a habitual imbiber of malt whisky. He greeted me warmly. The very first sentence he uttered was to the effect that he had brought along an extra bottle of Glenfiddich for Ho Chi Minh, who was partial to spirits from Scotland. Daly had been told this by a Scottish communist who had visited Hanoi in the fifties.

The other members of the team included Carol Brightman, editor of *Viet-Report*, a radical and effective anti-war magazine in the United States; Dr Abraham Behar from the Unified Socialist Party (PSU) of France, led at that time by Michel Rocard; and a slightly weird, incredibly gauche Canadian named Gustavo Tolentino, who is best described as a doctor on the eve of qualification. I had been hoping that it would just be a short stopover in Phnom Penh and then on to Hanoi, but we were informed that our tour of duty in Cambodia would extend to ten days.

Sihanouk was out of the country. In his absence we met some of his cabinet, numerous provincial governors and various other notables. Since they were all polite and formal the only method we had of differentiating between the pro-Sihanouk and the pro-American elements was their attitude towards our team. At one ultra-official banquet I had worn a giant Mao badge to relieve the tedium. The Governor of the Bank, who had been the chief host, had almost choked with rage and had not been able to eat properly. Our protocol chief suggested, without looking at me at all, that it was not customary for visiting delegations to wear badges. I feigned innocence. 'What?' I asked, 'not even the Chinese!' The man looked stern. 'Yes,' he replied, 'but they wear it because they are Chinese.' I started laughing and promised that I would never wear the offending button again on Cambodian soil.

At our first briefing, prior to our departure, the Cambodian military officer accompanying us informed us that 'today you will see Ho Chi Minh *piste*'. Lawrence Daly, whose command of French was limited, collapsed with laughter. The officer stopped. 'Did you hear what he just said?' Daly whispered in my ear. I nodded sagely. 'You obviously didn't,' Daly went on, 'he said we're going to see Ho Chi Minh pissed!' Now it was my turn to collapse as Behar explained to the extremely disturbed Cambodian that in future he should use the word 'trail'.

We drove off in our cars to see the non-existent trail. Where it got very rough we transferred to jeeps. We inspected an area where the Americans claimed that North Vietnamese planes landed with supplies for their southern armies. In the distance we could see the clouds of smoke from the other side of the Cambodian–South Vietnamese border – the result of American bombers getting rid of a day's supply of bombs. As we drove closer to the border we could actually hear the bombs. The trail that we were following had clearly been bombed by the United States, but how could we say that it had never been used by the Vietnamese resistance. I decided to question Wilfrid Burchett, the veteran Australian-born journalist, who had witnessed the effect of atomic weapons against Japan, and reported the Korean War, the second Vietnamese War and was one of the few Western journalists who could visit any communist capital whenever he wanted. Burchett was living in Phnom Penh at the time and one evening over drinks on his delightful terrace I asked him about the Ho Chi Minh trail. It was obvious that the North Vietnamese were supplying the South with weapons, food and medicines. One of the easiest routes lay through Cambodia. Why, I asked, could this not be publicly admitted? Why the absurd veil of secrecy? Burchett peered at me curiously through his spectacles. He smiled, but did not say anything. I persisted. Finally he agreed that this was indeed the case, but it did not suit Sihanouk to admit this and if Sihanouk wanted to play it that way why should the Vietnamese be disobliging?

Our non-stop travel was exacting a price. Lawrence Daly had uni-laterally decided that Ho Chi Minh would have to wait for another courier from Scotland and consumed his spare bottle of malt. One afternoon when we had returned from a particularly gruelling trip, we were informed that the Governor of the Province (Svay Rieng) had organized a banquet for us that evening. There was a loud groan from our ranks, but on these occasions protocol reigned supreme. Daly and I were seated on either side of the Governor. All our glasses were soon filled with the tepid Cambodian beer. Daly had already pronounced on this as being 'worse than piss', an assessment with which I whole-heartedly concurred. The Governor, however, was being served whisky. Even before dinner was served, I observed Daly downing the Gover-nor's whisky on two occasions while the man's attention was engaged elsewhere. This was observed by everyone except the Governor. Our delegation was finding it very difficult to maintain the decorum which is required on such occasions. The mirth was not restricted to our side. A number of Cambodians were giggling as well and finally the Governor was informed that there had been a breach of protocol. Daly had by this time consumed a third glassful of the amber liquid. Advised that unless he acted rapidly the entire evening might disintegrate, the Governor ordered another glass and had it placed in front of the Scottish miner, an action which the table applauded. Daly then stood up to propose a toast not to Sihanouk as custom dictated, but to Robert Burns, the anni-versary of whose birth he claimed fell on that very day. He then recited some lines from the bard, which could not be translated by me into English or anyone else into French. To a person, the entire table rose and Robbie Burns was honoured. After that the evening became extremely relaxed. Later we discovered that the Governor was one of Sihanouk's staunchest supporters. That explained his tolerance.

The ten days we spent in Cambodia were politically inconclusive and physically exhausting. Most of the real friends of the Tribunal were underground and official attitudes veered from antagonistic indifference to a restrained neutrality. On our side, too, there was a great deal of play-acting. We were, of course aware that the North Vietnamese communication routes to the National Liberation Front (NLF) forces in the South included one which cut through Cambodia. A pretence had to be maintained, however, that this might not be the case and some in our party were better actors than myself.

My impressions of the country itself were favourable. It had a small population by Asian standards. Many grotesque disparities were visible, but we did not see any signs of starvation. Phnom Penh itself retained the characteristics of a French colonial city, despite the Boulevard Mao Tse-tung and other exotic street names. The architecture, social habits and language of the elite continued to be French and Sihanouk was a great admirer of De Gaulle. On a number of occasions Lawrence Daly and myself abandoned our official cars with their 'protocol officers' and toured the town on our own. We ate on the streets in the circular market where the cuisine was far more satisfying than the bland pseudo-French fare on offer at our hotel. Often I used to wake up early in the morning and walk around the empty streets, which were still being sprayed with water and cleaned. The only people one ever encountered on these dawn outings were the saffron-robed Buddhist monks of different ages and sizes, walking briskly and silently to their destinations. After breakfast the picture became totally different: the streets were crowded with rickshaws and bicycles. These images returned very strongly after the forced evacuation of the town by Pol Pot's soldiery. There was much puritanical talk then of 'decadence' and the 'bloated city', a parasitic excrescence which had to be destroyed. It is true there were bars and brothels in the town, but their presence was not symbolic of Phnom Penh. If any capital was the brothel of Asia, it was Bangkok, a 'rest and recreation centre' for the war-weary American soldiers. Ironically, it is to that city that Pol Pot's zealots have now repaired, feasting on funds supplied by the United States and its allies.

A few days before we were due to leave for Hanoi, our Cambodian hosts took pity on us. A small plane was laid on to fly us to Angkor Wat, where we could marvel at the magic of the 850-year-old Khymer palaces. The occasion was slightly surreal. Next door a bitter and cruel war was taking place; we could hear the noise of the bombings from Cambodia. And yet these old ruins generated an unbelievable tranquillity. I walked silently through and around them. I observed their richness from every possible angle and gazed in awe at the rich repertoire of images. The beautiful reliefs on the plinths supporting the terraces were matched by the friezes of erotic groups and minor deities of traditional Hindu sculpture. Here in the middle of the Cambodian jungles one caught a glimpse of the myths and legends of medieval India. Here, too, a caste of military aristocrats must have established its control over tribespeoples and 'barbarians'. As I wandered, in a semi-daze, I thought of the polymathic qualities, skills and perseverance that must have been a hallmark of the architects, stonemasons, master–artists and their apprentices, the latter notorious for the outspoken eroticism of their sexual sculptures. And the slaves who carried the stones that made all this possible? What was their lifespan? I saw the sun set on Angkor Wat that evening and almost forgot the war. It is one of the wonders of the world, but impossible to record except in the mind's eye. No postcard or film could convey the richness of the Cambodian sky or the play of golden red shadows and reflections on the stones and statues of the ancient Khymer works.

The same night, in a neighbouring palatial ruin, we saw a moon rise and in its light witnessed an exquisite display of Cambodian folk dancing, once again a variation of the old dances of Southern India. In the background lay the darkness of the forest. The night was enveloped by silence. The technologies of the 20th century could neither be seen nor heard. We might easily have been part of a scene from a different epoch. The image of Angkor Wat remains vivid. When I shut my eyes I can still recall many pictures of the sun setting on the delicate and graceful reliefs. I thought of them a lot in the years that followed, first when Kissinger and Nixon embarked on their campaign and bombed the country into the Stone Age, resulting in a savagery which gave birth to the deranged squads of Pol Pot. Neither variant, I am happy to say, destroyed Angkor Wat. It is still there and I have not given up the idea of seeing it again one day.

The dream ended early in the morning with the by now familiar thud of bombs which began to fall in neighbouring Vietnam. We were off to Hanoi. The only flight to the North Vietnamese capital from the West in those days was on a plane belonging to a strange body called the International Control Commission (ICC), which had been set up in 1962 to monitor truce violations in Laos, the smallest member of the Indochinese triumvirate of nations. The members were Canada (USA nominee); India (choice of non-aligned states); Poland (USSR nominee). The only useful service this august body provided was the regular flight from Phnom Penh to Hanoi via the Laotian city of Vientiane. In 1965 an ICC plane had disappeared while flying over Laotian air space. Apparently, the communist Pathet Lao guerrillas who controlled three-quarters of the countryside and were subjected regularly to American bombing had developed a pathological hatred of all planes. They shot at anything that flew. As a result all visitors flying to Hanoi from Phnom Penh were a bit tense. The ICC must also have been nervous as just before boarding we were made to sign a document. This stated that we were flying at our own risk and in the case of our death none of our relatives were entitled to any compensation. I signed away my life quite happily, desperate for the wretched machine to get airborne.

It was a five-hour flight, but we had a three-hour stopover in Vientiane, a dump of a city crawling with CIA and other intelligence operatives who scrutinized every traveller to Hanoi and took photographs for the files back at Langley, Virginia. The long wait in Vientiane was in order to let the sun set. It was not safe to fly into Hanoi during the day and I experienced the strange sensation of flying over an invisible city. Hanoi was enshrouded in darkness as the plane began to descend. Nothing was visible. The French doctor Behar was a tiny bit nervous, but the pilot was experienced. Suddenly, just before the plane touched the ground, the airport lights were switched on to aid the descent and immediately after we had landed, they were speedily extinguished. This was Hanoi. The lights in the plane were switched off and we sat quietly in the blacked-out machine. The doors were opened, but outside seemed no different. As my eyes became used to the dimness I saw from the plane window a group of shadows moving towards us. Inside the plane they flashed torches as they recognized us and ticked off our names on a list. Then our hosts shook hands with us warmly and welcomed us to Vietnam.

The drivers of the Russian-built limousines which transported us from the airport towards the heart of Hanoi were just as expert as the ICC pilots. They could see in the dark and with deftness and skill they avoided the worst bumps. We arrived at the Reunification Hotel at about 9pm. Inside there were lights, but the black curtains remained drawn, yet another reminder that the Vietnamese capital was not immune to the B52 raiders. The hotel appeared empty, but a table had been prepared for us to eat with our Vietnamese interpreters and Mr Protocol, whose worried look never left his face once throughout our stay. The hotel itself was a pre-First World War construction in the French colonial style. It was large and our rooms were spacious with much of the old furniture intact, especially the large canopied beds. We washed, ate, drank a few toasts, thanked our hosts and prepared for the next day. Before we retired to our rooms we were shown the location of the hotel's air-raid shelter and instructed politely to get there quickly the minute we heard the warning sirens. In every action or gesture, however small, of our Vietnamese hosts there was the unspoken reminder that they were a people and country at war.

Sleep did not come easily that night. The buzz in my head was interrupted by a knock on the door. I opened it to confront a merry miner from Scotland bearing a nightcap. He, too, was extremely moved by our presence in Vietnam. We spent a few hours discussing the numerous tragedies of the British Labour Movement. Daly talked that night about his own past. His break with the Communist Party in 1956 had been a painful affair. Many close friends had regarded him as a traitor, but he had proved them wrong by carrying on the struggle through different channels. When we decided to halt the conversation I had a very clear picture of the richness and vitality of the political culture of the Scottish proletariat. Daly himself was addicted to books. He had nothing but contempt for middle-class socialists who thought that the way to win workers to socialism was by pandering to their backwardness. 'There is no substitute for political education and books', he remarked, just before I declared the discussion closed and guided him to his room next door.

I was woken at an unearthly hour by noises on the streets. It was barely light. I rushed to the window and saw people on bicycles pedalling fast in both directions. Occasionally a military convoy would appear. The cyclists would move to the sides so quickly that one could have been watching a tableau. I bathed, dressed and rushed downstairs. None of the others were up so I wandered outside and silently watched the inhabitants of Hanoi going about their business. When I returned to the hotel, breakfast was about to be served, but my colleagues had still not surfaced. Whilst waiting, I began to leaf idly through the hotel's Visitor's Book. Very few westerners had visited the country, but the American journalist Harrison Salisbury was an exception. He had written in the book: 'It is a curious experience to be a correspondent "behind the lines" of a land engaged in a heavy war with my country. But in this friendly, cheerful hotel none of that feeling comes through. It is a bright, pleasant and cool experience. And I thank you all for letting an American in wartime share that spirit. Yours for Peace, Harrison Salisbury.'

From the very first day we had observed that there were no official expressions of hostility to Americans as a whole. A sharp differentiation was made between 'the people' and 'the Government'. This made an interesting contrast with the official British and Russian attitudes to Germans during the First and Second World Wars or the North American internment and persecution of their own citizens of Japanese origin during the latter conflict. In his memoirs, *No Jail for Truth*, the Soviet dissident, Lev Kopelev (the man on whom Solzhenitsyn modelled Rubin in *The First Circle*), described how when, as a serving officer in the Soviet Army, he addressed German prisoners in their own language ('the language of Goethe, Marx and Beethoven') they could hardly believe their ears. Kopelev recalled the counter-productive nature of the chauvinistic Slav motifs, which Stalin had utilized during the war. He argued convincingly that an inter-nationalist approach to the German soldiers and prisoners–of–war could have had sensational consequences.

It is true that the circumstances were now different. There was a growing anti-war movement in the United States, but the amount of bombs dropped on Vietnam exceeded in quantity and 'quality' those deployed against the fascist states during the Second World War. There was a great deal for the Vietnamese to be angry about, but the regime's propaganda machinery carefully but firmly forbade crude anti-Americanism. In a sense this was one of the most amazing and unexpected discoveries on this trip. Carol Brightman was struck by this much more than myself. She had been prepared for hostility from ordinary people on the streets, but none materialized. In fact people used to crowd around Carol to shake her by the hand and ask her to convey their best wishes to ordinary people in America.

Our party was split up the next day. Lawrence Daly and Tolentino travelled to the three northern provinces of Phu Tho, Vinh Phuc and Bac Thai. Behar, Brightman and I went south to the Ninh Binh and Thanh Hoa provinces, where bombs fell like rain during the monsoon. What follows are extracts from my diary, which I wrote every day I was in Vietnam.

HANOI 26 January 1967

Tonight we are to leave for the south. P. and V. (two Vietnamese interpreters) have told us to pack a bag. We will travel only at night. During the day it is too dangerous and since we are being transported in old Soviet command cars they could easily become a target for the bombers. P. said it wasn't even safe at night as new infra-red devices could pick out human beings in the dark. After breakfast we were taken to the war museum where we saw a replay of the Battle of Dienbienphu. Amazing that in the middle of a new, more vicious war they still have time to think of the last one. Maybe it is to boost *our* morale and convince *us* that victories are possible. But the Americans are not the French.

At 10.25am, after the Dienbienphu display, we are taken to a small room, where Colonel Ha Van Lau is waiting for us. About forty years old, intense, not given to fake bonhomie and straightforward. He briefs us on war situation, opens with these words: 'You are well informed about Vietnam. My difficulty is how to explain the situation in a way that can be useful for you. Excuse if I repeat things you know. My purpose is to aid your understanding. Before saying anything else I wish to make it clear to you that in this war between US imperialists and the Vietnamese people, the latter will be the victors.' His quiet confidence is both convincing and, as a consequence, infectious. For two hours he talks but my concentration is solid, even though he speaks Vietnamese and P. translates it all into English. Very useful for taking detailed notes. Ha Van Lau analyses the recent history of his country and the reasons for US intervention. Then he challenges the contention that what happened was US intervention on one side in a civil war. 'Many of you even might believe that, but it is not true. If we say it is a civil war we must mean that the people have risen to overthrow a legal government which has become unpopular. But the Diem administration was never a government in any sense. It was a creation of the United States. The Saigon army consists of quislings and mercenaries who can be purchased in most countries. The war is one between the people and the United States, who have created and funded a puppet administration. Diem's successors, too, are hand-picked by Washington. That is why we are so sure that we will win. These puppet administrations do not have an independent social base. The Ap Bac victory in 1963 saw 200 NLF [National Liberation Front] guerrillas defeat a puppet contingent of 2000. By 1964 we were on the verge of major military victories. The US should have withdrawn then, but they decided to fight the war with their own troops. This was the clearest signal to all the people as to the character of this war.'

Ha Van Lau has very few notes. He often turns to large wall map to illustrate place-names and where the big US bases are located. His knowledge of the terrain in the South is such that I wondered as he was talking whether he had been to the South. This is the big unmentionable here. We know they're there and they know that we know, but it cannot be admitted. Ha Van Lau often spices his analysis with little aphorisms. After detailing several small NLF victories in different parts of the South, he paused, smiled and said: 'Little streams make a river.' His thesis, if true, explains the incredible optimism. He lists the five objectives of US policy: (1) wipe out main force of NLF army; (2) pacify South Vietnam; (3) consolidate puppet regime and army; (4) Isolate South Vietnam and (5) wage an air war of destruction to compel North Vietnam to surrender. He reviews all five and demonstrates convincingly that none of these are close to fulfilment. He says that every escalation is an admission of defeat. He says that bombing of Hanoi and Haiphong on 29 June 1966 was nothing less than terrorism and banditry. He repeats again that 'we believe that US imperialism can be defeated. For us this is now a practical possibility. Before the US entered this war this was only a theoretical possibility. No one really knew whether it was possible. After two years of direct war against the US expeditionary force we have come to the conclusion that this is a reality.'

After he finishes I question his confidence. How can he be so sure? America is the most powerful industrialized nation on earth. They have the firepower and the means to destroy Vietnam overnight. Ha Van Lau admits that nuclear weapons would end the conflict, but he doubts they will use them since they have half a million of their own troops in the country. And then there are the USSR and Chinese reactions to consider. On another level he explains 'that in the South the NLF have distributed two million hectares of land to peasants in the liberated zones. Even puppet soldiers who have families in liberated areas are given land which is cultivated by their families in their absence. In the North we have, as you will see, adapted ourselves fully to war conditions. The Americans bomb our big industrial centres. We develop local industries and decentralize operations. Of course the war waged against our people is cruel and savage. Toxic gases and napalm, defoliants and other chemicals, but the morale of our people has not been broken. In the end that will be the decisive factor.'

He wishes us well on our trips and hopes to meet us again when we return to Hanoi.

Back to the hotel for lunch. The waitress has put a decorative chilli plant on our table today. I inspect it carefully and, yes, it is the real thing. While eating the meat and rice I pluck a chilli and consume it in order to stimulate my somewhat bored palate. There is a peal of laughter. The waitress has observed me. Soon she and her fellow-waitresses surround our table. I oblige them again and end up consuming the entire output of the potted plant. Even Lawrence Daly is taken aback. He can easily empty a bottle of malt whisky in an evening, but is perturbed at my chilli-eating habits.

Rest after lunch. Then an early supper. I am supplied with more chillies by a new set of waitresses, who stand and watch to see if the tale they have heard about this madman is true. I oblige them and it is a delight seeing the formality disappear from their faces as they laugh or try and cover their faces in case I think it's rude. P. the more experienced of our interpreters (N. is his apprentice) questions me in some detail about chillies and the Indian subcontinent. I explain that it is largely a plebeian habit not mimicked by the aristocracy or the *haute bourgeoisie*. A peasant's midday meal in the subcontinent often consists of a piece of dried wheat cake (*roti*) and a few chillies, since they are rich in vitamins. Of course I eat them because I like the taste. It improves an insipid dish. P. rushes off to explain all this to the waiting women. They all come up and shake hands with me and wish us all well. I shall miss Lawrence Daly. We say our farewells and Daly mutters, 'I'm glad we're going North. Best of luck, comrade.'

27 January 1967

We travelled out of Hanoi after dark. I had imagined empty roads and a fast driver speeding us southwards. How wrong I was. The roads are crowded. The entire country seems to be awake. Our command car is allowed to overtake several military convoys and numerous other trucks and lorries and carts. At times, where bridges have been destroyed, our pace is considerably reduced as we wait in the long queues to cross the makeshift boat bridges that have been hurriedly organized to enable the traffic to keep moving. There are only three of us from the team going south, but we are taken in three separate vehicles. It seems a terrible waste, but P. explains that it is a security measure. If there is a direct hit only one of us will be hurt or die. 'Better than three', he explains with a smile. I protest strongly. Our lives are, if anything, less important than those of the Vietnamese. Why should we use two extra cars and take up more space on the road during wartime? I tell P. that we all were aware of the risks when we decided to come. He smiles, but does not reply. Soon he falls asleep, but I could not sleep. We reach an official rest-house at 3.30am. It is a cold night, made colder by the fact that one of the walls is missing – a target of the last raid! We unpack and sleep.

This is a small town, Phat Diem in the province of Ninh Binh. Was Catholic stronghold during French rule. Church owned 70 per cent of the land. Post-revolution land reforms distributed land to the peasants, but much of it lay fallow as Catholic bishop and priests fled south in 1954, claiming that they were following the Virgin Mary who had already fled to Saigon. Area considered soft by US, who dropped commandos here in 1963. All of them were immediately captured. Total of 119 Catholic churches and at least 40,000 Catholics. Fishing boats and churches have been bombed unremittingly since June 1965. I met a wounded priest and saw the damaged churches. I record these facts, but whispered to Behar: 'The Americans are doing us a favour, bombing these churches. The Vietnamese would never have dared to do so themselves.' He chuckles in agreement. I am pleased that the anti-clerical tradition is still strong in France.

28 January 1967

We spend another day in this province. I saw the wounds inflicted on children aged between two and eight. It is a painful sight. One four-year-old has lost an arm, but is still full of fun. His mother tells us how the local school was bombed one day and describes the agony of the children. As she talks and P. translates Carol Brightman and I both weep. What can one say? Even Thu Van, the intrepid wartime camerawoman, who has filmed a great deal and is accompanying us, begins to shake and has to put down her heavy 16mm camera so that she can wipe her eyes. The heroes in these small towns are the doctors and nurses. To see them at work and hear them talk is a deeply moving experience. An old doctor tells Behar in French: 'In this same area during French rule we had 3000 people per bed in the hospital. All the beds were for the wealthy. Today in Ninh Binh alone we have eight hospitals and a health centre in every village, however small. Our bed ratio is still not sufficient, but it is 300:1. So you see even the most unpolitical poor person knows what will happen if we are occupied again.' Behar replies with a torrent of abuse against the iniquities of French colonialism.

We leave, once again in the night, to move further south. The closer to the border we get, the greater the danger of being bombed. Surrounded permanently by stories of other deaths and the agonies of those who will soon die, death itself no longer worries me. If one has to die young, where better to fall than in Vietnam. Infinitely better than being shot by the Pathet Lao while travelling on a decrepit ICC plane. On this journey, too, we pass numerous military convoys. Encountered massive traffic jam at 2am. Got out of the car with P. He recognized the area. His father, a Viet Minh guerrilla, had fallen in battle not far from here in 1952. And now, I think to myself, P.'s generation is experiencing *its* war. For the last two decades this country has known no peace. Being here at this time is a much better education than any of the dozens of books I have read about this nation.

There is another panic as American planes have been sighted further south. We actually stop and take cover on one occasion. In the distance I can hear the noise of the bombs. Where? Who's the target this time? These are questions we all ask, but no replies. Interestingly no one asks why; living with the bombs seems to have become a part of everyday life. At 4am we reach a sheltered hamlet, about 6km from Thanh Hoa town. The village is clearly a command centre for the local administration. It is effectively camouflaged. We are shown our beds and there is an instant collapse. I was exhausted.

29 January 1967

Thanh Hoa is the largest province in North Vietnam. French were never able to recapture it after 1945, but bombed it mercilessly since its entire agricultural output supplied the armies of Vo Nguyen Giap during the siege of Dienbienphu. The coffee is excellent. We are welcomed by the Chairman of the Administrative Committee, who warns us to be prepared for anything. The bombing is very heavy. 'I hope you sleep well tonight,' he says, 'because the Americans have an annoying habit of waking us up at 3am.'

Our military escort is Major Van Bang. He is forty-two, deputy Commander of the province and fought at Dienbienphu. He briefs us on the local situation and introduces us to Dr Tran Van Quy, Director of Thanh Hoa hospital, which we are to visit that afternoon. We spend morning at our base. I see many scarred veterans of previous wars. In the evening we are told there will be a cultural performance in our honour. I exchange looks with P. and later in private I complain again. It is wrong to waste any resources on us. But P., who has by now got to know my instinctive reactions well, is prepared this time. He informs me that our visit is very good for local morale. It shows worldwide solidarity and the presence of a Frenchman and an American woman, in particular, is important for the town. It sounds convincing.

Just before lunch, Major Van Bang gives us a lecture. He is even more optimistic than Ha Van Lau: 'The Americans have no choice between victory and defeat. Their alternative is only between defeat and crushing defeat.' This is a slightly new variation and cheers me up enormously. Van Bang says that 'objective of attacks is simply to demoralize us. There is no other explanation. But they have failed to demoralize Thanh Hoa. How can they succeed against a province with such a history of resistance as ours? By their crimes they are only adding fuel to the fire.'

Lunch at 12.30. Local cuisine excellent and much to my amazement a plate of chillies is put in front of me. P. smiles and even Van Bang stares. I am deeply touched. Suddenly a flurry of messengers. Van Bang and Chairman Nguyen Van Truong leave the table. They return slightly shaken. A new bombing raid has begun and our visit to the town, scheduled for 2.30 that afternoon is off. I argue strongly that we should go, but suddenly the bombs seem very close. We can hear them. I plead again that we should move since this is our task: to report on what is being bombed and why. Van Bang refuses to permit us to leave. The Mayor of Thanh Hoa looks worried. He is convinced that they are bombing the heart of the town. Two hours later, after the raid, we visit the city. We were supposed to have been at the hospital at 2.30. At 3pm it was bombed. Several patients were killed by the first bombs. While they were being removed from the hospital and taken to the first-aid station there was another attack and the first-aid station was totally obliterated. Incendiary bombs had been used as well and we saw houses still smouldering. Mrs Nguyen Thi Dinh had rushed out of her house just in time to see her house and its contents burn to the ground. She was weeping silently when I spoke to her. 'Do you think I will ever forgive them for what they are doing to us? Never, never. They must be punished for this.' Two hundred dwellings have been destroyed. Dang Batao, the local Red Cross organizer was burnt to death. Ms Ho Thi Oanh is also dead, a few weeks before her wedding. Her trousseau lies scattered, half-burnt and scarred.

Impossible to visualize this agony in the West. I had not been particularly affected when I had heard the planes overhead, but this is too much. There are mangled dead bodies. There is a hospital with Red Cross markings, which has been singled out and destroyed. If the shelters had not been evacuated, the casualties would have been very high. I look for military targets. There are none. Sadness mingles with anger and rage. Would the Americans ever bomb a European city in this fashion today? The Vietnamese are clearly not human beings as far as Washington is concerned.

After seeing the ruins of the hospital, we drove four miles to inspect the Ham Rong (Dragon's Jaw) bridge, whose defenders have brought down many American planes. The bridge is known throughout the land and many songs have been written about it. It is defended by a platoon of young women. I saw them in their trenches, staring earnestly at the sky. The commander of the local militia is an 18 year old, Ngo Thi Truyen, who has taken part in over a hundred 'battles'. She was at the village near the bridge, which appeared to be a women's only settlement. The men were at 'other fronts'. She smiled shyly at us as we were introduced, but her first few sentences exuded a confidence, which is now becoming a familiar refrain. It is obviously the party line, but it is a widely held opinion as well. Talking to P. over long periods has convinced me of the popularity of the Vietnamese Communist Party. If it did not have mass support, there could not be such total support for the war against the United States. P. is not one of nature's extroverts. He does not talk much, but when I can draw him out I learn more about the country and its mood in one session than from numerous official lectures, useful though these are in many ways. It is interesting that none of the bombers which came today even bothered to bomb the bridge, which *is* a military target. I return to our concealed base emotionally exhausted.

Dinner tonight was a quiet business. The horrors were too recent for anyone to make jokes. Van Bang was in bitter mood. 'Did you see the military targets they bombed today?' I nodded silently. For once the Vietnamese present forgot our existence and talked to each other for a long time. I found this an immense relief. Formalities had been discarded.

No sleep tonight as we are travelling again. Our destination is the district of Tinh Gia at the southernmost extremity of the province. No foreigners have been there as yet for fear of casualties. We drive slowly. In the command car I asked P. what the discussion in Vietnamese had been all about that evening. He is not the least coy. The main talk was about the NLF campaign in the South and our casualties. P. explained that whenever there is a particularly bad bombing attack on the North, people generally tend to talk about conditions in the South which everyone knows are much, much worse. In conditions such as these it is, I suppose, not particularly surprising that a form of collective self-therapy comes into existence.

The second part of the talk had concentrated on the casualties in Thanh Hoa and some of the people at our base-village had lost relatives. 'That sense of loss is something impossible for me to appreciate,' I confessed to P., 'since the daily loss of friends and relatives must be a numbing emotional experience.' He agreed with a sad look on his face and then reverted to the subject of our security. 'It is a loss we do not wish your parents to experience. That's why we are extra careful.' But I did not accept the argument. We reached Tinh Gia safely. Slept for a few hours.

30 January 1967

This was the most depressing day I have had till now. I have seen bombed schools and hospitals. They had received direct hits. In the coastal village of Hai Nan, not far from the US Seventh Fleet, every single house has been destroyed. The attack took place four days ago. I spoke to a twelve-year-old girl, Nguyen Thi Tuyen, who had lost a leg. She described what had happened: 'I had just come back from school and was about to have a bath, when the aircraft came from the sea. They dived down and dropped lots of bombs. I grabbed my younger brother and rushed to the shelter, but I was too late. A bomb fragment hit him in the stomach. He died in my arms. Another fragment cut my leg off. Our house was destroyed. Now I live with some relatives. Will you please tell me why they are bombing us?' I mumbled something. She replied: 'You see how we suffer. I hate them, but now I can't even join the militia!' She said that if she survived the war she would be a teacher.

Other victims were not as mild. All swore revenge. It was the same story in several other villages I visited. In one place there was a makeshift school with the slogan, 'Good Homework is a Bullet in the US Aggressor'. I asked the teacher whether homework was possible in such conditions. The primary schoolteacher said that the children grumbled a lot every day about not being allowed to help the militia (they were all aged five to nine). Her concession had been to mark their homework in downed US aeroplanes rather than numbers. I saw the school books with the downed planes. Just as I was leaving I saw a young woman approaching. P. told her I had to leave, but I could see she wanted to talk. So I intervened. Her name was Nguyen Thi Hien. She was twenty-three years old. This is what she said:

'My 4-year-old son and 24-year-old husband were killed in the last attack. I lost my toes as you can see. I was three months pregnant at the time. I hate Americans. I really hate them. How can you expect me to forgive them.' She started weeping and screaming: 'There will be bitterness and hatred. What else can we do. I will wait for my two-year-old to grow up and then will send him to revenge his father.' She then broke down completely and was consoled by other women, who stroked her hair and hugged her. These are war crimes.

31 January 1967

Toured more villages in Tinh Gia. More horrors. More atrocities. Civilian targets are the aim of the American warmongers. These are not mistakes or accidents. It is systematic and deliberate bombing of the population as a whole.

Left after dinner to return to base in Thanh Hoa. Arrived back at 4am and were told to have a long sleep.

1 February 1967

Had a late breakfast and visited Quang Xuong district. Recorded details of horrors. Returned for late lunch to base. Afternoon was free and P. asked what we wanted to do. I suggested, if possible, a trip to the coast so that we could at least glimpse the sea. This was agreed by Van Bang and we drove off to the Sam-Son seashore, where we walked along the beach, observed the gulf of Tongkin and talked, mainly about the war, but also wondered what might be happening in the rest of the world.

In the evening the local administration had organized a banquet and a cultural evening. There were speeches after dinner and since P. was tired, his apprentice-interpreter translated. He was good and used more colloquialisms than P., though while translating the speech of the Chairman he made one mistake. 'I thank you for everything,' translated N., 'from the heart of my bottom.' Carol Brightman and I collapsed at this stage. And P. then translated the joke in Vietnamese. It was the first time that we had laughed collectively since our arrival in Thanh Hoa and the Vietnamese laughed louder than us. Poor N. was not able to live this down for the rest of the trip.

The cultural evening consisted mainly of songs, most of them ballads of the war sung in the most delicate voices by men and women of the militia.

2 February 1967

After visiting one more district and filling a lot more notebooks with details of bombing raids and atrocities, we talked for a long time with Dr Quy of the Thanh Hoa hospital. He admitted that the Vietnamese were short of elementary antibiotics such as penicillin. Behar's medical ethics now came into play and he expressed his dismay and promised to help speed up supplies from France.

During lunch we heard the noise of planes, the anti-aircraft response and then the thud of bombs. It sounded very close and we were forced to leave the room and hurry to the shelter with our helmets. Nothing happened. More noise of planes and I came out of the shelter and actually saw one, which was alarmingly close. I was dragged back to the shelter. My pleas that I be given a rifle and allowed to join the militia were ignored. This was the most frustrating part of the trip. I hate being holed up in a shelter when others are outside in trenches firing at the planes. One was downed that day, not far from our village. A local militia member returned from the wreckage with some metal and someone else made us rings on the spot with the date and place. This was my equivalent of getting homework marked in downed planes!

Afterwards we were given figures of the total number of raids on the province, types of bombs and weapons used and the composition (gender and age) of the casualties, which were mainly old people – men and women – and children. Throughout this trip I noticed that the administration on every level was kept going by the women. Some co-operative farms were being run completely by women. The war had also compelled the Vietnamese leadership to embark on a massive decentralization of authority. These measures had been welcomed by the populace and local party administrators seemed to be close to the needs of the ordinary people in the towns and villages.

Even in the few days here I have become very attached to the local comrades. We said our farewells and embraced. Then it was back to Hanoi. I wondered how many of them at the village-base would survive the war. For a few days that place had seemed like home.

Arrived at Hanoi in the early hours. The hotel was asleep with one exception. Ralph Schoenman was at the bar with a full glass. He rushed up to us. 'I've been waiting impatiently.' He was celebrating. The Vietnamese Comrade Protocol was sitting next to him looking very tired. I was too tired to do anything, but go to bed. I had not thought much of the rigours of the recent journey while in the middle of it, but Hanoi and the Reunification Hotel were welcome relief. And the bed was simply heaven.

One day before the Lunar New Year truce brought forty-eight hours of respite, there was a raid on Hanoi. I heard the sirens and rushed out on to the streets, unnoticed by Comrade Protocol or the others. I heard the planes and photographed people rushing into their shelters. The Vietnamese had built one-person shelters throughout the city. Shaped like manholes with concrete covers, they provided effective protection and reduced casualties considerably in the case of direct hits. It was when I heard the sound of exploding bombs that I made my way back to the hotel. The waitresses were all in combat gear, with rifles strapped to their shoulders and on their way to the roof to join the anti-aircraft battery. I begged once again to be allowed to go up with them, but P., who had emerged from nowhere gently dragged me down to the hotel shelter. Here was an interesting collection of people. The Asians – Laotians, Cambodians, Koreans – were, like me, angry at not being allowed to take part in the resistance. The Eastern Europeans giggled nervously, looking totally out of place, which made one feel that Hanoi must have been a punishment-posting for many a bureaucrat. The Canadians were all members of the ICC and later that evening in a bar one of them, in a state of advanced inebriety, remarked: 'I'm glad the Americans have started bombing again. They should be bombing the shit out of these bastards.' Lawrence Daly was beginning to move towards the drunk, when his colleagues took him away. The British Consul, whom I met for tea the next day, was very different. He said Hanoi reminded him of London during the war. The bombs had united the population and the regime. He was tactful, but his own views were at variance with those of the Wilson Government. He surprised me by confessing that his gut reaction when he heard the sirens was to join his Vietnamese employees and take a few shots at the planes. It was clear that his reports to the Foreign Office were simply being ignored.

The Americans were using a wide range of bombs. Of these the anti-personnel devices were the worst. There were two particular bombs which I was shown everywhere. They were nicknamed 'guavas' and 'pineapples' because of their shape. A small bomb the size of a guava was dropped. Each contained 300 steel pellets, which entered the body and were difficult to remove. Many victims died as a result or were maimed. The bombs had only one purpose: to kill and hurt civilians. Hundreds of thousands of these bombs had been dropped all over the country. Children had been the worst hit and this explained an odd feature of Hanoi. I had felt that something was wrong with the town. For days I tried to work out what it was that I found so odd. I mentioned this to P., who agreed and provided me with one clue after another. I finally got the message. There were no children in the city. They had all been sent to safe areas in the northernmost part of the country. I asked P. whether he worried about his child all the time. 'How can I? There is no time for worry. This is a cruel war. I am happy my child is safe. I would be more worried if he was here.'

All this changed during the Tet holiday. As I walked the streets I found them transformed. Hanoi was back to normal with a flurry of colour and fireworks. Children were temporarily reunited with parents. Lovers were cuddling on the benches at the edge of the lake. Bicycles laden with chickens and vegetables, which had been saved for weeks and months, were crossing the streets. Everything had come alive. We joined in the celebrations not knowing that in exactly one year's time, the Vietnamese guerrillas in the South would launch a military offensive that would herald the defeat of the United States. Even if someone had told me I doubt I would have believed the story.

The Vietnamese had asked me repeatedly if there was anything special I wanted during the trip. I used to reply with a name: Ho Chi Minh. I had wanted to write a biography of Ho and Anthony Blond had commissioned me to produce one. I had cabled the Vietnamese leader and he had replied: 'Thank you for message. Thought of you writing my biography never occurred to me – Ho Chi Minh.' They used to smile. Everyone who came to town wanted to meet the legendary Indochinese revolutionary. I told them that I really wanted to question him about his days as a chef in London, where he had worked in the kitchen of an old hotel during the twenties. This was important since it was the only vindication of Lenin's most utopian pamphlet, *State and Revolution*, in which he had coined the formula of the state withering away and a situation where even 'a cook could run the state'. This was a request which could not be met. He was old, easily tired and visitors had to be restricted since he wished to devote his energies to supervising the tactics being adopted to fight the United States. A meeting with the Prime Minister, Pham van Dong, was organized instead. It was not the same, but Pham van Dong, also a veteran revolutionary, was undoubtedly the person who was probably the best informed on the politico-military realities throughout Vietnam. I had been struck by the fact that there was no personality cult surrounding Ho. This was particularly noteworthy given the bizarre excesses of the Mao cult in neighbouring China. In fact there was probably less written of Ho Chi Minh in the Vietnamese press or heard on radio than the coverage accorded Churchill and Roosevelt in their respective countries during the Second World War. When I asked P. about this he said that Ho simply did not require a cult. He was genuinely popular. The other side of this being, of course, that the sort of blind worship encouraged by Stalin and Mao, for instance, indicated a lack of confidence.

We met the Prime Minister, Pham van Dong, soon after returning to Hanoi. Lawrence Daly's visit to the North had not been as eventful as our experiences, but he had seen enough and was horrified by the senseless destruction. Pham van Dong was dressed in the Vietnamese tunic and trousers worn by men throughout the country. He greeted us affectionately and said he was quite happy to answer any and all of our questions. I asked him why the Vietnamese did not invite international brigades. Some of us wanted to fight, but more importantly it would be an enormous propaganda victory to have Americans fighting side-by-side with the Vietnamese against a common enemy. Pham van Dong, who was seated at the other extremity of the large reception room, stood up and walked towards me. Surprised, I got up and waited. He embraced and kissed me as if to thank me for the thought. Then he returned to his chair. 'There are many problems with this proposal', he replied. 'First, this is not Spain in the thirties, where the technological level of combat was primitive. You have seen the scale of the US attacks on us. International brigades are no good against B52 bombers. In the South any brigade from abroad would not be able to function at all effectively. Many areas we control by night are overrun by the enemy during the day. We disappear effectively because, after all, we are Vietnamese. Just imagine trying to hide several thousand European faces in the forests of the South. That is one problem. Then there is the fact that we have two great socialist states in existence today, the Soviet Union and China. They might misunderstand the call for international brigades.' (I frowned at this stage not under-standing what he meant. He noticed and smiled). 'You see, my friend, they might think that it was our way of criticizing them for lack of sufficient support and we would not like them to think that, would we? The propaganda value, I agree with you, would be good but even if we had them to help repair bridges and roads and schools and hospitals we would be more worried about their safety and would have to expend more resources on housing and looking after them. But we appreciate the suggestion.'

I asked about the Geneva Agreements of 1954. Was it not the case that if they had continued the war then, instead of bowing to Sino-Soviet pressure, we might have been spared the most recent phase of the conflict. He nodded and was silent for a while. Then came his response: 'It was the unhappiest time in our history. We would not do it again.'

Like the many other Vietnamese with whom I had spoken, Pham van Dong was confident of ultimate success. He explained calmly that the United States could not shift the relationship of forces in the South. 'There is a limit to the number of troops they can pour into Vietnam. Most of their land forces are already here; one-third of their air force and one-third of their navy are deployed in the battle to defeat us. Remember there are over 14 million people in that country. So our forces can increase tenfold and next year, I promise, you will witness large-scale desertions from the puppet troops.' He then stressed the importance of the anti–draft movement in the United States. 'For them to raise their total from half a million to 1 million soldiers would create a major crisis in their own country. There is already a growing movement and soon even more Americans will be convinced that they can never win this war. The combination of that realization and our politico-military offensives will lead to their defeat.' For this reason the North Vietnamese leader was convinced that a land invasion of Northern Vietnam was virtually excluded. It would extend the Americans too far. When we discussed British policies, he was scathing about the Labour Government. 'They are chained like slaves to the financial heel of America, and under such conditions can only support American policy. It is very sad, but that is the logic of Britain's new place in the world. As far as we are concerned there is one bold and courageous Englishman. His name you know well ... Bertrand Russell. Vietnam will never forget the support he has given us. Never.' He told Carol Brightman that Vietnam was honoured by her presence. 'Thank the American peace movement. We respect them greatly. Internationalism is in our blood and we appreciate the sacrifices being made by many Americans for us.'

The most striking feature of that trip was the optimism and intellect that one encountered everywhere. The effect of this on Western

Europe could not be anything but dramatic. If a predominantly agricultural country could resist the world's most powerful nation, then
surely a determined working class in France or Italy could dislodge its
own bourgeoisie. Or could it? We were told in Hanoi of how Ho Chi
Minh had stunned a top-level delegation from the politburo of the
Italian Communist Party several months ago. After a long and con-
vivial session with the Vietnamese leader, the Italians had asked what
sort of help would be most useful for the struggle. Ho Chi Minh had
responded immediately: 'The best way you could help us is to make
the revolution in Italy.' The Italians had been stunned into silence, for
such language had not been heard in the world communist movement
for a long time. There was little doubt that the war had radicalized
Vietnamese society on every level. The country with which the
Vietnamese felt the greatest degree of solidarity was Cuba. In fact the
Cuban Ambassador was also a technician well-skilled in the capabilities
of the SAM missiles supplied at that time in very limited numbers by
the Russians in order to enable the Vietnamese to defend their capital
city. The Cuban had joked that it was just about enough to defend a
few embassies and not much else. As our interview with Pham van
Dong had ended he had stressed the role of solidarity and said that if
the Americans could be isolated globally it would shorten the war.
'Your struggle is very important for us,' he said as we parted, 'it is *our*
second front. Everything helps.'

One of the most harrowing days in Hanoi was spent at the Ministry
of Health, with the senior doctors of the country who had the
responsibility of caring for the wounded. We stayed with them for
nearly a day. Dr Behar would ask detailed questions and they would
reply with a sad look in their eyes. They told us of the substitute
medicines they had developed including one for penicillin. A young
doctor also explained how in order to make up for the shortage of
plaster of Paris they used bark from trees to heal cracked bones. We
heard them out and then the Frenchman exploded. 'I am aware of
what you are forced to do, but please friends don't pretend to us that
this is satisfactory. The real medicines would be infinitely better. Why
are you not getting them? Why? Why?' The Vietnamese looked at

each other, but did not reply. During lunch one of them told us with tears in his eyes that they had requested these medicines from the Eastern Europeans, but they did not have enough money to pay for everything. He told us that there was a large plaster of Paris factory in Poland, which could easily supply them, but ... he shrugged his shoulders. I was livid with anger. I had met a Polish member of the ICC at the hotel that week. I now recalled what he had told me: 'Many attitudes in Eastern Europe are coloured by racialism as far as Vietnam and China are concerned. Most East Europeans sympathize with the Americans.' He had insisted that he was not one of them, but listening to the Vietnamese doctor I wondered how far that attitude extended into the very heart of the ruling parties.

There was another explanation on offer as well, which illustrated the lack of *sufficient* aid much more clearly. The fact was that the USSR and its allies were providing more military hardware at that time to India and Egypt. The Vietnamese were perfectly well aware of this fact, but never commented on it publicly except through carefully veiled allusions in stray editorials in the Party daily, *Nhan Dhan*. One evening in Hanoi a senior Party official, angry at Kosygin's clumsy manoeuvres with Wilson in London at that time, decided to talk. 'The problem', he said over a glass of the killer-whisky, Moutai, brewed in China (and which in Urdu means 'death is near'), 'is that the Russians do not believe that we can win. They have forgotten what it is to win. Perhaps they would like us not to win because our victory is a blow against how many people practise peaceful coexistence. We are for peace and coexistence, but not if it means being occupied by an imperialist power. So they deprive us of military aid to bring us closer to their views, but this time we will not make concessions. Geneva has taught us that very well. We are prepared to negotiate an American withdrawal from our country at any time. Whenever they are ready they can stop the bombing and we can talk. But our big brother in Moscow wants *us* to make the concessions. We say no. Let them punish us. I know that our doctors have told you the medical situation. That, too, is part of the price we pay for preserving our independence.'

I was very pleased at being trusted in this fashion. 'Why', I enquired, 'don't you say this in public? It would be like a blast of thunder and might shame them into giving more help.' He shook his head. 'You know,' he began, 'we are at the beginning of a Chinese–Russian fight for hegemony in the communist movement. We don't want to take sides. There have been occasions when Red Guards have attacked Russian trains carrying supplies for us via China. We have complained privately. The Chinese are also helping us with arms and, more importantly, rice. So we have to be careful.'

When I told Lawrence Daly of this conversation he was not particularly surprised. He had felt similar undercurrents on his trip to the North.

The very day after the Tet ceasefire, Hanoi was bombed again, but it was a minor raid compared to the devastation I had witnessed in Thanh Hoa and Tinh Gia. It was strange how one became acclimatized to war and its consequences. I had been extremely upset during my first week in this country, but now after a month the war had become part of the landscape. It was there and it was unavoidable.

Behar had to return to France, but the rest of us prepared for the second phase of our investigation. We were to visit Haiphong and the mining towns of Ha Tu and Cam Pha as well what we were told was 'a surprise'. It was agreed that Lawrence Daly and I could travel in the same car. He was delighted as it meant avoiding Tolentino. (I have not really explained why this fellow was such a pain in the posterior. I think the reason was simply that he was not very bright and made up for his lack of confidence by putting on pompous airs. Thus when we used to visit hospitals, he would put on an awful pose as he inspected patients, much to their embarrassment. Often Daly and I were rude to him, but he never fully understood our irritation. There is a photograph of him in the Vietnam portfolio we were all given prior to our return. He is fingering the breast of a wounded woman. Lawrence Daly said that this was the best pose he could have struck and insisted on captioning the photograph with the remark: 'Tolentino feeling a right tit.')

We travelled out of Hanoi that night and reached Haiphong before dawn. The 'surprise' was a one-day rest in an old French bungalow overlooking one of the most beautiful bays in Asia. Halong Bay is distinguished for its amazing rock formation, which looks like a dragon that has just descended on the water. Hence the name of the bay. Even though it was sometimes bombed we were permitted a boat trip which was sensational. One could forget the war here as the incredible beauty of the coast enveloped the senses. The dinner that night at the bungalow was a feast of seafood. I have never tasted such delicious giant prawns anywhere else in the world. And, I suppose to show me that they still cared, I was presented with a special plate of chillies with the remark that 'they were much hotter than the ones in Hanoi'.

The idyll was broken the very next day. We saw the mining towns, high up in the hills overlooking the sea. Both the towns had been completely destroyed. Since it was difficult to score direct hits on the mines, the miners and their families were regarded as a legitimate target. The towns had been attacked after the night shift while the miners were having their breakfasts. They were evacuated to rapidly erected bamboo huts on the side of the hills near the mines, but these, too, were bombed. Then this most modern of 20th-century wars compelled the miners to live in caves. I recalled an American General arguing that the Vietnamese 'should be bombed into the Stone Age'. Yet morale was high, although Lawrence Daly wept as he saw the conditions under which the Vietnamese miners were living and working. He addressed a miner's rally in one of these giant caves. A marvellous orator, Daly spoke that night with great emotion. The cave was lit with hand-held torches. He talked as a miner who knew what pit-life was like and as he spoke I noticed that the entire audience was bewitched. As he neared the end of his speech, Daly's heart united with his intellect. 'I am shocked and angry', he roared, 'that while the US Seventh Fleet violates your territorial waters and sends its evil machines to bomb you every week, your allies do not send their fleet and air force to protect you. I talk now of the Soviet Union, whose navy is second to none. Why don't they send it to Vietnam and blow these bastards out of the water.' The miners could feel Daly's emotion and waited eagerly for the translation. The interpreter exchanged looks with the senior member of the Central Committee who had accompanied us on this trip. He nodded his head and the interpreter, relieved, translated Lawrence's final peroration in the same style. The miners rose to their feet and cheered and applauded till it seemed the roof of the cave would collapse. He was embraced and kissed by many Vietnamese that night for saying something that everyone felt, but dare not speak of in public.

A week later I left Vietnam. It was a formative experience; something I can never forget. The struggle was still approaching its peak, but I had no doubt that what I had seen was the most epic resistance ever witnessed in the sordid annals of imperialism. Many years later I was talking to a veteran communist leader in India. He was describing a meeting with Ho Chi Minh in 1964, two years before my visit. The Indian asked Ho Chi Minh to explain how the Indochinese Communist Party, which had been formed at roughly the same time as the Communist Party in India, had succeeded whilst they in India had failed. The Vietnamese had laughed and replied: 'In India you had Gandhi. Here I am Gandhi!'

The remark was more serious than one might imagine.

Chapter Five

Changing Times:
1967

You'll get food and even booze –
You've great prospects, on the level!
Just don't let some foreign devil
Tempt you to extremist views!

Heinrich Heine, Poems For The Times

'My God!' cried Gudrun. 'But wouldn't it be wonderful, if all England did suddenly go off like a display of fireworks.'

'It couldn't,' said Ursula. 'They are all too damp, the powder is damp in them.'

'I'm not so sure of that,' said Gerald.

'Nor I,' said Birkin. 'When the English really begin to go off, en masse, it'll be time to shut your ears and run.'

'They never will,' said Ursula.

'We'll see,' he replied.

D. H. Lawrence, Women in Love

London seemed very unreal after Hanoi. There is a brief passage in Orwell's *Homage to Catalonia* in which he describes his emotions on returning to England after his days on the front in Barcelona during the Spanish Civil War. He captures well the placidity and insularity of an island which is so aloof from the European cockpit. He writes half-sadly, half-scornfully of the fact that the milk will be on the doorstep as usual and the *New Statesman* will be delivered on time every week. And this makes Orwell angry for he is still full of Spain. I read the book some years after visiting Vietnam, but it summed up what I had felt on the day I returned, with one important difference. Orwell wrote as someone who belonged to Britain and half-appreciated its institutional eccentricities. I was an outsider congenitally incapable of such sentiments.

In contrast to the life-and-death struggles taking place in Asia and Latin America, politics in Britain appeared even more trivial than before. An unspoken consensus had paralysed the parliamentary arena. The Labour left had become willing, albeit unhappy, prisoners of Labourism. When Wilson succumbed to American pressure and decided to go for membership of the European Community, Edward Heath found it difficult to differentiate the Tory Front Bench from Wilsonism. A high-powered Tory cadre school therefore met at Selsdon Park to prepare a set of policies, which broke with the old consensus. The ultimate beneficiary of this was Margaret Thatcher. Respect for the House of Commons, never particularly high outside the war years, was at its nadir in 1967. Left-wing Labour MPs were quite prepared to admit that 'the real power of making decisions has been almost entirely withdrawn from Parliament', and that 'the House was an ideal arena for evasion, procrastination and delay', but they were incapable of action and extremely hostile to any notion of building an extra-parliamentary resistance to the Labour Government. It was this failure on the part of socialists in the Labour Party to campaign against what was now admitted by all to be a consensual conservative regime, that laid the basis for a small explosion of revolutionary politics in Britain over the next decade.

Immediately after my return from Indochina I had thrown myself into a wide-ranging set of activities. I had written a number of articles on my trip, the longest of which had been published with a selection of my photographs in *Town*, while the more polemical pieces had appeared in *Tribune* and the *New Statesman*. Even more pleasing was the fact that I had been rung by Tom Blau of Camera Press who had praised the quality of my photographs and bought the rights. I still receive the odd cheque from the agency. The result of this literary flurry was that I was deluged with invitations to speak from all over the country. They came mainly from the universities, but I was amazed at the number of sixth-formers who invited me to address them on Vietnam. This period of growing political awareness on Vietnam coincided with an office coup inside *Town* magazine. Michael Heseltine, for reasons which I never really discovered, had decided to dismiss his loyal friend and comrade, Julian Critchley, from the Editor's chair. The entire episode was over in a matter of hours. Critchley, an officer and a gentleman, never voiced his anger in my presence. He simply packed his bags and departed. His whole team was soon given its marching orders and with very little warning and no ex gratia payments we left as well. I cannot recall any tears being shed. Most of us were fairly relieved as the rumour-mongers were saying that *Town* was to be given one more chance to survive and then it would be closed down permanently. The only other Bolshevik on the magazine had been Ken Thomson, the Fashion Editor, a gutsy Australian copy of Dudley Moore, who kept one supplied with sample shirts and trousers during bad times. He left to become the PR person for Aquascutum from which vantage point in 1968 he presented me with a bright red raincoat, which was to keep me dry on many a demonstration.

The mood on the campuses was beginning to change rapidly. The size of my meetings was growing at a pace which took me by surprise. There were two reasons for this transformation. The first was a complete disenchantment with Labour because of Wilson's govern-mental record. The second was the international conjuncture. The examples of the Cuban and Vietnamese revolutions were, at the time, inspirational. A universal feeling was gaining ground: if the Vietnamese could successfully resist the Americans, then surely lesser enemies could also be vanquished. The first student occupation took place in March that year. Its venue was the London School of Economics, where the Board of Governors had appointed Walter Adams as the new Director. The students objected strongly because of Adams' past as a senior academic figure in Rhodesia, where Ian Smith had declared his settler-regime to be independent of Britain. Wilson, a staunch supporter of violent action in Vietnam, had decided not to use force against the Rhodesian whites. In this climate, the LSE decision to appoint Adams was a mindless provocation. There had been a boycott of lectures already in 1966, which had attracted little censure, but this time the authorities were outraged. Appointments and patronage was a jealously guarded preserve. How dare the students challenge such a time-honoured tradition.

The first LSE occupation lasted for a week and two of the activists involved, Adelstein and Bloom, were suspended. A gigantic meeting in the New Theatre refused to accept the suspensions, voted to continue the struggle against Adams and demanded the reinstatement of the two students. This was the first real sign of the turbulence that soon spread to campuses throughout the country. It has since become fashionable to decry every strike or struggle as being organized, led or 'manipulated' by a 'tiny minority'. Yet the most amazing feature of the LSE in 1967 was the degree of participation by ordinary students. It was obvious that a large majority was not in favour of Adams.

Campus radicalism had spread to Britain from the United States. The catalysts there had been the war in Vietnam and the burning question (in a literal sense) of race and segregation in the South. The American Students for a Democratic Society (SDS) had been founded in 1960, but had moved to the left in 1962 at its convention in Port Huron, Michigan. The Port Huron statement, drafted by Tom Hayden, was not a revolutionary manifesto by any stretch of the imagination, but it was radical in the sense that it declared war on the American Dream. The SDS perceived the Dream as a prison. At Port Huron they did not decide to tear down the prison, but they did agree that the walls needed to be scaled in order to glimpse the real world that lay outside. They did this and saw ugliness and violence. The SDS delegates were aware of their status as the children of the comfortable classes, but they voiced their anxieties aloud and hoped that liberal America would listen. It was a plea to the intelligentsia on the East and West coasts and its core was contained in this appeal:

As we grew, however, our comfort was penetrated by events too troubling to dismiss. First, the permeating and victimizing fact of human degradation, symbolized by the Southern struggle against racial bigotry, compelled most of us from silence to activism. Second, the enclosing fact of the Cold War, symbolized by the presence of the Bomb, brought awareness that we ourselves, and our friends, and millions of abstract 'others' we knew more directly because of our common peril, might die at any time. We might deliberately ignore, or avoid, or fail to feel all other human problems, but not these two, for these were too immediate and crushing in their impact, too challenging in the demand that we as individuals take the responsibility for encounter and resolution. While these and other problems either directly oppressed us or rankled our consciences and became our own subjective concerns, we began to see complicated and disturbing paradoxes in our surrounding America. The declaration 'all men are created equal ...' rang hollow before the facts of Negro life in the South and big cities of the North. The proclaimed peaceful intentions of the United States contradicted its economic and military investments in the Cold War status quo ...

The eruption of the Vietnam War and the despatch of half a million American troops had pushed the SDS further and further to the left. In 1967 it was engaged in helping draft resisters. That year 2000 young Americans publicly burnt their draft cards in an attempt to confront their government and challenge its right to pursue the war. The Berkeley students in California had spearheaded a nationwide movement against the war. They had proclaimed their campus to be a 'liberated zone inside the imperialist heartland' and the new resistance was being studied in amazement by students and professors in the major cities of Europe.

In Britain we had decided to form the Vietnam Solidarity Campaign (VSC) in order to promote a public resistance to Wilson's policies and mobilize support for the Vietnamese struggle. The actual decision had been taken by a handful of Trotskyist-Marxists, who produced a tiny, duplicated magazine called *The Week*. This journal had a very broad list of sponsors, including leading trade unionists, a sprinkling of left Labour MPs and other notables. The two guiding spirits behind the magazine were Ken Coates and Pat Jordan. Coates had been a miner and a member of the Communist Party. Jordan had served in the British Army as an engineer and had subsequently worked as a metal worker. He, too, had joined the Communist Party and become a paid full-time regional organizer, a sign that he was trusted by the apparatus. At different times both these men had left the CP and had decided to move to the left rather than the right. They had become Trotskyists and had initially worked with the Militant inside a common organization, but had finally realized that cohabitation with a political variant of Seventh Day Adventists was unsatisfactory. They had set up a small Trotskyist group, aligned to similar groupuscules in Europe and North America and known in the tiny world of that left as the Fourth International. This was not the only commodity with that name in the market, but it was undoubtedly the one closest to political reality. Most of the different Trotskyist currents at the time were embedded in the Labour Party, some more deeply than others. *The Week* had not looked kindly on Richard Gott's candidature in Hull, but unlike other publications it had permitted a healthy debate on the question. I had never encountered the magazine at Oxford. The two active groups there had been an ultra-orthodox sect, then known as the Socialist Labour League (SLL), run like a one-party statelet by the supreme leader, Gerry Healey, and the International Socialism (IS) Group, whose leading ideologue was a Palestinian, Ygael Gluckstein, who wrote under the pen name of Tony Cliff. Green I undoubtedly was in those days, but the particularly esoteric form of sectarianism espoused by the SLL left me cold. Every instinct in me rebelled against that style of absolutist politics.

The IS members were entirely different and, on most questions, were refreshingly undogmatic, but their view of world politics seemed to me to be bizarre and far too Eurocentric. When I first heard them talk amongst themselves they gave me the impression of being a weird breed of professional anti-communists. When I discovered that for them there was no qualitative difference between Chiang Kai-shek and Batista on the one hand and Mao Zedong and Fidel Castro on the other, I realized that I would always be a stranger in their house. Their hostility to the Chinese and Cuban revolutions and the possibility of further outbreaks of a similar sort in the future was, in my eyes, tantamount to writing off a large part of the globe. I was never attracted to them intellectually, even though many of their members became close personal friends. The SLL was so rigid that personal friendships with men or women who were not 'hundred percenters' were frowned upon by the apparatchiks. The style of the IS Group in the sixties was in polar contrast to such absurdities.

I was attracted to *The Week* by one simple fact. The people who ran it had decided to make solidarity with Vietnam a central priority, which came before everything else. This tied in well with my own preoccupations and I began to warm to their political approach to the rest of the world. When Pat Jordan rang me up and asked if I would be one of the founding members of the Vietnam Solidarity Campaign and help to build it in Britain, I agreed immediately. Bertrand Russell had blessed the initiative and the Peace Foundation agreed to provide some funds to help prepare the campaign. Just as I was about to embark on a whirlwind tour to try and win people over to the idea of VSC, I became ill with mumps.

The version of the disease that inflicted itself upon me was not mild. At first it was only my glands that were affected, but just as I thought I was recovering, I had a painful relapse. This time the virus decided to hit me below the belt. My testicles swelled up like balloons and the amused physician advised a sling. Observing my misery, a warm-hearted woman friend bought me some books to read. She was aware that I needed something strong to take my mind off the dreaded affliction and so she walked in one afternoon with Isaac Deutscher's three-volume biography of Trotsky.

I had of course heard of Deutscher. His biography of Stalin had even reached the bookshelves of my father's study in Lahore, but I had not been tempted to read that volume. The Trotsky trilogy, however, was a different matter altogether. It was, and remains, the sort of book which can change one's life. It certainly did mine. I was entranced. Friends who shared the house on the river's edge in Chiswick with me at the time will testify that I was incapable of paying attention to anything else. I stayed in bed till I had finished all three volumes. It took me a week, during which time my disease mysteriously subsided. The most arresting feature of the trilogy is Deutscher's flawless prose, which brings the Russian Revolution and its leaders to life as it describes the rise and fall of Trotsky. It is difficult to think of any other biography which has so brilliantly married the intellect of an outstanding Marxist historian to a literary style whose richness has often stunned connoisseurs. In describing the tragedy of Trotsky, Deutscher explained to me some of the reasons for the degeneration of the Revolution.

Deutscher was born in Cracow, Poland in 1907. He came from a strong rabbinical background and his early clashes with parental and religious orthodoxy have been described with honesty and humour in *A Non-Jewish Jew And Other Essays*. He joined the Polish Communist Party in 1926 only to find himself in a strange new world where theoretical confusion was rife. In May 1926, the Polish Party had supported Pilsudski's coup against the gentry. This decision had shocked the rank and file. A debate had begun on the Central Committee between leaders backing the rival factions of Zinoviev and Bukharin inside the Russian Party. Deutscher was not impressed by the level of the debate and was later to describe it as a 'quarrel of damned souls imprisoned within the enchanted circle of Stalinism'.

Deutscher severed links with the 'damned souls' after the rise of Hitler. He had read Trotsky's impassioned pleas from his exile in Prinkipo which prophesied both the victory of fascism *and* the holocaust and pleaded for social-democratic and communist unity against the Nazis. Deutscher agreed with this analysis, but he and his supporters were isolated. In 1932 they were expelled for the crime of urging on the Communist International a policy of working-class unity in Germany against fascism. Six years later, the entire leadership of the Polish Communist Party fled to Moscow to escape repression at home. They were regarded as too independent-minded. Stalin had them arrested and executed as 'fascist agents and traitors'. This was a shattering blow for Deutscher. He had disagreed with most of them in his time, but the manner in which they were so brutally eliminated was to prove a traumatic experience. Subsequently he was to recall his memories of one of the dead leaders:

I remember the image of Warski at Theatre Square on 1 May 1928. He was marching at the head of a huge banned demonstration, through the hail of machine-gun fire and rifle shots with which we were greeted (by Pilsudski's militia). While tens of hundreds of wounded were falling in our ranks, he held up his white-grey head, a high and easy target visible from afar; and he indomitably addressed the crowd. This was the image of him I had in my mind when, some years later, he was denounced from Moscow as a traitor, a spy and a Pilsudskist agent.

Hitler's victory in Germany had confirmed Trotsky's critique of the criminal sectarianism emanating from Moscow, but Deutscher did not think the time was ripe for launching the Fourth International and breaking completely with the existing communist movement. He decided to devote his energies to writing and retreated to 'the watchtower' as Marx had done after the defeat of the Paris Commune in 1871. Some months before the Nazi invasion of Poland, Deutscher left his native country and sought refuge in Britain. He was recruited to the Polish army-in-exile, but he spent most of the war as a journalist. He had read references in Marx's *Capital* to *The Economist* and it was that journal which accepted and published his first article. Deutscher had studied English only when he came to Britain. His mastery of the language amazed everyone and the inevitable comparisons with a fellow-Pole of the preceding generation – Joseph Conrad – were not long in making an appearance.

Deutscher began to write regularly for *The Economist* and the *Observer* on Eastern Europe and the USSR. It was a stimulating discipline, which enabled him to display his talents as a political analyst. The Trotsky trilogy had been completed at a time when the cold war was still raging fiercely. The biography, as I discovered for myself that summer, was a powerful assault on both the crude anti-Marxism of the CIA intelligentsia as well as the intellectuals bewitched by Stalinism in or around the communist parties. Deutscher was fiercely attacked by all sides. The Congress for Cultural Freedom hacks attacked his work; the official communist press denounced him savagely and the Trotskyist sects thought that he was too unorthodox in his approach. It was Deutscher's obstinate refusal to compromise with falsehood and half-truths that led to his isolation. He never received a grant from any

academic institution nor any university professorships. There was one
occasion when he applied for a job as a lecturer in Russian Studies at
the University of Sussex. The Vice-Chancellor, Asa Briggs, felt that it
was too lowly a job for such a great historian. He persuaded Deutscher
to apply for a professorship. Alas this elevated position required more
than Asa Brigg's approval. Deutscher applied reluctantly, only to be
blackballed by the great believer in freedom and democracy, Isaiah
Berlin, who was opposed to a Marxist being allowed to teach Russian
history.

Deutscher's repressed activism was aroused by the war in Vietnam.
He participated in the teach-ins in the United States in 1964–65 and
agreed to be one of the judges at the War Crimes Tribunal. I had
discovered Deutscher through the trilogy. Soon I would see him in
action at the Tribunal's hearings. My own report on the effect of the
bombings was ready. The only thing in doubt was the venue of the
Tribunal. The Labour Government had rejected Russell's appeal to
allow the session to take place in London. Roy Jenkins, the Home
Secretary, had said 'that it would not be in the national interest'.
Russell had complained to Wilson, who had referred to the 'one-sided
character of the Tribunal' and backed Jenkins' decision. In reality, the
United States had made it clear that it expected its allies to reject all
attempts to convene the Tribunal in friendly capitals. Jean-Paul Sartre
had written to De Gaulle asking that the Tribunal be permitted to hold
its sessions in Paris. In a lengthy reply to Sartre, the French President
said that he, too, was opposed to the Vietnam War. His refusal was cast
in a quasi-judicial cloak:

> Neither is it a question of the right of assembly nor of free expression,
> but of duty, the more so for France, which has taken a widely known
> decision in the matter, and which must be on guard lest a State with
> which it is linked and which, despite all differences of opinion, remains
> its traditional friend, should on French territory become the subject of
> proceedings exceeding the limits of international law and custom. Now
> such would seem to be the case with regard to the activity envisaged by
> Lord Russell and his friends, since they intend to give a juridical form to

their investigations and the semblance of a verdict to their
conclusions . . .

Sartre responded publicly and angrily in the pages of the *Nouvelle
Observateur*, tearing De Gaulle's argument to shreds and warning the
General that a worldwide movement from Tokyo to London was in
motion against the war. He admitted that France had not reached the
stage of general strikes as had Japan, 'but people are growing restless'.

Ultimately it was the Scandinavian social-democrats who provided a
home for the Tribunal. Olaf Palme, then a member of the Swedish
Cabinet and a strong opponent of the war, stated that his country
would welcome the Russell Tribunal. One reason for wanting the
venue to be in London was to enable Russell to attend since he was
now too frail to travel. In the event he sent a searing message which set
the tone for the proceedings. It was Jean-Paul Sartre who presided
over the event, aided by the Yugoslav historian, Vladimir Dedijer. The
members of the Tribunal included James Baldwin; Simone de Beauvoir; Lazaro Cardenas (a former President of Mexico); David Dellin-
ger, a veteran American pacifist; the Black Power leader, Stokely
Carmichael; Peter Weiss; Isaac Deutscher; the Philippines poet,
Amado Hernandes; the Pakistani jurist, Mahmud Ali Kasuri; Sara
Lidman; the French mathematician, Laurent Schwartz; as well as a
Turkish lawyer and a Japanese physicist.

When I arrived in Stockholm to present my report it seemed as
though the Swedish Government had declared the Tribunal to be an
official event. The entire city was talking about the indictment and it
received saturation coverage in the Swedish press as well as being
reported daily by Swedish television. As I arrived at the conference
centre, I ran into Ken Tynan. He was reporting the event for *Playboy*
and was anxious to meet some of the Tribunal members and get an
idea of what had happened in Vietnam. We met later and over dinner
Tynan cursed the Labour Government for its cowardice. 'After all,
Olaf Palme is also a social-democrat', he said as I was eating my steak.
'Why is he so different from bloody Wilson?' I suggested that the
difference might not be one of ideology, but of strategic location.

Britain was a crucial pillar of the NATO alliance, while Sweden had refused to accept membership. Olaf Palme was simply pushing through policies which Wilson had promised as Leader of the Opposition.

The next day I spoke at the Tribunal and was duly questioned. I remarked that there was an element of racism in the American war against Vietnam. I refused to accept that they would have behaved in such a fashion in Europe, especially after the horrors of the Second World War. I saw Sartre nod vigorously, but Deutscher frowned. He questioned me relentlessly. Why did I think that to be the case? If there was a revolution taking place in Southern Europe or Scandinavia did I really think the United States would treat it more kindly? I obstinately defended my position, but he was not convinced on this point. At the end of the session both Lawrence Daly and I tried to convince Deutscher that the disregard for Asian lives did have an extra component which added to the counter-revolutionary fervour of the Pentagon. The 'gooks' were only half-human. He smiled, but begged to disagree.

While I was explaining to Deutscher how much I had appreciated his Trotsky trilogy, a strange confrontation began to erupt in the background. Ralph Schoenman was being interviewed by Michael Barratt from BBC TV. The reporter had clearly been instructed to put the boot in without any mercy and, as a result, the questions abandoned all pretence of objectivity. Schoenman, no stranger to these tactics himself, responded in kind. His answers were deliberately couched in a language that made transmission impossible. Barratt would ask something like: 'Mr Schoenman don't you agree that this Tribunal is a propaganda exercise for the communist regime in Hanoi, and is utterly one-sided and irrelevant?' Schoenman's response: 'When did you last fuck your wife?' After three attempts interspersed with furious rows, the BBC gave up and went in search of less offensive victims.

Russell and Sartre had never sought to conceal their own views or to pretend that they were setting up a judicial body. How could they? They had no state authority. The entire event was viewed as a moral intervention to expose an immoral war. The bulk of the media in the

West – barring Scandinavia – denounced the two philosophers as well-intentioned dupes of Hanoi, but much more was at stake. The scale of atrocities revealed at Stockholm and later at Copenhagen was immense. The systematic destruction of the environment coupled with the planned attacks on non-combatants and the torture of prisoners was undeniable. All this was exposed two years before the My Lai massacres shocked the conscience of liberal America. Russell and Sartre were attempting to create a climate in which future My Lais could not take place. The most detailed report of the Tribunal was written by Tynan and published in *Playboy*. Alas his reference to the portly Pakistani barrister as a subcontinental Orson Welles – a compliment from Tynan – did not go down well in the home country. Kasuri's wife, an orthodox lady with strong religious leanings, was deeply shocked when she discovered a copy of the magazine concealed in his suitcase. His explanations were not considered satisfactory.

As far as I was concerned the Tribunal was a partial success. It had taken place. It had been reported, albeit with distortions, though these were much worse in Britain than in the United States. I had met Sartre and de Beauvoir, Melba Hernandes from Cuba and the Latin American novelist Alejo Carpentier. That in itself made the trip worthwhile for me. But Sartre's devastating indictment 'On Genocide' which concluded the Tribunal was a *tour de force*. The philosopher had collated his multiplicity of talents for this onslaught. It was a brilliantly argued case and at least he had understood the point I had been trying to make to Isaac Deutscher. Sartre pointed out that while the Nuremberg Tribunal was still fresh in people's minds, the French colonial administration in Algeria had massacred 45,000 Algerians at Setif to set 'an example'. In other words, the Nuremberg judgements could not apply to the peoples of the Third World. For they were not really human beings. It was an American tragedy that they could embark on a genocidal course and deceive themselves that they were doing so for a good cause:

> This racism – anti-black, anti-Asiatic, anti-Mexican – is a basic
> American attitude with deep historical roots and which existed, latently

and overtly, well before the Vietnamese conflict. One proof of this is that the United States government refused to ratify the Genocide Convention. This doesn't mean that in 1948 the US intended to exterminate a people; what it does mean – according to the statements of the US Senate – is that the Convention would conflict with laws of several states; in other words, the current policymakers enjoy a free hand in Vietnam because their predecessors catered to the anti-black racism of Southern whites. In any case, since 1966, the racism of Yankee soldiers, from Saigon to the 17th parallel, has become more and more marked. Young American men use torture, they shoot unarmed women for nothing more than target practice, they kick wounded Vietnamese in the genitals, they cut ears off dead men to take home for trophies. Officers are the worst: a general boasted of hunting 'VCs' from his helicopter and gunning them down in the paddy fields. In the confused minds of the American soldiers, 'Viet Cong' and 'Vietnamese' tend increasingly to blend into one another. They often say themselves, 'The only good Vietnamese is a dead Vietnamese', or what amounts to the same thing, 'A dead Vietnamese is a Vietcong' . . .

Total war presupposes a certain balance of forces. Colonial wars were not reciprocal, but the interests of the colonialists limited the scope of genocide. The present genocide, the end result of the unequal development of societies, is total war waged to the limit by one side, without the slightest reciprocity.

The American government is not guilty of inventing modern genocide or even of having chosen it from other possible and effective measures against guerrilla warfare. It is not guilty, for example, of having preferred genocide for strategic and economic reasons. Indeed, genocide presents itself as the ONLY POSSIBLE REACTION to the rising of a whole people against its oppressors.

The complete text of Sartre's closing remarks was published in *Le Monde*, but ignored by every other mainstream daily of the West. By contrast, lengthy extracts appeared in many Third World newspapers in India, Pakistan, Mexico, Chile, Uruguay, Algeria and Egypt. Sartre and Russell were generally caricatured by the establishment press in their own continent. In many Third World countries they were painted as giants in a land of pygmies.*

When I returned to London, there was an urgent message from Clive Goodwin to contact him 'the minute you return'. I rang him immediately and was summoned to dinner. In his sprawling office-cum-flat on Cromwell Road, we talked about the state of the world and also more concrete projects. The newspaper we had discussed before I went to Prague was foremost in Clive's mind and we agreed that he should convene a meeting of sympathetic people to raise funds and discuss the shape and thrust of our proposed publication. Then he mentioned the escalation of police repression against marijuana smokers. 'Of course it's the blacks who suffer the most, but they've started raiding the rich. This is the time to do something and reverse the trend. By the way, do you smoke?' I shook my head and told him that I simply loathed cigarettes and their filthy smoke. He laughed. 'Oh well, but the fragrance of grass is quite pleasant. Anyway it's a civil liberties issue. Every single medical expert has admitted that marijuana is less harmful than tobacco and alcohol. The big capitalist lobbies know this well and refuse to legalize it because they fear massive loss in profits on drink and tobacco.' There was (and is) a rational kernel in this argument. I agreed that we should do something. Clive's proposal was a full-page advertisement in *The Times* signed by 'well-known people' that would demand the legalization of the herb and shock bourgeois society. I agreed to sign and the ad did appear under a list of names, which included the Beatles, David Bailey, Humphrey Berkely, Graham Greene, Tom Driberg, Kenneth Tynan, Dr Stafford-Clarke and Jonathan Aitken. The Beatles followed this by issuing an LP,

---

* There is an interesting sequel. Exactly ten years later I ran into trouble with the Pakistani regime and they 'disembarked' me from three different planes at two different airports. Friends in the West mounted an immediate campaign and several Labour MPs sent cables, but it was a strong protest from Sartre and de Beauvoir which annoyed the country's ruler the most but had the desired effect. I was permitted to leave!

Sergeant Pepper's Lonely Hearts Club Band, with choruses like 'I'd love to turn you on'.

A great deal has been written on the popular culture of the period. The music, the new sexual permissiveness etc, have become the subject of numerous colour-supplement articles and television programmes. For some that, and a form of happy mysticism, represents the meaning of 1968. Politics tends to be ignored. In correcting this imbalance I do not wish to suggest that a Chinese Wall divided pop culture from revolutionary politics. In fact during the high points of the movement there was a potent and heady mixture of both. We imbibed some of the music and the devotees of the rock groups learnt a bit of politics.

In summer 1967, R. D. Laing and David Cooper organized a conference at the Roundhouse under the banner of 'The Dialectics of Liberation – towards a Demystification of Violence'. It was a gathering of Marxist intellectuals – Paul Sweezy, Ernest Mandel, C. L. R. James – and political activists. I had been asked to speak on the last day, but since I was planning to be out of Britain, I declined the offer. I was, however, able to attend one day of the conference. Stokely Carmichael was in full flow that day. It was exhilarating rhetoric. A defence of violence against a violent society and extremely black nationalist in tone. He was provided with important backing by Ronnie Laing, who argued for counterviolence against the system. I spoke to Carmichael during the lunch break. We sat in the sun outside the Roundhouse and chatted about what he had said in his speech. We were surrounded by a few black militants from Britain, who were not pleased when I questioned some of the assumptions of 'Black Power' in the United States and insisted that the situation of blacks in Britain was in any case totally different from that of the United States. Carmichael himself remained friendly as the banter continued, but some of his local acolytes would brook no criticism. Carmichael's main argument was that white America – including the white working class – was not going to concede any of their demands without a struggle. On this there was no disagreement, but when he began to discuss the possibilities of *black* revolution I was completely unconvinced.

Later in the afternoon the Trinidad-born writer C. L. R. James, whose physique and demeanour were in polar contrast to the American, came to the podium to speak. James hardly raised his voice that day, but he was heard in silence by an audience which had enthusiastically cheered Carmichael. C. L. R. James, an epitome of classical scholarship, proceeded without much effort to demolish the black nationalist case, while defending their cause. He did so elegantly, but without mercy. Sitting there listening to this black man with white hair I found myself agreeing entirely with his approach to this question. There could not have been a better antidote to Carmichael and when James sat down to polite applause – he had, after all, been swimming against the tide that day – I applauded loud and long in order to express my gratitude. That same week I started to read James' classic study of the 18th-century slave rebellion in Haiti, *The Black Jacobins*. Here was another historian of quality, different from Isaac Deutscher in many ways, but essentially from the same political tradition.

The Vietnam Solidarity Campaign was founded in the same period. We had hoped to unite all those in Britain who were prepared to declare their support for the Vietnamese in public. There was already an organization called the British Campaign for Peace in Vietnam (BCPV), which was a classic Communist Party front organization. In itself, of course, there was nothing wrong with this, but the BCPV believed in discreet pressure politics. Those who pulled the strings inside this organization supported the Vietnamese, but secretly and in whispers. In public they were simply for peace. Our approach was the opposite. We wanted a lasting peace and felt that this could only come about through a Vietnamese victory. We therefore stressed our solidarity with the Vietnamese struggle and planned a series of demonstrations to emphasize our way of doing things. The North Vietnamese were represented in this country by three semi-recognized representatives: Nguyen van Sao, comrade Ba and the redoubtable Linh Qui. The last-mentioned was married to Sao. She was the brains of the outfit. We had discussed the VSC's formation with them quite openly and invited them to attend the founding conference as observers. They realized what was at stake since the BCPV were the 'official' body in this regard. Nonetheless they attended our meeting and read a message from Vietnam. This made it difficult for the British CP to denounce us too viciously, but did not stop them from sniping consistently and arguing that *we* would narrow the base of opposition to the war by stressing our pro-NLF slogans. We responded by pointing out their failure to mobilize existing opposition to the Downing Street/White House axis and explained that their alliance with a layer of Tribunite Labour MPs seemed to be more important than the agony and suffering of the Vietnamese. We had received messages of support from various groups all over the world and an appeal from Berkeley to organize worldwide demonstrations against the war on 22 October 1967. The VSC conference agreed unanimously to make this a priority, but fully aware that not everyone was in VSC we decided to initiate, on the American model, a call for an Ad Hoc Committee to which all other organizations could send representatives and participate. As it turned out the bulk of the organizing was done by the VSC and its activists.

The week after the birth of VSC, there was a meeting at Clive Goodwin's flat to discuss the newspaper project. A number of familiar faces were present. All were eager to find out the whys and wherefores of VSC. I had membership forms and most of those present signed up immediately. That meeting was attended by the poets Adrian Mitchell and Christopher Logue; the playwrights David Mercer and Roger Smith; Ken Tynan; Sheila Rowbotham and a few others whom I did not know. Adrian Mitchell's poems on Vietnam were the staple diet of most Vietnam activists and he was a familiar figure at many meetings and demonstrations. Christopher Logue had produced a poster-poem entitled 'Why I Shall Vote Labour', which had evoked the growing disillusionment with the Wilson Government. Mercer was a Marxist playwright very well-known as a result of *Morgan: A Suitable Case for Treatment*.

It was agreed that the paper we wanted would combine politics and culture, help the Vietnamese, attack the Labour Government and act as a voice for the thousands of young people who were becoming more and more radical every day. Names were bandied around, but none was approved. Christopher Logue volunteered to go to the British Museum and search relentlessly until he had found a long-forgotten radical paper of the previous century whose name we could recover. Clive himself volunteered to take charge of the fund-raising, without which, alas, nothing was possible. We were all optimists. It was felt that if we raised enough money to produce two or three issues, the quality and success of the paper would generate its own funds. Since Clive was a literary agent, he knew perfectly well how much money all his clients were earning. He drew up a list with appropriate amounts opposite most names. One exception was Denis Potter. Would he or wouldn't he help? To this day I can't recall whether Potter ever made a donation to our Fighting Fund. Most of those approached, however, did oblige. Others agreed to write regularly in lieu of money. A few, very few, were sceptical and doubted whether the project would ever get off the ground. I myself had some doubts on this score, but Clive displayed a confidence that rapidly became infectious. He had already started talking at our founding meeting, while we were still nameless, about sales targets and subscription lists and offices.

The following week, at a smaller gathering, Logue returned triumphantly from his labours in the British Museum. He had found a name with a history. *The Black Dwarf* had been established in 1819 and closed down in 1828. Its editor, Tom Wooler, had been a Sheffield printer, who had first been charged with *writing* seditious material against the monarchy. Wooler argued that he had not *written* a single word, merely set it up in print. The charge had to be dropped. The law was subsequently altered. Wooler was a strong believer in political action. His paper was worn by miners in their helmets and his prose used to fill the street with demonstrators. In 1819 he was sent to Warwick Gaol for advocating universal adult franchise in Britain. Wooler was also an internationalist. He constantly urged his British readers to support rebellions and insurrection at home and abroad – in Latin America and among the slaves in the Caribbean. His slogan for the world was apposite: *The right of the People to resist oppression always exists and the requisite power to do this always resides in the People.* But if freedom could not be achieved by passive resistance, Wooler coined another slogan: *Peaceably if We May. Forcibly If We Must.* As for the programme of Wooler's *Dwarf*, it was close to all our hearts. *To lead a consistent struggle for the day-to-day interests of the working masses and ward off attacks on their standard of living,* while simultaneously, *to make use of every partial demand to explain the necessity of revolution and show the impossibility of even a moderately serious and lasting, let alone fundamental, improvement so long as the power of capital is maintained.*

This pre-dated all of the socialist classics. Wooler was also a theatre critic and he was wont to review the proceedings in Parliament and the Law Courts much as one would comment on a play. Every week he wrote a letter from *The Black Dwarf* to the Yellow Bonze of Japan in order to inform the latter of the ridiculous goings-on in the Britain of that period. We applauded Christopher Logue's discovery and decided to appropriate the name without further delay. It was registered in the same week. Our only doubt was whether we could live up to the great traditions of Tom Wooler. It was felt that we needed a super-professional journalist and D. A. N. Jones was mentioned. He was a radical socialist, wrote well and was a good sub-editor. He was approached and agreed to link arms with us on this project. Having found a name and an editor was a tremendous boost. Clive Goodwin now began to collect on the IOUs and promises that we had so far accumulated in great numbers.

At about this time news seeped through that Che Guevara, the Cuban revolutionary who had left Cuba some years ago, was in Bolivia. He was reportedly at the head of a band of guerrillas, who had clashed with the Bolivian Army. Moreover a young Frenchman, Régis Debray, who had theorized the experience of the Cuban Revolution in a book called *Revolution in the Revolution*, had reportedly been arrested while leaving the guerrillas to return to Europe. Debray's life was in danger. Bertrand Russell wanted a mission despatched to Bolivia in order to find out what was going on and to try to see Debray and attend his trial. I received a phone call from Ralph Schoenman, asking whether I would be prepared to leave within a week. In vain did I protest that I spoke no Spanish. They wanted 'reliable' people and, in my case, an additional advantage was that I could use a camera. My Vietnam photographs had amazed both friends and detractors. It was an offer that could not be refused.

Chapter Six

The Last Year in the Life of Ernesto 'Che' Guevara: 1967

In my time streets led to the quicksand.
Speech betrayed me to the slaughterer.
There was little I could do. But without me
The rulers would have become more secure. This was my hope.
So the time passed away
Which on earth was given me.

Bertolt Brecht, *To Posterity*

12 October 1967

It was a crisp and clear autumn day in London. We were in the midst of preparations for the first of the big Vietnam demonstrations. I was due to speak at two meetings that day. The *Guardian* of that morning had published the news of Che's death in Bolivia, together with a photograph of the dead body and a despatch from Richard Gott. There was no longer room for doubt. I sat at my desk and wept. The sense of loss and grief was overpowering and there was nothing else one could do but cry. Nor was I alone. On every continent there were many others who felt and reacted in a similar fashion. Everything associated with that day became unforgettable. I do not remember, if the truth be told, what I was doing when Kennedy was assassinated. But I can recall every small detail of the day that Che died. The conversation with Clive Goodwin. The speeches I made at the two meetings. The suggestion to Pat Jordan that we organize a memorial meeting at the Conway Hall. The long wait for the response from Havana. The anger I felt both at the manner of his death and our collective impotence. What made it marginally worse was that a number of us had been in Bolivia not so long ago in the region where Che and his tiny band of fighters were surrounded and trapped. I had not realized that his death was so close. The very thought had been inconceivable.

The secret of Che's appeal is not difficult to fathom. He was a successful revolutionary leader in Cuba, where he held high office. Yet he had left the relative safety of Havana to resume the struggle in other lands. In his person, theory and practice were in complete harmony. Such a display of internationalism had not been seen since the twenties and thirties, but even then none of the central leaders of the Russian Revolution had left their posts and departed for other storm-centres in Europe. It is true that at one stage the German Communist Party, deprived of Rosa Luxemburg and Karl Liebknecht, had appealed via the Comintern for Trotsky's talents to be made available to their party. Trotsky had been willing, even eager, but the demand had been rejected by the Soviet party on the grounds that Trotsky was needed more in his own country. In Cuba, too, Castro had been extremely reluctant to lose Che, but the veteran Commandante had insisted that in order to help Vietnam concretely it was vital to open new fronts and distract imperialism from Indochina. His departure from Cuba led to a great deal of speculation. His presence was at various times reported in the Congo, Vietnam, Guatemala ... Everywhere but where he was, deep in the heart of land-locked Bolivia.

The Che myth began in Latin America, but spread rapidly to North America and Europe. He was called a murderer and a pyromaniac by the oligarchies, but to the poor he was a Robin Hood, a modern Christ, a Don Quixote. He was not unaware of the mythology that surrounded his name. In his last letter to his parents in mid-1965 he bade them farewell, warning them that 'perhaps this will be my last letter. It is not my intention, but it is within the realm of logical probability. If so, I send you a last embrace.' He had begun the letter by a reference to Cervantes and a light-hearted identification with the fictional hero: 'Once again I feel Rocinante's bony ribs beneath my legs. Again I begin my journey, carrying my shield ...' He was not universally popular on the Euro-American left. The Maoists and sectarians of every hue united in their chorus of disapproval. 'Adventurer!', they screamed in unison, angry at his popularity. Guevara had foreseen such a charge and had replied to it in advance. 'Many', he had written, 'will call me an adventurer, and I am, but of a different kind – one who risks his skin in order to prove his convictions.'

The choice of Bolivia was not so foolish. The country had a strong revolutionary tradition; in the tin miners, it boasted one of the best organized trade unions of the entire continent; and the military oligarchs were corrupt to the core and racist in their attitude to the predominantly Indian peasants, who were the victims of super-exploitation. The fault did not lie in the country or its people, but in the form chosen for the struggle, without the existence of a strong and reliable urban network.

News of Che's presence in Bolivia had begun to circulate freely in Latin America within the ranks of the left, but it was not until Régis Debray's arrest that we obtained confirmation that this was indeed a fact. Debray, referred to as Danton in Che's *Bolivian Diaries*, was captured in May 1967 in the main street of a tiny town, Muyupampa. He was in the company of George Roth, an Anglo-Chilean photographer, and Ciro Bustos, an Argentinean painter. Debray had been lecturing in philosophy at Havana University and living in a room at the Hotel Habana Libre on the 21st floor. It was here that he received word from Che asking him to rush to Paris, where an urgent message awaited him. The place of assignment was a left-wing bookshop in the Latin Quarter, 'La Joie de Lire', owned by the radical publisher, François Maspero. Che had chosen Debray to be the first journalist to report first-hand on the establishment of a guerrilla base in the Andes. Debray's book-essay, *Revolution in the Revolution*, had been widely acclaimed in Cuba as a primer for extending the Cuban experience to the entire Latin American continent. Che offered the young Debray (he was 26 years old at the time) the opportunity to write on how these tactics were being deployed in Bolivia. The attraction of the offer was obvious. Debray returned to Paris, where a messenger handed him his instructions. He was told to proceed to La Paz, the Bolivian capital where, at 6pm every Tuesday, a courier named Andres would wait for him outside the Sucre Palace Hotel. Debray travelled under his own name, armed with official papers confirming his status as a writer and journalist from Maspero and the Mexican magazine *Sucesos*. These credentials were duly validated by the Bolivian authorities, as was his passport.

Debray duly met Andres, who took him to an underground guerrilla using the name 'Tanya'. She travelled with him by bus (a journey and vehicle that has few equals anywhere in the world) and eventually they arrived at the Hotel Grande in Sucre. Here they met Bustos and on the following day continued their travels till they reached the tiny oil town of Camiri. After a day's rest they proceeded northwards into the dense jungles until they reached an isolated ranch in the district of Nancahuaza. Up to this time there had been no clashes between the guerrillas and the troops of the Barrientos military dictatorship. In fact, Che's plan was to wait another six months before undertaking any action. While Debray was waiting for Che in the ranch, a military patrol was sighted heading in its direction. An oil engineer had reported some suspicious movements to the army. The guerrillas ambushed the patrol, killing three officers and capturing 15 soldiers. It now became impossible to stay on at the ranch and Debray and Bustos were taken to the mobile units in the jungles.

It was here that Debray met Che and interviewed him, but since the latter was more involved in commanding units, which found themselves suddenly at war, there was not much time for prolonged discussions. By early April, Debray had accomplished his task and both he and the painter attempted to exit via Gutierrez, but found that the city was already under military occupation. They marched with the guerrillas for another fourteen days. Here Debray must have pondered on what he had written two years previously: 'Bolivia is the country where the subjective and objective conditions [for armed struggle] are best combined. It is the only country in South America where a socialist revolution is on the agenda ...' There was little sign so far of the ripeness of subjective conditions. The peasants, destitute, but not stupid, remained unconvinced of the need for armed struggle. Che had realized that contact with the miners was critical and was attempting to achieve this objective, but the unforeseen discovery of their movements had made everything very difficult.

While the guerrillas were camped near Muyupampa, George Roth rode into the camp on a horse. Che was now seriously alarmed and felt that all three outsiders should leave as soon as possible since their presence was adversely affecting the capacities of the guerrillas. They walked into the town, unarmed except for cameras, where they were arrested by the local police. Fortunately for them they were seen by a Bolivian journalist and a French Dominican missionary. They might all have been released had it not been for the fact that a deserter from the guerrillas told the police that he had seen Bustos and Debray in the camp. The police panicked and informed the army. A military helicopter arrived and transported them to an army barracks. Here all three were badly beaten up. Debray was virtually unconscious when inspected by a doctor. Within days of the capture, an officer showed Debray his obituary which had been published abroad and taunted him with the words: 'The world already believes you're dead. Now it's easy for us to just shoot you.' More sinister was the fact that Debray was endlessly interrogated by CIA agents and Cuban exiles from Miami. Their logic was faultless: if Debray was there, could Che be far behind? Four days after the Frenchman's arrest, two American military men booked into the Hotel Beirut in Camiri. A few weeks later they were joined by others.

Debray was tortured regularly. His interrogators wanted information as to Che's whereabouts. He was often threatened with execution. What saved him was the worldwide concern. His father was a conservative Parisian lawyer; his mother a staunch Gaullist, well-known in local Parisian politics for her right-wing views. They moved into action rapidly to try to save their son's life. On 6 June, an American prelate, Monsignor Kennedy, a distant relative of the famous American clan, was permitted to see Debray in his cell. Kennedy told the outside world that he was alive and would soon be tried in a public court as a guerrilla-collaborator.

This information had reached us while we were busy preparing the

Tribunal. Sartre had suggested to Russell that the Peace Foundation should despatch a team of observers with the aim of ensuring Debray's safety and attending his trial. A few weeks later the Cubans had approached the Foundation with a similar suggestion. They were now concerned for Debray as well as Che and the others, whose where-abouts had been prematurely revealed. I was asked by Ralph Schoenman to purchase up-to-date camera equipment and take a large stock of film. He suggested that we, too, might have to establish contact with Che's units and therefore security was a prime con-sideration as far as the nature and circumstances of this trip were concerned.

The team was to consist of five people. Apart from Schoenman and myself, there were Perry Anderson and Robin Blackburn. Both were described in a Sunday paper as 'two young British dons', which was technically accurate, but very inappropriate. Anderson was editor of the *New Left Review* and Blackburn one of his closest comrades-in-arms on the editorial committee of the magazine. I had met both of them at social gatherings, one of which had been a party organized by Blackburn's Chinese wife, Fei Ling, at their Ladbroke Grove flat. I had been extremely impressed by Perry Anderson's frenetic dancing style, which went well with the music of the Stones, but my knowledge of his work was limited to his introduction to the Italian Communist Party documents which I had read while in Pakistan. I still had not at that stage studied the much talked about polemical exchange between Anderson and E. P. Thompson on the historical roots of the crisis in Britain. The debate had covered a wide range of subjects, including the nature of the English Civil War, the function and role of the land-owning aristocracy in Britain, the effects of Protestantism and Darwinism on English culture and history and finally the development of Marxist thought in this century. Thompson and Anderson were both experienced in the art of polemics and the rapier-like thrusts and counter-thrusts became the most celebrated and important battle of ideas that the left in Britain had ever experienced. I had, of course, noticed both Thompson's essay in the *Socialist Register* and Anderson's response in the *New Left Review*, but since the terms of reference were limited to Britain, I had simply not been interested, a philistine response which I was later to regret. Apart from anything else it would have enabled me to understand the complexities of Anderson's character much better while we were in Latin America.

I had first encountered Robin Blackburn through an article of his in defence of the Cuban Revolution. He was also a co-editor of *The Week*, though I do not recall ever reading anything by him in that tiny, but influential, magazine. His hair had turned white prematurely, but whereas others might have panicked, Blackburn converted this biological accident into a much envied sexual asset. I knew Fei Ling a little better since she was active in the Vietnam movement and was an enthusiastic partisan of the Vietnam Solidarity Campaign. In fact I first met Blackburn via Fei Ling and subsequently at one of Clive Goodwin's soirées.

The fifth member of our expeditionary team was a German leftist, Lothar Menne, who was camping at the time in Ladbroke Grove, together with Angela Davis and a few others including his lady-friend. It was felt that we needed a more mainstream continental representative, so Menne's amorous activities were abruptly terminated and he obtained credentials from the German magazine, *Konkret*, to cover Debray's trial.

It was an odd collection of persons that assembled at Heathrow Airport late one afternoon and boarded a flight for Rio de Janeiro. I had never visited the Americas and, in normal circumstances, my head would have been full of images of what we might or might not see, but tourism was very far from my thoughts on that day. It was the picture of that face under the beret that sustained me throughout the journey. I was sitting next to Schoenman, whose capacity to make conversation on a varied range of topics was legendary. He talked about sex and politics, world revolution, Russell's sudden interest in smutty jokes, the iniquities of British social-democracy and so on. Schoenman described how on one occasion he had spent the entire night outside the hotel suite of Richard Burton and Elizabeth Taylor. Burton, an admirer of Russell, had promised a donation to the Foundation, but, as is often the case with rich people, there was a delay between the promise and the execution. Schoenman had followed the couple halfway round the world, till he decided that an all-night vigil was the only solution. When Ms Taylor came out of the conjugal suite she had caught sight of Schoenman and screamed. In order to get rid of the menace, Burton had finally made good his pledge. This was one of the many scenes in *Who's Afraid of Ralph Schoenman*, one of the longest dramas to be staged by the Peace Foundation at the time.

I asked Schoenman why he had fallen out with Sartre and de Beauvoir. A slanging match between him and de Beauvoir had been witnessed at Stockholm and everyone was intrigued, but few knew the reasons. Schoenman said that the First Couple of the French Left were far too sensitive and some of his political suggestions had been rebuffed. Sartre had said that Schoenman 'always tries to make me feel guilty', while de Beauvoir had commented that Schoenman was 'the only man I know who grows a beard to hide a strong chin'. I never really managed to find out, however, whether it had simply been a clash of personalities or whether the differences were more fundamental.

During intervals in these conversations my thoughts would return invariably to Che. He was born in Argentina, but the wanderlust had gripped him at an early stage. He decided to tour the Andes on an old, clapped-out motorbike when he was still in his teens. He worked in a Chilean mine and as a volunteer in a leper colony in Peru. The condition of the lepers moved him greatly and compelled him to think about the state of medicine in the Third World. He decided to return to the place of his birth and qualify as a doctor. One reason for this decision was his knowledge that as a doctor he could practise anywhere in the Third World. The formality of frontiers in Latin America he had always found irksome. Che became a doctor, but soon realized that unless there was a total social and economic transformation, medicine would remain the preserve of the rich. Thus medicine became a stepping stone on the path to revolution.

When he heard that there had been a change of government in Guatemala and that the new regime of Jacobo Arbenz was planning to nationalize the United Fruit Company, Che decided to go to

Guatemala City. It was here that he met his first wife, Hilda Gadea, a militant from Peru. She told him about the Cuban exiles who belonged to the 26th July Movement and had led a heroic attack on the Moncada Barracks in 1953. She told him about Fidel Castro who was then in prison as a result of the failure of that attack. In Guatemala, Che went to the Ministry of Health and asked for permission to work in a hospital. He was told to join the Communist Party first. He was livid and walked out denouncing the suggestion as corrupt. When the CIA overthrew Arbenz, Che defended the regime, but was shocked at the lack of resistance. He later wrote that 'when the United States intervention occurred, I made attempts to organize a group of young men like myself to confront the United Fruit interests. In Guatemala it was necessary to fight, and yet almost no one fought. It was necessary to resist and almost no one wanted to do it.' To avoid the repression he took refuge in the Argentinean embassy, but was asked to leave after a few weeks. Hilda had been arrested, but released after she had gone on hunger strike. She had then swum across a small river and reached Mexico. After his expulsion from the embassy, Che followed her via the same route into Mexico. There he resumed contact with the Cubans and became a close friend of Raul Castro, who introduced him to his brother, Fidel. The Castro brothers were immersed in plans to launch a guerrilla war in Cuba. Their optimism was inspirational and the Argentinean was enrolled as the official doctor.

In 1956, eighty-two people boarded a decrepit old yacht named *Granma* and after six days at sea landed on a Cuban beach. They were spotted by Batista's air force and bombed. Twenty survivors finally reached the safety of the Sierra Maestra. As the months passed it became clear that the doctor was, despite his asthma, a tireless fighter and a skilful strategist. 'If, as a guerrilla, he had his Achilles heel,' Fidel Castro was to say later, 'it was this excessively aggressive quality, his resolute contempt for danger.' Che soon became a Commandante and led a unit of the guerrilla forces from the Sierra Maestra to central Cuba with the aim of cutting the island in two. In *Reminiscences of the Cuban Revolutionary War* he described, simply but eloquently, the success of this operation.

949 May Day in Lahore; the meeting was dominated by news of revolutionary victories in China.

'56 Chou-en-Lai, China's Prime Minister and Marshal Ho Lung (garlanded) with communist and dical intellectuals in Lahore.

1964 Malcolm X visits the Oxford Union. Richard Kirkwood (see Preface) is standing third from right.

964 With Vanessa Redgrave at an Anti-Apartheid event in Oxford.

1965 Michael Stewart, Labour Foreign Secretary, at the Oxford Teach-In on Vietnam. Stewart defended the US more ably than Henry Cabot Lodge.

1965 With Peggy Duff and Malcolm Caldwell at the Helsinki Peace Conference – all three of us heckled the Algerian representative of the regime that had replaced Ben Bella.

1966 Hanoi during a US bombing raid – manhole shelters were designed to reduce civilian casualties in case of direct hits.

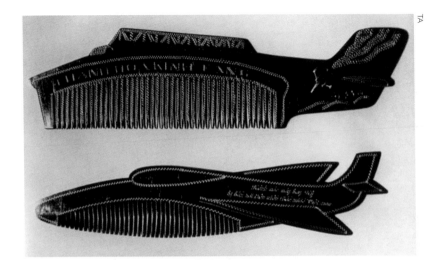

1967 Combs made from downed US warplanes (above) were a much treasured item, unlike the 'ghava' anti-personnel bombs (below) whose principal aim was to maim civilians.

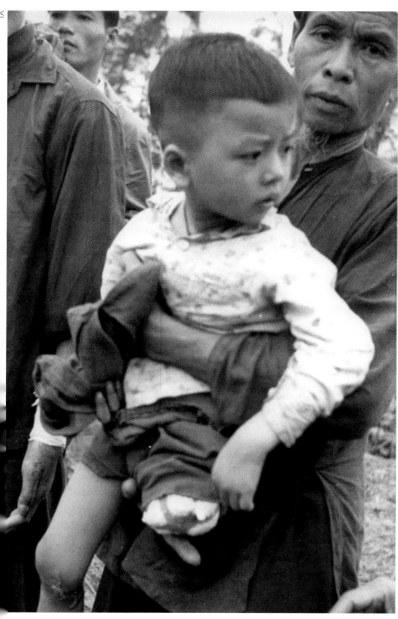

967 One of the many civilian victims of the Vietnam War.

1967 A Vietnamese guerrilla in Thanh Hoa Province.

1967 With Scottish miners' leader Lawrence Daly and Carol Brightman (extreme left) in Halong Bay, Vietnam.

967 War Crimes Tribunal: inspecting damage in the village of Diuh-tanh (in the province of Thanh Hoa).

1967 Palestinian refugees in Jordan after the Six-Day War.

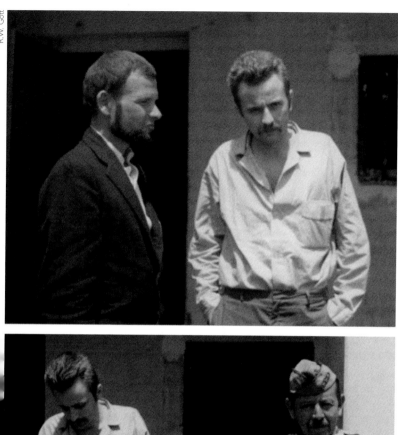

1967 (Above) Régis Debray with Ralph Schoenman outside the prison in Camiri, Bolivia and (below) with his captor, Colonel Reque Teran.

1966 Fidel Castro inspects a disguised Che Guevara's false passport.

1966 Pombo and comrades in the Bolivian jungle.

1967 Portrait of Pombo and identity picture of Tariq Ali in Bolivia (see p.228).

1967 Richard Gott, then Latin American correspondent of the *Guardian*, looks at Che's dead body (pictured below) – his despatch was the first confirmation of Che's execution.

1968 Vietnam demo in London.

1968 With Daniel Cohn-Bendit

968 An unpublished William Rushton cartoon.

1968 May Day in London.

1969 Addressing students in Pakistan.

969 Pakistan, after a three-month-long student–worker insurrection had toppled the military ictator.

1971 John Lennon and Yoko Ono photographed for *The Red Mole* interview, hence the T-shirts.

1971 John Lennon selling *The Red Mole* on a pro-Irish demonstration.

1971 A public rally in Tokyo against the Vietnam War.

1973 London: with Robin Blackburn (on right) protesting the visit to Britain of Portuguese dictator Caetano, who was toppled by a mass insurrection the following year

986 (Above) Robin Blackburn proposing a toast to Ernest Mandel (centre) and 'the World revolution' at a Verso official dinner to mark the publication of Mandel's *The Meaning of the Second World War*. (Right top, from left to right): with Marion Miliband, Perry Anderson and Susan Watkins discussing the Labour Party. (Middle) Tamara Deutscher listens as Mandel is toasted. (Bottom) Colin Robinson and Neil Belton reflect on Verso's future between courses.

1990 New Year's Day walk in north Norfolk: discussing the impending collapse of the Soviet Union with Ralph Miliband – hence the headgear.

1990 Co-writers of *Moscow Gold*: with Howard Brenton during rehearsals, Royal Shakespeare Company, London.

1993 Bandung Days: with Derek Jarman on the set of *Wittgenstein*.

2003 With Edward Said and Stuart Hall at a dinner hosted by Jaqueline Rose.

2003 Demonstrating against the Iraq War with school students including my daughter, Aisha (on my left).

In January 1959, the dictatorship fell and Che became the Commander of the La Cabana fortress in Havana from where he paid tribute to the Cuban peasants and pledged that justice would now be done. He became a Cuban citizen and travelled widely to Asia, Africa and Europe. His passion was concentrated on world politics, but he agreed to take charge of the economy. An apocryphal tale began to circulate in Havana, according to which, at a meeting of the revolutionary High Command, Castro had asked, 'Is anyone here an economist?' Che apparently misheard Fidel. He thought they were being asked whether anyone present was a communist, so he raised his hand and was appointed economic supremo. Despite his lack of experience he at once decided to convert Cuban gold and dollar reserves in Fort Knox into currencies which were immediately exported to Canadian and Swiss banks. It was a farsighted act since there was very little left for the United States to seize when they decided to expropriate all Cuban assets in the United States. A leading American banker, who had to negotiate with the Cubans on behalf of the United States Treasury in those early days after the revolution was surprised at Che's grasp of high finance. He was later to write: 'Guevara knows and understands foreign exchange, balance of payments, etc., and in fact he understands finance and economics, and he knows exactly where the hell he is going ... It was just like talking to another banker, except that the son of a bitch is an orthodox Marxist.'

Yet the attraction of the man lay in his refusal to accept the global status quo. His position in Cuba was unchallengeable. He was, like Fidel Castro, a national hero, though his style was very different to that of Castro, for whom he had great affection and whose leading role in the revolution he never let anyone forget. His personal life was settled. During the civil war he had separated from Hilda Gadea, who was in Mexico with their daughter, and established a relationship with a Cuban fellow-fighter, Aleida March, and they had two children. They say that power always corrupts and this is often the case, but it was not so for Che Guevara. He knew better than most what conditions were like during the first phase of a civil war. But he also knew that socialism on one island would always be a precarious affair. Cuba needed to

break the US blockade and the isolation. Simultaneously the Vietnamese needed help. He had visited Vietnam and realized that it was a
life-and-death struggle for that country. Castro tried very hard to keep
him in Havana, but none of his arguments worked on this occasion.
Che was one of the few leaders of the revolution who could argue and
disagree with Castro quite fiercely and the latter often came round to
his views. This time neither man could convince the other. In the
middle of 1965, Che wrote a private letter to Fidel, which was later
made public. In this he formally renounced all his positions in Cuba:

> I want it to be known that I do this with a mixture of joy and sorrow.
> Here I leave behind the purest of my hopes for building, and the dearest
> of my loved ones, and I leave a people that has accepted me as its son.
> This deeply hurts a part of my spirit. In new fields of battle I will bear
> the faith you instilled in me, the revolutionary spirit of my people, the
> feeling that I am fulfilling the most sacred of duties: to fight against
> imperialism wherever it may be. This comforts me and more than
> compensates for any regrets.
>
> Once again, let me say that I absolve Cuba from any responsibility,
> except for that which stems from the example it has set. If my final hour
> comes under distant skies, my last thoughts will be for this people and
> especially for you ... I have left no material possessions to my wife and
> children, and I do not regret it; I am happy it is this way. I ask nothing
> for them, since the state will provide for their needs and their
> education.

At the same time he wrote letters to his parents in Argentina, his
companion Aleida and his children. These are extremely moving
documents and reading them again, twenty years later, brings the tears
back. Che tried to ease the worry of his parents by confiding that 'My
will, which I have perfected with an artist's care, will now hold up my
shaky legs and exhausted lungs. I will do it ...' To his children he
explained his motives for leaving them and hoped that they would be
proud of him. His political reasons were spelt out in great detail in a
document which was his last political testament. It was a message to the

Tricontinental Conference in Havana and was published in April 1967. The title, 'Create two, three ... many Vietnams', became the battle-cry of delegates from Asia, Africa and Latin America. In his message from 'somewhere in Latin America' Che called for the breaking of the isolation of the Vietnamese. The core of his case was expressed with great passion:

> There is a sad reality: Vietnam – a nation representing the aspirations, the hopes of a whole world of forgotten peoples – is tragically alone. This nation must endure the furious attacks of US technology ... but always alone.
>
> The solidarity of all progressive forces of the world towards the people of Vietnam today is similar to the bitter irony of the plebeians coaxing on the gladiators in the Roman arena. It is not a matter of wishing success to the victim of aggression, but of sharing his fate; one must accompany him to his death or to victory.

Guevara called for a global revolutionary strategy to defeat the United States. He analysed defeats and victories in Latin America, Asia and Africa. He paid tribute to the martyrs who had fallen: Lumumba in the Congo, Father Camillo Torres in Colombia and numerous others in Asia. He predicted that when the black people of Rhodesia and South Africa started their struggle 'a new era will dawn in Africa'. He ended with an appeal that called for taking risks:

> Our every action is a battle cry against imperialism, and a battle hymn for the people's unity against the great enemy of mankind: the United States of America. Wherever death may surprise us, let it be welcome, provided that this, our battle cry, may have reached some receptive ear and another hand may be extended to wield our weapons and other men be ready to intone the funeral dirge with the staccato singing of the machine-guns and new battle cries of war and victory.

The man who wrote these words had abandoned everything, a triumphant revolution, his prestige in the world at large, his parents, the much-loved Aleida and his children, to put his theory into practice. The contrast with the leaders of the West, who calmly sent people to die without stirring themselves, could not have been more pronounced.

We spent a day and a half in Rio waiting for a connection to Lima, since there were no regular flights to the Bolivian capital. Ralph Schoenman and Perry Anderson disappeared for the best part of the day. Both had friends in town and were keen to reestablish direct contact. Robin Blackburn and I spent the day on Copacabana beach, observing the sights and reading newspapers. It was a slightly surreal interlude. I could not enjoy the sea. My mind was fixed on Bolivia. I wondered how long victory would take in the Andes. Cuba had taken four years, but Washington had been unprepared for Fidel Castro. They were now far more alert and I had direct experience of their technological skills from Vietnam. The struggle would never be as easy as in Cuba ever again. One could not afford to be sanguine, but the thought that Che could be defeated did not even enter my head.

We left for Lima the next day, but our flight was late and we missed the only connection to La Paz. The others had American, German, British and Irish passports, which did not require a transit visa to enter Peru. I still had only my Pakistani passport and I don't think that such a document had, at that time, ever been seen in Lima or La Paz. I pleaded with the airport authorities to issue a temporary visa. They declined. There was no Pakistan embassy in the country and so no consular appeal was possible. There was no other flight out of Lima that day. I was a prisoner of the Lima airport immigration authorities. So I parted company with my European comrades and we agreed a meeting place in La Paz. The night was extremely cold and there were no facilities of any sort at the airport. Fortunately there was the equivalent of a change of guard at 2am or thereabouts and the new team was much more friendly. I managed to explain my predicament and was, to my surprise, provided with a bed in the police room. Next morning they gave me breakfast and I caught the first flight to Bolivia.

La Paz, the highest capital city in the world, has an airport which is situated at a staggering altitude of 13,358 feet, more than two and a half miles above sea-level. As the plane was circling the airport, I suddenly became very alarmed. There were no buildings in sight and it felt as though we were going to land in the middle of a moon crater. Everything seemed unreal. The plane did land and, yes, there was a runway. As I stepped out of the plane and breathed in the Altiplano air, which was crisp and thin, I looked anxiously for the airport building. There was none to be seen. Finally we followed the stewardess and the more knowledgeable travellers. There in the distance was a tiny wooden shack. Inside was a makeshift desk, behind which sat the immigration officer. My passport was closely inspected. 'Pakistan? Pakistan?' The man looked genuinely bewildered. I explained that it was a new country near India. They knew where India was and since my visa from the Bolivian embassy in London was genuine, I went through without any problems. Customs, when the luggage finally arrived, was even less of a formality. I shared a taxi to La Paz with some fellow passengers and caught my first glimpse of the bowl-shaped valley that lay below. There at the very bottom was the capital city of Bolivia. On the way I saw the hovels clinging to the side of the mountain in which the Indian population lived. These homes were made of mud, like in large parts of India, but even from a taxi the poverty seemed much worse.

I booked into the Sucre Palace Hotel on the Avenida 16 de Julio. It was a large white building, probably constructed in the forties. The rooms were spacious and clean, but unfortunately there would be none available for the others when they arrived. I bathed, rested and then went for a walk on the streets. This was an Indian city in a country where a majority of the population consisted of Quechua and Aymara Indians. The former claimed descent from the Incas and the latter were the heirs of the pre-Inca inhabitants of this region. The Spaniards had conquered and occupied, but had not been able to either assimilate or destroy the indigenous population. The country was run by the mestizos, who are very proud of their Spanish blood and one of the more racist ruling groups in Latin America. They treated the Indians with contempt. The President of the country, Rene Barrientos, was a General who had toppled the civilian regime. He had been trained at

Randolph Field, Texas, and his cowboy flying style ultimately led to his death. Interestingly enough, however, Barrientos was half-Indian and spoke better Quechua than Spanish. This enabled him to communicate directly with the Indians, but did not lead to any fundamental changes. I wandered round the streets taking in the colours and the smells and testing the street-vendors' cuisine. The quality of a country's food can always be judged by what is being served on the streets. The best food is, more often than not, to be found in cheap eating-houses or cafés rather than the expensive restaurants. I am talking now of most countries of the Third World, though probably the same could be said of some of Mediterranean Europe.

When I got back to the hotel, I was told that someone had arrived to see me. This gave me a jolt as I was not expecting anyone. A man was waiting for me in the corner of the lobby. He did not look like a plainclothes cop so I felt a little less uneasy and went up to him. He introduced himself, but spoke no English. I took out my Spanish phrase book and a painful conversation ensued. After an hour I realized that he had been expecting all our party to arrive that day and that he was one of Schoenman's contacts. Every time I asked who he was and what he did the only response was laughter. Embarrassed by my inability to communicate I gave up. We sat and smiled at each other for another half an hour or so and then he stood up, shook hands and departed, leaving me bewildered.

We had been warned not to carry reading matter which might betray our political proclivities. This meant no Marxist literature, only novels and plays. That night after a lonely supper I retired to bed with Aeschylus' *Prometheus Bound*. A friend had happened to remark that it was the one play that Marx himself read at least once a year. I had always wondered what had attracted him to the Ancients. That night in the Sucre Palace Hotel, I read, reflected, read again and understood. Previously, Greek mythology, which had been a childhood favourite, I had always read as adventure yarns. Mars and Athena had been teenage idols. Now I read of how Zeus had punished Prometheus for stealing fire from heaven and imparting its secrets to the mortals. Prometheus' natural sympathy with the underdogs resulted in his excommunication by the Immortals. Marx must have identified his own situation with that of the deposed Greek god for had he not, too, given the wretched of this world the means to liberate themselves from the new deities of Capital. And that night it also became clear that the myths of Antiquity must have been related to class struggles on earth. The dynastic factional struggles of mythology must have been a reflection of real turbulence in these societies.

The rest of the gang arrived the next afternoon and booked into the much grander Copacabana Hotel a few blocks down on the same street. I went to meet them and there in the foyer I ran into my strange visitor of yesterday, deep in conversation with Ralph Schoenman. He was a trade union militant and from him we obtained an account of what was really happening in the country. We set about making plans for our trip to Camiri, but discovered that we needed a special pass signed by General Ovando, the second highest figure in the oligarchy, before we could be allowed to enter the 'military zone'.

The others had come well armed with the required credentials. Between them, they monopolized the handful of left magazines in Britain. I had come with my membership card of the National Union of Journalists, which did not count. What was to be done? Our Bolivian friend had a suggestion. I went with him to a tiny left-wing printshop in an even tinier backstreet in La Paz. Here I designed some notepaper with some skill, I might add, and the printer dug around for his best quality typeface and paper. Then before my very eyes I saw the sheets with *Town* magazine emblazoned boldly on the top with correct address and telephone number come sliding down the press, which must have been an antique captured during the Chaco Wars against Paraguay. We then went to the offices of a local daily, *El Diario*, borrowed their best typewriter and I typed out my credentials as a 'Special Foreign Correspondent' assigned to Latin America. I then paused to work out whose signature I should forge and decided on Michael Heseltine's. He was, after all, the publisher and deserved this privilege. An intermediary organized by Schoenman then began the process of getting us official permission to travel to Camiri. We had to wait two days.

One evening our Bolivian friend suggested that we go with him to a fiesta organized by various groups in the Indian quarter of the city. We were promised songs, music, dancing and an opportunity to see the district where the bulk of the population lived. This was the highest section of the town and on that cold night we ate at a local café and then went to the hall where the fiesta was in full swing. This was the real Bolivia. I felt both moved and elated by the sight of a largely proletarian and sub-proletarian assembly which was full of confidence and laughter. We joined in the celebrations. Later, in circumstances that I do not fully recall, some speeches were made. I felt the urge to say something to such a unique gathering. On the way to the quarter I had seen anti–Vietnam War graffiti and I thought that I must tell the Indians of what was really happening in Vietnam and how the NLF forces were fighting back. Unable to speak their language, I decided to explain my points in the form of a mime. There was complete silence as I enacted the war in gestures and body movements with the odd explanatory word. By the time I ended the entire hall was chanting, 'Vietnam Si, Yanqui No!' This brought a few policemen to the scene, at which point our Bolivian friends discreetly took us out by another exit and we made our way back to the other city. There was no time for Aeschylus now as we talked late into the night. I realized that my outburst at the fiesta had represented a deplorable breach of security, but interestingly enough none of the others reprimanded me and the Indian faces of that night accompanied me everywhere I went in Bolivia.

The next morning as we were on our way to collect our credentials from General Ovando's office I noticed the Bolivian Army on parade in full gear and with band. We all stood and watched in amazement. The soldiers were dressed in Prussian outfits, which was bizarre enough, but the tune being played by the band was distressingly familiar. It was the 'Horst Wessel Song', a favourite Nazi anthem. There could be no doubt at all. Later when we asked a local journalist about this he acknowledged the fact and told us that one of the Germans who had helped to train the Bolivian Army during the thirties was a Captain Ernst Rohm! What a strange ruling class possessed this unfortunate country, which Queen Victoria once had erased off every map in Britain after her Consul had been stripped naked by the then dictator and forced to ride through the streets on a donkey – a cross between Lady Godiva and Lord Christ.

We finally obtained our papers and rushed back to pack our bags. There was no flight to the tropical zones that day, but Schoenman was insistent that some of us had to get there immediately. No further delay was possible. I volunteered and Schoenman hired a twin-engined Cessna and a pilot to fly the two of us to Camiri. The deal was struck, though the blood-shot eyes of the pilot did not inspire confidence. The journey was sensational. Flying low across the Andes to the tropics we had a unique view of the country. I wondered as we approached our destination where the guerrillas were based and Schoenman and I would often point down and exchange knowing winks. There were no disasters *en route*, not even when the pilot handed me the controls, only taking them back when the plane began to nosedive a bit. We landed on a tiny military airport. Just as we were disembarking, a military helicopter landed and an officer stepped out to be immediately surrounded by soldiers. He stared at our plane, then at us and with a wave of his hand summoned us to his side. We walked towards the helicopter slowly. Colonel Reque Teran asked to see our papers, inspected them closely and asked why we had come to the war zone. We explained that we were there to observe the battle and report back to our respective journals. He appeared somewhat bemused, but gave us a lift to Camiri in his jeep, but this was only after he had posed for several photographs in front of his helicopter. Later he would pose for me with his stretched out arm pointing a revolver at the horizon. The Colonel wanted to become famous.

Arriving in Camiri escorted by Reque Teran meant that no one else asked us any more questions that day. We booked into a hotel and then walked down the main street. Camiri was surrounded on all sides by mountains and only a single dusty trail led to the town. It could easily have been the set for a Hollywood Western. The single-storey houses, rectangular streets and the saloon bars gave this small oil town a very odd character. That night in a restaurant we were told that the last civilian mayor was fond of firing shots into the air when the waiters were slow in serving his meal. So it was not just my imagination which insisted on these images of Dodge City. After dinner, Schoenman and I walked outside the prison where Debray was being held, talking loudly in English in the hope that he would realize that there were friends in town.

The next morning we registered our presence with the local police chief. He stared at me for a long time and then nodded knowingly. He then muttered some insult which neither Ralph nor myself understood, but which had his cohorts roaring with laughter. We stared back silently till he returned our papers and then walked out quickly. Reque Teran was free that morning and agreed to talk for the record. He spoke good English. He had been trained in Georgia and had served as a military attaché at the Bolivian embassy in Washington from 1964–66. He was in command of the Fourth Army Division's anti-guerrilla campaign and he confirmed much of what we already knew, though he was disturbed by the fact that 'there is contact between the miners and the guerrillas. Some of the people we kill are miners.' We questioned him about Debray and the other prisoners. He admitted that Roth was a genuine journalist, but 'Bustos is an agitator from Argentina. He came here to receive some instructions from Guevara. He knows many things about the guerrillas. He knows more than he says . . .' And Debray? 'Monsieur Debray is a well-known communist, an admirer of Guevara, a friend of Castro. I've read Debray's book. It is a good book for guerrillas. I would recommend it to you. Mao Zedong doesn't work here. He wrote for a country with a big population, though some principles can be used here, of course. But, Debray came to help the guerrillas and we caught him. I hope it's death. Not just thirty years. If you have a snake you kill it immediately.'

It was a tremendous strain listening to talk of this sort without being able to reply in kind and since self-control was not a virtue for which Ralph Schoenman was best-known, we decided that it would be best to continue the interview on another occasion. As soon as we were out of the Colonel's earshot, Schoenman exploded and the bile poured out without restraint. That afternoon the remaining three members of our party arrived and we briefed them on the special qualities of this zone.

Our aim was to see Debray in his cell so as to reassure ourselves that he was alive and to make him feel that he was not alone. He had met Robin Blackburn in Havana and it was therefore essential that Blackburn was one of the visitors. I asked Reque Teran whether I could go in and photograph Debray. Surely, I pleaded, it is in your interests to let the world see that he is alive and permitted to receive visitors. The Colonel said that this was too important a matter for him to decide, but he would make the request known to higher authorities. In the meantime he advised us to be patient and invited me to accompany him on one of his missions to Lagunillas the following week. The very thought filled me with nausea, but there was no way out and I agreed with a fake enthusiasm. He promised that he would let me photograph captured guerrillas that day.

Meanwhile, all that we could do was wait till La Paz sanctioned permission for us to see the prisoner of Camiri. The town was full of officers, soldiers and, increasingly, US officers, who refused to speak to us. We must have seemed a pretty odd bunch to the Bolivians. We certainly did not behave as journalists are supposed to in these circumstances. If they had decided to spy on us or place hidden microphones in our hotel rooms, the Bolivians would have received a serious shock. For in private we talked endlessly about world politics, Marxist theory, the fate of the Russian and Chinese Revolutions and similar topics. One of the most heated exchanges took place between Schoenman and Anderson on the practice and nature of Stalinism. Perry Anderson insisted on putting the record of Stalinism in some overall perspective. Both he and Robin Blackburn, who, much to Schoenman's great annoyance, tended to agree with each other on most questions, were sympathetic to the positions of the pro-Moscow CPs in Western Europe. This was, in Anderson's case, moderated by a particular interpretation of Isaac Deutscher's writings on the USSR. Schoenman was, I suppose, a libertarian Trotsko-Marxist slightly infected by anarchism.

My own political formation was in a state of flux, but having recently read Deutscher, I was fascinated by our debates. It is difficult to describe Lothar Menne's orientation at that time. He said very little and tended to become passive when the political temperature rose in our small rooms. He did, alas, chain-smoke, thus breaking the united front against tobacco in our group. At one stage the noise of debate reached such a crescendo that the guests in the neighbouring rooms complained by knocking on our door. We had been discussing the scale of the repression in Stalin's Russia. Schoenman had the facts and statistics at his fingertips, but he also insisted on describing the most gruesome tortures inflicted on political prisoners, who included tens of thousands of veteran Bolsheviks, by the torturers of the NKVD. At the end of his peroration, he stared hard at comrades Anderson and Blackburn as if challenging them to reply. Perry Anderson responded by reprimanding him for reducing everything to 'a moral question'. At this point Schoenman erupted. 'Stalin killed millions including the majority of old Bolsheviks and you say this is a fucking moral question. We're talking about one of the biggest crimes against socialism this century.' Robin Blackburn and myself acted as responsible seconds on that occasion and took our respective pugilists back to their chambers.

I was much more sympathetic to Schoenman during these battles, and the arguments that underlay his freak-outs appealed far more than the icy logic of Perry Anderson. There was one time, however, when both men backed each other up against Blackburn and myself. The argument that night was on the events which led up to the success of the Chinese Revolution. Both Schoenman and Anderson dismissed Maoist pretension and the cult around Mao far too brusquely as far as I was concerned. Anderson then suggested that if there had been no Japanese occupation of China, the Maoists would never have succeeded. I responded by saying first that the argument was somewhat pointless since it could be argued that without the First World War there might not have been a Bolshevik victory in Petrograd in 1917. 'Not so,' said Schoenman, 'because Lenin's party had the correct ideas and understanding and would have won in the end. That cannot be said of Mao. He was a total confusionist.' We defended Mao vigorously, but the discussion ended as all such things do, not because we resolved anything, but because it was time to retire.

There was no food of any sort at the hotel. We used to breakfast on large helpings of fresh fruit juice at the various juice-bars and then sup at a rather good Italian bistro without a name, owned by a Sr Giuseppe. The only other eating place was a pretentious café, which served unrecognizable chunks of meat and charged a fortune. There were, alas, no street-vendors as in La Paz, so our choice was restricted. One night, the owner of the Italian restaurant joined us underneath the big tree where we normally ate. Small talk flowed as freely as the wine. Then we asked why he had left his native Italy and settled in Bolivia. It was a long story. Sr Giuseppe had been a leading fascist in Mussolini's party, had fought hard and well for the Duce, but rather than face arrest afterwards he had fled to Latin America and sought refuge in Bolivia. We became silent. So our jovial host was part of the postwar fascist emigration from Europe. I wonder what crimes he had committed. They must have been fairly horrendous for him to hide in this particular hole. He left our table after this, not realizing the terrible moral dilemma we now had to confront. A discussion followed his exit. Could we carry on eating there? I was in a minority of one. The others decided that Giuseppe's had to be boycotted. I accepted the status of a 'loyal minority' and trailed behind them the next day as we made our way to Café Rubbish. One meal there was sufficient to enable me to reopen the question. The previous day's decision was unanimously reversed. The boycott was over.

Every day after supper we would stroll down the main dust track of the town. As we passed the prison quarters we would whistle the 'Internationale', hoping that Régis would hear and recognize the tune. One morning permission arrived, but only for a photograph and not any interviews. This posed a problem since the local authorities knew that it was *I* who was the photographer. I insisted that I needed someone to carry my camera bag and telephoto lens and, much to my amazement, this was agreed. Robin Blackburn followed me in to Debray's cell as an assistant. Debray recognized him immediately and acknowledged him with a nod. The look of relief on his face had made it all worthwhile. During the time I was photographing him I managed to mutter that more and more people were arriving in this country and there was no way they would kill him. He nodded again and we were then ushered out.

In the square that day I began to photograph every military officer in sight. I did so with a powerful telephoto lens. Unknown to me I was being watched by another Colonel from the Fourth Division. As he walked out of his office I took several photographs of him as well. When I saw him striding towards me, I took the roll out and put it in my pocket. He marched straight up to me and demanded the film. I showed him an empty camera. He pointed to my camera bag. I put my hand in blind, took out an exposed roll from the very bottom and handed it over to him. He grunted, said he would have it developed and if his image was on it he would return to have a word with me. He then took out a revolver, pointed it at my chest and warned me that if I took any more unauthorized photographs of military personnel he would not hesitate to shoot me dead. He was not joking. In fact he appeared to be suffering from rabies, since he was frothing at the mouth. In any case I agreed. The next day Colonel Juan Delgado Molanoz, for that was his name, returned the developed film. As luck would have it, the roll had only contained some scenic views of the Andes photographed from the air.

The next morning I accompanied Colonel Reque Teran on one of his helicopter missions, hoping against hope that I would not have to witness any brutality against the guerrillas. Once or twice the helicopter swooped down at the sign of some movement, but they were false alarms. We landed at Lagunillas, a village where the guerrillas were known to operate. Reque Teran was saluted by the officer in command of the local military post. He was not wearing insignia. I asked him for his estimate of guerrilla strength. 'Those who serve a foreign interest', he replied, 'are called bandits not guerrillas.' It was an interesting distinction, but I could not help replying that if that was so then the Bolivian Army could be characterized in the same way given that some people said they were operating in the American interests. He hurriedly changed the subject and reverted to my original question. He forgot his earlier strictures and used the forbidden word. 'The guerrillas have suffered serious losses, but we can't reveal this as yet.'

Reque Teran interrupted him with an odd aphorism: 'If you want the fly to enter your mouth, you mustn't close it too soon.' Both officers roared with laughter. Then the junior man explained that there were lots of little groups of guerrillas, but no fixed force. He spoke, too, of 'Operation Cynthia', which he described as a mopping-up exercise. He told me that Che was 'somewhere near here, but we cannot tell you the exact location'.

While he had been talking, Reque Teran had wandered away to speak to some local soldiers. I could see them pointing at me from a distance. I did not pay much attention since my appearance – very long hair and a droopy moustache – often excited adverse comment. The day before, a fat, fascist comedienne, who had arrived from Sucre to entertain the troops had shouted: 'You need a haircut, you ...' I had responded in kind: 'You badly need a diet, fat lady ...' There was a great deal of nervousness about the guerrillas and long hair was viewed as an insignia of rebellion. Suddenly Reque Teran sent a messenger to get me. I walked over to him. The two soldiers stared at me. Then the Colonel asked if they could see my watch. I rolled up my sleeve and allowed them to inspect it from every angle. Reque Teran then asked me some trivial questions and I gave equally trivial answers.

Reque Teran was planning to stay there overnight, so I returned to Camiri in a jeep. As the vehicle entered the town, we were stopped. Two soldiers asked me to get out and accompany them to their office. I did so and was taken to a tiny room, without windows. Inside was a chair and a table. They asked me to wait and locked the door, leaving me in total darkness. I don't remember how long I was left there alone, but it was definitely over an hour. As I sat there I tried to work out the possible reasons for my arrest. It was unlikely to be the fake credentials. Perhaps they had discovered that we had been sent by the Russell Foundation, but if so why pick on me alone? To say that I was scared would be an understatement. After a few weeks in the 'war zone' I had no illusions as to the capacity of the Colonels to do whatever they liked. The rabid Colonel had said as much during the fracas in the square.

At last the door opened. Two men walked in, sat opposite me and started asking me questions in Spanish. I repeated several times that I did not speak the language. One of them spoke English and muttered in classic B-movie style that 'we have ways of making you talk Spanish'. I replied calmly that I did not speak Spanish, but if he was suggesting that a few days of torture might lead to my acquiring a new language, then I would be eternally grateful. The sarcasm was not totally wasted and the man informed me that I had been recognized by two soldiers at Lagunillas. These men had been captured and then released by Che's group. I was amazed, and the incredulity must have convinced them to some degree. 'Are you saying', I shouted 'that I am a Cuban guerrilla?' Both men nodded. 'Then why in heaven's name should I travel on a Pakistani passport? Surely it doesn't make sense, does it?' The English speaker actually smiled and I sighed with relief. 'You are not any Cuban guerrilla', the inquisitor continued. 'You are Pombo, Che Guevara's bodyguard.' At that point I wished I had been Pombo somewhere in the jungle. To their faces I simply grinned and told them that if they were foolish enough to charge me on that score they would make a laughing stock of themselves since it would not take me long to prove my identity.

Outside, unbeknown to me, Ralph Schoenman was mobilizing support. A stringer from the New York Times had filed a despatch claiming that another journalist had been arrested and the military were incredibly stupid. The local censor had not permitted the report to be filed, but my release was ordered. I was told to report to the police the next day. When I went back in the morning I was made to walk past all the guerrillas held prisoner, including Bustos. Slowly they all shook their heads in the negative. Later that day we went to see a Captain Reuben Sanchez, who had been captured and released by Che. He had made sketches of the guerrilla fighters. When we went in, he showed me his drawing of Pombo and there was a certain likeness. Sanchez had clearly been impressed by the conduct of his captors, even though they had released him without any clothes and he had been found naked. Even at that time one felt that this officer had been won over by Che. Five years later he fell resisting the Banzer dictatorship. Prior to that he had announced his defection to the ideas of Che Guevara.

Later that night Schoenman insisted that I return to Europe. He was worried that this incident might not be the last and the fact that the military had blundered might provoke some young blade to take individual action. As Debray's trial had been further delayed, I agreed, albeit reluctantly. Schoenman accompanied me to Cochabamba. We spent a day there and in the evening watched *Cat Ballou* in the local flea-pit. It had no subtitles in Spanish, let alone Quechua, even though the audience was largely Indian. The next morning I said farewell to Schoenman and flew back to La Paz. I had to wait a few days before I could get a flight out of the country. The Sucre Palace was booked out, so I stayed at the Copacabana. As I was waiting for the lift, I suddenly saw Richard Gott. We embraced and I told him my tales. He was off to tea with some other journalists, including a man from *The Times* at the British embassy. I was dragged along and the jovial diplomat happily conferred honorary citizenship to me for the occasion. Richard asked about the real situation of the guerrillas. I said that the Colonels were fairly confident that they had Che cornered and repeated Reque Teran, who had told me that 'It is difficult to leave the country when the whole of Bolivia is hunting for Che Guevara.' This was rubbish, however, as Pombo and two other Cubans did escape the dragnet and reached Havana safely many months later. Che had refused to leave the field. We talked into the night and Richard regaled me with the latest crimes of the Labour Government. The next day he left for Camiri. Little did we know that in a few months he would be asked to identify the dead body of Che, whom he had met in Cuba. I also met Régis' mother, Madame Janine Debray, in La Paz and told her that I had seen her son with my own eyes and that he was safe. She had brought an appeal from De Gaulle and the Pope to Barrientos, asking for his release. It was a strange experience for her, a right-wing Gaullist, being compelled to hobnob with the left-wing mafia, who were the only people actively and systematically campaigning for Debray's freedom.

On my last day in La Paz, I witnessed the arrival of the left-wing Italian publisher, Feltrinelli, with a lady-friend. They had been in town for only a few days but had already created a scandal in Rome.

Feltrinelli's companion was photographed with him and the news-papers captioned her as his wife, upon which the real Signora Fel-trinelli had raised a tempest back home. When I went to greet him in the lobby of the hotel Feltrinelli was attired in a large fur coat. He was poring over a large map of Bolivia and had marked the guerrilla zone with red stars. He told me that he had come with money, lots of it, to help buy arms and medicines for Che's fighters. This was said in a loud voice. His bejewelled lady-friend seemed oblivious to the world. Within twenty-four hours both of them had been declared *personae non gratae* and expelled from the country.

Some ten days after my departure, Ralph Schoenman devised a plan to hire a jeep, buy food and medicines and locate Che's camp. He had bribed some officers to discover the region in which the veteran revolutionary was meant to be operating. I have often wondered how I would have responded to such a plan. I have a feeling that one's heart would have overridden reason. This was also Robin Blackburn's secret reaction, but Perry Anderson's intellect was in command. He realized that it was a madcap adventure which might get them all killed. Schoenman was now in a minority of one. He ran after the jeep transporting Messrs Anderson, Blackburn and Menne to the airport, on their way home, waving his fist in anger. He did carry on regardless, almost got himself killed but was finally deported. The Labour Gov-ernment declared him an 'undesirable alien' and prevented him from returning to Britain, presumably on instructions from the State Department.

I reported to the Peace Foundation, gave them dozens of rolls of film, which they certainly used, but which mysteriously disappeared. One set went to the archives in Havana. There is no trace of the others. After a few week's rest, the Foundation pestered me to go on another trip. The Six Day War in the Middle East had resulted in more Palestinian refugees and there was enormous pressure on the Foun-dation to record their experiences. I resisted on the grounds of battle-fatigue. This was regarded as an act of gross insubordination. I capi-tulated. We spent three depressing weeks listening to the tales of woe that fell off the tongue of every Palestinian, young or old, man or woman. Nothing could justify these expulsions and as we toured the West Bank in Jordan, the Palestinian encampments in Syria and spoke to the most articulate representatives of the Palestinian nation in the calm luxury of Beirut, the picture became very clear. Anti-Zionists of Jewish origin had never entertained any illusions about Israel, but I was so hostile to the parasitical monarchs who, backed by the West, ruled large parts of the oil-producing Middle East, that secretly I had even hoped that the Israelis might topple them, if not through a frontal assault, then indirectly. These were crazy illusions. For what that trip revealed was that the Sheikhs, Shahs and Kings were the natural allies of the Zionist regime. The only state that the survivors of the Holocaust could construct contained inbuilt discriminations against the native Arabs and was based on the displacement of the Palestinians. This multiplication of tragedies could only lead to renewed violence and bloodshed. There would be no peace till the Palestinian Arabs found a home.

One question dominated interviews and discussions. 'Why', the anguished Palestinians would ask, 'are they punishing *us*? Their fight is with Europe, which let them die, or with America, which restricted Jewish immigration. Why take their revenge on us? Why?' The situation was chaotic everywhere except the Lebanon, which appeared to be an oasis of sanity and culture in a region traumatized and bitter as a consequence of the recent war. Defeats in the Middle East and uncertainties in Bolivia. What happened in Vietnam now would have a crucial effect on the balance of power in three continents.

I returned to London and discovered that Isaac Deutscher had died of a heart attack at the age of sixty. I had met him at Stockholm, but I hardly knew the man. Yet having read his work only recently I felt an enormous sense of loss. Deutscher had been working on a biography of Lenin, but had only finished the first chapter of the first volume. Its posthumous publication some years later gave one an idea of the intellectual loss that had been inflicted on our generation. For Deutscher would have eschewed both hagiography and blind anti-Marxism. The Vietnam War had forced him to leave the 'watchtower' and resume political activity. One can only imagine how much he would have enjoyed the year that followed his untimely death. Interestingly enough, Deutscher's last published interview was with the *New Left Review* on the recent Arab–Israeli war. Deutscher had not been unsympathetic to the foundation of Israel and had known Ben-Gurion well. In his last testament he was angry, though perceptive. He used an old German saying, '*Man kann sich totsiegen*' ('You can rush yourself victoriously into your own grave'), to warn the Israelis of the trap they had set themselves. Then this son of a rabbi went on to make two important points among many others. First, he insisted that:

> We should not allow even invocations of Auschwitz to blackmail us into supporting the wrong cause. I am speaking as a Marxist of Jewish origin, whose next-of-kin perished in Auschwitz and whose relatives live in Israel . . . It was only with disgust that I could watch on television the scenes from Israel in those days; the displays of the conquerors' pride and brutality; the outbursts of chauvinism; and the wild celebrations of the inglorious triumph, all contrasting sharply with the pictures of Arab suffering and desolation, the treks of Jordanian refugees and the bodies of Egyptian soldiers killed by thirst in the desert. I looked at the medieval figures of the rabbis and khassidim jumping with joy at the Wailing Wall; and I felt how the ghosts of Talmudic obscurantism – and I know these only too well – crowded in on the country, and how the reactionary atmosphere had grown dense and stifling.

These words, in such contrast to the triumphalist rhetoric of the intellectual Jewish mafia of New York (many of them former socialists, but turned by the cold war) were coupled with a warning:

> The war and the 'miracle' of Israel's victory have, in my view, solved none of the problems that confront Israel and the Arab states. They have, on the contrary, aggravated all the old issues and created new, more dangerous ones. They have not increased Israel's security, but rendered it more vulnerable than it had been. I am convinced that the latest, all-too-easy triumph of Israeli arms will be seen one day, in a not

very remote future, to have been a disaster in the first instance for Israel itself.

The rapidly changing pace of world politics during the late sixties made it virtually impossible to reflect on one episode for too long. The despatches from the war zones in Vietnam demanded immediate responses. The Vietnam solidarity campaign and its needs totally dominated my existence for the next year, as these extracts from my diary demonstrate.

15 October 1967

We were immersed in preparations for the first of our Vietnam actions. Groups of VSC supporters throughout the country were out flyposting, booking transport and gathering support in the colleges and universities.

22 October 1967

It was a nice Sunday. No rain and not too cold. We had expected a few thousand people at most, given that none of the established groups such as CND or various front organizations of the Communist Party had supported our call. When I arrived in Trafalgar Square for the rally, I saw a much larger crowd which had virtually filled the Square. A number of us spoke and then, carrying NLF flags and placards proclaiming 'Victory for Vietnam', 'Victory to the NLF', we began the march to Grosvenor Square. The plan had been to picket the American embassy, hand in a petition, chant slogans, sing pro-NLF songs and end the demonstration. The size of the crowd grew as we marched and by the time we approached the embassy there were about 10,000 people behind our banners, predominantly the young and largely students. The police, on their part, were equally surprised at our numbers. Their intelligence, which was usually based on ours, had let them down. We marched right up to the steps of the embassy before a thin blue line emerged to defend the citadel. A few shoves and we were through. We actually reached the doors of the embassy before police reinforcements dragged us back. There were hardly any arrests and very little violence.

We were amazed that we had got so close to the enemy fortress. On the way back we talked about what we would have done if we had managed to occupy the embassy. The most popular view was to open the files and embarrass the Labour Government by publishing the list of MPs and journalists on the payroll or otherwise involved with the more sinister aspects of the embassy. This was a utopian hope, but it was very strong at the time. We also dreamed of using the embassy telex to cable the US embassy in Saigon and inform them that pro-Vietcong forces had seized the premises in Grosvenor Square.

The demonstration was judged to be a major success. Both its size and militancy were a reward for all the hard work of VSC activists and a vindication of our political approach. The professional petition-wallahs, the pathetic politics of pressure through pleading with nota-bles, had not mobilized as big a demonstration as ours. The Vietnam Solidarity Campaign doubled the size of its branches as a result and money began to come in from sympathetic donors, who belonged to virtually every social strata in British society. We received letters from Spanish Civil War veterans, from rank-and-file members of the Communist Party, from trade unionists (including a young Yorkshire miner named Arthur Scargill) and from students' unions. A few Labour MPs, including Frank Allaun and the late Anne Kerr also sent us offers of help. The actors Robert Shaw and Vanessa Redgrave made it known that they would speak for us in public. Edna O'Brien wanted to know when the next march was being planned and Viscountess Dorothy Head wondered whether she could provide more concrete help. Dorothy Head was married to the former Tory Defence Min-ister, Lord Head. She had accompanied her husband to Malaysia where he had been High Commissioner for a period and had been radicalized by the Vietnamese struggle. She loathed the United States. I had first met her when she had attended an Oxford Union debate on the motion that 'American political friendship is the kiss of death'. Her husband and son had opposed the motion, but Lady Head, sitting in the gallery, had applauded the other side very ostentatiously, much to the embarrassment of her son. She had kept in touch with me afterwards and became very attached to the VSC. Her estate in Wiltshire was just next to that of the Marquess of Salisbury. She drove me round it one weekend, pointing to her neighbour's fences and wondering whether she should encourage African guerrillas from Rhodesia to use her place as a launching pad to raid Salisbury's farm. It was a joke, of course, but it could just as easily have been a serious offer. In any event the fact was that the *élan* displayed by VSC had attracted wide-ranging support, which would multiply rapidly over the next six months.

The birth of VSC had also brought us into contact with likeminded groups throughout Western Europe and North America. Many letters and invitations to each other's demonstrations and events were exchanged. The one that appealed to me the most was an event being prepared by the German SDS (Students for a Democratic Society) in Berlin, the capital of the cold war. I agreed to go and speak at the Berlin Congress, which was being prepared for January 1968.

I had decided that it would be nice to end the year with a tenth birthday party for the NLF. The local Vietnamese representatives, comrades Ba, Sao and Linh Qui, agreed to grace the occasion. The cake, I thought, should be in the shape and colours of a NLF flag, together with an inscription which read 'Victory in 1968'. Much to my surprise the local baker, Dunns, refused to accept the order. Three other bakers refused likewise. The diarist at the *Guardian*, a young whippersnapper called Peter Preston, put the story in his column. It worked wonders. I was deluged with offers from various bakers. It was only fitting that the cake be baked by Floris ('By Appointment to ...') and so it was, with all the necessary frills. The party was a modest success. At the stroke of midnight comrade Sao, the senior Vietnamese diplomat, cut the cake and blew the candles. We sang the 'Internationale'.

Chapter Seven

The Year: 1968

Everywhere I hear the sound of marching, charging feet boy
'Cause summer's here and the time is right for fighting in the street boy
so what can a poor boy do, 'cept to sing
For a rock n' roll band, cause in sleepy
London town there's no place for a
Street Fighting Man
they said the time is right for a palace revolution
But where I live the game to play is compromise solution . . .

Mick Jagger, 'Street Fighting Man', Summer 1968

January

The year began like any other. There was nothing to suggest the upheavals that were on their way. In a tiny Paris office overlooking the Seine, a short, stout man in his late fifties with the look of an obstinate bulldog was addressing the Central Committee of the PCI (Parti Communiste Internationaliste). This minuscule organization had less than a hundred members. The name of the man was Pierre Frank. He had been one of Trotsky's secretaries during the Russian leader's first exile on the Turkish island of Prinkipo. Frank had survived the vicissitudes of the thirties. He had been imprisoned in Britain for part of the war as an 'undesirable alien', but had returned to France following Liberation and helped to build a Trotskyist organization. His group had carried out effective solidarity work with the Algerians and had organized the flow of funds, medicines and arms to the FLN (Front Libération National). For these acts of 'treachery' the OAS (Organisation de l'Armée Sécrète) had paid him the supreme tribute of bombing his offices in Paris.

The PCI was small, but its youth supporters, who had been expelled from the Young Communists, had organized themselves into the Jeunesse Communiste Révolutionnaire (JCR) and were recruiting many students because of their support for Che Guevara (vilified and slandered in the official Party paper, *L'Humanité*), and their militant solidarity campaign for Vietnam. The main leaders of the JCR, with the exception of Daniel Bensaid, were also members of the Central Committee of the older and virtually moribund PCI. It was to this gathering that Pierre Frank confided his belief that he 'smelt change in the air' and that France could be engulfed in a massive strike by the end of the year. Pierre Frank's sense of smell had never been in any doubt. Even his factional opponents acknowledged the uncanny way his instincts had a habit of merging with reality. One of the half-serious jokes that circulated among the younger comrades was old Pierre's ability to sense a split before anyone else and change all the office locks in order to prevent his faction being moved out if it transpired that he was in a minority.

When challenged on his latest pronouncement, he defended his olfactory talents by explaining that the five-year-old wage freeze had created tensions in the factories, that the growth of unemployment had shaken the complacency of workers and that the student strike of last November had seen 10,000 people on the streets. This indicated a change in mood and the combination might well prove to be explosive. Gérard Verbizier, who was present on this occasion, later told me that not a single person seated round the table had taken Frank's predictions too seriously.

In Britain we were preparing the next Vietnam demonstration, scheduled for mid-March. Pierre Frank's co-thinkers in Britain, Pat Jordan and Ernie Tate, were insistent that the momentum of last October be maintained and we discussed various details of organization. I agreed to commit myself to a virtually non-stop speaking tour for three weeks which would consist of a lunchtime meeting on a campus, an afternoon gathering at a polytechnic or possibly a school, and a public assembly in the town at night. This was planned for February and they asked me to cancel all other activities. I agreed, but with one proviso. I insisted that *The Black Dwarf* planning meetings were equally important and I would not forego them for any public meeting unless it was a matter of life and death. This compromise was duly signed and sealed.

I was beginning to ask myself whether I should join one of the two far-left groups who were backing VSC – they were grouped behind two journals: *The Week* and *International Socialism* – but decided against it for the moment. The groups which appealed to me were the German and American SDSes and the French JCR. They did not have any equivalent in Britain and, as a result, I decided that a single-issue movement like VSC remained the only answer.

The headquarters of *The Week* group were at 8 Toynbee Street, in the heart of the most deprived section of London's East End. It was here, too, that the organizing work for VSC was concentrated. The premises where *The Black Dwarf* was preparing to be reborn were situated in Clive Goodwin's office-apartment in South Kensington and the journey from Liverpool Street to Gloucester Road soon became a familiar underground route. Clive had inaugurated a concerted drive to make friends, raise money and line up future contributors. He would organize lunches to impress writers, glittering social evenings to intimidate the people of wealth and early evening sessions to plan the launch of the paper. I would, in normal circumstances, be present at all these occasions. Our routine was well established. Clive would report on the paper and what would be in it if, for instance we had been coming out that fortnight, and we would talk around the themes. Then I would report on the level of mobilization for the VSC's marches and distribute leaflets, posters and stickers. On one such occasion Kathleen Tynan asked for a large amount of stickers. She was attending a special lunch which was being hosted by Mrs David Bruce, the wife of the US Ambassador in Britain at their stately residence in Regent's Park. The stickers were provided and during the luncheon, Kathleen excused herself and went round the house pasting the stickers everywhere. They bore the NLF emblem and the words: 'Victory to the NLF. All out on March 17th. March to Grosvenor Square.' Other guests soon began to notice these strange intrusions and the demonstration became a talking point. Kathleen Tynan admitted that she had been responsible and left soon afterwards. The event made the news and Clive was delighted that our little meetings in Cromwell Road were beginning to produce practical results.

At the VSC headquarters we had received an invitation to send a representative to speak at the Vietnam Congress in West Berlin, which was being organized by the German SDS. It was agreed that I should go, speak and establish contact with representatives of VSC-type movements from the rest of Europe. The anti-war movement was growing all over the world. Leading figures in the Democratic Party of the United States were beginning to get extremely worried. While President Johnson and his cabinet continued to escalate the war, a peace candidate from within the party, Senator Eugene McCarthy, had declared himself for a coalition government in Saigon, which included the NLF, something which would have led to the immediate collapse of US strategy in Indochina. Other Senators, Wayne Morse and Fulbright in particular, were beginning to air their misgivings in public. Morse declared that the war was 'an illegal, immoral, wholly unjustifiable military intervention'. Fulbright was more measured but used his authority as Chairman of the powerful Senate Foreign Relations Committee to challenge the official version of what was happening in South Vietnam.

February

West Berlin was the capital of the cold war. A few years ago, a Congress for Vietnam in this city would have been unthinkable. And yet the events of 1967 had changed some attitudes. The overwhelming majority of the population was still extremely pro-American, but a growing section of the student population had broken with the dominant ideology. In 1967 a demonstration had been organized by the West Berlin SDS against the visit of the Shah of Iran, the head of a torturer's regime which relied on a secret police whose chiefs boasted that they were the most effective network of repression since the collapse of the Gestapo. The police had been instructed to clear the streets and on the police radio a message was broadcast saying that 'two policemen had been stabbed by students'. This was a lie and inevitably led to violence. A member of the SDS, Benne Ohnesborg, was beaten badly and fell, semi-conscious, on the street. As he lay there, another policeman came and shot him dead. The Burgomaster of West Berlin, a Herr Albertz, was deeply shocked at the incident and even more upset when he heard of the fake radio message. He made his displeasure public, thus committing political suicide. He was replaced by an insipid Social Democrat, Schütz, but everyone in Berlin knew that the real power in the city lay in the hands of the Senator in charge of the Interior, Neubauer, who the SDS accused of being a 'national-socialist'. He was on the far-right of the German SPD and extremely authoritarian. This much I knew as I arrived in Berlin that February to speak at the Congress.

I went straight to the Republican Club, where I met the Berlin SDS leaders and was briefed on the local situation. The social-democratic administration of Schütz-Neubauer had banned a projected demonstration on the grounds that it threatened the security of the city. The plan was to march to the American sector and demonstrate opposition to the war. In response, Schütz had declared that his police would 'sweep the streets with an iron broom'. Everyone was tense as a crucial decision had to be taken by the SDS high command. Should they defy the ban or not? If they did, there was no question but that it would be a violent and bloody affair. The students were in an angry mood. The scar left by Ohnesborg's murder was still raw and many talked of revenge. For my part, I had not realized that a demonstration had been planned, let alone that it could be banned.

While I was listening to the debate, which was being simultaneously translated for me by Elsa (she was for defying the ban and this meant that she was not inclined to interpret the other side's position with any enthusiasm. They realized this and supplied me with an extra person, who supported their views), the SDS leaders walked in and introduced themselves. There were three of them: Rudi Dutschke, who had left East Berlin and was a student of theology; Gaston Salvatori, a Chilean nephew of Salvador Allende, studying in Berlin; and Karl Dietrich

Wolf from Frankfurt. They took me into a separate room and explained the seriousness of the situation. Unbeknown to me another subterranean argument was taking place. Should they appeal to the courts in West Berlin to override the ban or would such an act be seen as capitulating to the very institutions that needed to be overthrown? I had refused earlier to be drawn in on the discussion about breaking the ban. I had stated that it was a purely tactical decision and could only be taken by the Congress. There was no dispute on that, but what, they asked, would I recommend? I explained gently that I would not say anything since I was ignorant of many things as far as the situation in West Berlin was concerned and I thought that this would also be the position of most of the people coming from outside. As far as a court appeal was concerned, however, I had no such doubts. A sympathetic lawyer should be briefed and a case against the local administration should be put to the judge. They exchanged looks and smiled. Dutschke then said that he agreed with me completely. The others did not say anything.

The next day when the conference opened, it was announced that the decision of the Burgomaster was being appealed against in court. There was hardly a murmur of protest from the audience, which was, to my pleasure and surprise, very large. There were thousands and thousands of students inside and outside the Free University, where we were in session. A further crisis broke out within the city administration. Neubauer had told the Chief of Police: 'It doesn't matter if a few people are killed, a thousand heads must be bloodied.' The Chief of Police refused this instruction and resigned. His deputy, another right-wing Social Democrat, replaced him and declared that he would 'hit them so hard that they would run all the way to Moscow'. These were the methods by which German social-democracy was preparing to defend freedom and democracy.

The emergence of the SDS had marked a turning point in German history. Traditionally, students had been supporters of the right, and the two main political parties of postwar West Germany, both of whose leaderships had been chosen by the United States, were not unhappy that this was the case. The generation born during or soon after the war was, however, very different from that which had preceded them. There had been no thorough purge of fascists after the war. The new enemy was already visible and old enmities had to be transcended. Germany in the fifties had on the surface been acquiescent and passive. Yet the memory of the war could not be erased so easily for any of the generations that co-existed in the Bundesrepublik. The students on the campuses in the sixties were very aware of the failure of their parents' generation to resist the rise of fascism. The fact that Hitler had come to power, wiped out all vestiges of democracy and destroyed the two largest working-class parties in Europe had left a political and psychological imprint on the children of the fifties. Even when silence reigned supreme, they knew something was deeply wrong. The war in Vietnam became a catalyst. 'We are an *active minority*', the SDS used to chant at meetings and demonstrations. In this way they shouted their defiance of the past which was present in every family. Better an active minority than a passive majority blind to the crimes being committed every day. That was the message of the German SDS which, in the years that followed, would be taken by some of its supporters in desperate and self-defeating directions. The 'active minority' theses were ultimately interpreted to justify 'urban guerrilla warfare' in German cities with tragic consequences.

I spoke on the second day of the Congress about the war and solidarity. The NLF had launched a new military onslaught in South Vietnam to mark the Vietnamese New Year (Tet). The Tet offensive had begun even while we were preparing to open the Congress. Every fresh victory was reported to the Congress amidst louder and louder applause. The Vietnamese were demonstrating in the most concrete fashion imaginable that it was possible to fight and win. This fact was critical in shaping the consciousness of our generation. We believed that change was not only necessary, but possible. Thus the theme of international solidarity seemed more vital than ever before and I attacked strongly the Glassboro Summit in the United States where Kosygin and Johnson had toasted each other, while Vietnam was being devastated by US bombers. This was, I said, an obscenity. Most speeches were applauded and interrupted with chants of 'Ho, Ho, Ho

Chi Minh', a slogan which crossed every frontier in Western Europe that year.

I was sitting next to the Belgian Marxist, Ernest Mandel, on the podium and he was interpreting other speeches for me. I had not met him before or read his two-volume classic, *Marxist Economic Theory*, which had not yet been published in English. (It was to appear later that year under the imprint of the valiant Merlin Press.) But Mandel's facility with languages was truly amazing. Then he spoke himself, putting the war in a global perspective and assuring the assembly that the United States would be defeated, if not in 1968, then in a few years time and 'it will be a far bigger defeat than Dienbienphu'. He spoke, too, of the changing mood all over Europe and defended the SDS against its slanderers and detractors in the SPD. He spoke in fluent German and his audience responded warmly. He was followed by Alain Krivine from the JCR in France, who described the growth of the student movement and the rise of a movement of solidarity with Vietnam. Then Dutschke stood up and made a powerful speech linking the struggle against the United States in Vietnam with the battles against the bourgeois order in Europe. He talked of extending the base of the student movement by the 'long march through the institutions', a phrase that was much used and discussed by the SDS. Dutschke's theory was derived largely from Herbert Marcuse, the veteran philosopher from the pre-war Frankfurt School, who exercised a big influence among German students. The long march did not mean 'boring from within' but gaining experience on every front: education, computers, mass media, the organization of production, while simul- taneously preserving one's own political consciousness. The aim of the 'long march' was to build counter-institutions. Liberated zones in bourgeois society, which would be the equivalent of the areas freed by Mao's partisans in China during the long civil war and run by the Chinese communists. The university was decisive in such a process as it was here that an alternative cadre could be trained and prepared to replace the cadres of the governing class. It was a utopian project and Mandel and others pointed out gently that change in Western Europe was impossible without the mobilization of the working class. This was certainly true and in the West Germany of February 1968 it appeared as unrealizable as it would have in Britain, though not as inconceivable as it must have seemed in the United States.

One of the high points of the Congress came when two black Americans, both of them Vietnam veterans, mounted the platform. Even before they spoke they were given a standing ovation. Then they briefly described the war and how blacks were being used as cannon fodder. They told us that black America was on the verge of great disturbances and both of them linked arms and began a chant which we had not heard before, though it was common in the United States:

> I ain't gonna go to Vietnam
> Because Vietnam is where I am
> Hell no! I ain't gonna go!
> Hell no! I ain't gonna go!

The cheering lasted for several minutes as the veterans gave the clenched fist salute.

Everyone was by now waiting for the court's ruling on the demonstration. I have little doubt that the judge had received reports of the mood and the size of the Congress. The Austro-German poet Erich Fried was speaking, when he was interrupted by the chair. The court had permitted us to march provided that we did not approach US soldiers or barracks in the city. It was a victory and greeted as such, but then Rudi Dutschke demanded the floor and stormed to the podium. He was delighted with the result, but wanted to defy the restriction. It was intolerable that we should not try and speak to American soldiers. His voice rose: 'But comrades, it is just that that we must do. If the enemy fixes the rules of the game and we accept them it means, as Herbert Marcuse has often told us, that we play by *their* rules.' Once again the Congress was divided. Then Fried, himself a veteran anti-Nazi who had been forced to flee Austria and seek asylum in London, sent Dutschke a written message: 'Our victory lies in the fact that we got the demo. No provocations, please! I have spoken and saved my soul!' Dutschke stopped and read the message to himself. He paused and then informed everyone of its contents and admitted that his own response had been wrong. Everyone heaved a sigh of relief.

We marched that afternoon. It was a sight that had not been seen in Berlin for over three decades. Fifteen thousand, predominantly young, people, a sea of red flags and gigantic portraits of Rosa Luxemburg and Karl Liebknecht, who had been brutally murdered in the same town in 1919 on the orders of the political forebears of Schutz and Neubauer. There were also large posters of Ho Chi Minh and Che Guevara, whose image dominated that march. We walked and ran down the Kurfurstendam, ending with a massive rally, where some of us were asked to speak again. We had raised our banners in the very heart of American-dominated Europe. The Berliners had been told by the Springer press that there would be violence and blood, that Dutschke was the 'Public Enemy No. 1' and that the citizens should be prepared to defend Berlin. In the event the march remained peaceful.

Of all the slogans chanted that day, the one which appeared closest to reality was 'Victory to the NLF'. As for the least probable one, there was a choice, but 'All Power to the Soviets' seemed the remotest of possibilities in Berlin, where Neubauer still commanded support. (Years later he was found guilty of large-scale corruption and involvement in crime and lost his position, but he remained unrepentant and defended his authoritarian rule in the city.) We celebrated the success of the demonstration and I invited the SDS leaders to send a contingent to our demonstration next month in London. They agreed, as did Alain Krivine. One felt that the unity of the European left against the war was important in order to isolate the United States.

A week later the Berlin City Senate organized a counter-demonstration to show its support for freedom and democracy. All employees of the city were ordered to attend and were promised overtime payments for doing so. The hysteria whipped up by the local press was such that anyone who was young and not dressed 'properly' was regarded as a menace to Western civilization. A young English woman, who had been staying in Berlin as the guest of *Observer* correspondent Neal Ascherson, went to observe the 'silent majority'. She was sighted, denounced as a 'student whore' and was beaten up and trampled on. A Protestant pastor and a right-wing lawyer who went to help her were both abused and physically assaulted by the fanatics, who were desperate for a fight with the students. In the latter's absence they found alternative objects on which to release their frustrations and pent-up anger.

The Berlin Vietnam Congress was an important turning point for the Vietnam movement in Europe. It was the first real gathering of the clans and it reinforced our internationalism as well as the desire for a world without frontiers. The whole experience had been deeply exhilarating. There had also been a strong symbolic side to the Congress. We had collectively raised one big fist and pushed it through the ideological barriers of the post-1948 cold war, which had begun in Berlin. The gang in power on the other side of the Berlin Wall were just as perturbed as the right-wing Social Democrats. It was all getting out of control. The playwright Peter Weiss had been in East Berlin, working on a play with the Berliner Ensemble. He was needed at our Congress and the demonstration. His cautious and worried hosts warned him against getting involved with Dutschke's barbarians. They, too, read the West Berlin press and were influenced by its propaganda, when it suited their purposes. The SDS despatched Ulrike Meinhof across the Wall to 'rescue Weiss' and bring him back to us, a mission which she accomplished. She was sent because she was one of the few supporters of the SDS who was a member of the clandestine and ultra-orthodox West German Communist Party. She was a columnist for the left-wing magazine *Konkret* and was married to its editor, Klaus-Rainer Roehl. I had met her one evening at the Republican Club and had been very impressed by her intensity and intelligence. She had talked about the NLF's recent triumphs in Vietnam with an irrepressible joy. I thought of her often in later years as she embarked on a different political trajectory.

March

In order to succeed, a movement has to have some successes. The anti-war battalions of Europe and North America had received a tremendous fillip from the Tet offensive in Vietnam. This was a time when it really seemed as if our actions in the West were co-ordinated with what was happening on the actual battlefields in Vietnam. 'The movement against the war in the United States and Europe', the Vietnamese leaders were fond of saying at the time, 'is our Second Front and just as valuable as our struggle here.' The Tet offensive was never designed to win an outright victory. Its purpose was to puncture completely the myth that the American-backed regimes had any real indigenous support and simultaneously to demonstrate that there was no way, short of nuclear annihilation, that the United States could win the war. The three-pronged assault of the NLF armies had already, in early March, resulted in large-scale mutinies by the conscripted soldiers of the puppet forces, cut off the strategic highway No. 4 which linked Saigon to the Mekong Delta, and laid siege to the US fortress of Khe Sanh, where from 20 February to 8 March the Americans had lost 2000 soldiers and 200 planes and helicopters, most of which had been destroyed on the ground. The US General in command of the expeditionary forces, which numbered over half a million soldiers and technicians at this time, called for more troops to be sent to Indochina. A more astute General De Gaulle replied from Paris with the observation that in the kind of war being waged in Vietnam, the more powerful a country was and the more horrendous the means of destruction at its disposal, the less chance it had of winning. He demanded that the Americans withdraw their forces. He was backed by Robert Kennedy, who denounced Westmoreland's objectives as 'immoral' and 'intolerable'.

What was really immoral and intolerable for liberal America, however, was the fact that this war could not be won rapidly. If the United States had succeeded in establishing a South Korean-style regime, buttressed by a permanent US presence, many of those who came out against the war would have been silenced into acquiescence. That was the real meaning of the Tet offensive. It convinced at least half of America that the war could not be won. In two important interviews at the time, the legendary Vietnamese strategist, Vo Nguyen Giap, left no doubt that he was planning a total victory. He was not opposed to talks in Paris, but talks were for diplomats and he was a General in command of a winning army. Asked by a visiting American woman journalist whether he was planning to inflict a Dienbienphu on the United States one of these days, Giap replied:

Dienbienphu, madam? Dienbienphu! History doesn't always repeat itself. But this time it will. We won a military victory over the French, and we'll win it over the Americans, too. Yes, madame, their Dienbienphu is still to come. And it will come. The Americans will lose the war on the day when their military might is at its maximum and the great machine they've put together can't move any more. That is, we'll beat them at the moment when they have the most men, the most arms and the greatest hope of winning. Because all that money and strength will be a stone around their neck. It's inevitable.

It was this amazing confidence that infected a whole layer of young people in every country in the world, including Europe. I saw this with my own eyes all over Britain as I toured the country to mobilize support for the March 17th demonstration. The meetings had suddenly got larger. They had doubled and trebled in size and the mood was one of triumph and defiance. The Tet offensive had shown the vulnerability of US power and the contrast with the shameful capitulations of the Labour Government was so sharp that there was a wave of disillusionment. I recall how the audiences at those meetings expressed their anger at the failures of Labourism. Of course there was always the sectarian from the Socialist Labour League (SLL), who had been instructed to attack the VSC, myself and the entire movement. The speech he (and it was always a him) made at my meetings was predictable and dreary. I got to know that sectarian refrain so well that at some meetings when the man from the SLL stood up I used to sit back and mouth the words with him, much to the amusement of those present. This would send the SLLer into paroxysms of rage and abuse would fall on my head like drops of polluted rain. The charge against us was always the same. We were guilty of having entertained any illusions about Wilson in the first place. The fault therefore lay in our own defective systems of thought rather than in the blotted copybook of the Labour Government. It followed that we were victims of self-deception and the only possible mechanism to salvage our lost souls lay in joining the SLL and preparing a general strike to overthrow the Labour regime. At this stage laughter used to erupt, leading the SLL man to launch a big attack on the VSC and urge students not to go on its 'adventurist' demonstrations. The logic here was interesting. A march to Grosvenor Square was a crazy 'adventure', whereas sober realism dictated an immediate general strike by the British working class to topple Wilson and pave the way for an insurrection. Such incantations were lost at VSC meetings, but it did give one the opportunity from the platform of studying the faces, gestures and the well-rehearsed displays of mock anger that emanated from these people. Of course it was a sectarian mask, but what really lay underneath?

The SLL said it was a Trotskyist party and it undoubtedly paraded under that flag, but its political style and internal regime at the time of our encounter was totalitarian. No internal dissent was tolerated, the main enemies lay within other groups on the left and there was a surreal personality cult around the 'leader' of the sect. The model on which they based their style of polemic and organization seemed to be derived from Stalinism. They had recruited some of the post-1956 layer of dissident CP intellectuals like Cliff Slaughter and Peter Fryer. How could these two, amongst others, have simply exchanged one form of monolithism for another? They were intelligent people, aware of what was taking place inside their organization. Fryer had left after a period, but most of the others stayed for a long time. They were, of course, privileged in some ways, since they were on the leading bodies of the sect, but what of the members and who were the members? What sort of person joined such an organization? Did they really believe that in so doing they were accepting the 'discipline of the proletariat'?

Some years later, after I had travelled a great deal to other parts of Europe and Asia, the full answer to these questions began to emerge. It seemed that the particular ideology espoused by such a group was not the most important feature of its daily life. The SLL claimed Trotsky as its patron saint. In Norway, Sweden and Germany there were groups with exactly the same behaviour patterns and an identical form of organization. But in these countries they wore Mao badges and sold the collected works of J.V. Stalin. In Japan a similar group based itself on a post-Trotskyism derived from the works of an American woman, Raya Dunayeskaya. After I had observed members of all these organizations in action at different times and in different worlds, it was difficult to accept that politics was in command. For all their ideological differences, the sort of members they attracted were people who were heavily imbued with a sense of masochism and/or guilt, who saw in such groups a way of exorcizing other ghosts. A self-isolation and sectarianism became part of their pseudo-political therapy. The tough and authoritarian Central Committee either replaced other authority-figures or provided for the lack of one. It worked both ways. The treatment did not and could not work for ever. A large proportion of ordinary recruits left after a limited stay. The turnover was high in all these organizations. Another characteristic was that many of those who left were cured of politics for life, burnt-out shells who were a shadow of their past selves. Politics of this sort had alienated me from the SLL at Oxford. One of the members at that time had been barred from living with his female companion because she was not a member of 'the party'. I often used to wonder what a state would be like if it were run by this crowd and the images that arose in response were those of Stalinist Russia.

Nonetheless, I could not evade all political responsibilities. It was becoming clear that a sizeable proportion of those who came to hear me speak wanted answers that went beyond Vietnam. They accepted that a campaign which concentrated on one issue of global importance was vital, but not sufficient. There were other questions being posed and they demanded responses. I was constantly being approached by people at the conclusion of a meeting and asked my advice on what form of political activity I could recommend to them. We had all, by now, left the Labour Party. What was the alternative? The 'deep-entryism' of Militant was deeply unappetizing. Moreover, their hostility to VSC and certain organizational similarities to the SLL were extremely unattractive. My own attitude was that if one had to work in the Labour Party, the only effective method was to do so in conjunction with all other socialists who were in there. To create a sectarian divide within a social-democratic party seemed to me to be crazy, but then I must confess that I was still new to the politics of the left in Britain. The model of *The Week* appeared to be the most productive if one was to continue in the Labour Party. But the youth who were now embracing a new form of radicalism were not the least bit interested in the Labour Party. This fact limited the political choices available at the time. I discussed the problem on more than one occasion with Pat Jordan, but we were all so immersed in the Vietnam movement that everything else took second place.

I had returned from a nationwide speaking tour and reported to the Committee that the size of the demonstrations would be at least twice as big as that of last October and probably even larger. We agreed a list of speakers for Trafalgar Square and it was suggested that two of these (Vanessa Redgrave and myself) should hand in a letter to the American embassy. That was decreed to be the official objective of the march, but what were to be our unofficial aims? These were not discussed at the larger meetings, since we had little doubt that informers were present and active. But amongst a smaller group we spent a very long time discussing what was possible. I presented an analysis of the previous demonstration. If we had been prepared we could have occupied the embassy, which would have had a tremendous propaganda value. However, we had been taken by surprise by the militancy and the extent of our own support. This time the militancy would be greater as a result of the NLF successes in Vietnam and so would our size. A serious attempt should therefore be made to occupy the embassy. There was virtually no disagreement as to the desirability of such an outcome. Then Pat Jordan spoke and said that it would be extremely foolish to imagine that the state would be unprepared. 'We were taken by surprise last October. True. But so were *they*. This time they have been able to witness all our pre-activities.' He was convinced that every single one of my speeches on the recent tour had been noted and

studied by Special Branch. I protested. I had not discussed any street-
fighting tactics at any of the meetings. 'That's not the point', Jordan
responded. 'It's your tone that matters. They're not fools.' Someone
else asked me if I was prepared during the course of my speech in
Trafalgar Square to state loudly that the object of the demo was to
storm the embassy. I nodded in the affirmative. There was silence.
Then the plan was vetoed. I could be charged with incitement or
conspiracy and either locked up for a few years or, given that I had
only been resident in Britain for four and a half years, they could
deport me out of the country. It was decided to make the decision
at the last possible moment when we had been able to assess the
balance of forces on the ground. Everyone knew that this was an
unsatisfactory 'neither fish nor fowl' variant, but the majority of the
twelve people present had been insistent that there was no other
realistic possibility.

Three days before the action, we interrupted twenty theatre per-
formances in London. VSC activists climbed on to the stage, usually,
though not always, at the end of a scene and told audiences about our
movement. There was a great deal of sympathy from both those on
stage and in the audience and we left after distributing leaflets. The one
place where the audience had been extremely hostile was the *Black and
White Minstrel Show*, but here the situation was saved by the 'minstrels'
who turned out to be sympathetic and insisted the audience give us a
hearing. There were other less pleasing aspects, which smelt of *agents
provocateurs*. Someone had been going round London and super-
imposing the following two words on the VSC posters: 'Come
Armed'. We felt that this was the act of some arm of the state, which
was trying to isolate and weaken our support, but in the absence of any
proof, all we could do was to deny that this was anything to do with
the VSC or the groups that were supporting the demonstration. *The
Economist*, edited at the time by Alastair 'Bomber' Burnett, was a
staunch and uncritical defender of US activities in Vietnam. As such it
was especially hostile to the American anti-war movement. It had no
doubt as to the identity of the sinister elements who had defaced our
posters: 'The American group who *probably* [my italics] overprinted the

organizer's stickers with the stamp "Come Armed" should be caught hold of and deported: British and Commonwealth militants are on the whole both less violent and less efficient.'

On the day before, the German SDS contingent arrived, or rather marched in to Conway Hall, where we in the middle of preparing last-minute plans, with their familiar chant of 'Ho, Ho, Ho Chi Minh'. They were warmly welcomed and joined in the proceedings. They had come well prepared with helmets and their own banner. They had also brought me an SDS helmet as a gift. They insisted on hearing our battle-plans. We said there were none. They expressed anger and shock. Were we not planning to occupy the embassy? I was chairing the meeting and spelt out our official position, but the SDS came straight to the point: 'We understand what you say, but we now ask you another question. If the masses spontaneously decide to storm the American embassy will you stop them or join in?' Feeling that this questioning was getting too close for comfort I declared the meeting closed, came down from the platform and dragged the leaders of the SDS contingent to another room. Here I explained what the position of VSC was and why we could not publicly call for an occupation. They argued long and hard. I was sympathetic to what they said, but I insisted strongly that the view of the majority had to be upheld. I reminded them that in Berlin last month they had accepted a court order restricting their own objectives. I pointed out that those of us attending the Congress had decided to accept *their* right to determine tactics in a situation which they had known better than visitors such as ourselves. I pleaded some reciprocity and goodwill. This argument finally won the evening and we adjourned to an Italian restaurant for badly-needed refreshments.

Earlier that afternoon I had been summoned by the Redgrave clan to a family conclave at Vanessa Redgrave's house in Hammersmith. Here I was asked by Corin in the presence of Vanessa and Lynn as to what our intentions were regarding the demonstration. It was a bit like a father questioning a future son-in-law as to his prospects, but it was a friendly occasion and I assured them that whatever might or might not happen we would ensure that Vanessa was well protected. I then told them about various other people who would be speaking or marching with us that day. A few more pleasantries were exchanged and I then returned to the VSC headquarters. By the end of the day I was exhausted, but the arrival of the SDS from Germany had revived me. Several of them were sleeping on the floor of my tiny flat in Crouch End. We stayed up talking until the early hours. Their news was disturbing. The hysteria against them and, in particular, Dutschke, had escalated since the Berlin Congress and this had led to the emergence of an ultra hard-core within the SDS who wanted more effective direct action. Dutschke was resisting this trend, as were others, but the hardliners were gaining support.

When a number of us arrived at Trafalgar Square the next day, an hour and a half before proceedings were due to start, we were amazed by the sight that greeted us. The square was already full and the NLF tricolour dominated the large crowd. More and more people began to arrive and the stewards who were counting the numbers reported just as the speeches began that there were over 25,000 people present already. Vanessa Redgrave had brought greetings from other actors, actresses and film directors. The speeches were short and to the point and every speaker attacked the complicity of the Labour Government. Two days previously a number of left MPs had written to *The Times*, expressing their support for Harold Wilson. They, too, were verbally savaged and the response of the crowd indicated a contempt for these clapped-out supporters of *Tribune*.

As we led the march towards Oxford Street, the main VSC contingent was in the lead with a marvellous display of red flags and banners, flanked with gigantic NLF emblems. Just behind us were the German SDS with their banner. It was an impressive sight and the mood was one of optimism. If the conversations of those who came that day had been recorded, I am sure that the overwhelming majority wanted more than just a victory in Vietnam. We wanted a new world without wars, oppression and class exploitation, based on comradeship and internationalism. The wealth of the First World, if properly utilised, could help transform the Third World. Moreover, if a meaningful socialism was successful in the West, it would not just be the

City of London and its state that would tremble, but also the bureaucrats in Moscow, who were equally scared of change from below. We were aware that a new spring had arrived in Prague and that many exciting discussions were taking place at Charles University and in the Czech Communist Party. But it was not just talk. It was also a feeling that change was possible. That was what Vietnam had taught all of us.

We filled Oxford Street, then turned into South Audley Street and marched into the square. The police tried to hold us back, but we were many and they were few and their first lines crumbled, permitting us to enter Grosvenor Square and occupy the area directly in front of the embassy. They were not going to let us deliver a letter and so we asked stewards to escort Vanessa Redgrave to safety. Then we saw the police horses. A cry went up that 'The cossacks are coming', and an invisible tension united everyone. Arms were linked across the square as the mounted police charged through us to try and break our formation. A hippy who tried to offer a mounted policeman a bunch of flowers was truncheoned to the ground. Marbles were thrown at the horses and a few policeman fell to the ground, but none were surrounded and beaten up. The fighting continued for almost two hours. An attempt to arrest me was prevented by a few hundred people coming to my rescue and surrounding me so that no policeman could get very near. We got close to the imperialist fortress, but by 7pm we decided to evacuate the square. Many comrades were badly hurt and one pregnant woman had been beaten up severely.

Our phones kept ringing till late in the night as we collated more and more information. It was undoubtedly a violent confrontation. Alain Krivine had been amazed at our militancy, which he said was somewhat lacking in France. On the other hand, the German SDSers were displeased. They felt we should have prepared our supporters, provided them with helmets and battled it out with staves. We explained that one of our aims was to win support and we were not as isolated from public opinion on Vietnam as were the Berlin SDS. Our different tactics reflected this. In fact, one of the opinion polls carried out after the Grosvenor Square demonstration revealed that a majority were opposed to US policies in Vietnam, and, to our great delight, nearly 20 per cent wanted a Vietnamese victory.

There had been a number of trade union banners on the march. Those who had led the attack had been a group of striking building workers from the Barbican. Their shop steward, the late Frank Campbell, was a staunch supporter of VSC and his tiny contingent had been invaluable on the frontline that day. Few of those who had marched with us thought that we had behaved incorrectly. One of them, Mick Jagger, would a few months later write 'Street Fighting Man', indicating, if anything, his disappointment at our lack of battle-readiness. During the fighting in Grosvenor Square I had caught sight of the comrades from the *New Left Review* and had seen Perry Anderson, wiping his spectacles and remarking loudly to one of the others, '*This* is our constituency, man!' I warmed to him much more on hearing that than I had on our Bolivian journey.

The coverage on the television news gave me an idea of what to expect from Fleet Street the next morning. The cameras had, at least, recorded and shown some fairly grisly incidents of police isolating and beating up demonstrators. The press was, in general, one-sided, with the tabloids devoting much space to the plight of the poor horses. Over the next few days I was singled out as *the* instigator of the entire demonstration. Tory MPs and the Tory press demanded that heads should roll and they accorded a privileged place to my head in parti-cular. The *Evening News* reported three days after the demonstration that the Director of Public Prosecutions had ordered an investigation into my 'activities' and that 'Today a detective superintendent was detailed to conduct an inquiry. A record of Tariq Ali's past speeches and pronouncements was being studied by a team of Special Branch men. But among the Yard experts the feeling is that it will be difficult to bring a case of sufficiently incontestable evidence to make a pros-ecution possible.' On reading this I thought of our meeting where Pat Jordan had warned against any public call for occupying the embassy. How right he had been.

The fact that Special Branch had a record of my speeches interested me a great deal. I wasn't particularly surprised, but it was nice to know that my speeches were being preserved for posterity, especially as I never write a speech. It would have been useful to have the right to see this record for the purposes of this book, but, alas, given that there is no Freedom of Information Act in Britain, that, and a great deal else, remains inaccessible.

At a *Black Dwarf* gathering at Cromwell Road the next day it was gratifying to discover that everyone involved with the paper had been in Grosvenor Square. David Mercer was outraged at the press reports and had crafted a letter to *The Times*, which that august organ of ruling-class opinion, as it then was, had decided not to publish. In his unpublished missive, the playwright had lambasted the press for its posturing and hypocrisy and had attacked Labour and Tory MPs for their motion in Parliament recording their respect and admiration for 'the conscientious and commendable restraint of the police'. Mercer had argued our case with great eloquence and passion:

> With quite extraordinary obtuseness you recommend demonstrators once more to those constitutional procedures which they know perfectly well will have no results. According to the democratic formula then, they can placate their consciences by jogging along with their futile charade – or retiring with honour before the will of the majority, as expressed by the present elected government. You admit that 'the adaptation of constitutional procedures has not fully kept pace with recent changes in social conditions and customary assumptions' but show little sign of recognizing how fundamental the discrepancy is, or how inevitably social conflict will break the impasse maintained by frightened authorities and moribund institutions to preserve a rotten society intact for its unwilling inheritors.
>
> In addition, three-fifths of the world and its people are in a pitifully worse condition. Everywhere – from Venezuela to Mozambique, from Rhodesia to Vietnam – there is a people's struggle to liberate themselves from humiliation, despair and degradation. It would be cynical indeed for us to expect them to look upon our social systems in the West as paradigms of social justice. They want land, resources and social and economic control in their own hands and are prepared to fight for

these objectives. Like American Negroes, they have made the discovery that no one will implement revolutionary social change on their behalf, but themselves. Experience has taught them that negotiation and compromise lead at best to pseudo-democracies wretchedly tied to the economic and political systems of exploiting countries; at worst to a brutal and oligarchical despotism which opposes power derived from Western approval and capital to the needs of poor people in a desperate search for dignity and national identity.

... The truth of the matter is that capitalism is now more seriously embattled than at any time since the thirties. And the police who cordoned off the American Embassy on Sunday faced not exhausted men from Jarrow, nor orthodox Communist militants in a re-enact- ment of Cable Street, but an educated and informed spectrum of opinion which will tolerate dissimulation no longer.

The violence on Sunday was not some kind of discreditable lapse from decent standards of public expression in a democratic society – it was the dramatic outcome of profound and irreconcilable differences cutting across young and old, Right and Left, or any other convenient antithesis to which a threatened order still clings. So long as it takes place in Vietnam or elsewhere, most people are not unduly disturbed, except to click their tongues at the horror of it all. When it happens in Grosvenor Square, there is a sense of public outrage – and columns of self-righteous drivel in the newspapers. The unreality of the response is amazing. Carrots are handed in to the police for those poor horses. Under a photograph of a young woman with her thighs exposed being manhandled by the police, there is a caption remarkable for its gloating Victorian ambiguously erotic term of 'spanking'. Our media of mass communication avidly dig their jaws into the entrails of dissent, and come up smug and self-satisfied as usual. After all, the morality of violence is clear: it's wrong, committed by whoever and anywhere at any time – except against demonstrators. Entrenched 'authority' looks everywhere to place the blame for public disorder except within its own tangled and complex responsibilities.

If policemen persist in physically defending (after all they are paid and demonstrators are not) a society whose assumptions and values are rapidly becoming meaningless to anyone who can think – then their injuries are no more regrettable than those who at least have some idea what the fracas is all about.

But such letters were destined to remain unpublished. None of us was particularly surprised. David Mercer had now agreed to become part of the working group which was producing *The Black Dwarf* and this was far more important to us than getting worked up about Fleet Street. Mercer was not one of those who felt that great art or literature transcended politics. He was for the unity of aesthetics and political commitment, as were a number of other writers and playwrights at that time. The working group at the time consisted of Clive Goodwin, Mercer, Adrian Mitchell, Mo Teitelbaum, the designer Robin Fior, D. A. N. Jones and myself. The events of Grosvenor Square had now convinced large numbers of people that we had an audience for the paper and preparations for publishing the pre-launch broadsheet were well under way.

The repercussions of the demonstration continued to have a ripple effect. At VSC we were simply deluged with requests for information and speakers from all over the country. Pat Jordan noted that if I had accepted every invitation for the months of April and May 1968, I would have been speaking at six meetings per day. The ferocious personal/political attacks on me by the media and a wide range of Labour and Tory MPs, as well as papers such as *Tribune* and the SLL rag of the time made me think more seriously than ever before about joining a political organization. The three musketeers of the Fourth International – Pierre Frank, Ernest Mandel and the Italian Livio Maitan – had recently spoken at a meeting in London. I had also by this time bought and read Mandel's *Marxist Economic Theory*, as well as a number of pamphlets by him and others on world politics. Mandel, Frank, Maitan, Jordan *et al* were staunch upholders of the Trotskyist tradition, but unlike the Fifth Monarchy Men of the SLL or similar sectarian brethren, I found them remarkably open, creative, relatively undogmatic and not totally devoid of a sense of humour. These were subjective considerations. On the level of objectivity I had to concede that this was the only group which had decided to make defence of the Vietnamese revolution the central priority as long ago as 1965. Moreover, they had or had tried to build organizations all over the world, which meant that I could remain a member even when I returned to Pakistan. The only serious competitor was the IS Group, which included many personal friends, but whose politics I had always felt were entirely Eurocentric. This view had been reinforced by common work within VSC in a number of ways. At some local meetings IS speakers would insist on equating the epic resistance of the Vietnamese with something that was happening in Britain. A classic example of this occurred when an IS leader referred to a minuscule and irrelevant, though very worthy, rent strike on a tiny North London council estate and claimed that 'it was part of the same struggle as that being waged by the Vietnamese'. The impulse was undoubtedly decent, but the political logic was truly bizarre. In 1967–68, however, the IS had one big advantage over the others: their internal regime was very relaxed and their tactical pragmatism was equally refreshing, but this began to change as they grew in numbers.

Once I make up my mind I tend to be fairly decisive. This some-times gives rise to errors on my part, but I still prefer this way of acting to interminable delays, indecision, dilly-dallying and the like. Now that I had decided to throw in my lot with *The Week* or rather the group behind it, I did not waste any more time. I told comrades Jordan and Tate that I would like to join the Fourth International and since they held the franchise for Britain I would be happy to become one of their tiny band. The two men looked at each other, seemed slightly embarrassed as well as pleased and said they would discuss it with 'the others' and inform me of the outcome. I waited a day, two days and finally a week passed without a response. I wondered whether my political literacy was in doubt and rapidly read Trotsky's amazing *History of the Russian Revolution*. This has remained the most riveting account of any revolution that I have ever read and what struck me, apart from the politics, was the sheer beauty of the language. This was not simply a historical but also a literary masterpiece. It was this aspect of Trotsky that had attracted a chunk of the New York intelligentsia during the thirties. Edmund Wilson, Irving Howe, Mary McCarthy, Dwight Macdonald and others had all fallen prey to Trotsky's artistry and skill. The quality of the prose was devastating and I remember that after I had finished his history I felt extremely sad at the thought that because this man had been anathematized by Stalinism, his writings had not been read by millions of people who had been under the influence of Moscow. What better book to explain 1917 to the new generations in China and Vietnam than Trotsky's magisterial account, without precedent in the annals of revolution. The mental blockage created by Stalinism went very deep and many, many intellectuals who broke with official communism in 1956 found it very difficult to read Trotsky, whereas someone like Michael Foot had read both Trotsky and Deutscher and paid tributes to the genius of both men.

I finished the book in a week, but still no reply from the comrades. Eventually I invited Pat Jordan to lunch at the Ganges on Gerrard Street. This was a favourite haunt of many a leftist because the owner, Tassaduque Ahmed, described himself as a Marxist and often joined in the debates during meals. It soon became clear why my membership application had taken such a long time to process. Pat Jordan explained, after a few beers, that since I was so used to speaking at big meetings and conferences they felt that I might not be aware of the small size of the group. Since the numerical strength of Pat Jordan's battalions had not really been my worry I just laughed and asked what the membership of the group was at the time. 'It's much, much smaller than IS', came the reply. I tried again. 'I know that, Pat, but how many bodies do you have?' A long pause followed. 'Er, er, about fifty,' he replied, 'and of these thirty are in Nottingham. You know, of course, that we've had a split with Ken Coates ...' I must confess that I was astonished, since I had assumed that they had about twenty members. 'Are you sure it's really fifty, Pat?' I enquired. Another long pause. 'Well, I think it might be nearer forty, but there are lots of contacts and we'll grow fast.' I told him that I wasn't particularly bothered whether they were ten or twenty and I still wanted to join. 'In that case consider yourself a member', he said and we toasted the future of the International. I did ask whether the group had a name and, to my relief, it did, as well as a constitution, which I picked up the very next day. I had joined the International Marxist Group, affiliated to the Fourth International.

April

The ferocious press attacks on the Vietnam Solidarity Campaign and the half-truths, lies and slanders which were repeated against myself had not increased the isolation of the movement. The opposite had happened and the size of meetings had now quadrupled on the campuses and in the towns. We had already decided that a massive show of strength was necessary in October 1968 and we decided to hold a number of regional conferences in Yorkshire, Scotland, Wales and the Midlands to plan our strategy. This meant another month or so on the road for me, but it was already becoming part of a daily routine. The Easter rituals of CND were also approaching and we had decided not to ignore their march, but to join it with our banners and win support for VSC and the October mobilization.

Late one night I received a phone call from Berlin. It was a friend from the SDS and she could not speak for a few minutes after hearing my voice since she was sobbing uncontrollably. I was paralysed with worry and pleaded with her to explain what had happened. Rudi Dutschke had been shot by a right-wing fanatic. Was he still alive? How serious was the injury? Where was he? He was under intensive care and unconscious. The bullet had entered his head and they were going to operate soon, but the chances of survival were slim. The SDS had called for demonstrations throughout Germany and were informing friends all over Europe. This was on the eve of the CND assembly in Hyde Park. I rang various VSC committee members and we agreed on the phone that something had to be done, and soon, but we agreed to make the final decision when we had the London VSC contingent present and ready on the following afternoon. I was positive that my phone was tapped and my mail was being opened before being delivered, but since I was not engaged in any plots to bomb any buildings I was not unduly worried. It did prevent one from discussing the detailed tactics of demonstrations on the phone, though even this self-discipline was often difficult to enforce.

That night the phone did not stop ringing. It was friends from Germany, Ernest Mandel from Paris and lots of VSC supporters in Britain. The attempted assassination of Rudi Dutschke had moved everyone into action. I tried that night to remember every detail of the man. His shock of long hair, his intense eyes, his powerful oratory, which could often make one forget the strong Christian streak that had always played a part in his life. He had been born in Eastern Germany, which had become a separate state while he was a child. He had been deeply influenced by Protestantism and wanted to study theology in East Berlin, but this choice was not greatly encouraged at the time. Young Dutschke had not liked the atheistic ritual devised by the new state for schoolchildren under the age of sixteen, which had replaced Christian confirmation. Those who did not accept it were denied a party career and were often conscripted into the army before being permitted to go to university. Dutschke had not wanted to join the army and had, instead, left for West Berlin. Here he had come under the influence of radical theologians and the literature of the Frankfurt School, especially Marcuse. The combination of the latter with his own brand of Christianity had imparted to his utterances a Messianic flavour, which delighted the SDS, but antagonized the establishment. He was living with Gretchen, an American woman also a theologian, and they had a child who had been named Che.

The Springer press was notoriously reactionary. It was a product of the cold war and its newspapers ran effective campaigns against its political enemies. A defeated nation is *often* frustrated, aggressive and sullen. Axel Springer's publications sought to channel the postwar despair into an anti-communist crusade. The character of the regime in East Germany undoubtedly aided the process, whose target was the left in West Germany. I had noticed some of this in Berlin a few months ago. The vicious caricatures of Dutschke, the presentation of him as a crazed Bolshevik murderer, were common practice. The would-be assassin, Bachmann, told the court later that his entire image of Dutschke had been formed by the Springer press. He had detailed the newspaper commentaries which inspired him to kill the red maniac. In Berlin the students attacked the Springer buildings to make their feelings clear.

On 15 April, the day after the attack, the VSC banners were raised in Hyde Park and we started appealing to CND members to join us on a march to the West German embassy and the Springer offices in London. The SDS had left us their banner after the Grosvenor Square demonstration and we now mounted it on two poles and gave it pride of place behind the platform. When we had gathered 2000 people (about one-sixth of that CND march) we marched out of Hyde Park and went to the German embassy in Belgrave Square. There were a few token scuffles with the police, but a senior embassy official agreed to see us and I led a deputation inside. Naturally the official was deeply shocked by the incident. Was he also 'deeply shocked' by the year-long campaign mounted by Springer's tabloids I asked in a very soft tone? He did not reply. I went on to inform him that if the German SDS was banned there would be a permanent siege of the West German embassies in Europe. This had not happened during the thirties, which is why we would ensure the rights of the SDS as a mass student organization.

We then left the embassy and marched to the Springer offices, which were housed in the *Daily Mirror* buildings on Holborn Circus. 'Springer Today, King Tomorrow' (a reference to Cecil King who owned the Mirror group at the time) was inscribed very large on *The Black Dwarf*'s first banner, proudly carried that day by Clive Goodwin and David Mercer. Outside the *Mirror* building there was a much bigger police presence than there had been outside the German embassy, an interesting reflection on the priorities of Scotland Yard. A contingent of militant hippies was being led by a long-robed Sid Rawle who wanted to take his followers into the building. They were marching behind a banner which simply said 'Cannabis Martyrs'. 'Right,' Sid told the hippy platoon, 'you've seen the fucking *Mirror* building. I don't want to see it, I want to take it . . .' They charged, but the police presence was very strong that day. Finally, Commander Lawlor came and told me that the Springer representative had agreed to see me. Six of us were escorted into the building and taken to the offices of George Clare, UK Director of the Springer Group. We spoke. He listened. I accused his organization of having instigated murder. He said he would pass on our views to his head office in Hamburg. Someone else from our deputation said that if they carried on in this way the German SDS would be passing them more than just messages. He shrugged his shoulders. We left.

Outside the mood was disturbed. Twenty people had been arrested. I stood up on a van to speak. All I was planning to say was that we should march away and disperse in Lincoln's Inn Fields. Before I could utter a single word a posse of policeman charged towards me and grabbed my legs, but simultaneously I was pulled in the other direction by dozens of VSC activists. Fortunately, the police let go and I was dragged to safety. Lawlor then came and asked what our intentions were and received a mouthful for his stupid attempt to arrest me. As he left us, we marched away and dispersed as planned.

Despite the fact there had been only a tiny scuffle in Belgravia, *The Times'* front page headline the next morning was 'LONDON MARCH ON SPRINGER OFFICE: Hundreds In Clash At Embassy'. The careful reporter who wrote the story underneath, however, was far more accurate.

In this fashion we paid our tribute to the German socialist Rudi Dutschke, who survived his injuries and began to stage a slow recovery, but found it difficult to live in his native Germany any longer. He had left East Germany voluntarily; he also felt unable to live in West Germany after the bullet entered his brain.

These events clearly had some effect on Cecil King. On 17 April, two days after our demonstration, the *Daily Mirror* announced on its front page that it was offering space to what the large headline stated would be 'The Uncensored Voice of Protest'. Two days later they invited me to write a front-page article to explain our views to their 'audience of five and a half million'. After explaining why we were disillusioned with the Labour Government and the paralysis of the parliamentary left, I outlined the main reasons for our protests:

1. To break the silence. There is no real opposition in the country. The Press opposition is largely a sham. To Socialists it seems that the entire 'democratic' process is on the side of reaction.

The House of Commons is simply a rubber stamp which is not consulted on important matters (many remember that the decision to make the atom bomb was not taken by Parliament). A recent blatant example is the sight of international bankers vetting the Budget and telling Mr Jenkins how much unemployment he should create.

More and more power is being vested in fewer hands (note all the recent industrial mergers) and this is destroying the democratic process. We must also keep in mind that 90 per cent of the national press is controlled by five men.

2. The sight of a small peasant army inflicting heavy casualties in the jungles of Vietnam on the mightiest Imperialist nation in the world has had an energizing effect on many militants. The nineteen guerrillas who died after capturing the US Embassy in Saigon for a few hours are widely admired. It is felt that if, during the Occupation of France, a group of British commandos had done the same to the Nazi Embassy they would have received posthumous VCs.

Moreover in social-democratic Sweden we see Swedish Cabinet ministers marching with demonstrators to protest at the American Embassy – their arms linked with representatives of the National Liberation Front and Hanoi.

In this country these representatives are not even allowed in and British social democracy continues to support American policy in Vietnam. British troops are training US marines in Malaya...

The pages did not remain open for too long, but it showed that even press magnates were susceptible to mass pressure. More importantly, I received hundreds of letters in response, the bulk of them favourable and over half wanting to know how they could join the Vietnam Solidarity Campaign. It was clear that the coupling of Springer and Cecil King on our placards did lead to a softening of tone on the part of the *Daily Mirror* and it was regarded by us as a small victory.

Chapter Eight

The Year 1968:
The French Revolution

Revolutions are festivals of the oppressed and the exploited . . . At such times the people are capable of performing miracles, if judged by the limited, philistine yardstick of gradualist progress. But it is essential that leaders of revolutionary parties, too, should advance their aims more comprehensively and boldly at such a time, so that their slogans shall always be in advance of the revolutionary initiative of the masses, serve as a beacon . . . and show them the shortest and most direct route to complete, absolute and decisive victory . . .

V.I. Lenin, 1905

On May Day in 1968, we celebrated spring and commemorated working-class martyrs throughout the world. There were a few trade unionists present, veterans of past struggles, and we marched to Transport House in Smith Square. The slogans were a combination of old and new. A pre-launch *Black Dwarf* broadsheet was distributed free and since it could be carried as a poster – it depicted Enoch Powell in the peaked cap of an SS officer – many demonstrators held it to show their contempt for the Tory politician. Powell had recently come out with his notorious 'rivers of blood' speech which attacked the presence of black faces in his white and pleasant land. At Transport House a number of us had spoken on various themes and then dispersed. As I was walking away with some friends from the Cartoon Archetypal Slogan Theatre – an agitprop troupe which pioneered the birth of radical fringe theatre in the sixties – we noticed an ugly demonstration in support of Powell by Smithfield meat porters and, to our horror, dockers from Tilbury. The British fascists had always had a strong base in Smithfield. I suppose the sight of that blood-red meat encourages fantasies of one sort or another, but the dockers represented a new wave. Unfortunately they had seen me as well and indicated in gestures and words that I should be lynched and decapitated, though the moderates amongst them merely called for my deportation. This last idea was not original. They had picked it up from Robert Mellish, a Labour minister, who had publicly written to James Callaghan, the Home Secretary, calling for my expulsion from the country. Callaghan had expressed great understanding and sympathy for Mellish, but had regretfully informed his cabinet colleague that unless I was arrested, charged with some criminal offence and found guilty, he was powerless to act. I was a Commonwealth citizen and entitled in those days to automatic permanent residence and nationality after I had completed five years in this country. There were still five months left before I was safe and many VSC activists had felt that Callaghan's remarks were an open invitation to the police and judiciary to do their duty. In any event it was this fact that resulted in a spontaneous defence of my person during demonstrations. On that May Day there were very few of us and as a group of meat-porters and dockers, their faces contorted with hate and a frenzied look in their eyes, ran to get me, Roland Muldoon, never one for false heroics, decided that the time had come to retreat. We ran away.

Three days later, the French students began to get restless again and the birth-pangs of a new movement were heard all over Europe. Prior to the Second World War, France had only 60,000 students in a population of 42 million. In 1958, when De Gaulle had seized power and disbanded the Fourth Republic, their numbers had increased to 175,000. In 1968, France had grown to 50 million and the number of students had risen dramatically to 600,000. The university system faced a dual crisis: its buildings, student quarters, and amenities were insufficient and the quality of education was suffering. These were the surface phenomena which provided the material basis for the revolt that followed, helped by an authoritarian structure and a foolish attempt to impose rectorial discipline. It backfired badly, but if it had not provided the spark something else would have done. The truth was that France was ready to explode. Ten years of Gaullism had choked French society. The growth rate had slowed down and unemployment had risen to 2.3 per cent. This was coupled with a wage-freeze. The size of the working class had risen by 30 per cent. National discontent found its first voice among the students. Pierre Frank had been right after all.

We were preparing to produce the first proper issue of *The Black Dwarf*, but it was becoming clear that we would not be able to meet the deadline of 15 May 1968. We had planned to produce a newspaper the size of *The Times*, but virtually every printer we approached refused to handle our paper. One managing director told us that 'your tone is all wrong'. Several printshop owners also refused us and so finally we had to come down in size and go to Goodwin Press, who agreed without preconditions, which was hardly surprising since they were the printers for CND. This came as a relief, but it did mean that we had to change our style and design rapidly. Robin Fior and D. A. N. Jones were working on the paper when the news from Paris began to get warmer and warmer. I rang up a friend, who asked me to go there as soon as possible. Nanterre had been closed down. There had been battles on the streets and the Sorbonne was occupied. The descriptions were magical, but I had a whole set of speaking engagements in different parts of Britain and this, coupled with the *Dwarf* launch, made it impossible for me to travel that week. Instead I asked a million questions on the phone in order to report back to the meetings that I was due to address.

The two groups playing a major role in the student movement were the 22nd March Movement, which had emerged in Nanterre and taken the name of its mobilization date, just as Fidel Castro and Che Guevara had formed the 26th July Movement, and the JCR. The first was a spontaneous umbrella grouping whose main spokesman was Daniel Cohn-Bendit, a brilliant sociology student in his twenties. He was a libertarian anarchist, extremely hostile to the French Communist Party. He was flanked on his left by Daniel Bensaid, a gifted theoretician and orator, who was also a leader of the JCR. Cohn-Bendit and Bensaid, despite doctrinal differences, found it fairly easy to work together. They were united against the assorted sectarians who mocked the student movement from the sidelines.

On 6 May the students at the Sorbonne held out for twelve hours against two police forces, the *gardes mobile* and the much-hated CRS. They defeated an attempt by the police to end the occupation. The Latin Quarter was named the Heroic Vietnam Quarter. The main auditorium in the Sorbonne was renamed Che Guevara Hall. Several student leaders had been arrested and the main demand now became their immediate and unconditional release. A 22nd March Movement banner was held aloft on 7 May and behind it tens of thousands of students held the streets of Paris till dusk. A new movement was born. A 22nd March Movement leaflet headed 'We Will Not Be The Watchdogs Of Capital' was distributed in hundreds of thousands over the next two days. It announced that it wanted revolutionary change in society and that the students would refuse to permit the normal functioning of the universities until the imprisoned students had been released and all sanctions had been withdrawn. It called for a mass demonstration on Friday 10 May and asked people to assemble in Place Denfert Rochereau under the gaze of the bemused statue of the lion. The call was backed by the French equivalent of the National Union of Students (UNEF) and the JCR.

At 6.30pm on 10 May 1968, over 30,000 students assembled at the agreed spot and blocked traffic for two miles. Cohn-Bendit addressed the demonstrators and asked them where they would like to go. Three targets were named: la Santé prison, the ORTF (French BBC) and the Ministry of Justice. Several thousands joined the march *en route* to the prison, which was defended by armed policemen. The demonstrators then turned towards the right bank and the ORTF, but the police outwitted the marchers by forcing them to go up the Boulevard Saint-Michel instead of down St Germain. On the Boulevard Saint-Michel, the student vanguard found itself surrounded on all sides by the police. The choice was to disperse or to stay and fight. Cohn-Bendit suggested that they occupy the Latin Quarter 'without bothering the police' and hold the Quarter till the police had left. Then the march could proceed to the ORTF. The student militants were already digging up the cobblestones in order to construct barricades. This was, after all, France, and the submerged consciousness of past revolutions had risen to the surface yet again. Two women militants later wrote: 'As others were twenty when the Nazi hordes swooped down on France, as others were twenty when Algeria shook off the feals of a foetid colonialism, we were twenty in May.'

And they might have added, *pace* Wordsworth, that the bliss of existence itself was transcended by their youth, which was 'very heaven'. The cobblestones of the Latin Quarter (now covered with ugly asphalt) were treated with great love that night. Barricades were going up everywhere and by midnight militants were looking at each other and remarking on which barricade deserved the Engels award. Some of them had been built double: one three-foot high row of cobblestones, an empty space and then a ten- or even twelve-foot high wall consisting of cars, metal posts and dustbins. The citizens of the Latin Quarter, the people who actually lived there, proved to be extremely sympathetic. They provided food as well as water, sugar and cloth to make masks as a protection against the inevitable use of tear gas. Older citizens observing the students from their apartment windows remembered something from their past and came down attired just in their pyjamas, and helped construct the odd barricade. Red flags were hoisted on the barricades. Many of them were the old tricolour after the blue and white had been torn off. Some citizens mounted their roofs to see if they could sight the enemy and came down to report every movement to the students.

The police attack came at 2am on Place de Luxembourg. The CRS units sent to end the occupation launched gas grenades to try and blind and suffocate the students. Initially the students remained on the defensive. Then they decided to counter-attack. To their amazement they realized that they had defeated the police while onlookers cheered from the pavements. The fighting continued till 4.30am. Two hours later all police units were withdrawn. The Latin Quarter remained liberated. The very next day the French Government accepted the main demands of the students. In normal times this would have been sufficient to defuse the movement, but France in May 1968 was suffocating under the Fifth Republic. The students had shown the rest of the country that it was possible to start breathing again.

In London, *The Black Dwarf* despatched Clive Goodwin to Paris the day after the night of the barricades. He rang me back excited out of his mind. 'There's a revolution going on here. The paper must reflect that . . .' He had seen slogans painted on the walls of the Latin Quarter. *I take my desires for reality, because I believe in the reality of my desires.* 'The workers?' I asked Clive. 'The workers? Are they going to move or not?' But the workers had already moved. JCR comrades tell me that lots of young workers were already present on the night of 10 May. As were the intellectuals. Jean-Marie Vincent, Nicos Poulantzas, Ernest Mandel, Denis Berger and others had also constructed barricades.

The best-informed reportage in Britain had been provided by Patrick Seale and Maureen McConville from Paris in the *Observer*. I packed my bags, desperate to join the JCR on the streets. A newspaper published the fact that I was preparing to visit the French capital. That same day I received a phone call. It was an 'elderly' man (in his forties I thought at the time), from a call box who would not give his name. He spoke briefly but with tremendous authority: 'I work for the Home Office. If you go to France today, they will not let you back into this country again. I suggest you do not leave here till your five years are up.' That was all he said, not giving me the chance to question him further. It was his terseness that convinced me it wasn't a practical joke. A jester would have kept up the pretence and tried to stretch the frontier of incredulity. For that, after all, is the function of a good jape. Since I am, or, to be accurate, used to be, an expert on such matters I was ever determined not to be caught out myself and, therefore, I was suspicious of the call. I consulted a senior barrister, while Ken Tynan informally asked John Mortimer. Both men gave me the same advice. The anonymous caller, prankster or not, had given very sage counsel. Given that two cabinet ministers had publicly discussed my deportation, it would be playing into their hands to be debarred on a legal technicality. Pat Jordan and the IMG reinforced this view and so, reluctantly and angrily, I bowed to collective pressure. Any doubts that I may have had regarding the seriousness of the mystery phone call were resolved when my five years expired. The London *Evening Standard* reported that there 'were rueful faces in the Home Office' that day because I had escaped the net. Nonetheless I am still not sure whether or not I made the correct decision. To have missed Paris that spring was unforgivable.

The student upheaval developed into a revolt against French capitalism and its values. The Odéon Theatre was occupied by the Parisian intelligentsia and became a place of daily debates and discussions. Jean Genet mocked from outside that it was all a drama. He wanted the state to be confronted and felt it could not be done via the Odéon. The students responded with the slogan, 'When the General Assembly becomes a bourgeois theatre, we must make bourgeois theatres into a General Assembly'. But could it go any further? It did. The factory occupations began and spread to the whole of France. Only one worker in five belonged to the unions, split along political lines, unlike Britain. The factory takeovers united unionized and non-unionized workers. Here, too, it was the young who took the lead. 'You lot,' they shouted collectively at the veteran trade union organizers of the CGT (Confédération Generale du Travail) and the CFDT (Confédération de la Force Démocratique du Travail), 'you've been telling us that we can't do anything. That we're not strong enough as yet. That we should wait a bit longer. And look at these students. They fought on the barricades and they won. They won!'

As the Vietnamese successes inspired the students, so now the triumph of the students inspired the workers. France slipped into a pre-revolutionary solution without an awareness on the part of the workers who made it possible that their actions had begun to pose the question as to who ruled France. The upsurge swept the whole country. Ten million workers went on strike. It was the biggest general strike in the history of capitalism and the scale of the events was much greater than the 1905 upheavals in Tsarist Russia. It was no longer just the students and the workers who were involved. Farmers and peasants brought their tractors and compost on to the streets; lawyers and magistrates, architects and astronomers came out for change. They were backed by the newsreaders of ORTF, who declared that they were fed up with feeding 'shit' to the population. And, as if to stress the truly national character of the discontent, the striptease artistes of the *Folies Bergére* joined the big marches, chanting 'De Gaulle assassin!' The French ruling class was by now extremely nervous, but in order to demonstrate their sang-froid the Prime Minister, Georges Pompidou, went on a state visit to Afghanistan, where he was received by cheering students, and the General paid a state visit to Rumania, where he was greeted by workers waving flowers. In France itself, the students had handed their banners to the workers who were demanding self-management and workers' control.

The French events led to the first split in the tiny ranks of *The Black Dwarf* working group. Our ambassadors to Paris returned with revolution shining from their faces. D. A. N. Jones had produced the first issue of the paper, but it did not capture the spirit of the French May. Jones had meant well, but he did tend to be somewhat hostile to students and the paper reflected his lack of enthusiasm. It could have been distributed, but we would have exposed our weaknesses. An emergency meeting convened at Cromwell Road and we went through every page of *The Black Dwarf*. A lot of material was in there, but it was the presentation that was lacklustre. We decided, reluctantly and sadly, to incinerate the entire print run of 20,000 copies and simultaneously part company with D. A. N. Jones. It was Clive who communicated our views to him and I do not know what was said and whether or not Jones parted with bitterness in his heart.

In this way the very first issue of *The Black Dwarf* became a collector's item because it was destroyed. I kept a copy, naturally, and when I disinterred it to refresh my memory, I felt that, apart from the cover, it was not so bad as we had thought. Apart from anything else it had an article by myself, which the second first issue also unceremoniously discarded. This had been my own decision since David Mercer had proposed that I take over as Editor and proceed rapidly to produce the paper. We worked late into the night for the next few days. Clive Goodwin had brought back articles from France and Patrick Procktor had sketched a street-fighting scene from Paris. I designed the cover on a piece of notepaper and showed it round the table. It was a poster-cover, simple and easily comprehensible: *We Shall Fight, We Shall Win, Paris, London, Rome, Berlin*, to be printed in red and black. Below it, our designer, Robin Fior, placed a photograph of French students clambering on the statue of the lion and underneath the words spoken by a French shipyard worker to Daniel Cohn-Bendit: 'Listen, I'm forty-three, and at that age a worker is too old to learn a new job. My children have got education, and they look down on me. But I can remember when I was your age. We wanted to change the world, too. Go on, you lads.' Inside, the paper contained a detailed diary of the French upheaval, a brilliant polemic by David Mercer against 'Respectable Man' and a defence of the revolutionary road by Eric Hobsbawm, the distinguished communist historian. Hobsbawm's piece was a witty and effective attack against the French Communist Party which had turned its back on the movement and was negotiating a return to normality. His concluding paragraph summed up what a large section of the Western European left was whispering to each other in a bit of a trance:

> We knew – though the politicians didn't – that people are not con-tented. They feel that their lives are meaningless in a consumer society. They know that, even when they are comfortable (which many of them are not), they are also more powerless than before, more pushed around by giant organizations for whom they are items and not men. They know that the official mechanisms for representing them – elections, parties, etc – have tended to become a set of ceremonial institutions going through empty rituals. They do not like it – but until recently they did not know what to do about it, and may have won-dered whether there was anything that they could do about it. What France proves is that when someone demonstrates that people are not powerless, they may begin to act again. Perhaps even more than this: that only the sense of impotence is holding many of us back from acting like men and not zombies.

We printed 25,000 copies of *The Black Dwarf*, but not a single main-stream distribution network agreed to stock or circulate our paper. It was sold by small newsagents or by sellers on the streets. One such person, appropriately named Mick Shrapnell, used to sell 2000 copies on a tour of Central London every week. On launch night, we were given a very generous welcome on BBC2's *Late Night Line-Up*, where Claud Cockburn and myself were interviewed about *The Black Dwarf*. Claud paid us a handsome tribute and said that we were the true heirs of his own legendary broadsheet of the thirties, *The Week*. Later, over supper, he wondered whether his own editor, Richard Ingrams, would take kindly to that remark, since a 'quarter of Richard thinks that *Private Eye* is the successor to *The Week*!' I doubted this since I thought that *Private Eye*, just as disillusioned as all of us about Wilson and the Labour Government, had decided, unlike us, to move right-wards, Claud's excellent column and Paul Foot notwithstanding. Patricia Cockburn, a remarkable person in her own right, then changed the subject. She was very critical of the tactics used in Grosvenor Square in relation to the police horses. Patricia, an expert horse-breeder herself, offered me the following piece of equestrian advice: 'It's silly to throw marbles or chilli powder at the animals. They're not policemen! [Guffaws from Claud.] The simplest way of disrupting a cavalry charge is by getting two of your men to get a piece of strong nylon wire and tie it to a railing or something strong on either side of the Square or wherever. As the charge commences they should lift the wire so that it touches the horse just above the knee [here she demonstrated where on Claud's knee, oblivious to the fact that the neighbouring tables were expressing distaste, since I had been recognized]. This will cause the horse to stumble, if not actually come down and the mounted policeman will be thrown off, causing great confusion.' I thanked her profusely and later transmitted the infor-mation to those who were expert in such things. They were equally impressed, but whether the Cockburn method was ever deployed in action or not I do not know.

In France, the general strike was not so much defeated as side-tracked. The powerful engine of the French Communist Party and its trade-union front, the CGT, shunted the movement aside and did a deal with the government. The French Communists had attempted throughout to keep the workers and students apart, occasionally by force. They had denounced Cohn-Bendit as a foreigner, stating that the French workers did not need lessons from a 'German Jew'. In response 50,000 people had assembled on the streets and chanted in unison: 'We are all German Jews.' But the movement, which had brought France to a pre-revolutionary crisis, did not have its own organizations and it could not create an institutionalized dual power. The French Communist Party could have, but chose to go along with the other side. De Gaulle had not been so sure that the French Communists would be able to derail the revolution and De Gaulle was many things, but he was not a fool. He made a secret trip to Germany where he met the non-conscript units of the army, who agreed to come and liberate Paris from the rabble, but charged a high price. De Gaulle agreed to rehabilitate some of the men behind the extreme right-wing OAS which had tried to kill him for his treachery in agreeing to Algerian independence. General Massu, torturer and semi-fascist, was accordingly back in favour and received the 'royal' pardon.

It was Pompidou who worked with the French CP and CGT to end the strike. A revolution takes place when no other solution can be seen on the horizon. But when the leaders of the big battalions promise that there are other ways and different solutions it is not possible to create a dual power, let alone the plans for an insurrection. Paris was not Petrograd, but France had come perilously close to a sudden transformation. The chanceries in other capitals of Western Europe were fearful. Robert Escarpit provided an accurate summary of the fears abroad. *Their nightmares are our dreams*, a poster in Paris had proclaimed in May. Wrote Escarpit in July:

A Frenchman travelling abroad feels himself treated a bit like a con-valescent from a pernicious fever. And how did the rash of barricades break out? What was the temperature at five o'clock in the evening of May 29? Is the Gaullist medicine really getting to the roots of the disease? Are there dangers of a relapse? Even if those questions are not put directly, one can read them on the headlines displayed in all the news-stands and bookstalls.

But there is one question that is hardly ever asked, perhaps because they are afraid to hear the answer. But at heart everyone would like to know, hopefully or fearfully, whether the sickness is infectious.

And of course it was, as Italy, Pakistan and Argentina were to discover. It was an amazing feature of 1968, that the spread of the revolt embraced every continent. The combination of Saigon and Paris had resulted in a global radicalization without precedent in the history of capitalism. The ingredients of the brew were different in every country, but the pattern of mobilization was not dissimilar, with the exception of the United States where the anti-war movement coincided with the wave of black rebellions that shook Detroit, Chicago, Washington and Los Angeles and created the conditions for the birth of groups like the Black Panthers, whose simplistic chants, such as *The Revolution Has Come, Time to Pick Up Your Gun*, were only one side of the debate. The other was the Word. Eldridge Cleaver's *Soul on Ice* had become an international bestseller, to be followed by George Jackson's masterpiece, *Soledad Brother*, a devastating critique of American society. Both men were greatly inspired by the Vietnamese and proudly acknowledged their debt. The war was beginning to affect life at home for many Americans.

In France at the height of the movement, Pompidou instructed French television to put three student leaders, Cohn-Bendit, Alain Geismar and Jacques Sauvageot on a programme which directly preceded his own Prime Ministerial broadcast. In his speech to the nation Pompidou referred to the *enragés* by telling his viewers that 'we have shown you some of them', but the plan misfired. The three radicals refused to play the part assigned to them. Instead they had appeared reasonable and audacious, witty as well as serious and had succeeded with great flair in turning the tables on the journalists who had been instructed to make them appear as blood-thirsty fanatics. The only outcome had been that the French Communist Party had denounced the ORTF for allowing them to appear in the first place and had denounced Cohn-Bendit as the agent of a sinister international network.

In Britain, Hugh Greene was Director-General of the BBC and with one unfortunate exception – he had not allowed the Corporation to screen Peter Watkins' first-rate anti-nuclear film, *The War Game* – he ran it in a remarkably libertarian fashion, resisting attempts by the

Labour Government to censor dissident opinions. In late May he personally approved an idea by Anthony Smith, a BBC producer at the time, to invite radical leaders from several countries and give them a peak-time audience. I was asked to appear on the show and was told that several acquaintances of mine from other countries were being approached. When news of this was leaked there was the usual storm in a beer mug with Conservative MPs demanding that heads should roll. Labour ministers also considered banning the entry of Cohn-Bendit and the others. We had planned a welcome party for all the visitors at Clive Goodwin's apartment on Cromwell Road, where a number of people who worked for, but were deeply suspicious of, the BBC were waiting to give us advice on how to prevent the programme from being manipulated. Cohn-Bendit arrived on 11 July at Heathrow and was detained for detailed questioning by Special Branch and immigration officers. We rushed to the airport in four or five cars, with placards to the ready. Simultaneously, Fenner Brockway started chasing the Labour ministers responsible to the Home Office. So did the Liberal MP, Eric Lubbock, who buttonholed a junior minister, David Ennals, at the House of Commons. We began an impromptu political meeting at the airport as more and more people began to arrive and listen to what we were saying. Finally, Labour agreed that Cohn-Bendit could enter for twenty-four hours to participate in the programme. In the fatuous words of David Ennals: 'If he wasn't going to create a revolution in Britain, I didn't think there was any danger.' If only revolutions could have been made simply because a few people desired them...

We collected Cohn-Bendit and drove him directly to Cromwell Road. A party designed to discuss ideological battle-plans had become enlarged to a gathering of over 200 people. We met in a small room for an hour to discuss tactics for the *Students in Revolt* programme. Tony Garnett and Kenith Trodd were of the view that we should insist that the programme was live and not permit any editing after it had been recorded. The look of surprise on Cohn-Bendit's face led Garnett to become more explicit: 'The BBC', he shouted, 'will fuck you. It will fuck you!' As the other veterans of encounters with the Beeb nodded their heads sagely, Cohn-Bendit attempted to work out how we could be raped by a corporation. There were many that evening who were only too ready to explain the mechanics. We agreed not to permit interviewer Robert Mackenzie to manipulate or divide us and my proposal that as the programme came to an end we should rise and sing the 'Internationale' was accepted. Then we joined the party next door, where a harassed but friendly Tony Smith was waiting to hear what we had decided. He agreed to our demands and while wine was being consumed and unmentionables were being inhaled, Ken Tynan pointed out that 'a representative of the bourgeois press was present'. It was 2am, but the presence of an intruder brought us to our feet. Where? Who? Why? It was Richard Davy from *The Times*, whose reportage had been somewhat more sympathetic and more accurate than the *Guardian* of those days. Davy, enjoying himself immensely, refused to leave. Clive Goodwin suggested a vote on the question, but it was felt that there had been insufficient discussion and a debate ensued. Davy decided to leave voluntarily, which ended the affair.

The next day I took Cohn-Bendit and the others to Highgate Cemetery where we rehearsed the 'Internationale' in front of the ugly, socialist-realist bust of Karl Marx and then went off to address a large rally at the London School of Economics. I had not met Cohn-Bendit prior to this meeting. Our politics were radically different, but I liked him instinctively. He possessed an impish sense of humour and was remarkably open. At one point as we were surrounded by photographers he said, 'I like all this. It's like a drug. I don't know how I would live without it . . .' I pointed out that he might not feel that way if he had been in Britain or Germany.

We talked of the absence of Rudi Dutschke from our ranks that week and I told him that the press campaign against me had led to real problems on the streets or while using public transport. He understood, of course, but the French experience had been completely different. He was vitriolic on the role of the French CP, which he said had in the last instance emerged as a 'pillar of the system', openly used by Pompidou to derail the movement. 'The French bourgeoisie', Cohn-Bendit insisted that day, 'will use the Stalinists like a contraceptive and then . . . into the toilet.' He had been deported from France, had returned illegally in disguise, but was resigned to living in Germany, where he had many friends in the SDS. At the LSE later that day the response was very positive as the meeting agreed to use British campuses to provide refuge to American deserters and draft-dodgers, a growing phenomenon in the United States.

There was an unfortunate incident at the LSE that day, which left a very bad taste. I had by now become accustomed to racist abuse from the right-wing press and Tory and Labour MPs. I was also getting used to being attacked in the sectarian press of other left-wing groups, but they had remained two distinct forms of personal attack. The International Socialists (later the Socialist Workers Party) were, unsurprisingly, not well disposed to the International Marxist Group. Which set of initials one supported was important. I had always been friendly towards other initials, even to the extent of recommending to people in those towns (and they were a majority) where there was no IMG that people should join the IS. Anything was better than remaining outside at the time. So when an IS member stood up and shouted 'Why don't you go back to Pakistan?' I was deeply shocked since this was the verbal assault one normally associated with the far-right. The tabloids often used phrases like 'foreign scum'. The IS heckler was heckled by the audience, but was not publicly reprimanded by his own group at the LSE. Many of my black nationalist friends, heavily influenced by Stokely Carmichael and the American Black Panthers, often derided me in private for working with the 'white Left'. Their argument was that racism ran very deep in British society and there was no way in which being an ideological leftist helped to clean the slate. I had always criticized this view as being based on individual psychologies and not a serious analysis and I would still insist that I was right, but this incident did give me a great deal to think about. The main leader of the IS, Tony Cliff, was shocked and disgusted by the incident. He apologized many times over, but could not explain the occurrence. I suggested that this was the logic of dead-end sectarianism. Anyone who refused to join the IS was to be treated as an enemy and warned of the consequences of such behaviour. Cliff replied that none of this would have happened if I had joined IS rather than the IMG, which was sweet of him, but only confirmed my opinion of what had taken place. I was angry and fed-up enough to contemplate a total withdrawal from any involvement in British politics, but realized that this was an immature and individualistic response. There was the big October march and *The Black Dwarf*, which required my services, and both Clive Goodwin and Pat Jordan were appalled at any notion of capitulating before sectarian or racial prejudices.

The BBC programme itself went ahead and was, naturally, an anticlimax for those who had thought that its transmission might lead to insurrection. For those of us who participated it was far too short, though watching the embarrassment on the late Robert Mackenzie's face as we sang the 'Internationale' made it worthwhile. Cohn-Bendit was allowed to stay for a fortnight and then returned to Frankfurt. The person who had, in some ways, interested me even more was a quiet young Czech student named Jan Kavan. His father, a senior communist, had been a victim of the purges in the late forties. He had suffered solitary confinement and other tortures, but had survived. His family for some time had to live with the opprobrium of being the 'family of a traitor'. Jan's mother, a formidable Englishwoman, had kept the household going despite every privation, of which there had been many in those years. Kavan told us that there was a great deal of ferment in his country. Many changes were taking place and a process of democratization was under way. I had already seen newsreels of May Day 1968 in Prague, which had moved me a great deal. Unlike the heavy, ritualized celebrations which were a hallmark of Stalinism, here one could see a spontaneous outpouring of joy and happiness. The workers and students had not been dragooned to this march and I even spotted a large poster-portrait of Che, which was regarded as contraband in Eastern Europe and the USSR at the time. The Czech leader, Alexander Dubček, had been touched by this display of support, unprecedented in Eastern Europe, and had been seen wiping a tear off his cheek. 'Socialism with a human face' was what Dubček and his comrades had called the Prague spring. We had been preoccupied too deeply with France to pay serious attention to the developments in

Czechoslovakia. And yet Prague was to become as much a part of our 1968 as Paris and Saigon.

Jan Kavan told us about the Czech student leader Jiri Müller whose arrest had radicalized him, Karel Kovanda (who I met later) and many others. They were all initially suspicious of the Party's reform programme. Had it not come out of the bowels of the same infernal beast that had produced rigged trials and executions, justified every Stalinist atrocity and loyally defended every prevailing orthodoxy in Moscow? They were sceptical and they had every right to be, but things were changing. They were anxious to avoid the mistakes of their fathers and therefore they rejected every new dogma, but elections were taking place in the universities and the factories and good people were being elected. There was a new mood in the Party and especially its youth sections. The latter had started broadening their horizons. Isaac Deutscher's prose was being translated into Czech and published in the pages of official communist magazines. Once despised newspapers were now in great demand because the journalists had cast off their soiled shirts and were publishing the truth. Czech television had also flowered and every evening there was a special programme on which former political prisoners confronted their jailers and told the viewers what they had suffered. The result of all this was to turn the world of the bureaucracy upside down. Bureaucratic rule depended for its stability on a depoliticized and passive mass. Dubček and his supporters were desperately searching for new forms which could marry socialism and democracy without offending the men in the Kremlin too much. The results were being watched as closely as France in May. It was July when Jan Kavan told us of the popular support in the country for the new Czech leaders and his quiet enthusiasm had made a big impression.

One of the central myths of bourgeois ideologues in the West was to equate the socialist project with the crimes of Stalinism. Since there was no other model of existing 'socialism' it was always difficult to demonstrate in practice what we were fighting *for* in those days. Everyone knew what we were against, but positive models could not be found in any advanced country. Since the bureaucrats in Moscow agreed with the political lieutenants of capitalism in the West that what existed in Eastern Europe was socialism, it was hardly surprising that millions of working people identified socialism with single-party authoritarian rule. The logic was to suggest that democracy could only exist in a free-enterprise market economy. Of course this did not take account of Hitler, Mussolini, Franco, Salazar and the numerous banana republics in Latin America and Asia, but these double-standards were not universally appreciated.

The changes in Czechoslovakia from March 1968 onwards enabled one to argue that socialism and democracy were, in fact, far more compatible than freedom and capitalism. Once again my desire to travel abroad was frustrated by lawyers. I could not go to Prague as I was planning to in August because my five years in Britain would only be completed in October. Even if that had not been the case I would not have been welcome since Russian tanks had got there before me. Behind-the-scenes bullying of Czech leaders had failed to produce the necessary results. The Kremlin refused to tolerate the variant of socialism that had become uniquely popular in the Second World. They were scared and with good reason, for if the Czech model was allowed to exist then it would not be long before the clamour of angry voices was heard elsewhere in Eastern Europe. If socialism and democracy could coexist in Prague, then why not in East Berlin or Budapest, Warsaw or Sofia or Bucharest and ultimately Moscow itself? The example of Prague had to be crushed overnight and here the Czech tragedy saw the inauguration of a new act. The Czechs had depended on the West to safeguard their independence from Nazi Germany. The British and French ruling classes had, instead, done a deal with Hitler and sacrificed Czechoslovakia. After the war the Czechs, grateful at being liberated by the Red Army, had hoped that Moscow would respect the traditions and advanced economic basis of their country. Once again they had been proved wrong. Jean-Paul Sartre expressed that aspect of the tragedy extremely eloquently:

Czechoslovakia could have been the first power to accomplish a successful transition from an advanced capitalist economy to a socialist economy, offering the proletariat of the West, if not a model, at least an embodiment of its own revolutionary future. It lacked nothing, neither the means nor the men; if genuine workers' control was possible anywhere, it was in Prague and Bratislava.

To its misfortune, the manipulators in Moscow, manipulated by their own manipulations, could not even understand the idea of such a socialism. They imposed their system instead. This imported, dis-adapted model, with no real foundations in the country, was sustained from the outside by the solicitude of the 'elder brother'. It was installed as an idol – that is to say, a fixed sort of unconditional demands, indisputable, undisputed, inexplicable, unexplained . . .

The Stalinist model of 'socialism without tears' was another disaster and an important layer of Czech communists understood this from the very beginning. In 1968 they acted, only to be told that their very crime was that they had become popular. Too popular! The Dubček experiment was watched just as nervously by Washington and the NATO capitals in Western Europe. For if he had succeeded, there can be little doubt that the echoes would have been heard throughout Europe, East and West. The insurgents of May had been disarmed, but troubles lay ahead in Italy and Portugal was to hover on the brink of revolution several years later. A functioning socialist democracy in Czechoslovakia could well have affected the outcome in both coun-tries. When the tanks went in there was very little real anger expressed by the West. If one compares the reaction to Soviet intervention in Afghanistan or the declaration of Martial Law in Poland, then it could almost be said that sighs of relief could be heard if one listened carefully in Western capitals during the invasion of Czechoslovakia.

This was the third act in the Czech tragedy. It is now fashionable to treat such events as inevitable. Political fatalism became very popular after 1968. Yet the Russians need not have invaded and could have been prevented from doing so by a firmer authority in Prague. It was clear then, as it is now, that if Dubček had mobilized the people and the army and told Brezhnev and his imperial cohorts boldly and publicly that Czechoslovakia would resist the re-imposition of bureaucratic rule, it is very possible that the Soviet Generals might not have sanctioned a military invasion. After all, Tito had broken with Stalin in 1948 and had armed his own people politically, by conducting the debate in public, while at the same time warning Stalin privately that any attempt to impose Moscow's will by force of arms would be met with armed resistance. Dubček and his comrades did not wish to take the risk.

I heard of the invasion of Czechoslovakia when I was rung at 7am by Pat Jordan, always an early riser. Within an hour I was at the new offices of *The Black Dwarf* on the second floor of 7 Carlisle Street in Soho, just below the *New Left Review*, which appropriately occupied the lofty heights of the top floor. I spent three hours solidly on the phone as people began to pour into our office and prepare placards. Five thousand demonstrators responded to our call and we marched to the Soviet embassy the same evening to record our protest in the name of Marx and Lenin, Luxemburg and Trotsky, whose portraits were carried, together with red flags. It is a matter of some pride to record that it was the Marxist left in Britain that organized the largest demonstration against the destruction of socialism with a human face. A Labour Party rally in Hyde Park that weekend could only collect a few hundred bystanders. We had been constantly attacked for our one-sided attacks on the United States. The press labelled us as dupes of the Kremlin. Reactionary workers often told us to go and live in Moscow. For once they were silenced, embarrassed by the passivity of their own side.

The invasion of Czechoslovakia had other repercussions as well. The Cuban Ambassador in London, Alba Grinan, was a great friend of *The Black Dwarf* and I had been negotiating with her for the rights to publish Che Guevara's *Bolivian Diary*. This document had been captured by the Bolivians, copied and sent to Washington, but the Bolivian Minister for the Interior, Arguedas, had been unable to stomach American control of his government any longer. He had left Bolivia and handed the diaries to Havana, which published them rapidly. They included a passage where Che confided that 'I must write letters to Sartre and Bertrand Russell, so they can organize an

international fund to raise money for the Bolivian liberation movement . . .' Arguedas had told Castro of the circumstances of Che's death
and the Cuban leader revealed these in the course of his long introduction to the diaries. Che had been captured alive and taken to the
village of Higueros. After twenty-four hours they decided to kill him.
Castro described the scene thus:

> Major Miguel Ayoroa and Colonel Andres Selnich, two Rangers
> trained by the Yankees, ordered a non-commissioned officer, Mario
> Teran, to murder Che. Teran went in completely drunk, and Che, who
> had heard the shots which had just killed a Bolivian and a Peruvian
> fighter, seeing the brute hesitate said to him firmly, 'Shoot. Don't be
> afraid.' Teran left the room and his superiors Ayoroa and Selnich had to
> repeat the order which he finally carried out, firing his machine-gun at
> Che from the waist down . . . Che's agony was thus cruelly prolonged
> until a sergeant, who was also drunk, finally killed him with a pistol shot
> in the left side. The whole procedure was in brutal contrast with the
> respect Che never once failed to show for the life of many Bolivian
> officers and soldiers he had taken prisoner . . .

Three Cubans, one of them Pombo, had escaped the encirclement
and made their way back to Havana, where they confirmed the
authenticity of Che's diaries. These were to be published in English by
the radical US magazine, *Ramparts*, and rights in Europe had been
assigned to various left-wing publishing houses – Maspero in France,
Feltrinelli in Italy, Trikont Verlag in Germany – and we succeeded in
getting Cuban permission to publish the diaries as a special number of
The Black Dwarf. Jonathan Cape had decided to publish a hardback at
25s. We scooped them by using the *Ramparts* artwork and our
introduction 'spat on those publishers' who were out to make money.
In the event we sold 25,000 copies within two months at 5s a copy,
returned the money we had borrowed from various people, including
£250 from Peggy Ramsey, who was David Mercer's agent, and put
the rest in our general funds.

Money for the magazine was a perennial problem in those days.

Apart from Clive's appeals in our pages (Lenin in 1917: Land, Peace and Bread; *Black Dwarf* in 1968: Bread, Bread and Bread!) we occasionally had art sales of paintings donated to us by Hockney, Kitaj, Patrick Procktor, Jim Dine and others. Then there was a stall-holder from the Portobello Road, with hair that reached his waist, who used to walk in every fortnight, smile at me, put his hands in his apron and bring out fifty five-pound notes, which was an enormous amount of money in those days. I would thank him. We would both smile and he would go away. The fourth time this happened I asked him in the most friendly fashion possible why he gave us this money. He looked at me as if I should have known better, smiled again and said after a short pause: 'Capitalism is non-groovy, man' and left. On another occasion after one of our appeals – we owed printing bills – I got a phone call from a woman in Wales. She gave me her name and asked how much we needed. I thought if I gave her the actual amount she might not donate a penny so I was mumbling incoherently when she said, 'Please, just tell me exactly how much you need'. It was in the region of £2,500. She promised a cheque in the post the same day, but I managed to stop her from ending our conversation and asked what we had done to deserve this mercy. 'Christopher Logue once saved my life,' she replied, 'and I like the paper.' She was a potter by profession and had recently inherited a small sum of money. She was to help us out on two subsequent occasions. Christopher Logue was uncharacteristically modest when we informed him of this windfall. All he could remember was that he had encountered her in a distressed state on a mountain road in the South of France. She had broken off with her lover and was standing on the edge of the road, looking down meaningfully at the ravine below. Logue had talked her out of her depression and she had not forgotten the kindness. Clive Goodwin was not disposed to give the poet too much credit on this occasion. 'The key fact', he suggested, 'is that she read our paper in the first place. Otherwise how could she have known that Logue was on our board?'

Relations with the Cubans were, alas, about to deteriorate. Fidel Castro had finally spoken on the Soviet intervention in Czechoslovakia. It was a clever speech and there were several strands contained in it, including an important subtext, which was very critical of Eastern European socialisms, but he had finally come down on the side of the degenerate Muscovite papacy against the Reformation. David Mercer and myself went to see Alba to express our regret and to inform her that we would soon be publishing 'An Open Letter to Fidel' making our criticisms public and distancing ourselves sharply from his analysis. She was very sad and wept. We, too, were sad, but the tears of Czech socialists and reformers had to prevail in this debate. She pleaded with us to send the letter to Havana via an embassy courier if necessary, but not to make it public. But a socialist principle was at stake and politics had to remain in command. I realized that it was goodbye to any trip to Havana in the near future. I had received two invitations, but until October, lawyers had advised against travelling anywhere and I cursed the Wilson–Callaghan regime that day. We returned to the office and I drafted the letter to Castro, which was signed by Mercer, Clive Goodwin, Roger Smith and myself. The issue containing this and our special edition of Che's diaries were published simultaneously. One small, though not unforeseen, result of this business was that my name was removed from the official guest list of the embassy for their annual beano to mark the success of the revolution. It was farewell to tamarind juice and the potent mixtures contained in the Havana Libres.

Chapter Nine

The Year 1968:
The New Revolutionaries

Know thy enemy,
He does not care what colour you are
provided you work for him;
he does not care how much you earn
provided you earn more for him;
he does not care who lives in the room at the top
provided he owns the building;
he will let you say whatever you like against him
provided you do not act against him;
he sings the praises of humanity
but knows machines cost more than men;
bargain with him he laughs and beats you at it;
challenge him
and he kills;
sooner than lose the things he owns
he will destroy the world.

Christopher Logue, 1968

The continuing Vietnamese offensive had created a major crisis inside the United States. Impending defeat in a war being fought several thousand miles away had split the Democratic Party. At its convention in Chicago that year, the delegates had been surrounded by anti-war demonstrators, inspired largely by the SDS and various anti-war coalitions. The veteran Mayor Daley had used excessive force, but when he realized that half the delegates inside the convention were sympathetic to the peaceniks and were about to refuse the Presidential nomination to the Vice-President Hubert Humphrey, he panicked and turned his truncheons and tear gas on them. The Democratic Party tore itself apart in public as a peace candidate, in the shape of Senator Eugene McCarthy, challenged Humphrey and polarized the convention. Daley was denounced as a 'Hitler of the stockyards', as a McCarthy delegate told TV cameras that 'you can only be pissed on for so long before you realize it's not rain'. As the predominantly white demonstrators were beaten bloody outside the International Amphitheatre that summer many of them began to realize the treatment that was the daily lot of the underprivileged black Americans.

Yet in some ways the most exciting news came not from Chicago, but from Fort Hood in Texas, where forty soldiers had been arrested and put in the stockade for refusing point-blank an order to proceed to Chicago and confront the anti-war demonstrations. The black comedian, Dick Gregory, who was in London at this time, had got very excited by the soldiers' revolt. We were discussing the situation in the hospitality room of a TV station, prior to appearing on the *David Frost Show*. The programme's researchers were somewhat frazzled, but trying not to show it as we ignored their efforts to elicit what we intended to say when interviewed by Frost. Instead we discussed the latest news from the home-front. Gregory predicted that with the conscripts in a state of disaffection, there was very little chance of the United States winning the war. He said that the Tet offensive had demoralized the rank and file of the American Army and Vietnam would win. Gregory was particularly pleased at the effect the war was having on black consciousness in his country. 'In all other wars,' he said, 'including the genocidal wars against the native Americans, blacks fought as patriots. A man with a black skin had to fight extra hard to prove he was a patriotic American. Now that's over.' What he told me that evening tied in with the reports in *Ramparts* and other radical journals of the time. Some of the most effective snipers during the black rebellions had been black war veterans.

Both Martin Luther King and Robert Kennedy had recently been assassinated and Gregory referred to their deaths as 'executions'. Martin Luther King's death was felt as a personal loss by the whole of black America, but it was also mourned by a significant section of white

society. It appeared that any black leader who attacked the Establishment and acquired nationwide popularity had to be summarily despatched. King, unlike Malcolm X, had never espoused violence. Yet
he, too, was defeated by the bullet rather than the ballot. Gregory felt
that Kennedy would have won and pulled out of Vietnam. As for
Senator McCarthy, he would lose. Gregory was very critical of
McCarthy's record and as he described the past of the Senator who was
the peace candidate my heart sank. McCarthy had voted in favour of
every appropriation for the war; he had voted consistently against the
admission of China to the UN; voted to wage war against Cuba; voted
to back the House of Un-American Activities Committee; and voted
against withholding of federal school aid from segregated schools in
1961. In the space of a few minutes, McCarthy's liberal credentials
were torn apart, but just as I was about to throw them into the ever-
present dustbin in history, Gregory muttered: 'Of course he might
have changed. People do change . . .'

Just before the murder of Bobby Kennedy, the London Bureau of
the *Washington Post* had written to a few dozen people in Britain asking
us to explain in a hundred words who we would vote for in the US
Presidential elections and the major reason for so doing. My choice
was simple and, I must admit, simplistic. I chose the only far-left
candidate in the ring at the time, Fred Halstead of the Socialist
Workers Party. Paul Johnson, Hugh Thomas, Dee Wells and Arnold
Wesker opted for Kennedy. McCarthy received the votes of Michael
Foot, Harold Pinter, Iris Murdoch, A. J. Ayer and Robert Shaw. The
official war candidate, Hubert Humphrey was backed by a literary
triumvirate consisting of Kingsley Amis, Elizabeth Jane Howard and
J. B. Priestley. Nelson Rockefeller obtained just one vote, from Nigel
Lawson. Richard Nixon's only supporter was Auberon Waugh. The
novelist Brigid Brophy insisted on voting for Coretta, the widow of
Martin Luther King and Bertrand Russell stated that he was against all
the major candidates, but found McCarthy the 'least attractive'. In the
event, because of the Kennedy death, the *Washington Post* decided that
it would be in poor taste to publish the survey, thus sparing American
readers the tedium of our thoughts.

What was happening in the United States was vital for all of us who were following the progress of the war in Indochina. The two battlefields were very different, but the two struggles were closely interconnected. The military failure of the United States in Vietnam produced a major political crisis at home. Mayor Daley tried to exorcize this spectre by attempting to crush it physically, but the movement had not yet reached its peak. It was getting stronger by the day and we monitored it very closely from Europe.

Not that we were isolated. There were large numbers of Americans visiting Europe and from the SDS militants who came to *The Black Dwarf* offices to exchange experiences we got a very clear idea as to the intensity of the struggle against the war. I remember an SDS woman, who stated in a matter-of-fact way one afternoon that the *only* way to defeat the war-machine in her own country was to emulate the NLF guerrillas who had attacked the US embassy in Saigon. What she was suggesting was a campaign of bombings in the United States directed at military installations and the headquarters of Dow Chemicals (the manufacturers of napalm) and other corporations who were maximizing profits at the expense of the dead in Vietnam. I argued against this course very strongly. Perhaps I was tougher than I might have been because we were in the middle of plans for the VSC's October demonstration and ideas not completely dissimilar to what the SDSer was saying had been publicly aired. Such a course was not simply wrong on principle, and foolish, it was suicidal in every sense of the word. I must confess that whenever something like this was suggested I had to think very hard whether the person who wanted to embark on such a course was somewhat deranged or a straightforward provocateur. This was not paranoia. We knew full well that phones were tapped, mail was opened and there were Special Branch infiltrators in VSC. This was part of the routine functioning of a capitalist democracy. In fact on one occasion a postman had dragged me out of the office and told me that our letters were opened every day before being delivered. He declined to be interviewed for the obvious reason that he would lose his job. Years later I was accosted by a young man on a platform on Brighton railway station. He had been a postman who sorted the post near my home and told me exactly the same tale regarding my personal correspondence. After the general strike in France, there was a definite sign of panic in Britain. This made us more careful than usual. But the woman from an SDS chapter in New York was neither nutty nor an agent of the state. She was horrified by what her government was doing and she felt powerless. I reminded her of Lenin's description of a terrorist as 'a Liberal with a bomb'. She looked puzzled. I explained: 'Liberals believe in pressure politics. They think that if you apply pressure on the rulers in a nice way they will change. Terrorists apply pressure in not-such-a-nice-way, but it is pressure unrelated to the masses or their moods. Hence total failure and isolation and repression.' She replied that this was a very Liberal argument. She got angry with me and shouted that America was basically a one-party state, run by different segments of the ruling class. She banged her fist on my desk and insisted that the blue-collar workers had been integrated into the system. Only blacks and students were fighting the war criminals. I mustered every authority possible to convince her that she was wrong. Rosa Luxemburg, Lenin and Trotsky had all favoured mass action and new popular institutions as the way to overthrow the old regime. Mao, Fidel and Ho Chi Minh had succeeded or were in the process of doing so because they had the support of a sizeable majority of the population. She heard me out, smiled and said without rancour: 'But none of them ever tried to make a revolution in the States.' Then a new round began and others joined the debate.

Our offices had now become a regular port of call for visiting revolutionaries from all over the world. One night a group of hippy anarchists slept in our distribution office. While eating lotuses that night they painted a large diagram of how to make a Molotov cocktail on the wall. When I arrived the next morning they were still fast asleep. I woke them up and persuaded them to depart. They did so, but not before trying to empty their bowels in the lavatory we shared with the *New Left Review*. A full-scale verbal battle then ensured on the landing. The toilet was occupied by a Hungarian revolutionary, a veteran of 1956, Nicolas Krasso, who was happily reading his batch of newspapers when the door was pushed open by these interlopers from 1968. Krasso had not bothered to lock the door. He told the Dutch contingent, by now bursting to the seams, that he was likely to be another fifteen minutes. This resulted in a furore and abuse was generously exchanged. I have no idea how the matter was resolved, but we covered up the offending drawing on the wall with a large poster and it was agreed to paint it out as soon as possible. The very next day our offices were raided by Scotland Yard. A team of Special Branch men and a woman went straight to the poster covering the drawing, removed it and photographed the crudely drawn diagram. Chief Inspector Elwyn Jones then interviewed me at length and warned me that they would be preparing a report for Sir Norman Skellhorn, Director of Public Prosecutions. He then ordered a search of the offices. They examined all our files, looked through our address books and took away various documents, especially material in French and Spanish. A letter from a reader asking how he could obtain a helmet of the sort worn by demonstrators in France was treated as extremely sinister. Since our offices had been broken into twice, without anything being removed one had assumed that the Special Branch already had a copy of everything on our files.

The reason for this particular raid was to help create an ugly atmosphere for the October demonstration, which was due to take place the following month. I had been speaking throughout the country once again for VSC and it was clear that the demonstration would dwarf all previous assemblies. The size of my meetings had taken a qualitative leap and students were occupying campuses in different parts of the country, choosing as their enemy the remote and unaccountable bureaucracies which ran the universities. To the traditional methods we counterposed a university where students and lecturers had equal rights and elected a body to administer all institutions of higher education. 'Student Power' had become a rallying cry throughout Britain. Its aim was to begin the process of change immediately and at the place where one worked or studied and then move outwards. The necessity to transform the bourgeois universities into a 'red base' was theorized by Robin Blackburn in the *New Left*

Review, and a Penguin book edited by him and Alexander Cockburn, enticingly entitled *Student Power*, sold tens of thousands of copies at the time. The French events had given the indigenous movement a tremendous impetus which worried those in authority. They openly expressed fears that the VSC's October demonstration might turn into a French-style insurrection. The very thought was absurd. Britain was not France. Labour was in office and the working class was restive, but quiescent. A minority of workers were involved in VSC, but none of us ever believed that anything remotely resembling France could happen in Britain that year. The organs of the state were not as sure as we were and two days after the raid on *The Black Dwarf*'s offices a police-inspired report was published in *The Times*, then owned by Lord Thomson. It was obvious the police had leaked disinformation to the authors of this fiction, Clive Borrell and Brian Cashinella, who were assigned to cover crime. Their story opened thus:

> A small army of militant extremists plans to seize control of certain highly sensitive installations and buildings in central London next month, while 6000 Metropolitan policemen are busy controlling an estimate crowd of 100,000 anti-Vietnam war demonstrators...
>
> This startling plot has been uncovered by a special squad of detectives formed to track down the extremists who are understood to be manufacturing 'Molotov cocktail' bombs and amassing a small arsenal of weapons. They plan to use these against police and property in an attempt to dislocate communications and law and order...

This was pure fabrication, designed to excite passions and keep people away from our demonstration. A leader in the same paper backed these lies and warned the public about the menace posed by demonstrations. Two days later, as a VSC member was walking out of the campaign's headquarters in the East End of London, a blue van drew up and somebody shot at him. The evidence of this was visible as the street sign bore the marks of the bullet. Yet it was unanimously agreed that reporting it to the police would be a complete waste of time.

Labour and Tory MPs called on the government to ban the march and sections of the press built up a nationwide hysteria. I was by that time used to receiving at least three or four death threats a week, but since all our phones were tapped, I assumed that Special Branch was aware of them as well. There was one important tactical question facing the Vietnam campaign. Should we or should we not march to the American embassy in Grosvenor Square? There were differences of opinion on this question and it was agreed to take a decision at our National Committee meeting in Sheffield on the weekend of 8–9 September.

We were due to meet at Sheffield University, but at the last minute the Secretary of the Students' Union, a supporter of the Labour Government, insisted that the meeting could only take place if he was allowed to attend. Since he was not even a member of the VSC we declined his offer and left. None of the pubs in the town was willing to rent us a room; the publicans had clearly read the more lurid accounts in the tabloids and did not want to be seen providing facilities for insurrectionists. Our search was not made easy by the fact that we were being openly followed by a posse of police cars. Ultimately, we pretended to leave the town and the police gave up the chase. In fact we took advantage of the good weather and decided to meet on the moors outside Sheffield. The VSC leadership finally met in a bomb crater near Ringinlow, a dozen miles from Sheffield. The discussion commenced and it soon became obvious that an overwhelming majority was of the view that 27 October should be a show rather than a test of strength. We discounted the possibility of occupying the US embassy, even with a hundred thousand people. The police were now well prepared, the Labour Government had engendered a national hysteria, the media were still very strong on their line of subversive plans to seize the Stock Exchange and any real attempt to take the embassy would, we were convinced, lead to bloodshed. None of us was prepared to play with anyone else's life. We did, nonetheless, agree to take over the streets and not tolerate any heavy police presence. After we had made the crucial decision to disperse in Hyde Park, the local police arrived and instructed us to move since we were trespassing on private property. A debate commenced on our common law rights, but as they appealed on their intercom system for reinforcements, we decided to leave. This time they followed our convoy to the motorway.

The October demonstration created a strange polarization in this country. It was as if, deprived of a real revolution, the state was determined to treat VSC as a substitute in order to ram their views down several million throats. Raymond Williams, a distinguished Marxist writer and scholar, commented on a TV programme that the British ruling class had always believed in the theory of 'nipping all threats in the bud'. English pragmatism even on that level refused to accept the underlying causes of dissension and unrest. Williams was amongst the few from the older generation of the left who defended VSC on television in debates with the Police Federation and actually spoke on our platforms whenever we asked him to appear. It was extremely important to demonstrate to the children of '68 that not all the socialists from the preceding generations were hostile to us, though it often appeared to be the case.

In the month prior to the demonstration there was an amusing incident which illustrated the depth of the divisions in Britain at the time. Norman Swallow of the BBC had approached Clive Goodwin, who was also my literary agent, with an interesting proposal for their *Omnibus* programme. The aim was to show that our ideas were irrelevant as far as 'ordinary people' were concerned and that we were completely out of touch with the realities of rural England. The BBC suggested that I should speak on 'Why Revolutionary Socialism?' or a related topic in a medium-sized village in the countryside. They would prepare large posters, advertise the meeting, film me addressing an empty village hall, show the locals carrying on their everyday life totally unconcerned at the intrusion and then interview me in the very heart of this sea of indifference.

We discussed the matter seriously and I felt that it was a challenge that should be taken up. Apart from anything else it gave us an opportunity to talk about the British aristocracy, its large landholdings, its pampered life-style and its strong grip on the way in which the upper echelons of British society were organized. It would have been a good moment to discuss the English Revolution of 1640 and its failure to create lasting republican institutions or to crush the economic power of the landed gentry. Even as Clive and I talked the speech I would make to half a dozen agricultural workers was running through my head like a film.

The BBC chose a village whose name I forget, and everything was organized for the meeting. Then there was silence. Finally Norman Swallow rang, extremely embarrassed, to explain that they had run into problems. The posters had gone up in the village and created an immediate storm. There were some supporters, but a minority, whereas the local farmers had organized what amounted to a lynch-mob to burn me at the stake. In other words the BBC's political initiative had backfired and the entire village had been able to talk of little else. This seemed to me to be an ideal moment to make the film. Clive concurred. The BBC after a lot of hesitation finally decided against the project on the grounds that there might be violence against my person and their insurers refused to insure me. The risk was too great. And so the viewers were deprived of the sight of a trouble-making foreigner entering a peaceful English village to stir up hatred.

During the same period BBC radio's *Any Questions* rang to ask whether I was prepared to be on the same platform as Enoch Powell and debate him during the course of the programme. I had always wanted a public debate with Powell, but he had consistently refused to contemplate the idea. He did the same on this occasion and the BBC, regretfully of course, withdrew my invitation. Powell, quite naturally, went ahead after approving the list of those who could appear with him.

As 27 October approached, state-engendered tensions grew and sections of the press began to talk of the 'October Revolution'. We were informed by a tiny Maoist group that they were intending to march to Grosvenor Square and the embassy and would split off from our march and take as many people as they could. We shrugged our shoulders and ignored their antics. I had spoken at the big mobilizing meetings in Scotland, Wales and England for three continuous weeks.

I knew the mood because I had helped create it and the view of most people was clear. Grosvenor Square was a 'death-trap' and had to be avoided. We would march past Downing Street and then to Hyde Park. At every press conference during this period I had stressed that VSC did not want any violence and there would be none provided the police kept away from the march. Scotland Yard believed that something sinister was being planned and increased Special Branch surveillance. I was followed almost everywhere and the pub near *The Black Dwarf* offices in Carlisle Street was always full of Special Branch men.

What worried us a great deal was that the police might provoke a confrontation by blocking off streets and then the anger of the marchers would become uncontrollable. The students at the London School of Economics had decided to occupy their institution for the whole weekend and a first-aid unit staffed by VSC doctors and nurses was set up to deal with victims of violence. A special issue of *The Black Dwarf* with a print run of 50,000 was being prepared for the demonstration. The BBC had banned Mick Jagger's latest song, 'Street Fighting Man'. I rang and asked whether he would write the words specially for us so that we could print a facsimile in the paper. He agreed immediately and the handwritten song arrived the same day. (I was delighted that the handwriting was legible. We photographed the sheet of paper and I threw the original into the wastepaper basket. No one in the office thought this sacrilegious. The cult of the individual is always, in the last resort, a substitute for collective action. Jagger sang well and he was being helpful. That was all.) Amongst other contributors to that issue who were listed on the front page I added 'Mick Jagger and Fred Engels on Street Fighting'. Together with the song, I had decided to publish an extract from Engels on the difficulties of fighting on the barricades.

The week before the march *The Black Dwarf* offices became the organizing centre of the big demo. Journalists were flooding in from all over Europe, hoping that the next act after Paris might be London. Olivier Todd from France was very cross with me for suggesting that his journey might have been unnecessary. We were extremely busy producing the paper and organizing the march. Consequently one avoided as much as possible granting 'exclusive' interviews to individual journalists, who all tended to ask the same type of questions. For that reason we held VSC press conferences at regular intervals. The *Sunday Times* was convinced that something 'big' would happen in London on 27 October. They had persuaded the American novelist and critic, Mary McCarthy, to cover the demonstration for their colour magazine. She was paid a gigantic fee and clearly felt that some research was necessary. She arrived in London a week before the 'event' and rang me the same day. She only had one evening for pre-demo interviews and could I see her. I had an intensive speaking schedule, which was running at the time to three meetings a day, followed by an organizing committee every evening which monitored everything connected to VSC. I explained all this, told her when and where our press conferences were and declined to see her. She rang Ken Tynan. He rang Clive Goodwin, who gave me one of his special pleading looks and I caved in, but we limited her time to five minutes, enough to enable her to say she'd visited our offices and asked a question, but no more. I saw no reason why she should be afforded any more facilities than what we were offering journalists from Brazil, India or Egypt, who were pestering the office all the time.

I was in the middle of an organizing committee when she arrived the next day with Don McCullin, the photographer. She waited and looked around, while the item under discussion was dealt with and then I offered to answer her questions. She was livid at being restricted to five minutes, which I could understand. I have no doubt that if she had tried to engage me intellectually the conversation would have breached the agreed time limits. Her first question was banal beyond belief and I had answered it thousands of times on radio, TV and press interviews. The reply must have been on every press clipping she had read before coming to see us. Her own description of the visit ran as follows:

'What do you hope to accomplish by this demonstration?' I had been asking Tariq Ali in the offices of *The Black Dwarf* on Carlisle Street,

which was placarded with art work of Fidel and Che, previous issues of
the magazine, provocative slogans. There were photos of the enemy:
Axel Springer, Paul Getty, Howard Hughes. There was a striking photo
of US marines in bristling combat formation resembling a human
porcupine ready to throw its quills. There was another photo involving
a discarded condom, and a typed list of first-aid stations by districts. In
this window-case of pop politics, like a vision from another world,
hung a very big photograph of Trotsky with his clear, intelligent,
spectacled professorial eyes ('What you here old friend?'). A new issue
of the magazine had just been printed, and young distributors were
hurrying out with it ...

The Dwarf Offices, temporary staff headquarters for the Vietnam
Solidarity Campaign .. suggested a stage set of revolution, with
supernumararies like spear-bearers entering stage right and left, bit
players speaking lines of studied rudeness as in some up-dated Wildean
comedy, breathless messengers, and a general atmospheric litter, the
floor serving as a communal ash-tray. I could not resist the feeling that I
had been cast in the role of audience and ought to have paid an
admission ... The words 'What do you hope to accomplish', etc. had, I
quickly discovered, the effect of a negative password. It virtually invited
the bum's rush.

It is true that when she asked the question there was a collective
groan from everyone in the room, which annoyed her a great deal. I
replied that if she had been specially hired to come here she could have
been a tiny bit more original and since the answer to her question was
on record everywhere it might be better if she did not waste any more
of our time. She left in a huff and went to see the Maoists who had
nothing better to do and spent several hours with her. Her critical
sense must have deserted her because she retailed their slanders
wholesale in the pages of the *Sunday Times*. Her own reasoning was
influenced by how *she* as famous person was treated. We genuinely did
not have time to massage her ego that particular day. She wrote of how
kind the Mao–Stalinists were: 'Though we came from the bourgeois
press, we were not treated as trespassers but simply as guests – the

reverse of what had happened in Carlisle Street. It was even possible, as I did, to take exception to the icon of Stalin.' Exception may have been taken to the icon, but the lies peddled by the Stalinist school of falsification coincided with her own prejudices. After reading her article Tynan rang up to apologize: 'Your instincts were sounder than mine. She should have been kept out.'

On the eve of the demonstration I went to speak to a very large rally at the London School of Economics. There were over a thousand students present and their solidarity was very moving. This time there was no sectarianism. In fact one of the chants that evening, 'We Are All Foreign Scum', provided a united front against the blatant racism of most of the tabloids and various Labour and Tory MPs. A Peruvian Maoist who pleaded for head-banging in Grosvenor Square was ignored. The mood of the LSE was euphoric, but disciplined. I stressed that what we had to demonstrate on the morrow was not an exercise in urban guerrilla warfare, but the presence of a new model army. It was obvious that many of our own VSC branches would have preferred a set-piece confrontation outside the US embassy, but they accepted the views and feelings of the majority.

I went straight from the LSE to Carlisle Street to complete a discussion on the distribution of the paper on the march with Roger Tyrell, the circulation supremo, and others. At 7.30pm I left to get a taxi to go to the final VSC planning meeting. On the way I met Malcolm Southan, a journalist on the pre-tabloid *Sun* and the only Fleet Street person to have reported our side fairly. He asked for a lift and got into the taxi with me. Suddenly three men, thickset and pugnacious, smelling of alcohol burst into the taxi, shouting 'This is our cab'. They dragged me out and two of them started hitting me on the head. I resisted and soon Roger Tyrell and others from the office arrived and the thugs ran to a white Cortina, parked on the corner, which was intended as the kidnap vehicle and speeded away. We got the number, which was duly handed to the police, who, as usual, did nothing, preferring to treat the whole affair as a joke.

News of what had happened spread rapidly and when I arrived at the VSC meeting I found Pat Jordan and Ernie Tate extremely worried about my safety on the march itself. In the two weeks preceding the demonstration, the number of threatening calls had reached a crescendo, but we had ignored them. The kidnap attempt did shake me, but not enough to accept the advice of some that I should not march all the way. This was a grotesque suggestion and I refused. The campaign against us had been so strong that a National Opinion Poll sample showed that 56 per cent of the population were for banning *all* political demonstrations and 65 per cent favoured the use of tear gas against demonstrators. This did not surprise me at all. There was an extremely reactionary streak in Labour corporatism and Callaghan as Home Secretary was shameless as far as pandering to backward political instincts was concerned. In that sense the style of the present leader of the Labour Party, Neil Kinnock, resembles the authoritarian populism of Callaghan much more than the technocratic arrogance of Wilson.

On the day of the demonstration I was awakened by an early morning call from an *Evening Standard* person who asked a Mary McCarthy special: 'What's the first thing you did this morning?' Furious at being woken at 6am my reply was slightly apolitical. 'Masturbated!' I shouted into the phone. Long silence, followed by a hurt 'Oh!' and end of conversation.

When I arrived at the Embankment where we were assembling the sight was joyous. The VSC levies were all there and the red flags and NLF banners intermingled with posters from the French May and anti-capitalist placards in their hundreds. This was much more than a demonstration of solidarity with the struggle of the Vietnamese. It was an assembly of those who regarded the capitalist order in Europe as doomed. The significance of the turnout (over 100,000) was not lost on the state. This was the largest explicitly revolutionary demonstration in Britain since the twenties. A survey showed that an overwhelming majority of those who marched that day were hostile to capitalism. Vietnam had mingled with a pre-revolutionary crisis in France and Prague had proved that change in Europe would have to create a system that was infinitely more *democratic* than that which existed already. This was the mood that day. We were not crazed utopians and the ruling classes in Western Europe did not see us as such, but as the advance guard of a new order. We wished to transform Western civilization because we regarded it as politically, morally and culturally bankrupt. That was the hallmark of 1968. And as tens and tens of thousands of predominantly young people came together that day they expressed an optimism about the future. The world had to be changed and France and Vietnam proved that it is possible to move forward.

I had been rung up that morning by a few Labour MPs, including the late Anne Kerr, who had asked whether it would be safe for *them* to join us that day. I said they would be welcome and some were there. I remember the diminutive figure of Frank Allaun, whose voice had been one of the most critical of Wilson in Parliament. There was no hostility to him and we only wished that he had been able to bring more of his colleagues out that day. The whole demonstration was reported live for two hours by London Weekend Television, who had cameras placed at strategic points all along the route of the march. As we were about to start, a few extremely tough-looking and burly men came to the front and linked arms with me on both sides. Since the experience of the previous day I was slightly nervous and a number of IS and IMG comrades were also close by to prevent a mishap. But these were London dockers and had been sent by the Communist Party to stay close to me throughout the long march to Hyde Park. I was extremely moved by their protective presence and made a mental note to thank the old Party, which had by now realized that boy-cotting VSC had been an error and had decided to support this par-ticular demonstration.

The police were hardly present and we took over the streets completely. We saw them in large numbers for the first time as we marched up Whitehall. They were ensuring that there was no assault on Downing Street. In fact I was so preoccupied with other matters that I had forgotten Downing Street. It was the police who stopped the march and reminded me that we had informed them of our intention to hand in a letter of protest at Number 10. The truth was that Wilson was rather low on our list of priorities for that day and, character-istically, no one had remembered to draft a letter. Everyone was waiting for us to deliver something or other. We had at one stage discussed unloading a truckful of cow-dung on the steps, but given the hysterical climate this had been rejected as impractical. There had been several yippy-style volunteers who had offered to be part of a deputation which would puke outside the door of the Prime Ministerial residence. Various methods of making themselves sick had been aired, but this proposal had been rejected on the grounds that they might not succeed. There was no other alternative but to deliver a written protest. I had a scruffy little notebook in my pocket. I hastily scribbled a message which read: 'Dear Harold, 100,000 people came to tell you to stop supporting the Americans and start backing the NLF. What about it? Yours, TA for VSC.' Since no envelope was available I folded this note and gave it to the minion behind the door. A few days later I received the usual reply. I was savagely attacked by the zombies of the Socialist Labour League (who did not march that day, but instead distributed leaflets explaining 'Why the SLL is not Marching') for addressing the Labour leader as 'Dear Harold'. This, wrote the sectarian hacks, demonstrated beyond doubt the 'revisionist character' of the VSC and the political organizations who backed its mobilizations.

After Downing Street, the Maoists split off with a few hundred supporters and proceeded to Grosvenor Square. Our march turned into Hyde Park an hour later and it took the entire demonstration over three hours to enter. Ken Tynan was perched on a railing, counting the numbers coming in, determined to refute underestimates by the police and press, which he did in the week that followed. We heard that there had been a tiny fracas at Grosvenor Square, but that the remnants on both sides had ended up singing 'Auld Lang Syne', though the Maoists denied that they had joined in the chorus.

For our part the demonstration had gone according to plan. *The Times* had alleged that we were planning to overthrow the state. They were to mock us the next day for having been so peaceful. The newspaper did not need Murdoch to sink low. Shamelessness knows no bounds. Nor was it a pure accident that its Editor was William Rees-Mogg – a staunch defender of every US policy in Vietnam. When Washington bombed Hanoi, Rees-Mogg was in favour. When they stopped bombing, Rees-Mogg applauded their statesmanship.

When they started again, Rees-Mogg wrote that they had no choice. When they opened peace talks in Paris, Rees-Mogg deemed it to be a prudent move. There was a shift of personnel in the White House. Rees-Mogg became a born-again Republican. Nixon bombed Cambodia. Rees-Mogg regretfully understood. Saigon fell. Rees-Mogg mourned in silence. Watergate commenced and while the *Washington Post* and the *New York Times* became agitational newspapers, demanding a thorough cleansing of the stables, good old Rees-Mogg backed Nixon to the hilt. Then Nixon left the White House. Soon after Rees-Mogg vacated his editorial chair at *The Times* and moved to other pastures. During his editorship *The Times* had already become a banana-newspaper, wedded heart-and-soul to whichever devil occupied the White House.

On our own internal front the weeks before the demonstration had been taken up by another discussion, which never became public. We had felt that if only we could offer the possibility of a united and non-sectarian revolutionary youth organization to the tens of thousands who had been radicalized over that year, it would represent a small leap forward for the left in Britain. Tony Cliff and John Palmer of the International Socialists had been engaged in semi-permanent discussions with Pat Jordan, Ernie Tate and myself on the possibility of a joint appeal for a JCR-style organization. Cliff favoured making the call for such a group at the end of the march with myself calling for its formation from the platform. I was opposed to the latter course, but was strongly in favour of the initiative. Alas my own comrades were opposed to the whole idea. Their reasons were somewhat spurious as they explained them to Messrs Cliff and Palmer, but the real fear was that given the small size of the IMG (we had grown from 40 to 200 since April) we would be swamped by the larger IS group. No agreement was reached, which I always regarded as a big tragedy because if we had succeeded, I was convinced that the new members would have rapidly swamped both of our groups and created a different balance of forces. This could have created an exciting new opening on the left, which might have benefited many different projects in the years that followed 1968.

I never thought a great deal about the year as such when we were living it, because while it had been a momentous twelve months on three fronts – Third World in revolution, crisis in capitalist Europe and turmoil in the 'socialist camp' – it symbolized the period and some of us knew that battles might have been lost but the war was still raging. As if to prove this, I began to receive telegrams and letters from student organizations in Pakistan in November informing me that they had begun a movement to topple the military dictatorship of Ayub Khan and inviting me to return and speak at their rallies. I was desperate to return, but officialdom in Islamabad let my parents know that I would not be allowed in the country, even though the only passport I possessed at the time was one issued by the Government of Pakistan. By December it had become clear that the student rebellion in Pakistan was on a much larger scale than France and was spreading from city to city quite spontaneously. The Ayub regime had been presented by the United States as a model of economic success and political stability. This fiction had been taken seriously by the regime itself and it was celebrating its 'decade of development' in great style when the students hurled a dagger at its heart. The weapon was deflected, but the audacity infected the entire country.

I suppose I should have had an inkling of this a few years beforehand, when I had been rung up by the then Pakistan Ambassador to France, the late J. A. Rahim, and invited to lunch at a Parisian restaurant. He also sent a plane ticket and it was an offer I could not refuse. Over an unbelievably *ancienne cuisine* lunch and the most exquisitely full-bodied clarets, His Excellency asked me for my views on Pakistan. I was cautious since I had never met the man before, but straightforward. I think I lectured him for half an hour on the iniquities of the military dictators. Then I waited to be rebuked. He did nothing of the sort. Instead he lambasted the Government which he represented in France and provided me with information which should be used to expose the regime. Rahim was a close friend of the former Cabinet Minister Zulfiqar Ali Bhutto, and he told me that day that a new party was needed to bring socialism to Pakistan. Towards the end of the lunch he had leaned forward conspiratorially and asked me,

'Don't you think the time has come to get rid of this bastard?' This was a reference to Ayub Khan. I assumed, naively as it turned out, that he meant removing him by political methods, but he made a gesture which left no doubt in my mind that what he was proposing was something far more serious and permanent. I thought that this was the appropriate time to return to London and on the plane back I replayed the conversation to myself a number of times. No, it had not been my imagination or the claret playing tricks. The Ambassador to France had actually suggested assassinating his President. When regimes begin to crack up at the top it is usually the case that the more farsighted among them have realized that trouble from below is not far away. So it was with Pakistan in 1966–68.

Chapter Ten

◆

Much Maligned Movements: 1969–75

The call to abandon their illusions about their conditions is a call to abandon a condition which requires illusions.

Karl Marx

The birth of the civil rights movement in the United States had raised black consciousness everywhere, albeit unevenly. The birth of the modern women's movement also took place in the North American continent. The women who had been radicalized by the anti-war movement and SDS began to question their own subordinate position within these groupings. The first manifestos and novels of the women's liberation movement were produced by SDS activists, and American women visiting Western Europe were constantly expressing their amazement at the backwardness of their sisters on this continent.

The ideas had, like everything else in those days, begun to cross frontiers, and at a time when all the traditional values of bourgeois society were being questioned by a new generation it would have been very strange if questions related to gender and sexuality had remained unmentionables. The editorial board of *The Black Dwarf* was constantly changing in those days and everyone was delighted when Sheila Rowbotham joined us and in this way doubled the representation of women. I had known Sheila at Oxford where she had been a member of the Communist Club and subsequently she had worked as an activist in VSC. She was primarily a socialist historian, always interested in history from below.

I cannot now remember what triggered the discussion we had on the oppression of women. It may well have been Christopher Logue whose zany ideas for our covers tended to be conversation-stoppers. In

1969 it had become clear that the Labour Government was preparing to impose a new set of wage restrictions, but the entire Labour Movement had been taken aback by Barbara Castle's proposals to restrict the right to strike via the statute book. Logue had rushed in to an editorial board meeting and declared: 'I've got it. The next cover of *The Black Dwarf* is obvious. We have an ugly fat, naked capitalist standing over Barbara Castle. She's on her knees and is just sucking him off. The caption below should simply state *In Place Of Strife*.' The latter was the title of the draft White Paper proposed by Mrs Castle at the time. Everyone first stared at Logue in silence and then came the laughter. We unanimously decided against the idea for reasons of taste.

Sheila Rowbotham proposed that our first issue for the New Year should be on the theme of women's oppression. The Cubans had begun a tradition of giving every year a political title. They had proclaimed 1968 to be the 'Year of the Heroic Guerrilla', in honour of Che Guevara and the Vietnamese. We decided to make 1969 the 'Year of the Militant Woman' and begin the arduous task of explaining the problems to our readers. There were more problems than we had imagined. The editorial of that issue, 'Women, Sex and the Abolition of the Family', was the first serious attempt by a radical paper in this country to discuss hitherto hidden agendas. We felt that all this talk of an alternative society was flawed without discussion of personal relations and the family, which lay at the heart of women's oppression. Political, juridical and economic inequalities between man and woman could be solved within the existing order, but the transformation of sexual relations was not possible without social revolution. The editorial, written by Fred Halliday, was sharp, but without a trace of demagoguery or self-flagellation. The centre-spread was a manifesto drafted by Sheila and entitled 'Women: The Struggle For Freedom'. It was written with great verve and passion and set out to explain to both sexes what self-liberated women were demanding and why they would not give up this time. The appeal was direct and the opening paragraphs self-explanatory:

We want to drive buses, play football, use beer mugs not glasses. We want men to take the pill. We do not want to be brought with bottles [a reference to 'bird and bottle' parties common on the left at the time] or invited as wives. We do not want to be wrapped up in cellophane or sent off to make the tea or shuffled into the social committee.

But these are only little things. Revolutions are made about little things. Little things which happen to you all the time, every day, wherever you go, all your life.

Here the subordinated relates to dominator, here discontent focuses and here the experience is felt, expressed, articulated, resisted – through the particular. The particular pummels you gently into passivity. So we don't know how to find one another or ourselves. We are perhaps the most divided of all oppressed groups. Divided in our real situations and in our understanding and consciousness of our condition. We are in different classes. Thus we devour and use one another. Our 'emancipation' has been often merely the struggle of the privileged to improve and consolidate its superiority. The women of the working class remain the exploited of the exploited, opposed as workers and oppressed as women.

Sheila Rowbotham's socialist-feminist declaration of independence ended with a firm, but moving appeal to the other gender:

Men! You have nothing to lose but your chains. You will no longer have anyone to creep away and peep at with their knickers down, no one to flaunt as the emblem of your virility, status, self-importance, no one who will trap you, overwhelm you, no etherealized cloudy being floating unattainable in a plastic blue sky, no great mopping up hand-kerchief comforters to crawl into from your competitive, ego strutting alienation, who will wrap you up and SMOTHER you.

There will only be thousands of millions of women people to dis-cover, touch and become, who will understand you when you say we must make a new world in which we do not meet each other as exploiters and used objects. Where we love one another and into which a new kind of human being can be born.

We had all been affected by this text, probably the most important and formative ever published by *The Black Dwarf*, and it made one think a great deal. Sheila, knowing the abysmal proof-reading standards of the paper, had insisted on checking the final proofs herself since she knew that errors in this particular article would be hard to live down. A few days before publication I received an anguished phone call from her asking me to drop everything and join her at the offices where the paper was being designed. Our political designer, Robin Fior, had left us a long time ago and we had employed a young hippy, who was a talented designer, but not very political despite his strong support of VSC and the paper. I had told him that Sheila Rowbotham's article was extremely important and he should design it with sensitivity and care. It was, I informed him, on women's liberation and he should find the necessary illustrations. When I arrived I saw why Sheila was out-raged. Her manifesto was overprinted on a naked woman with the most enormous pair of breasts imaginable. Our hippy friend had designed it so that the key denunciations of male chauvinism were imprinted on the two breasts. It was obvious that it was neither the dialectic that was at work here nor an ultra-subtle deconstruction, but ignorance.

I asked him to scrap the whole design and do it again. Sheila sug-gested some positive images such as a Mexican woman guerrilla from Zapata's army. Neither of us were nasty to the designer, but I did take him aside and explain why what he had done was unacceptable. He did not take the point and was sullen and sulky for the rest of the day. When the paper finally came out, I noticed that, unbeknown to us all, he had slipped in a last-minute boxed advertisement. This read as follows: 'DWARF DESIGNER SEEKS GIRL: Head girl type to make tea, organize paper, me. Free food, smoke space. Suit American Negress. Phone ...' This was his last fling. The next day we parted company.

Nineteen sixty-nine did not become the year of the militant woman, but it did see important new beginnings, which grew in the years that followed and ultimately gave birth to a women's movement in this country. Many revolutionary women, like Sheila Rowbotham, were active in it at every level. That the women referred to themselves as the Women's Liberation Movement (WLM) indicated their political origins, which lay in the movements of 1968 and especially the struggle of the National Liberation Front in South Vietnam. The importance of this movement for women was manifest, but the very fact that many of its founders were members or sympathizers of left-wing parties or groupuscules meant that male socialists had no choice but to discuss the new ideologies seriously and serious attempts were made by women to change the style and functioning of the groups, with varying degrees of failure. The sub-Victorian characteristics of the men who led such groups were far too ingrained to even consider the problems posed by their own sexuality. Elsewhere the more grotesque internal practices which reproduced what happened outside were altered and women were supported when they demanded institutionalization measures to correct the balance of male domination. This required a struggle, but there could be no excuses since everyone was in the same political organization. As a result, the IMG won over a layer of socialist-feminists who played an important role in the development of the broader women's movement, as did an important group of women from the British Communist Party, in particular Elizabeth Wilson whose literary gifts enabled her to exercise considerable influence. I think it is fair to say, however, that it was Sheila Rowbotham's powerfully argued books, *Women, Resistance and Revolution* and *Hidden from History*, which did more to win a new generation of women and men to understand both socialism and feminism than any other writer of the period. Re-reading them again, almost two decades later, I am surprised and slightly startled to discover that they have lost none of their richness and passion or even the freshness which distinguished them from so much else that was published at the time. That is the sign of a true classic and how well they compare to much of the post-feminist writing that is currently on offer in the bookshops of Europe and America.

I do not wish to suggest that everything about the WLM, not to mention the Black Panthers in the United States or their mimics in Britain, was wonderful. The theoretical and practical contradictions were not easily surmountable and the burning urge to breach the walls of monogamy and storm the palaces of patriarchy created new problems. Many experiences were painful. The one feature which I personally disliked a great deal was the notion that the 'style' and 'ways of relating' of the WLM were qualitatively superior to the hierarchized structures of the left. That there were grave problems with the latter was undeniable, but the growing clashes between radical feminists and socialist feminists at WLM conferences were not couched in a language that could serve as an example to anyone of sisterly solidarity. In fact it reminded one of the worst excesses of sectarianism. I recall how several socialist-feminists returned from one of these conferences in a state of great emotional and political shock. On that occasion they had been physically assaulted and spat upon by the radical feminist faction. Their crime: working in groups with male socialists. In reality, sections of the WLM produced their own variant of demagogy whose sole purpose was to crush any attempt to formulate a national or international political strategy. Others used the cover of the WLM to attack far-left groups. It was much easier to do this as feminists rather than as members of a right-wing caucus within the Communist Party. The experts in this form of polemic were soon taken up by sections of the press which found in them a useful cudgel to batter the rams.

The Women's Movement, alas, did not figure in the big debate between the Old and the New Left in Central Hall, Westminster on 24 January 1969. I had received a letter some months previously from Michael Foot, who had suggested that perhaps the time was approaching when the debate should leave the streets and return to the meeting halls. On behalf of *Tribune* he challenged *The Black Dwarf* to a debate on the theme of Reform or Revolution. We both agreed that Lawrence Daly should chair the debate. On the day, almost two and a half thousand people packed the hall to hear Bob Rowthorne and myself defend the revolution against Foot and Eric Heffer. Even before the meeting commenced, excited *Dwarf* sellers were sending me notes to say that we had sold over a thousand copies, which was *Tribune*'s entire print-run for that week. The battle of ideas was, as these things invariably are, perfectly predictable. A large majority of the audience was on our side, as was Lawrence Daly. The outcome was inevitable.

We received massive support, whereas Foot and Heffer were consistently, and sometimes unfairly, heckled. Heffer's attempt to utilize his working-class origins to defend his case ('Four years ago I worked at a bench . . . I know more about the class struggle than 90 per cent of the people here . . .') was drowned in laughter. The main argument was between us and the Labour left. Not a single speaker from the other side defended the record of the Wilson Government. The reports in the press the following morning were virtually unanimous in awarding the prizes to the Dwarves. The odd person out was Ian Aitken in the *Guardian*, a close personal friend of Foot and a one-time member of the *Tribune* staff, though even his report did not attempt to deny that the Labour left were hopelessly outnumbered and outflanked that night.

The audience was not confined to the young. Our side, too, had its elderly supporters, veterans of the thirties and forties, who made no secret of their support. It was Kingsley Martin's last public appearance. Michael Foot had introduced me to him before the debate, but he had maintained a diplomatic and uncharacteristic silence when I asked which side he was backing today. He died a few months later.

During the debate from the floor we were judicious in allocating speakers from both sides and nobody was surprised when the militant brigade made a savage attack on the VSC, something that neither Foot nor Heffer had done. In some ways the most dramatic event was the arrival of a breathless contingent from the London School of Economics, led by a lecturer, Robin Blackburn. He spoke during the floor discussion and told us that there had been a battle at the LSE and that the students had torn the gates down despite a strong police presence. A march to the police station was planned that night and he appealed to the audience to join them after the debate. We cheered him for a long time, but our applause did not help him a great deal. His speech at the Dwarf–Tribune debate was one of the main charges against him when he was sacked by the college authorities a few months later, an event which brought his academic career to a premature conclusion.

Politics in Britain at the time, and even more so in Europe, were very exciting. It was now clear beyond any doubt that there was a massive process of radicalization under way, which had in France and Italy transcended the campuses and entered the factories. A new generation of young workers was deeply affected by the politics and culture of the period, as were the many political activists then in exile from their respective dictatorships in various Western European countries. Spanish, Portuguese, Nicaraguan, Brazilian and Southern African militants, to name only a few, were all apprenticed to the revolutionary process in Western Europe. Chenhamo Chimu-tengwende, a refugee from Ian Smith in Southern Rhodesia, was a member of *The Black Dwarf* editorial board. He was a partisan of Robert Mugabe in 1969–70 and is now a senior figure in the post-colonial administration in Zimbabwe. A Nicaraguan woman refugee in Switzerland was a member of the Revolutionary Marxist League and is now a minister in the Sandinista Government. There are many other examples. Despite the amazing shift in Europe, however, the call from Pakistan had become too loud to resist.

The student movement in Pakistan (which then included Bangla-desh) was in its fourth month of struggle and the revolt had extended to every town in the country. I was determined to see it all for myself. Letters from afar were totally unsatisfactory. The Student Action Committees from Rawalpindi and Dhaka were pressing me to return. They had said that when I came they would ensure that the airport was occupied so that there would be no question of my entry being pro-hibited. I did not entirely believe this, but I prepared to go back nonetheless. Friends and comrades felt that the security risks were too great and that it would be advantageous to encourage a few trust-worthy journalists from Britain to accompany me. Clive Goodwin had provided a graphic summing up of this position: 'If you are going to be assassinated let's at least see it on TV . . .' The only person I fully trusted in the TV world at that time was Gus Macdonald at Granada Tele-vision. Gus had grown up in working-class Glasgow, become a shop steward, and joined the IS, which had been his university under the able vice-chancellorship of one Tony Cliff. He had subsequently joined Granada and was a producer on *World in Action*, the only current affairs programme which had seriously attempted to explain the case of the VSC. Gus Macdonald had been instrumental in bringing that about and so I approached him about Pakistan. He took a few hours to consult his superiors, but they agreed with one condition. The departure must be kept secret or else they would lose their scoop. This was in everyone's interest since I felt (wrongly as it turned out) that the students would not be able to takeover any airport. There was another advantage. Granada had kindly suggested that they would pay my fare, thus saving the very poor IMG the burden of raising the money.

On the Lufthansa flight to Karachi, Gus Macdonald prepared his crew for emergencies. My head was full of wild thoughts. If my reading of the situation in Pakistan was correct, the state was confronting its most grave crisis. Neither the army nor the police had succeeded in crushing the revolt and the casualty lists indicated the seriousness of the enterprise. People were prepared to die for land, bread, socialism and democracy. The problem was that the traditional left had succeeded in discrediting itself completely. The Maoists had over the past three years ceased to oppose the Ayub regime because it had developed friendly relations with China. Ayub had visited Peking and met Mao and other Chinese leaders who had, for cynical reasons of real-politik, welcomed the Field Marshal as an 'anti-imperialist', which had amused him greatly. The pro-Moscow left had tied itself to the apron-strings of explicitly bourgeois parties who were wedded to achieving power, without social change. As a result the new political party formed by Z. A. Bhutto, the Pakistan People's Party, was leading the mass opposition. Bhutto himself had been locked up in prison for a few months. His leading lieutenant was J. A. Rahim, the former Ambassador to Paris, who had drafted the Party manifesto.

I thought back on that flight to the time when Bhutto had rung me up in London and invited me to dinner. I had forgotten the first time, which annoyed him greatly, but he had rung again and the second time I had gone to have lunch with him at Claridges. J. A. Rahim had also been present and I had told Bhutto of our lunch when Rahim had proposed disposing of Ayub. He had laughed a great deal and teased Rahim, but then both men became serious and we retired to Bhutto's room for a conversation. Here Rahim had handed me the typewritten first manifesto of the Pakistan People's Party and asked me to read it there and then, sign it and become a founding member of the Party. I had read the document rapidly and then declined the offer. 'Why? Why?' Bhutto had shouted. 'What else do you want?' I had pointed out two serious shortcomings. The first was a failure to separate religion from the state as the country's founder, M. A. Jinnah, had proposed, and as some parties, such as the National Awami Party and the Awami League of Mujibur Rehman, actually practised. Secondly, I had argued that a half-way house on the economic front would satisfy nobody. It would raise the expectations of the oppressed without being able to satisfy their needs and would simultaneously antagonize Pakistan's capitalists. Rahim had begun to agree with me, stating that he had favoured such a course but Bhutto had instructed him to moderate the statement. Bhutto took my criticisms very well, at least on that occasion, but he would not budge on fundamentals. 'Our biggest problem is going to be these bloody mullahs', he had argued. 'Your purism would have me go into battle with one arm tied behind my back.' I had responded by insisting that it was he who was playing into the hands of the mullahs by resorting to meaningless formulae such as 'Islamic socialism'. The mullahs would hit back by screaming that he was a *kafir* for mentioning socialism and Islam in the same breath and he would then be forced to hire scribes to discover hidden meanings in the Quran. 'If you do this,' I told him, 'you will end up by fighting the war on a battlefield that the mullahs have chosen. And then *they* will win.' Rahim nodded more when I was speaking, but kept silent while the argument raged. In the end we parted amicably, but without either of us having convinced the other. This had been in 1966.

Two years later as the plane circled over Karachi, I debated whether I should have joined and fought from within, but rejected the thought immediately. I had been right. The People's Party could not overthrow the state machine. As the plane landed, nervous tension gripped my stomach and I wondered whether or not they would let me in the country. The minute the immigration police saw my passport, they escorted me to the VIP room and asked me to wait. They were extremely polite. Gus MacDonald and crew hovered outside and finally came in to clandestinely film a senior police officer informing me that they were waiting for instructions from senior authorities. I cursed myself for not having informed the students of my arrival and even Gus agreed that it might have been more sensible. Finally, the permission came and I caught the next flight to Lahore. Two days later the Field Marshal relinquished his office, and handed over power to a military successor who pledged new elections within a year.

The movement had tasted blood and now the mood of the meetings became more radical. I embarked on a speaking tour of the country. As my plane was hovering above Rawalpindi, I looked out of the window and saw a large crowd assembled on the tarmac. The pilot told me that he could not land safely unless they moved back. He circled the airport for half an hour until the students were convinced that I was actually on the plane and agreed to vacate the landing strip. The plane had barely landed when they charged forward again. A few dozen of them clambered up the steps and garlanded me with what seemed like several hundred flower necklaces. Then as I finally got off the plane they lifted me on their shoulders and carried me triumphantly through the airport to the front of the building. Here there were more students and several dozen large lorries festooned with red flags and banners denouncing imperialism. I boarded one of these and we began the slow march to the city centre where a rally had been planned.

As the march progressed, I was truly amazed to see how large our entourage had become and, as if this was not enough, there were extended friendly waves and shouts from bystanders. As we went through the cantonment area lots of soldiers came to the perimeter and greeted me warmly. At times like this one is so overpowered with emotion that it is difficult, in a very literal sense, to think straight. I was, nonetheless, staggered at the size and warmth of the reception. I had thought that they would be ultra-nationalistic and resent my European activities, but in fact it was their nationalism which made them proud of the fact that one of them had become well known in Europe. A few weeks before I had arrived a large circulation, right-wing Urdu weekly had published a scurrilous attack on me, laced with anti-Semitism of the crudest variety. This dreadful magazine (like its Editor, now safely defunct) had manufactured a story involving me and the 'communist-Jew Cohn-Bendit' in a non-stop orgy in a large country house in France at some indeterminate time in the recent past. It was a swimming-pool extravaganza and both of us were accused of having fornicated with 'dozens of Jewish girls in one afternoon'. I was questioned about this in great detail by almost everyone I met. I used to get incredibly exasperated denying the story, but I was even more irritated to discover that my disavowal of this fiction was not taken seriously. A student leader then told me that far from damaging me, the tale had strengthened my image in the Punjab, where male virility is an important status symbol. It was the scale of the orgy that had impressed them and they pleaded with me not to deny it so angrily. They begged me for a more modest rejection.

As we approached the meeting place, I noticed an even larger crowd. Suddenly I felt a revolver against my ribs and froze. But it was only one of my student escorts telling me that they were armed and if the religious students made any attempt on my life they would not hesitate to shoot them dead. I had been warned that the right-wing students were going to present me with a copy of the Holy Book of Islam and my hosts were fearful that I might denounce this as a pro-vocation and call for a jihad against the religious maniacs. I promised not to do anything so foolish, but all they wanted was an assurance that if I did denounce religion I would warn them in advance since it might provoke a civil war on the streets of the city. I reassured them that I was not that out of touch with the country.

In my speech, I explained the worldwide revolt against United States imperialism, spoke about my trip to Vietnam and then on a softer note explained that we were in a pre-revolutionary crisis in Pakistan, but that problems lay with the lack of will on the part of the parties leading the revolt. This and other stray reflections were well received. Just as the meeting ended, a right-wing student leader clambered on to the platform. I handed him the microphone and he told the crowd that he was welcoming me to the city and presenting me with a copy of the Quran, which he then handed over to me. It was a tiny edition. I accepted it, thanked him for his thoughtfulness, put it in my top pocket and told the silent and tense crowd that I was looking forward to reading it again. A sigh of relief on the platform and the people relaxed. I did, however, wonder aloud as to why it was that those who treated the Quran as a divine monopoly in Pakistan, the Jamaat-i-Islami, were also on the payroll of the American embassy. This led to a loud roar of approval and chants of 'Death to the hired mercenaries', etc.

There were no clashes that day, but at two subsequent meetings in Multan and what was then Lyallpur, the Islamic gangs attacked our processions and were beaten off. In Multan the public rally was massive with tens of thousands of people. We had been stoned on the way by a few hundred Jamaat-i-Islami students. Everyone was angry and for once I lost my temper, pledging that we might have to avenge the deaths of the Indonesian left in Pakistan. It was a silly remark, but I did make it and the right-wing press used it as much as they could. The whole atmosphere was very different from much of Europe for in this situation one could smell power. That is what the struggle was about and the only party in West Pakistan in a position to take over the army was Bhutto and his People's Party. He had encapsulated his Party's manifesto in the slogan of 'Food, Clothing and Shelter' for everyone. He talked about expropriating the landed gentry and the urban rich and feeding the poor in town and countryside. The mullahs had denounced him fiercely inside and outside the mosques, but the radical appeal of his speeches coupled with the promise of social and economic reforms had neutered the men with beards. Their appeal, in any event, was always restricted to petty-bourgeois circles in the big towns. In the countryside, the mullah was not a greatly revered figure and Bhutto's proposed land reforms made the landlords tremble with fear.

I was invited to speak to Bar associations, to segregated assemblies in women's colleges, to doctors and medical students and to working-class meetings. The entire country seemed to be crying out for change, but before I could accurately estimate the possibilities I had to visit East Pakistan, the distant province of Bengal, separated from the West by a thousand miles of India. The majority of the population lived there, but the ruling classes, the bureaucrats and the senior army officers all belonged to West Pakistan. Bengal had been left to stagnate, treated like a colony and governed by proconsuls from the West. When I arrived in Dhaka, there was still hope that the rebellion would make the rulers in the West see sense; that a new harmonious and egalitarian structure could preserve the state of Pakistan, but here, too, the local Maoists had become isolated from the people and the forces of Bengali nationalism had been harnessed by Sheikh Mujibur Rehman and his Awami League. I had nicknamed him the Chiang Kai Sheikh of Bengal and when I met him for breakfast one day he referred to this and said: 'I have never pretended to be anything else. But your problem is that there is no Mao here. All the little Maos have been working with the military. They're finished.' Yet even Mujib would not talk about independence; all he wanted was his share of the cake. I told him that it was utopian to expect the bloated defence budget to be cut for Bengal. He said that I was 'too extreme'.

I was only in Dhaka for a few days, but it became very clear that this was a different world. Linguistically, culturally and politically it was a separate nation. Its oppression made it difficult not to become a separate state. And yet I felt much more at ease, intellectually and politically, in Dhaka than in Rawalpindi. The political culture was far more advanced. I spoke at a large student meeting underneath the famous Amtala tree on the campus of Dhaka University. They refused to let me speak in Urdu, a sure indicator of their anger against West Pakistan. The popular cry was 'English, English!' and even though one of the voices demanding this was that of Nicholas Tomalin of the *Sunday Times*, unmistakeable in the back row, I had to cave in to popular demand.

I spoke that afternoon of the struggle in Pakistan, but I went further and warned them that their demands for regional autonomy would never be conceded by the army. 'Rather than grant you that, they will crush you. The only serious option is independence. A Red Bengal could become the Yenan of our subcontinent.' These ideas had never been stated in this form in public and I felt the excitement of the

audience. Even the Awami League students were stunned. Was I not
after all a Punjabi? How could I talk in this fashion? But they recovered
soon and cheered me till they were hoarse. Afterwards I was mobbed
and the one question everyone wanted to discuss was how they could
achieve their goal. If, at that stage, the political leaders had realized the
holocaust that was to follow they could have politically armed their
supporters and prepared them for the inevitable civil war. When I left
Dhaka hundreds of students came to say farewell with clenched fists
and cries of 'Lal salaam!' ('Red salute') and invitations to come back,
but live in Dhaka. I had been thinking of returning permanently later
in the year and Dhaka did seem the ideal place, but would it still be
there?

I had to get back to Europe to attend the Ninth World Congress of
the Fourth International, but I promised to return soon. The World
Congress was the first real opportunity to meet like-minded comrades
from the rest of the world. The Fourth International (FI) was an
attempt to continue the work of the early Comintern and had been
founded by Trotsky in 1939, after the victories of Hitler and the
liquidation of the Old Bolsheviks by Stalin. As midnight had descended on Europe, Trotsky had decided to raise the flag of internationalism. It was this determination that had appealed to a small layer
of left communists repulsed by the purges and bloodbaths of Stalin. In a
private letter to a friend who wrote complaining that she was utterly
pessimistic (this was on the eve of the Second World War), Trotsky
replied:

> Indignation, anger, revulsion? yes, even temporary weariness. All this is
> human, only too human. But I will not believe that you have suc-
> cumbed to pessimism. This would be like passively and plaintively
> taking umbrage at history. How can one do that? 'History has to be
> taken as it is'; and when she allows herself such extraordinary and filthy
> outrages, one must fight her back with one's fists.

The formation of a new International – the first had disbanded, the
second had collapsed because of the First World War and the third had

become an instrument of Soviet foreign policy – was a bold step at a time when every stream was flowing in the opposite direction. Trotsky had thought that the outcome of the Second World War would split the Stalinist formations in Europe just as the first conflagration had split social-democracy. If he had been permitted to see the end of the war he would probably have altered his view, but he was assassinated on Stalin's orders in August 1940. One of his last predictions was to warn the USSR that Hitler was preparing Operation Barbarossa. Trotskyism had survived, but had been restricted to a handful of people in most countries. During the war they had suffered at the hands of both the Gestapo and Stalin. There are many, many stories of the courage which Trotskyists displayed in the face of repression and torture. One Greek Trotskyist intellectual made such a powerful speech to his firing squad of Italian soldiers that they refused to shoot. Finally they were disciplined and a few officers came and executed the veteran communist.

Repressed during the war and isolated in its aftermath, most of the groups retreated into a complacent and self-satisfied sectarianism, not dissimilar, in some ways, from the primitive Christian sects or the later Jesuits. In Pakistan I had been asked about Trotskyism and after my explanation a veteran cadre of the communist movement had laughed and said: 'We've got enough here already. We've got *Shias* and *Sunnis* and now you want to bring the *Wahhabis* in here as well ...' The *Wahhabis* are, in theory at least, an ultra-orthodox and puritanical Muslim sect.

Nonetheless the group around Ernest Mandel and Pierre Frank had, during the passive fifties, maintained the closest contact with reality and after 1968 they gained a great deal of support in Western Europe and Latin America. When I arrived at the Ninth World Congress in Rimini in 1969, the gathering was a strange mix of old and new in every sense. Mandel acted as a bridge both politically and gen- erationally between the veterans and the new recruits. The Congress itself was euphoric and registered the importance of 1968 in Europe, but failed to learn the lessons of Che's defeat in Bolivia. When one of Trotsky's secretaries from the United States, Joseph Hansen, had attempted to call a halt to the uncritical support of guerrilla war in that continent in order to reflect on the recent débâcle, he was denounced as a pessimist and his document was defeated. Hansen, however, was the only person from the American Socialist Workers Party to make any impression on me. Behind him was the new guard, which had taken over the organization. They struck me as apparatchiks pure and simple, obsessed with inner-party manipulations, factional intrigue and an unbelievable sectarian attitude towards everyone else on the American left. The SDS had won over the cream of American youth in the late sixties. The youth adjunct of the Socialist Workers Party had recruited the leftovers. Even these proved to be too independent as far as Hansen's successors were concerned and most of the '68 levy did not last long in their ranks. I now understood what so many SDSers had told me on their visits to London in 1967–68: 'If we were in Europe, we'd join with you, but in the States the SWP is unthinkable. It's bureaucratic and ultra-cautious in its approach ...' Of course some of the attacks were simple slanders, but there were more than two grains of truth and at that Congress I had to admit to myself that if I had been in Berkeley rather than Oxford I would not have joined this International.

When I had joined the IMG in Britain, I had been given a number of books to read by Ernie Tate and Pat Jordan. Most of these were a delight, but one had totally puzzled me and I wondered what I was meant to learn from its pages. This was a volume by an American communist turned Trotskyist: *The Struggle For a Proletarian Party* by James P. Cannon. I had not expected this to be a non-fiction version of Hemingway or Dos Passos, but the single-minded and relentless pursuit of an oppositional current within the same organization until it was defeated, demoralized and expelled, had shocked my sensibilities. I suppose I was far too naive and idealistic to appreciate this great work, which was, I later discovered, used as a 'key, cadre-building text' by the American SWP, the British SLL, and even the much-dreaded dogmatists of the Lambertist sect in France (they had distinguished themselves in France during May 1968 by advising everyone to stay away from the barricades). Cannon himself had been an impressive figure and he had played an important part in the big strike wave of the late thirties, but he had relied too exclusively on Trotsky to provide the theory and after the latter's assassination there were few intellectuals left inside the SWP. This was not all the SWP's fault, but they theorized the flight of the New York literati into an unfortunate anti-intellectualism. During Cannon's lifetime the disease was still controllable, but the second generation, whom I met in Rimini in 1969, seemed to be walking and talking parodies of Cannon. In the decades that followed they would adopt internal party norms that made them virtually indistinguishable from the Stalinism that they were supposed to be combating in every way. In this fashion the hopes and aspirations of thousands of young idealists were confiscated and crushed by men (and they were, in the main, men) whose control of tiny apparatuses – a printshop, a few dozen full-time workers, a building – gave them a power and authority which they shamelessly misused. It was a deadly virus. The only antidote to all this was mass activity, but when the movements receded, the disease gained ground rapidly and even organizations which had been relatively immune, including the one to which I belonged, were slightly infected.

I returned to Pakistan later that year and travelled throughout the country, interviewing politicians, trade unionists, peasant leaders, poets and students for a book that had been commissioned by Jonathan Cape. I had met Bhutto at his house in Karachi and he reproached me once again for not having joined forces with him. He was confident that he would win a big majority throughout the country. 'And then what?' I asked. He looked at me long and hard as our whisky glasses were replenished. Then as the amber liquid went down his throat he got a bit angry. 'The problem with you is that you're a purist. This is Pakistan. There are only two ways to fight. Like me or then there is Che Guevara. Great man. Why don't you go to the hills of Baluchistan like him and launch a bloody guerrilla war?' I refused to accept the dichotomy. I pointed out that the people were behind him in West Pakistan, but he had promised them fundamental change. If he did not deliver the consequences could be nasty. As we were talking a fat, ungainly youth walked into the garden. One of Bhutto's aides-decamp was sent by him to whisper the oaf's identity in my ear. It was the son of General Yahya Khan, then in command of the army and dictator of the country. Political discussion ceased. Yahya's son was complaining to Bhutto about a recent 'Letter from Pakistan' in the British satirical magazine *Private Eye*. My heart sank. I had written the 'Letter' and it contained a savage attack on the dictator and the imbecility of his offspring. Did this fool know I was the author? Evidently not, but Bhutto had noticed the look of panic on my face and his mischievous streak was uncontrollable: 'I don't know,' he said to Yahya junior, 'but Tariq here knows England well. Maybe he knows who wrote the article?' By this time I had recovered and so I suggested a possible author: the British High Commissioner in Islamabad. Bhutto roared with laughter but the corpulent son of a corpulent father took me quite seriously and said he would make further enquiries.

It was when I visited East Pakistan that I realized how close to coming to fruition were my 'prophecies' under the Amtala tree a few months previously. I travelled all over the countryside with the seventy-year-old peasant leader, Bhashani. We used to walk for miles every day and he would point out the similarities between the topography in Vietnam and parts of East Pakistan. East Bengal was on the verge of a major explosion and it was not difficult to see that the old state was on the verge of disintegration. I wrote as much in *Pakistan: Military Rule or People's Power?* The book was favourably received even in journals such as *The Economist*, but most reviewers in Britain and the United States were extremely sceptical of my assertion that a renewed military intervention in the East would result in an insurrection, civil war and the break-up of Pakistan. A year later that is exactly what happened.

The doubts were not confined to Asian scholars in the West. While in Pakistan I received an invitation to visit North Korea as a guest of the Korean Journalists' Union. I flew from Dhaka to Canton and then to Peking. The Chinese capital was in the last throes of the Cultural Revolution. I spent two days sightseeing and then went by train to Pyongyang. At one point a couple of Chinese army officers came into my compartment. When they heard I was from Pakistan they embraced me warmly. For, after all, General Yahya Khan, according to the Chinese mythology, was at the head of an 'anti-imperialist' regime. I soon disabused them of this illusion as I recounted what was happening in the country. They were shocked and left me soon afterwards.

At Chinese railway stations I had witnessed groups of school-children led by teachers bowing before giant portraits of Mao. It was a nauseating sight. A day and a half later the train crossed the Yalu river and I was in Kim-il-Sung's Korea. At the border station I was greeted by officialdom. A Korean interpreter asked whether I had had any problems in China. I said it had all gone smoothly and he then volunteered: 'The personality cult of Mao Zedong is bad.' I agreed, but I suddenly noticed that we were sitting below a life-size statue of Kim-il-Sung, the 'Great and Beloved Leader of 40 million Korean people'.

In Britain itself, the October '68 demonstration had represented the last big assembly of revolutionary forces. The failure of the left groups to transcend their own divisions and provide the levies of VSC with meaningful political activities led to a certain atomization and dispersal. The movement was visible in the continuing wave of student occupations, followed soon after by a spate of factory seizures by workers, which culminated in the historic 'work-in' by the workers of Upper Clyde Shipbuilders in Scotland and the victory of the miners in 1972. Nonetheless, the decline of the movement on the streets led to a debate amongst ourselves on the future of *The Black Dwarf*, which had been very dependent on the movement. I felt that the newspaper should begin to politically organize its readers. We had established some Black Dwarf Readers Groups and in Scotland they had attracted a group of young workers. A number of members of the editorial board had joined the IMG and others were sympathetic. I believed that the newspaper needed an organization to sustain it. Others, however, including Sheila Rowbotham, Clive Goodwin and Fred Halliday, felt that its independence from every left group should not be compromised. Ultimately, there was a split and those of us in or sympathetic to the IMG (this latter category included Neil Middleton and Chenhamo Chimutengwende) established *The Red Mole*. The actual scission was fairly civilized considering everything, but even though I had considered the break necessary, this did not totally banish the pain. Fred Halliday and Sheila Rowbotham were two people I had known since we were all together at university and, despite odd disagreements, I respected their work enormously. Clive Goodwin was a very close personal friend and he was extremely upset by the whole business. We did not speak to each other for several years, apart from saying 'hello' and exchanging ghost-like smiles at some demonstration or social gathering.

The Black Dwarf did not survive the break and collapsed a few months later. Its editors set up an excellent weekly called *Seven Days*, which was designed as a broad left intervention in politics and culture. This could have survived as an independent weekly, but it was mismanaged and the left lost another big opportunity to establish a magazine that would outlive the upsurge of the late sixties. *The Red Mole* continued for some years and then gave birth to *Red Weekly*, which later became *Socialist Challenge*. I was its first Editor and to my great delight Clive liked it so much that he started writing again and our friendship resumed. We talked frankly of the past and the hurt it caused both of us and we determined never to let this happen again. He had not changed at all and our daily conversations resumed, resulting in an astronomical increase in my phone bill. I wonder sometimes whether the Special Branch destroys tapes of conversations that it deems useless or keeps them safely in some archive. I hope the latter is the case because when all the files are one day opened they will constitute a magnificent treasure-trove.

Towards the last days of my *Black Dwarf* I had started receiving phone calls from John Lennon. He would ring me once or twice a month and talk about the state of the world. We had published a critique of his song 'Revolution' and Lennon had replied in very angry terms. In the Beatles versus Stones line-up at the time I was a partisan of Mick Jagger and not just because he marched with VSC. I preferred the music, though I did not agree with the critic Richard Merton who defended the narcissism of the Stones and justified their sexism by pretending that 'Under My Thumb', 'Stupid Girl', and 'Back Street Girl' were hymns designed to expose sexual exploitation. This was certainly a novel point of view, which Merton argued as follows:

> The enormous merit – and audacity – of the Stones is to have repeatedly and consistently defied what is a central taboo of the social system: mention of sexual inequality. They have done so in the most radical and unacceptable way possible: by celebrating it. The light this black beam throws on the society is too bright for it. Nakedly proclaimed, inequality is de facto denounced. The 'unmitigated triumph' of these records is their rejection of the spurious world of monadic personal relationships.

This was a bit like arguing that wife-battering, if carried out on the streets, would, in reality, be nothing more than a simple activity designed to raise feminist consciousness. Merton's craven apologia notwithstanding, the rhythm of the Stones' music captured the spirit of '68 much more than did that of the Beatles. I did not say all this to Lennon, but I did hint at it and he was shrewd enough to get the message. On one occasion I told him that I had hoped that he would come on the VSC demos and sing for us. 'But you know,' he replied, 'I didn't like the violence.' These conversations were open-ended, but one day when he and Yoko turned up at my tiny flat in North London with Japanese food, we talked into the early hours. He was a reader of *The Red Mole* and when I suggested that we interview him for the paper he agreed immediately, but wondered whether he was 'high-powered enough'. I suggested that Robin Blackburn, who had recently joined the IMG and was an editor of *The Red Mole*, might join us and he agreed. One morning his custom-built limousine arrived outside our offices and transported us to Lennon's large mansion in the country, Tittenhurst, near Windsor. We talked on tape for the best part of a day and returned exhausted. It had been a stimulating occasion and marked a shift in John Lennon's politics. The major influence on him was Yoko Ono. She introduced him to feminist concepts and the general reaction to her in British society made Lennon very aware of the chauvinist and racist poison which he insisted ran very deep in the ruling classes. He told us that 'I've always been politically minded ... and against the status quo. It's pretty basic when you're brought up, like I was, to hate and fear the police as a natural enemy and to despise the army as something that takes everybody away and leaves them dead somewhere ... I've been satirizing the system since my childhood ... I was very conscious of class, they would say with a chip on my shoulder.'

He had just finished writing 'Working Class Hero' and he read some of the verses, among the most radical that he was to compose. He was very critical of American rock groups for their failure to tackle the question of class and repeated many times what was then an obsession of the New Left, namely, the crucial importance of building links with workers: 'All the revolutions have happened when a Fidel or Marx or a Lenin or whatever, who were intellectuals, were able to get through to the workers. They got a good pocket of people together and the workers seemed to understand that they were in a repressed state. They haven't woken up here yet ... You should get these left-wing students out to talk with the workers, you should get the school-kids involved with *The Red Mole*.'

He was equally intransigent on the subject of women and acknowledged his debt openly: 'Of course Yoko was well into liberation before I met her. She'd had to fight her way through a man's world – the art world is completely dominated by men – so she was full of revolutionary zeal when we met. There was never any question about it: we had to have a fifty–fifty relationship or there was no relationship, I was quick to learn. She did an article about women in *Nova* more than two years back in which she said "Woman is the nigger of the world".'

After we had edited the interview into shape we took it to Abbey Road, where he was recording, and he interrupted a session to read it through and muttered about not understanding why we wanted to publish it in the first place.

It would be silly to pretend that our interview marked any decisive turning point. It was the period that had politicized John Lennon, but he had clearly been very pleased with our long session. The day after the interview he rang me up at *The Red Mole* and said: 'Look, I was so excited by the things we talked about that I've written this song for the movement, so you sing it when you march.' I expressed delight. 'Well,' he said, 'don't you want to hear it?' I said I was waiting. He had laughed and then 'Power to the People' was sung to me on the telephone. I said nothing, still trying to recover from the surprise. He asked: 'Well, what do you think?' I said it was an ideal marching song. It marked a shift from 'Revolution' in which he had stated: 'You say you want a revolution', and had ended by expressing his refusal to join it: 'Count me out.' In 'Power to the People', he started by saying 'We say we want a revolution/Better get it on right away', and went on to defend a socialist strategy, ending with an explicitly feminist verse which united the personal and the political:

> *I'm gonna ask you comrade and brother*
> *How do you treat your own woman back home*
> *She got to be herself*
> *So she can free herself*

John Lennon was, in fact, passing through the most radical phase of his life. He had seen a *Red Mole* special issue on the UCS (Upper Clyde Shipbuilders) work-in in Scotland. Our cover was a reprint of a 19th-century caricature of a fat, ugly, bloated capitalist confronting a strong, handsome and noble-looking worker. He loved that cover more than the convoluted articles on the inside and later showed it to Phil Spector and others at Tittenhurst. After he had finished *Imagine* he rang and asked Robin Blackburn and myself to come down for tea. They were making a video of *Imagine* and he wanted us to be filmed chatting to him.

That very day Régis Debray, freed from prison a month previously, turned up in London. He had come to *The Red Mole* offices, walked up the rickety stairs, seen a dusty poster with his image on it underlined with the slogan 'Libérez Régis Debray', smiled and taken it down. He had come to thank us for our support and talk about the changes in Europe. He had heard about '68 in his prison cell in Camiri and had wondered whether or not it had been that serious. Robin and I sat down with him in a transport café near Kings Cross station and described the movement. He was sceptical. Then he asked us: 'But why have you become Trotskyists? Why?' We explained our reasons, pointing out to him that theory and reality had come close together and Mandel's influence on us had been very strong. He muttered something about the 'greatness of Trotsky' and the 'smallness of the sects that claimed his heritage'. As time was short we asked Debray whether he wanted to accompany us to see Lennon. He was amazed that we mixed in such circles and as the Lennon limousine was cruising to Tittenhurst we tried once again to explain how the politics of the period had affected its culture as well, and on every level.

When we arrived, I told John who our guest was and he received him warmly. Then I took him aside and explained that this poor comrade had been locked up and tortured in a Bolivian prison and had been a friend of Che. That did the trick and Lennon warmed to him and they were filmed together. Listening to the tracks on *Imagine* for the first time was a pleasant surprise. The quality of the songs was extremely high and, fortunately, politics had not smothered art. Lennon had not done a Jean-Luc Godard. (The more recent work of Godard, when he embraced an ultra-radical world view heavily coloured by a European Maoism, had waged war against all artistic forms and conventions in the name of revolutionary politics. The result had been, at least as far as I was concerned, both a political and an aesthetic disaster.) Lennon's politics and music in *Imagine* were cemented together by artistic necessities. Other rock groups, most notably The Doors and Jefferson Airplane, sometimes insisted very loudly that rock equalled revolution. Lennon refused to accept that there was any natural equation between rock music and politics. In 'Working Class Hero', a track which I got him to play three times that afternoon, he reached the opposite conclusion. The working-class superstar was nothing but a convenient safety-valve for bourgeois society. Listening to that LP was very moving because the music and the songs were in a harmony and flowed out of Lennon's deeply-felt and often repressed personal experiences: oppression and neglect in childhood became transformed later into their obverse as he became naked Emperor of the Dream. These were Lennon's 'Songs of Experience', where childhood themes reinforced his political instincts.

A few months after this he rang to say that he and Yoko had decided to go and live in the United States. The reasons were personal. Yoko's child had been kidnapped by her former husband and she was desperate to find and reclaim her daughter. It proved to be an ill-fated decision. His own cult status and the nutty side of America (as observed by Patricia Highsmith and Wim Wenders) were bound to collide, even though no one could have predicted the form and manner of his tragic death. On the political level, he left Britain on the eve of the 1972 miners' strike, which inaugurated a shift in working-class perceptions and seriously worried the British ruling classes. In New York, Lennon met the yippy leaders, Jerry Rubin and Abbie Hoffman, whose remoteness from the working class was celebrated. The young miners who marched on Saltley Gates in Birmingham would have been far more satisfying to Lennon and, I am sure, he would have responded generously to their calls for solidarity.

It was a sign of the times that a number of universities were occupied during that strike and that the miners were offered the use of the facilities as long as the strike continued. I spoke to a large meeting of students and miners at the University of Essex in Colchester and got a rare feeling of real, rather than theoretical, unity of workers and the dwellers on the campuses. The mood was euphoric and the miners appeared confident of victory, which did indeed come a few weeks later. Wilson had been replaced by Edward Heath in 1970; workers who did not wish to strike against Labour had no qualms about dealing Heath a severe body-blow. It was the second miners' strike in 1974, however, which led to the fall of the Heath Government and laid the basis for the subsequent victory of Margaret Thatcher.

Robin Blackburn had breached left-wing convention and got married just as Heath was crumbling to the ground. At his wedding dinner, we had been simultaneously celebrating and berating him for this act of treachery. Clive Goodwin, in particular, was outraged that Blackburn had let the side down. The jollities were interrupted by the appearance of a late guest. This was young Mary Furness, who was full of the previous night's dinner party she had attended. She had been a guest of the Tennants in the country when, much to her surprise, the other guests were announced and the small gathering rose to bow before the Queen and her consort. Some minutes later Harold Macmillan arrived and dinner was served. What was interesting about the tales was that the conversation during dinner had been dominated by the miners' strike and the evil antics of Mick McGahey and Arthur Scargill. The monarch felt that civilization was approaching its demise, while her consort chimed in with suggestions as to how such a calamity could be averted. The reactions were similar to the panic felt by Queen Victoria when Europe was engulfed in the revolutions of 1848. Victoria had replied to a frightened letter from her uncle, the King of Belgium, thus: 'Since 24th February [date of the revolution in France] I feel an uncertainty in everything existing, which one never felt before. When one thinks of one's children, their education, their future – and prays for them – I always think and say to myself, "Let them grow fit for *whatever station* they may be placed in – *high or low*." This one never thought of before, but I *do* always now ...'

In reality, both Queens were being unduly pessimistic. At the Tennants' dinner, as Mary Furness told us that evening, it had been Harold Macmillan who had calmed the royal nerves by lecturing the assembled guests on British exceptionism: 'In our country we have a political pendulum', the shrewd old fox had said. 'It has moved very far to the left, but I already detect a movement back. Nothing to worry about Ma'am ...' Macmillan's pendulum was to move in the other direction soon and with a vengeance.

The period which opened up in 1967 was about to come to an end in Europe. The last uprising also came the closest to success. The overthrow of the *ancien régime* in Portugal was the direct result of radicalization in the armed forces. We were excited out of our minds. Most people thought that Spain would erupt first and none of the theoreticians of the European left had paid a great deal of attention to

Portugal. History took them completely by surprise. They failed to appreciate the effect of the colonial wars in Africa on the young conscripts from Lisbon, Oporto and the Alentejo, which had brought them into contact with radical ideas. They had read the manuals of Che Guevara and Mao after confiscating them from their guerrilla prisoners. That, coupled with the futility of the conflict, created the Armed Forces Movement which toppled the dictatorship. For a year Portugal was on the brink of a socialist revolution as soldiers and workers marched together in street demonstrations. Henry Kissinger wanted a destabilization programme put into effect, as had been carried out in Chile to topple Allende. In the coup that followed, 30,000 trade unionists, communists and socialists were massacred by General Pinochet. In Portugal, however, the army was split and therefore unreliable. Mario Soares and the Portuguese Socialist Party were able to derail the revolutionary process. Soares promised his supporters the overthrow of capitalism *coupled with* democracy. His radical opponents failed to understand that in order to win they had to show that they believed in a socialist democracy, not a one-party bureaucratic monstrosity on the Eastern European model. They could not evolve a viable socialist strategy, thus allowing Soares to monopolize the democratic banner.

We had demonstrated in London in 1973 against the visit of the then Portuguese dictator, Caetano, and I had been arrested outside Buckingham Palace with others for picketing an official banquet. In 1974–75 we built a solidarity movement with the Portuguese revolution, chanting 'No Chile in Portugal', which, as it turned out, was not the real danger at all. Ernest Mandel had addressed a very large meeting in Lisbon, reminding the Socialist Party of Saint-Just's formula in post-1789 France: 'Those who make the revolution halfway are only digging their own graves.' He had been wildly applauded, but Soares knew he held the winning card: the promise of socialism through democracy. In November 1975, a foolish attempt at a *putsch* by the far-left resulted in an inevitable defeat. There was no Lisbon Commune. Nor was there a Pinochet-style coup. What was missing in France, Italy and Portugal were carefully prepared goals which could capture and reflect popular enthusiasm while exploding the social order from within and demonstrating to millions of workers in struggle the reality of *socialist democracy*. It was impossible for the movements in advanced capitalist societies to make a *single* leap from a capitalist state to a socialist system. Lenin had built his party in specifically Russian conditions which he described as 'the gloom of the autocracy and the domination of the gendarmerie'. No group on the left succeeded, with the partial exception of the Italian far-left, in constructing new types of parties which reflected the societies in which we were functioning rather than Tsarist Russia. Even Portugal, where there had been a dictatorship, had preferred the certainties of parliamentary democracy to the jump in the dark with groups who themselves had differing conceptions on democracy. And yet the same year that saw the end of 1968 in Europe and North America also witnessed the liberation of Saigon and the final defeat of the United States. The seeds of Watergate were sown on the day that the United States lost a war for the first time in their entire history.

Late that year I went to collect my daughter, then almost three years old, from her grandmother's house in Ambleside in the Lake District. As we were waiting to get the morning train from Windermere to return to London, the guard on the platform smiled and said: 'Chilly morning isn't it.' My daughter had heard the catchword. She replied: 'No Chile in Portugal. No! No! No!' The bemused guard had just stared in amazement wondering what language the child spoke. It was, in its way, an appropriate epitaph to one of the stormiest phases in the postwar history of Europe and North America. In the other three continents the movements may have stopped for a pause, but could not afford a long rest. Too many lives were at stake. As 1975 came to an end I was banned from entering France, the United States, Thailand, Hong Kong and the Philippines. The Turkish regime had declared that Sartre, Russell, myself and a few others were 'mental and political degenerates' and should not be allowed to sully the soil of their country. General Reque Teran in Bolivia had told a leading British historian of the Andean republics that 'if we had realized who *he* [a reference to me] was when he was here, we would have killed him', which was a comforting demonstration of the General's disregard for the process of history. It did not occur to him that in 1967 I might not have been the person I became after 1968.

Chapter Eleven

Heretics and Renegades

In honoured poverty the voice did weave
Songs consecrate to truth and liberty —
Deserting these, thou leavest me to grieve,
Thus having been, that thou shouldst cease to be.

Shelley to Wordsworth, 1815

Twenty years after the political turbulence of the sixties, a surface calm appears to have enveloped the world of advanced capitalism. How could this have happened? Are not conditions worse now than they were two decades ago? Was it all real in the first place? Were we not the victims of our own illusions? Where have all the hopes and idealism generated during the sixties disappeared to?

These are not irrelevant questions, but many of those who raise them do not want any answers. The questions themselves contain a reply. Mocking the sixties became a European pastime in the late seventies and eighties. That was a small price to pay for our defeats. Many of the *flambée soixante huitards* of France felt so betrayed by history that they renounced their pasts. So it always was and shall always be.

Whenever the revolutionary tide has receded it has left behind its imprint, but also a great deal of flotsam and jetsam. Many erstwhile revolutionaries have, in periods of downswings and retreats, been transformed into their opposites. In his book *The Experience of Defeat*, Christopher Hill, the outstanding historian of the English Revolution of 1640, has written of how the last years of the Commonwealth and the Restoration led to a significant number of revolutionary ideologues, including some radical Levellers, making their peace with the exiled head of the Stuart dynasty on the continent. Milton remained solid, but some of his contemporaries found it difficult to ride against the wind. A similar process took place after 1789 in France, especially with Napoleon's assumption of power, and ex-Jacobins were transformed overnight into anti-Jacobins. Coleridge and Wordsworth were the most distinguished examples of this trend in Britain and the former went so far as to denounce a Bill for the prevention of cruelty to animals in the House of Commons as the 'strongest instance of legislative Jacobinism'. Isaac Deutscher pointed out in an essay reviewing *The God That Failed* – an explanation of their new world view by Koestler, Silone, Gide, Louis Fischer, Richard Wright and Stephen Spender – that 'our ex-communist, for the best of reasons, does the most vicious things. He advances bravely in the front rank of every witch-hunt. His blind hatred of his former ideal is leaven to contemporary conservatism. Not rarely he denounces even the mildest brand of the "welfare state" as "legislative Bolshevism" ... His grotesque performance reflects the impasse in which he finds himself. The impasse is not merely his – it is part of a blind alley in which an entire generation leads an incoherent and absentminded life.' Most, if not all, of the editors of the Reaganite American magazine *Commentary* were the radicals of preceding generations.

In France, ten years after May 1968, a new group emerged and took over the cultural and analytical pages of *Le Monde*. These were the 'new philosophers' whose leading lights consisted of former Stalinists and Maoists who had savagely denounced all attempts in the past to settle accounts once and for all with the legacy of Stalin. In the late seventies they suddenly discovered the Gulags and the extent of the purges. Having refused to countenance any critique of Stalinism from the Marxist left, they now adopted the Slav nationalist, Solzhenitsyn, as their new guru. 'The Dante of our time', said Bernard-Henri Levy to wild acclaim, while André Glucksman, former 'friend of the people' and one-time theoretician of French Maoism, now stated that Marxism equalled the world of concentration camps. Stalin was seen as the only true Marxist and socialist. Not surprisingly the new philosophy made its biggest impact on the Western media. The publicity it received was without precedent. *Time* magazine developed a new interest in the French intelligentsia. Long articles were published in the *Sunday Times* and the *Observer* and there were several hundred interviews on American and European television. They said very little that was new or had not been said for many decades by magazines such as *Encounter*. What gave them an immediate value was their hatred of '68. Given that most of them were participants it was useful to have them denounce socialist 'illustrations' for all time in the future. Paris, once the beacon of the left, had by the early eighties become the capital of European Reaction. The combination of Mitterrand and the 'new philosophers' created an atmosphere which was far more viciously right-wing than Thatcher's Britain.

There were others in France, who were equally demoralized, but chose a different way out of the new crisis. They committed suicide. Nicos Poulantzas had become extremely depressed by the turn of events in Kampuchea. The bleakness of the horizon in France, coupled with the horrors unleashed by Pol Pot proved to be too much for this man, who had helped to build barricades in 1968 and had subsequently written a number of important works on the state. It was not necessary to agree with him in order to realize that he possessed a very fine brain. None of my close comrade-friends in France joined the queue waiting for the autographs of the 'new philosophers'. One of the main leaders of the JCR, Henri Weber, had, it is true, felt rebuffed and wasted by his own far-left organization. He first moved to yuppiedom and ended up as a close confidant of the Socialist Prime Minister of France, but just as he was on the verge of an electoral defeat. Weber, too, is now grateful that 'we did not seize power in '68', but where his journey will finally take him remains to be seen.

Régis Debray became an adviser to the French President Mitterrand. In this capacity I rang him one day at the Elysée Palace and suggested that since the ban on my entry to France was still in force, I would be grateful if this order was now rescinded. He was surprised that this was the case, but within a fortnight I received a message from the French embassy in London informing me that I was now free to travel to France. It would, however, be extremely subjective to read anything into this kindness. The sad fact was that the author of *Revolution In the*

Revolution, the man confined to a solitary cell in Camiri, had now become a prisoner of French nationalism. He toured Third World countries as an unofficial ambassador, helping to sell French Mirage jets and Exocet missiles to regimes whose budgets were grotesquely inflated by military expenditure. Debray defended French policies in Africa and the retention of the Bomb. He had become a pompous and shifty functionary of the French state. A friend who met him in Paris in May 1982 wrote that 'he was plump from banquets at the Palace, possibly also power'. After describing Debray's shameless justification of France's imperial pretensions in Africa, the same friend continued:

Asked what the Mitterrand regime had done at home to enthuse anyone for it. Answer from Debray: we don't want to enthuse anyone, we intend to construct something that will last . . . While I was leaving, Elizabeth [Debray's wife, who maintains her old political positions to this day] was showing him a little handwritten letter and evidently asking for his intercession in some matter. The air with which he half-registered and half pushed it away was indescribably, but infinitely official.

After his departure, Elizabeth told me that the letter was a request from a Bolivian writer who had helped and sheltered her when Régis was in Camiri, simply for a visa to come to France when a book of his was published there. This lot are terrible, she said, no better than their predecessors in the treatment of Latin Americans trying to get into the country. Their arrogance is frightful . . .

It was much easier to remain a heretic during this period than it had been, for instance, in the thirties. The victory of Hitler resulted in a pessimism even amongst those who were usually full of hope. The great German critic Walter Benjamin committed suicide at Port Bou on the Franco-Spanish border in September 1940 after he was told that he would be handed over to the Gestapo on the next day. His death, which his friend Brecht claimed was the 'first real loss Hitler had caused to German literature', had an extremely depressing effect on the playwright. He wrote on hearing of Benjamin's suicide:

> Tactics of attrition are what you enjoyed
> Sitting at the chess table in the pear tree's shade.
> The enemy who drove you from your books
> Will not be worn down by the likes of us.

One reason for Brecht's pessimism was his knowledge of what was taking place in Stalin's Russia. The purges had obliterated some of the finest military commanders of the Red Army, including the legendary Marshal Tukachevsky who, in a series of lectures to Soviet military strategists, had predicted the methods and style which the new Germany would use in the war that lay ahead.

The poet Mayakovsky, the theatrical innovator Meyerhold, the talented politician, Adolphe Joffe, had all committed suicide in the twenties. They had caught a glimpse of the Stalinist future and the sight was unbearable. In later years the dictator in the Kremlin would not afford too many people the chance of taking their own lives. Suicide came to be frowned upon as a luxury. Osip Mandelstam, the real heir of Pushkin, recited 'The Stalin Epigram' only amongst friends, but such was the power of the poem that it spread by word of mouth. For this 'crime' Mandelstam was killed, one of the many losses Stalin caused to Soviet literature. The message of the poem was simple:

> Our lives no longer feel ground under them.
> At ten paces you can't hear our words.
> But whenever there's a snatch of talk
> it turns to the Kremlin mountaineer,
> the ten thick worms his fingers,
> his words like measures of weight,
> the huge laughing cockroaches on his top lip,
> the glitter of his boot-rims.
>
> Ringed with the scum of chicken-necked bosses
> he toys with the tributes of half-men.
> One whistles, another meows, a third snivels.
> He pokes out his finger and he alone goes boom.

He forges decrees in a line like horseshoes,
One for the groin, one the forehead, temple, eye.
He rolls the executions on his tongue like berries.
He wishes he could hug them like big friends from home.

It was in those times that heresy meant death in large parts of Europe. What we have experienced over the last decade is a series of setbacks, which are far removed from the cataclysmic defeats inflicted by fascism. Economic crises have, as always, been accompanied by apolitical recession. The new reaction has, in the name of 'radicalism', begun the process of demolishing the gains embodied in the postwar reforms all over Western Europe and North America. Some leaders such as the semi-late President Reagan or Margaret Thatcher have attempted to make a virtue out of this by stating that ordinary people wanted to be rid of the state. Freedom from the welfare state, modernized public utilities and privatization of many services are presented as victories against centralized bureaucracy. Elsewhere, similar measures have been pushed through by social-democratic leaders such as Mitterrand in France, Gonzales in Spain or the radical populist Papandreaou in Greece. All this is extremely reprehensible, but it would be unbalanced to compare even the most right-wing regime in the West to fascism. In fact if one were to make an overall balance sheet it would be essential to stress that the senile successors of fascism have been replaced by more traditional bourgeois-democratic regimes in both Portugal and Spain while the pro-fascist regime of NATO torturers in Greece has given way to an elected government. The torture laboratory has been shifted to Turkey, which is the only country governed by a *de facto* military administration.

Of course times have changed. The politics of the sixties *appear* to be far more remote than a mere two decades and the wreckages of those individuals or political organizations who preferred to pretend that nothing had altered can be seen in a number of European cities. The post-'75 period was one of history's enforced pauses, designed to make us think and reflect before the next wave, whose pattern is as unpredictable as its timing. The conditions that will produce it are already present and one perceptive observer of the British scene has forecast, albeit in a work of fiction, a great deal of clandestine and subversive action by minorities. In his novel *The Volunteers*, Raymond Williams foresees the total evaporation of the Labour Party and the exercise of governmental power by a National Government. Mass resistance to Capital has become impossible. There are no longer any mass politics on the left and working-class militancy is limited to the regions. The left then turns to minority actions on the German and Italian models. Williams sketches a scenario which is a classic case of left adventurism. Questioned about this by the *New Left Review* he replied:

> *The Volunteers* plays out one set of consequences, if the British working class were contained into a local militancy, managed and by-passed and pretty thoroughly defeated by a repressive right-wing government. Then I think you would probably get violent clandestine actions. I wouldn't want them ... I didn't want to underwrite that model – call it terrorist if you will. But neither did I simply want to oppose it with the old pieties, because I don't think we can rely on them. The prospects, of course, could change.

Williams, even at his most pessimistic and that too in a novel, nonetheless tempers this view by not excluding the possibility of a sudden change in mass consciousness. It is an interesting fact that the heretics of Williams' generation have, by and large, retained their political beliefs and, in his own case, the passions that accompany them. As I write, I think of John Saville's seventieth birthday party given in his honour by Ralph Miliband and Marion Kozzack. It was a small gathering but it consisted largely of veterans. In his speech of thanks, Saville expressed an admirable intransigence, a refusal to accept that we have lost. He thanked his lifelong companion Constance: 'Every time I read some speech by Kinnock I say "Oh God! Isn't he awful. He's worse than Wilson", and Constance reminds me that I used to say that Wilson was worse than his predecessor and he was worse than Attlee and he was worse than ... [laughter and cheers for Constance].' Miliband himself remains a powerful exponent of socialist democracy. Christopher Hill, retired now as Master of Balliol, defends the socialist cause with a freshness that is as remarkable as it is rare.

Ernest Mandel was not at all pleased when I left the Fourth International. I was tired of endless factional struggles. I thought they had made a series of irreversible errors. The thought of waging another internal battle inside a small organization filled me with dread and despair. I withdrew without public recriminations. 'Your generation does not have our stamina', Mandel said to me in early 1987 after a dinner given in his honour by the *New Left Review*. Perhaps he is correct, but is it just a question of stamina? Mandel himself had become a militant at the age of sixteen in Belgium in 1939. Born of Jewish parents he had despaired at the inability of many right-wing Jewish organizations either to fight against or defeat Hitler. His father, Henri, had been a member of the German Communist Party and the young Mandel had read at an early age many old communist books. He had also seen the newer stuff annotated by his father with remarks in the margins. Usually it was a single word: 'Lies!' Thus Mandel was not attracted to the local Communist Party, but had joined a small group of Belgian Trotskyists, whose leader, Abram Leon wrote a classic work *On The Jewish Question*. The entire group became part of the Resistance. Leon was captured by the Gestapo and executed. Groups such as these were hated because they refused to treat all Germans as Nazis. Mandel's comrades regularly distributed propaganda in German to the soldiers explaining the bestiality of fascism and calling on them to desert. Mandel himself had been arrested twice by the Nazis. On the first occasion he had escaped. He was rearrested, 'tried' by a Nazi court and deported to a concentration camp in Germany in 1944. Earlier that year he had participated in the first European conference of the clandestine sections of the Fourth International. The Allied victory saved his life and that of many others. This experience was qualitatively different to anything experienced in 1968 in Western Europe. Perhaps it is this that explains the 'lack of stamina' in the West.

For me, however, the most depressing after-effects of 1968 were not related to politics. Rudi Dutschke died while having a bath at his home in Denmark. He had recovered from the old bullet wound, but doctors had warned him that there remained a danger of fainting fits and said that he should never have a hot bath without an attendant. Doctors say many things and since he had never fainted since the assassination attempt he ignored the advice. That day, however, he was tired, and he did faint. Death was painless and swift, but the loss was irreparable. I had met him a few months before he died at a conference in London where we were both speaking. I was leaving as he arrived, but we had stopped and embraced each other. Then he had insisted we have a talk and we had disappeared for a while to some café on High Holborn. 'And you?', he had asked, 'You are well? You are the same? You have not changed?' His enthusiasms were undiminished. We talked a great deal of Mandel who was a close friend and an influence on him. 'He is amazing', Dutschke had said, 'He never changes.' He made me promise to visit him in Denmark and was cross that I had not done so on my last trip to Copenhagen. His death left a void in Germany. How he would have appreciated the Green challenge and how his own views are expressed within its ranks.

There was an additional sad footnote to his death. The son of the German press magnate, Axel Springer, whose newspapers had persecuted Dutschke, had become a great admirer of the wounded student leader. When Dutschke was travelling abroad for treatment, Springer fils had sent generous donations for the 'children's clothes'. A short time after Dutschke's death, he committed suicide, having told friends that he did not feel that life had any more to offer. His father never really recovered from the shock.

Malcolm Caldwell died in the capital of Pol Pot's Kampuchea. He had been amongst a handful of Pol Pot's apologists in the West and I had argued with him on a number of occasions. He was due to meet the Kampuchean dictator a day before he was mysteriously gunned to death in the room of his guest-house. Was it a rival faction? We never found out and Pol Pot was overthrown soon afterwards.

The death that affected me most, however, and created a vacuum in my life was that of Clive Goodwin. He had rung me the day before he left for Los Angeles in 1977, asking whether I wanted anything, talking about 'the hell and heaven in one place' aspect of LA and promising to write another long article when he returned. He never came back. He had gone to negotiate with Warren Beatty on behalf of Trevor Griffiths. What was under dispute was Griffith's script for the film *Reds*. Clive was dressed in his normal style, which was a T-shirt and a pair of jeans, not the sort of attire encouraged by the management of the Beverley Wiltshire where Beatty had an apartment. Clive had completed his negotiations and was on his way out when he felt ill. He staggered to the toilets where he was sick. Then he fell. The management imagined that he was drunk and called the LA police rather than an ambulance. The cops took him to the Beverly Hills police station and locked him in a cell. My friend Clive was, in fact, suffering a cerebral haemorrhage. He died that night without receiving any medical treatment whatsoever. I was staying with friends in mid-Wales working on a book when Robin Blackburn rang and gave me the news. For two days I was paralysed with shock. I would disappear for long walks on my own, find a suitable place, sit and weep. For years afterwards I would lift the receiver and dial his number, quite unconsciously. The lost years when we had not met acquired an even greater poignancy.

Even if I had wanted to, I could not expunge Clive from my memory. He was born in Willesden, not far from Grunwick's Photoprocessing Factory which had been the scene of a militant strike in the year of his death. His last political act had been to join the mass pickets. His father was a waiter, dependent for a living on tips from the rich and in later years Clive would say that he too was dependent on tips – his ten per cent fees from his clients. As usual he was mocking himself, for he was a person of many talents. He had started life after conscription as an actor, playing Jimmy Porter in Osborne's *Look Back in Anger* in London and Yorkshire. He had helped to launch a cultural magazine, *Encore*, in the fifties, in which Pinter's *The Caretaker* was first published. His friendship with Ken Tynan had led to a collaboration which resulted in a radical arts magazine, *Tempo*, for Granada Television. *Tempo* was a success and specialized in introducing to the screen what John McGrath has referred to as 'exponents of a counter-ideology'. These included R.D. Laing, Joan Littlewood and Adrian

Mitchell. It was also on *Tempo* that British viewers first caught sight of a young Australian woman named Carmen Callil.

Before I knew him, Clive had married a young painter and socialist, Pauline Boty. His friends of that period have all told me that it was an extremely happy and intellectually stimulating union. When Pauline was pregnant, however, they discovered that she was suffering from leukaemia, and she died soon after the birth of her daughter, Boty Godwin. I don't think that Clive ever recovered emotionally from that blow. He talked about it to me on one occasion and I realized that the scars would always be there. Pauline's paintings remained in his Cromwell Road flat, serving as both a tribute to her talents and a permanent reminder.

His literary agency was not just a money-making machine. He realized the critical importance of television in late-capitalism and was determined that socialist playwrights had to get on to the small screen. He fought hard for them and writers and directors such as Denis Potter, Ken Loach, Jim Allen, Trevor Griffiths, Jack Gold, Snoo Wilson and Cherry Potter all owe him a debt.

It is ten years since Clive died, but the pain still remains. Nor am I the only one of his friends who feels this way; a number of us have talked about those qualities which still make him part of our lives. I missed him enormously in 1985 when I wrote a set of three plays for the BBC which the Head of Drama at Pebble Mill had already begun to cast before the Corporation got scared and shelved them. I had an imaginary conversation with Clive about the whole affair one morning as I was jogging around the circumference of Hampstead Heath.

I am often asked these days, by interlocutors of one sort or another, whether I have any regrets about the sixties. Would I rather, some of them enquire politely, prefer to forget it all and concentrate exclusively on the present? It is a question that never fails to irritate. Whether my questioners realize it or not, their queries are not really about the past, but the future. I regret nothing. Many mistakes were made by individuals (including myself) and collectives. There was a great deal about that period which was shrouded in mysticism and fantasy. The dominant theme, however, was a passionate belief that we needed a new world. How can one possibly believe anything different today? No Orwellian nightmare has gripped the globe. The lessons of Vietnam have not been totally forgotten, except by Hollywood, and, despite repeated attempts by the White House to encourage and induce a political amnesia, a large majority of the population of the United States remains opposed to direct military intervention against the Sandinista Republic of Nicaragua. The Reagan administration's policy of portraying a collection of gangsters, cocaine pedlars and torturers of the *ancien régime* in Nicaragua as freedom-fighters has backfired badly. The *New Yorker* magazine pointed out in a shrewd editorial that just as Watergate was the punishment inflicted on Nixon for the mess in Indochina, Irangate was the price paid by Reagan for his Nicaraguan policies.

A sizeable proportion of Europeans, both East and West, are hostile to the nuclear arms race. They do not want their continent to be used as a testing ground for new and more devastating weaponry. This view has found its most dramatic political expression in the German Greens, but the success of the latter has had a tremendous impact inside the German Social Democratic Party. I do not think that we are today on the edge of a new '68, but a change in mood is perceptible all over Europe. One reason for this is the collapse of the Reaganite model in the United States, but an even more powerful spectre is beginning to haunt the European powers. Its name is Mikhail Gorbachev.

During the fifties and sixties there were uprisings in favour of socialist democracy in East Germany, Hungary, Poland, Czechoslovakia and then Poland again in the eighties. With the exception of Poland, they were all crushed by Soviet tanks. But whose tanks will topple Gorbachev? The reform programme of the Soviet leaders currently in power represents the most advanced set of proposals for the democratization of the USSR since the twenties. The West is nervous, but the real irony lies in the fact that outside the Soviet Union the main opposition to the Gorbachev reforms comes from the decrepit old men who were placed in power by Soviet tanks: Honecker in East Berlin, Kadar in Budapest and Husak in Prague. They are soiling their pants in fear lest Gorbachev is successful. For then the dam will overflow and their own populations will rise and demand that what is good for the Soviet Union is also good for them. Ever since the defeats in Prague and Warsaw, oppositionists in Eastern Europe have been despondent. Many of them, having fought and lost, were engulfed by a sense of hopelessness. They were not prepared to risk sacrificing their lives again only to be crushed by the Soviet bureaucracy. In private they admitted that the only lasting basis for change lay in some movement inside the Soviet Union.

Who could have predicted with certainty that such a strong reforming thrust would emerge from within the top layers of the Communist Party of the Soviet Union? Was not this party, from top to bottom, a totally degenerate collection of time-servers and bureaucrats? A parasitic excrescence? A corpse? The late Isaac Deutscher was the only left theoretician who was convinced that sooner or later a genuine reformist current would emerge from within this party. Gorbachev was foreseen by Deutscher. One hopes that the Soviet leader will soon repay the compliment by publishing Deutscher's monumental histories in the USSR. It is, of course, always possible that he might not succeed. The countervailing pressures are strong, but the Soviet population is unlikely to tolerate a reversion to Brezhnevite corruption, let alone Stalinist barbarism. The process begun by Gorbachev might be completed by others, but at least it has begun. Gorbachev reflects the hopes of a people long denied elementary freedoms. We have still to see whether he will confiscate or fulfil their aspirations, but it is difficult to remain unmoved by the changes announced every day in Moscow.

In the face of this forward march of history, despite all the detours and retreats, how can one hide behind a mask of passivity or cynicism? Very few of the people I have discussed in this book have become renegades. Many of them, it is true, are not now members of any political organization, but whenever we meet it is a reunion of heretics. I met Ralph Schoenman in Los Angeles in December 1986. He was exactly the same as I remembered him twenty years previously. He told me in his inimitable fashion of how his attempts to arrange a Peace March from Jerusalem to Tel Aviv had been frustrated by various individuals and organizations. He had lined up prominent intellectuals of Jewish origin from North America to show their hostility to the expansionist policies of Israel. As a result Schoenman was now barred from entering Israel. 'I think', he said with a proud grin, 'I'm the only Jew not allowed into Israel apart from one well-known Mafia chieftain.' To my great regret I forgot to question him about David Horowitz, once a leading Marxist scholar and co-editor of *Ramparts*, and now a supporter of Reagan's foreign policy and an unabashed defender of capitalism.

There are others as well. Henri Weber is now a permanent fixture in the boudoir of Fabius, the former French Prime Minister, and mocks his own past. Pat Jordan remained solid as only he could until he was cruelly felled by a stroke while speaking at a political meeting. He is paralysed on one side. He can still read and communicate. He has not lost the will to live. Robin Blackburn and Perry Anderson are still editing the *New Left Review* and we meet regularly at meetings of its Editorial Committee. Since the Bolivian days, Anderson has produced four amazing books on the history of the Ancient World and Marxism and his reputation is higher than ever before. Blackburn is completing his life's work, a history of slavery in the New World and the forces that eventually swept it aside.

The German poet, Erich Fried, who fled Austria after the Anschluss and sought exile in Britain, has made this country his base. Fried is in the great German tradition of political satire and is widely regarded as the heir of Heine and Brecht. He is in *his* sixties, but he still defends *our* sixties. We talk occasionally of times past and present and Erich, despite three cancer operations, continues to be optimistic and appears far more youthful than the 'young fogeys' of contemporary politics. In February 1987 we met and talked about Rudi Dutschke and the phenomena of renegacy. The French, Chinese and Spanish students had taken to the streets again and, though it was a different mood than that of '68, they had scored some victories.

'How can they give up so quickly?' he wondered aloud, talking about the mercurial behaviour of the French intelligentsia which symbolized the worst excesses of the retreat from the ideals of '68.

Erich Fried is now treated as the greatest living poet writing in the German language. His poems circulate widely in Germany, crossing the Berlin Wall with ease and he draws large audiences in both parts of the country. In the autumn of 1986, he told me, he had been invited to a prestigious literary salon in Paris. Hundreds of *glitterati* were present. Fried had composed a poem especially for this occasion, which had been translated into exquisite French under his supervision. He recited it to me in German and then translated it for me into English. I raced against him to get it all down in my notebook. The poem was entitled, 'A Prayer For the Left' and this is what Fried read to me that afternoon.

Dear God in whom I still do not believe,
Perform once again a miracle
Because it is high time
Or better still a few miracles simultaneously
(Because one alone would already be too little)
And help these god-forsaken French intellectuals
That at long last it should become fashionable amongst them
Not to have to go in for every intellectual fashion.

Help them to lose the stylistic momentum
Which turns them in a split-second
From heretics that are good and necessary
Into miserable renegades
Help them not to be blinded
By the splendour of their brilliant formulations
So that they no longer notice the poverty of the contents.
And, let them not play the devil's advocate so well
That they grow horns and cloven hooves
And only at the back a long tail!

Have them recognize that no argument in the world,
Can be so clever as to make forgivable snobbism, arrogance and racism
For example anti-Semitism or anti-Arabism.

And that all justified criticisms of the stupidities, crimes and mistakes of
the Left
Cannot by any stretch of the imagination, justify a turn to reaction
Because the direction in which the Right marches or slides
Is no way out for France and the world.

Help them to see
Even if Marchais obstructs their sight
That Gorbachev is not the same as Stalin
And that however horrible the débâcle of Afghanistan is,
It still remains idiotic and a crime,
To simply shout Afghanistan or Gulag when one speaks of Nicaragua
Or South Africa.
And to believe that thereby anything has been achieved.

Help them, dear God, before it is too late,
To see that even the most elegant way of licking the arse of
Reagan or Weinberger
Can be no substitute for the naive search
For some way to save human beings
And to save the world

'And', I asked, 'the reaction after you finished?' Had they hurled
wine glasses at him, called him a scoundrel, a dupe, a knave, an old fool
and then walked out? 'No,' replied Fried, 'much to my surprise many
of them applauded very enthusiastically.'

History has not yet given us her final verdict on the century that is
approaching its end. Most of the world is passing through bad times,
but however fragile and precarious the advances that have been made
sometimes seem, hope itself cannot be abandoned.

An Open Letter to John Lennon

Dear John

So they've done you after all. I didn't think they ever would.
It's a nasty experience, and I offer you my sympathy, for what
it's worth. But I hope you won't be depressed about it. In fact I
hope this experience will help you understand certain things
that you seemed a bit blind to before. (That sounds patronising
But I can't think how else to put it . . .)

Above all: perhaps now you'll see what it is you're (we're)
up against. Not nasty people Not even neurosis, or spiritual
undernourishment. What we're confronted with is a repressive,
vicious, authoritarian <u>system</u>. A system which is inhuman and
immoral, because it deprives 99% of humanity of the right to
live their lives their own way. A system which will screw you if
you step out of line and behave just a tiny bit differently from
the way those in power want.

Such a system – such a society – is so racked by contradiction
and tension and unhappiness that all relationships within it
are poisoned. You <u>know</u> this. You know, from your own experience, how little control over their lives working-class people
are permitted to have. You know what a sick, evil, and brutal-
ising business it is to be a 'success' in this kind of rat-race.
How can love and kindness between human-beings grow in such a
society? It can't. Don't you see that now? The <u>system</u> has got to
be changed before people can live the full, loving lives that
you have said you want.

Now do you see what was wrong with your record 'Revolution'?
That record was no more revolutionary than Mrs. Dale's Diary.
In order to change the world we've got to understand what's
wrong with the world. And then – destroy it. Ruthlessly. This

is not cruelty or madness. It is one of the most passionate forms of love. Because what we're fighting is suffering, oppression, humiliation – the immense toll of unhappiness caused by capitalism. And any 'love' which does not pit itself against these things is sloppy and irrelevant.

There is no such thing as a polite revolution. That doesn't mean that violence is always the right way, or even that you should necessarily turn up on the next demonstration. (There are other ways of challenging the system. But it does mean understanding that the privileged will do almost anything – will murder and torture and destroy, will foster ignorance and apathy and selfishness at home and will burn children abroad – rather than hand over their power.

What will you do when Apple is as big as Marks and Spencers, and one day its employees decide to take it over and run it for themselves? Will you let them get on with it? Or will you call in the police – because you are a business-man, and Business-Men Must Protect Their Interests?

One last thing. You've written some marvellous, honest, beautiful music. (And it's an indication of the weird effect capitalism has had on you that you felt it was necessary to pretend that in doing so you were only conning people.) But recently your music has lost its bite. At a time when the music of the Stones has been getting stronger and stronger. Why? Because we're living in a world that is splitting down the middle. The split is between the rich and the poor, the powerful and the powerless. You can see it here, and in the jungles of Vietnam, and in the mountains of South America, and in the ghettos of the U.S. and in the Universities all over the world. It's the great drama of the second half of the twentieth century – the battle for human dignity fought by the exploited and the underprivileged of the world. The Stones, helped along a bit by their experiences with the law, have understood this and they've understood that the life and authenticity of their music – quite apart from their personal integrity – demanded that they take part in this drama – that they refuse to accept the system that's fucking up our lives. You did it for a bit when you were taking acid – the only time in your career when you stepped outside the cheeky chappy slot the establishment had slid you in to, and the time when your music was at its best. But they didn't bust you (Why not, John?), and the way was open for you to come to represent not rebellion, or love, or poetry, or mysticism, but Big Business . . .

But after all, they still hate you, even if you are a company director. They hate you because you act funny and because you're working-class (in origin at least) and you're undisciplined and you weren't in the army and, above all, you've been going out with a foreigner. So now it's happened.

As I said before, don't be too upset about it. In an unjust and corrupt society there is no dishonour in being arrested, and certainly none of us on the left are going to think any the worse of you for it.

But learn from it, John. Look at the society we're living in, and ask yourself: why? And then – come and join us.

Yours fraternally,
John Hoyland

A Very Open Letter to John Hoyland from John Lennon

Dear John,

Your Letter didn' t sound patronising – it was. Who do you think
you are? What do you think you know? I' m not only up against the
establishment but you, too, it seems. I *know* what I' m up
against – narrow minds – rich/poor. All your relationships may
be poisoned – it depends how you look at it. What kind of system
do you propose and who would run it?

 I don' t remember saying Revolution was revolutionary – fuck
Mrs Dale. Listen to all three versions (Revolution 1, 2 and 9)
then try again, dear John. You say 'In order to change the world
we' ve got to understand what' s wrong with the world. And then –
destroy it. Ruthlessly.' You' re obviously on a destruction
kick. I' ll tell you what' s wrong with it – People – so do you
want to destroy them? Ruthlessly? Until you/we change your/our
heads – there' s no chance. Tell me of one successful revolution. Who fucked up communism – christianity – capitalism –
buddhism, etc? Sick Heads, and nothing else. Do you think all
the enemy wear capitalist badges so that you can shoot them?
It' s a bit naive, John. You seem to think it' s just a class war.

 Apple was never intended to *be* as big as Marks and Spencers –
our only reference to it was to get the kind of deal we used to
get from this nasty capitalist shop when we were downtrodden
working class students and bought a sweater or something which
was reasonably cheap and lasted. We set up Apple with the money
we as workers earned, so that we could control what we did
productionwise, as much as we could. If it ever gets taken over
by other workers, as far as I' m concerned, they can have it.

 When I say we con people – I mean we' re selling dreams.

Friends of mine like Dylan and Stones, etc who are doing *their* bit would understand what I said – ask them – then work it out.

The establishment never slotted us into a 'cheeky chappy' bag, dear John – WE DID – to get here to do what we' re doing now. I was there, you weren' t. So suddenly the papers told you we were taking acid – two years after the event! So you decided that our music was best then. You' re probably right about why they didn' t bust me before – they, like you, had me 'tagged'. I' ll tell you something – I' ve been up against the same people all my life – I *know* they still hate me. There' s no difference now – just the size of the game has changed. Then it was school masters, relatives, etc – now I' m arrested or ticked off by fascists or brothers in endless fucking prose.

Who' s upset about the arrest? OK. I' ll have a cup of tea. I don' t worry about what you – the left – the middle – the right or any fucking boys' club think. I' m not that *bourgeois*.

Look man, I was/am not against you. Instead of splitting hairs about the Beatles and the Stones – think a little bigger – look at the world we' re living in, John, and ask yourself: why? And then – come and join *us*.

Love,
John Lennon
PS – You smash it – and I' ll build around it.

'Power to the People!'

JOHN LENNON and YOKO ONO

talk to ROBIN BLACKBURN and TARIQ ALI

T.A. *Your latest record and your recent public statements, especially the interviews in* Rolling Stone *magazine, suggest that your views are becoming increasingly radical and political. When did this start to happen?*

J.L. I've always been politically minded, you know, and against the status quo. It's pretty basic when you're brought up, like I was, to hate and fear the police as a natural enemy and to despise the army as something that takes everybody away and leaves them dead somewhere. I mean, it's just a basic working-class thing, though it begins to wear off when you get older, get a family and get swallowed up in the system. In my case I've never not been political, though religion tended to overshadow it in my acid days; that would be around '65 or '66. And that religion was directly the result of all that superstar shit – religion was an outlet for my repression. I thought, 'Well, there's something else to life, isn't there? This isn't it, surely?' But I was always political in a way, you know. In the two books I wrote, even though they were written in a sort of Joycean gobbledegook, there's many knocks at religion and there is a play about a worker and a capitalist. I've been satirizing the system since my childhood. I used to write magazines in school and hand them around. I was very conscious of class, they would say with a chip on my shoulder, because I knew what happened to me and I knew about the class repression coming down on us – it was a fucking fact but in the hurricane Beatle world it got left out – I got farther away from reality for a time.

T.A.   *What did you think was the reason for the success of your sort of music?*

J.L.   Well, at the time it was thought that the workers had broken through, but I realise in retrospect that it's the same phoney deal they gave the blacks, it was just like they allowed blacks to be runners or boxers or entertainers. That's the choice they allow you – now the outlet is being a popstar, which is really what I'm saying on the album in *Working Class Hero*. As I told *Rolling Stone*, it's the same people who have the power, the class system didn't change one little bit. Of course there are a lot of people walking around with long hair now and some trendy middle-class kids in pretty clothes. But nothing changed except that we all dressed up a bit, leaving the same bastards running everything.

R.B.   *Of course, class is something the American Rock groups haven't tackled yet.*

J.L.   Because they're all middle class and bourgeois and they don't want to show it. They're scared of the workers, actually, because the workers seem mainly right-wing in America, clinging on to their goods. But if these middle-class groups realise what's happening, and what the class system has done, it's up to them to repatriate the people and to get out of all that bourgeois shit.

T.A.   *When did you start breaking out of the role imposed on you as a Beatle?*

J.L.   Even during the Beatle heyday I tried to go against it, so did George. We went to America a few times and Epstein always tried to waffle on at us about saying nothing about Vietnam. So there came a time when George and I said 'Listen, when they ask next time, we're going to say we don't like that war and we think they should get right out.' That's what we did. At that time this was a pretty radical thing to do, especially for the 'Fab Four'. It was the first opportunity I personally took to wave the flag a bit. But you've got to remember that I'd always felt repressed. We were all so pressurized that there was hardly any chance of expressing ourselves, especially working at that rate, touring continually and always kept in a cocoon of myths and dreams. It's pretty hard when you are Caesar and everyone is saying how wonderful you are and they are giving you all the goodies and the girls, it's pretty hard to break out of that, to say 'Well, I don't want to be king, I want to be real.' So in it's way the second political thing I did was to say 'The Beatles are bigger than Jesus.' That really broke the scene, I nearly got shot in America for that. It was a big trauma for all the kids that were following us. Up to then there was this unspoken policy of not answering delicate questions, though I always read the papers, you know, the political bits. The continual awareness of what was going on made me feel ashamed I wasn't saying anything. I burst out because I could no longer play that game any more, it was just too much for me. Of course, going to America increased the build up on me, especially as the war was going on there. In a way we'd turned out to be a Trojan Horse. The Fab Four moved right to the top and then sang about drugs and sex and then I got into more and more heavy stuff and that's when they started dropping us.

R.B. *Wasn't there a double charge to what you were doing right from the beginning?*

Yoko You were always very direct...

J.L. Yes, well, the first thing we did was to proclaim our Liverpoolness to the world, and say 'It's all right to come from Liverpool and talk like this.' Before, anybody from Liverpool who made it, like Ted Ray, Tommy Handley, Arthur Askey, had to lose their accent to get on the BBC. They were only comedians but that's what came out of Liverpool before us. We refused to play that game. After the Beatles came on the scene everyone started putting on a Liverpudlian accent.

T.A. *In a way you were even thinking about politics when you seemed to be knocking revolution?*

J.L. Ah, sure, *Revolution*. There were two versions of that song but the underground left only picked up on the one that said 'count me out'. The original version which ends up the LP said 'count me in' too; I put in both because I wasn't sure. There was a third version that was just abstract, musique concrète, kind of loops and that, people screaming. I thought I was painting in sound a picture of revolution – but I made a mistake, you know. The mistake was that it was anti-revolution. On the version released as a single I said 'when you talk about destruction you can count me out'. I didn't want to get killed. I didn't really know that much about the Maoists, but I just knew that they seemed to be so few and yet they painted themselves green and stood in front of the police waiting to get picked off. I just thought it was unsubtle, you know. I thought the original communist revolutionaries coordinated themselves a bit better and didn't go around shouting about it. That was how I felt – I was really asking a question. As someone from the working class I was always interested in Russia and China and everything that related to the working class, even though I was playing the capitalist game. At one time I was so much involved in the religious bullshit that I used to go around calling myself a Christian Communist, but as Janov says, religion is legalized madness. It was therapy that stripped away all that and made me feel my own pain.

R.B. *This analyst you went to, what's his name . . .*

J.L. Janov . . .

R.B. *His ideas seem to have something in common with Laing in that he doesn't want to reconcile people to their misery, to adjust them to the world but rather to make them face up to its causes?*

J.L. Well, his thing is to feel the pain that's accumulated inside you ever since your childhood. I had to do it to really kill off all the

religious myths. In the therapy you really feel every painful moment of
your life – it's excruciating, you are forced to realize that your pain, the
kind that makes you wake up afraid with your heart pounding, is really
yours and not the result of somebody up in the sky. It's the result of
your parents and your environment. As I realised this it all started to fall
into place. This therapy forced me to have done with all the Godshit.
All of us growing up have come to terms with too much pain.
Although we repress it, it's still there. The worst pain is that of not
being wanted, of realizing your parents do not need you in the way
you need them. When I was a child I experienced moments of not
wanting to see the ugliness, not wanting to see not being wanted. This
lack of love went into my eyes and into my mind. Janov doesn't just
talk to you about this but makes you feel it – once you've allowed
yourself to feel again, you do most of the work yourself. When you
wake up and your heart is going like clappers or your back feels
strained, or you develop some other hang-up, you should let your
mind go to the pain and the pain itself will regurgitate the memory
which originally caused you to suppress it in your body. In this way the
pain goes to the right channel instead of being repressed again, as it is if
you take a pill or a bath, saying 'well, I'll get over it'. Most people
channel their pain into God or masturbation or some dream of making
it. The therapy is like a very slow acid trip which happens naturally in
your body. It is hard to talk about, you know, because you feel 'I am
pain' and it sounds sort of arbitrary, but pain to me now has a different
meaning because of having physically felt all these extra-ordinary
repressions. It was like taking gloves off, and feeling your own skin for
the first time. It's a bit of a drag to say so, but I don't think you can
understand this unless you've gone through it – though I try to put
some of it over on the album. But for me at any rate it was all part of
dissolving the Godtrip or father-figure trip. Facing up to reality instead
of always looking for some kind of heaven.

R.B.   *Do you see the family in general as the source of these repressions?*

J.L.   Mine is an extreme case you know. My father and mother split and I never saw my father until I was twenty, nor did I see much more of my mother. But Yoko had her parents there and it was the same . . .

Yoko Perhaps one feels more pain when parents are there. It's like when you're hungry, you know it's worse to get a symbol of a cheeseburger than no cheeseburger at all. It doesn't do you any good, you know. I often wish my mother had died so that at least I could get some people's sympathy. But there she was, a perfectly beautiful mother.

J.L. And Yoko's family were middle-class Japanese but it's all the same repression. Though I think middle-class people have the biggest trauma if they have nice imagey parents, all smiling and dolled up. They are the ones who have the biggest struggle to say, 'Goodbye mummy, Goodbye daddy'.

T.A. *What relation to your music has all this got?*

J.L. Art is only a way of expressing pain. I mean the reason Yoko does such far-out stuff is that it's a far-out kind of pain she went through.

R.B. *A lot of Beatle songs used to be about childhood . . .*

J.L. Yeah, that would mostly be me . . .

R.B. *Though they were very good there was always a missing element . . .*

J.L. That would be reality, that would be the missing element. Because I was never really wanted. The only reason I am a star is because of my repression. Nothing else would have driven me through all that if I was 'normal' . . .

Yoko . . . and happy . . .

J.L.   The only reason I went for that goal is that I wanted to say: 'Now, mummy-daddy, will you love me?'

T.A.   *But then you had success beyond most people's wildest dreams . . .*

J.L.   Oh, Jesus Christ, it was a complete oppression. I mean we had to go through humiliation upon humiliation with the middle classes and showbiz and Lord Mayors and all that. They were so condescending and stupid, everybody trying to use us. It was a special humiliation for me because I could never keep my mouth shut and I'd always have to be drunk or pilled to counteract this pressure. It was really hell . . .

Yoko   It was depriving him of any real experience, you know . . .

J.L.   It was very miserable. I mean apart from the first flush of making it – the thrill of the first number one record, the first trip to America. At first we had some sort of objective like being as big as Elvis – moving forward was the great thing, but actually attaining it was the big let-down. I found I was having continually to please the sort of people I'd always hated when I was a child. This began to bring me back to reality. I began to realize that we are all oppressed which is why I would like to do something about it, though I'm not sure where my place is.

R.B.   *Well, in any case, politics and culture are linked, aren't they? I mean, workers are repressed by culture not guns at the moment . . .*

J.L.   . . . they're doped . . .

R.B.   *And the culture that's doping them is one the artist can make or break . . .*

J.L.   That's what I'm trying to do on my albums and in these interviews. What I'm trying to do is to influence all the people I can influence. All those who are still under the dream and just put a big question mark in their mind. The acid dream is over, that is what I'm trying to tell them.

R.B. *Even in the past, you know, people would use Beatle songs and give them new words. Yellow Submarine for instance had a number of versions. One that strikers used to sing began 'We all live on bread and margarine', at LSE we had a version that began 'We all live in a Red LSE'.*

J.L. I like that. And I enjoyed it when football crowds in the early days would sing *All Together Now* – that was another one. I was also pleased when the movement in America took up *Give Peace a Chance* because I had written it with that in mind really. I hoped that instead of singing *We Shall Overcome* from 1800 or something, they would have something contemporary. I felt an obligation even then to write a song that people would sing in the pub or on a demonstration. That is why I would like to compose songs for the revolution now . . .

R.B. *We only have a few revolutionary songs and they were composed in the nineteenth century. Do you find anything in our musical traditions which could be used for revolutionary songs?*

J.L. When I started, Rock and Roll itself was the basic revolution to people of my age and situation. We needed something loud and clear to break through all the unfeeling and repression that had been coming down on us kids. We were a bit conscious to begin with of being imitation Americans. But we delved into the music and found that it was half white Country and Western and half black rhythm and blues. Most of the songs came from Europe and Africa and now they were coming back to us. Many of Dylan's best songs came from Scotland, Ireland or England. It was a sort of cultural exchange. Though I must say the more interesting songs to me were the black ones because they were more simple. They sort of said shake your arse, or your prick, which was an innovation really. And then there were the field songs mainly expressing the pain they were in. They couldn't express themselves intellectually so they had to say in a very few words what was happening to them. And then there was the City blues and a lot of that was about sex and fighting. A lot of this was self-expression but only in the last few years have they expressed themselves completely with Black Power, like Edwin Starr making War records. Before that many black singers were still labouring under that problem of God, it was often 'God will save us'. But right through the blacks were singing directly and immediately about their pain and also about sex, which is why I like it.

R.B. *You say Country and Western music derived from European folk songs. Aren't these folk songs sometimes pretty dreadful stuff, all about losing and being defeated . . .?*

J.L. As kids we were all opposed to folk songs because they were so middle class. It was all college students with big scarfs and a pint of beer in their hands singing folk songs in what we call la-di-da voices – "I worked in a mine in New-cast-le" and all that shit. There were very few real folk singers you know, though I liked Dominic Behan a bit and there was some good stuff to be heard in Liverpool. Just occasionally you hear very old records on the radio or TV of real workers in Ireland or somewhere singing these songs and the power of them is fantastic. But mostly folk music is people with fruity voices trying to keep alive something old and dead. It's all a bit boring like ballet, a minority thing kept going by a minority group. Today's folk song is Rock and Roll. Although it happened to emanate from America, that's not really important in the end because we wrote our own music and that changed everything.

R.B. *Your album, Yoko, seems to fuse avant-garde modern music with Rock. I'd like to put an idea to you I got from listening to it. You integrate everyday sounds, like that of a train, into a musical pattern. This seems to demand an aesthetic measure of everyday life, to insist that art should not be imprisoned in the museums and galleries, doesn't it?*

Yoko   Exactly, I want to incite people to loosen their oppression by giving them something to work with, to build on. They shouldn't be frightened of creating themselves – that's why I make things very open, with things for people to do, like in my book [*Grapefruit*]. Because basically there are two types of people in the world: people who are confident because they know they have the ability to create, and then people who have been demoralised, who have no confidence in themselves because they have been told they have no creative ability, but must just take orders. The Establishment likes people who take no responsibility and cannot respect themselves.

R.B.   *I suppose workers' control is about that . . .*

J.L.   Haven't they tried out something like that in Yugoslavia, they are free of the Russians. I'd like to go there and see how it works.

T.A.   *Well, they have, they did try to break with the Stalinist pattern. But instead of allowing uninhibited workers' control, they added a strong dose of political bureaucracy. It tended to smother the initiative of the workers and they also regulated the whole system by a market mechanism which bred new inequalities between one region and another.*

J.L.   It seems that all revolutions end up with a personality cult – even the Chinese seem to need a father-figure. I expect this happens in Cuba too with Che and Fidel ... In Western-style communism we would have to create an almost imaginary workers' image of *themselves* as the father-figure.

R.B.   *That's a pretty cool idea – the Working Class becomes its own Hero. As long as it was not a new comforting illusion, as long as there was a real workers' power. If a capitalist or bureaucrat is running your life then you need to compensate with illusions . . .*

Yoko   The people have got to trust in themselves.

T.A. *That's the vital point. The working class must be instilled with a feeling of confidence in itself. This can't be done just by propaganda – the workers must move, take over their own factories and tell the capitalists to bugger off. This is what began to happen in May 1968 in France ... the workers began to feel their own strength.*

J.L. But the Communist Party wasn't up to that, was it?

R.B. *No, they weren't. With ten million workers on strike they could have led one of those huge demonstrations that occurred in the centre of Paris into a massive occupation of all government buildings and installations, replacing De Gaulle with a new institution of popular power like the Commune or the original Soviets – that would have begun a real revolution but the French CP was scared of it. They preferred to deal at the top instead of encouraging the workers to take the initiative themselves ...*

J.L. Great ... but there's a problem about that here you know. All the revolutions have happened when a Fidel or Marx or Lenin or whatever, who were intellectuals, were able to get through to the workers. They got a good pocket of people together and the workers seemed to understand that they were in a repressed state. They haven't woken up here yet, they still believe that cars and tellies are the answer. ... You should get these left-wing students out to talk with the workers, you should get the school-kids involved with *The Red Mole*.

T.A. *You're quite right, we have been trying to do that and we should do more. This new Industrial Relations Bill the Government is trying to introduce is making more and more workers realise what is happening ...*

J.L. I don't think that Bill can work, I don't think they can enforce it, I don't think the workers will co-operate with it. I thought the Wilson Government was a big let-down but this Heath lot are worse. The underground is being harassed, the black militants can't even live in their own homes now, and they're selling more arms to the South

Africans. Like Richard Neville said there may be only an inch of difference between Wilson and Heath but it's in that inch that we live ...

T.A. *I don't know about that; Labour brought in racialist immigration policies, supported the Vietnam war and were hoping to bring in new legislation against the unions.*

R.B. *It may be true that we live in the inch of difference between Labour and Conservative but so long as we do we'll be impotent and unable to change anything. If Heath is forcing us out of that inch maybe he's doing us a good turn without meaning to ...*

J.L. Yes, I've thought about that, too. This putting us in a corner so we have to find out what is coming down on other people. I keep on reading the *Morning Star* [the communist newspaper] to see if there's any hope, but it seems to be in the nineteenth century; it seems to be written for dropped-out middle-aged liberals. We should be trying to reach the young workers because that's when you're most idealistic and have least fear. Somehow the revolutionaries must approach the workers because the workers won't approach them. But it's difficult to know where to start, we've all got a finger in the dam. The problem for me is that as I have become more real, I've grown away from most working-class people; you know what they like is Engelbert Humperdinck. It's the students who are buying us now, and that's the problem. Now the Beatles are four separate people, we don't have the impact we had when we were together ...

R.B. *Now you're trying to swim against the stream of bourgeois society, which is much more difficult ...*

J.L. Yes, they own all the newspapers and they control all distribution and promotion. When we came along there was only Decca, Philips and EMI who could really produce a record for you. You had to go through the whole bureaucracy to get into the recording studio.

You were in such a humble position, you didn't have more than twelve hours to make a whole album, which is what we did in the early days. Even now it's the same, if you're an unknown artist you're lucky to get an hour in a studio – it's a hierarchy and if you don't have hits, you don't get recorded again. And they control distribution. We tried to change that with Apple but in the end we were defeated. They still control everything. EMI killed our album *Two Virgins* because they didn't like it. With the last record they've censored the words of the songs printed on the record sleeve. Fucking ridiculous and hypocritical – they have to let me sing it but they don't dare let you read it. Insanity.

R.B.   *Though you reach fewer people now, perhaps the effect can be more concentrated.*

J.L.   Yes, I think that could be true. To begin with, working-class people reacted against our openness about sex. They are frightened of nudity, they're repressed in that way as well as others. Perhaps they thought 'Paul is a good lad, he doesn't make trouble'. Also when Yoko and I got married, we got terrible racialist letters – you know, warning me that she would slit my throat. Those mainly came from army people living in Aldershot. Officers. Now workers are more friendly to us, so perhaps it's changing. It seems to me that the students are now half-awake enough to try and wake up their brother workers. If you don't pass on your own awareness then it closes down again. That is why the basic need is for the students to get in with the workers and convince them that they are not talking gobbledegook. And of course it's difficult to know what the workers are really thinking because the capitalist press always only quotes mouthpieces like Vic Feather any-way. So the only thing is to talk to them directly, especially the young workers. We've got to start with them because they know they're up against it. That's why I talk about school on the album, I'd like to incite people to break the framework, to be disobedient in school, to stick their tongues out, to keep insulting authority.

Yoko We are very lucky really, because we can create our own reality, John and me, but we know the important thing is to communicate with other people.

J.L. The more reality we face, the more we realize that unreality is the main programme of the day. The more real we become, the more abuse we take, so it does radicalize us in a way, like being put in a corner. But it would be better if there were more of us.

Yoko We mustn't be traditional in the way we communicate with people – especially with the Establishment. We should surprise people by saying new things in an entirely new way. Communication of that sort can have a fantastic power so long as you don't do only what they expect you to do.

R.B. *Communication is vital for building a movement, but in the end it's powerless unless you also develop popular force.*

Yoko I get very sad when I think about Vietnam where there seems to be no choice but violence. This violence goes on for centuries, perpetuating itself. In the present age when communication is so rapid, we should create a different tradition, traditions are created every day. Five years now is like a hundred years before. We are living in a society that has no history. There's no precedent for this kind of society so we can break the old patterns.

T.A. *No ruling class in the whole of history has given up power voluntarily and I don't see that changing.*

Yoko But violence isn't just a conceptual thing, you know. I saw a programme about this kid who had come back from Vietnam – he'd lost his body from the waist down. He was just a lump of meat, and he said, 'Well, I guess it was a good experience.'

J.L.   He didn't want to face the truth, he didn't want to think it had all been a waste...

Yoko   But think of the violence, it could happen to your kids...

R.B.   *But Yoko, people who struggle against oppression find themselves attacked by those who have a vested interest in nothing changing, those who want to protect their power and wealth. Look at the people in Bogside and Falls Road in Northern Ireland; they were mercilessly attacked by the special police because they began demonstrating for their rights. On one night in August 1969 seven people were shot and thousands driven from their homes. Didn't they have a right to defend themselves?*

Yoko   That's why one should try to tackle these problems before a situation like that happens.

J.L.   Yes, but what do you do when it does happen, what do you do?

R.B.   *Popular violence against their oppressors is always justified. It cannot be avoided.*

Yoko   But in a way the new music showed things could be transformed by new channels of communication.

J.L.   Yes, but as I said, nothing really changed.

Yoko   Well, something changed and it was for the better. All I'm saying is that perhaps we can make a revolution without violence.

J.L.   But you can't take power without a struggle...

T.A.   *That's the crucial thing.*

J.L.   Because when it comes to the nitty-gritty they won't let the people have any power, they'll give all the rights to perform and to dance for them, but no real power...

Yoko   The thing is, even after the revolution if people don't have any trust in themselves, they'll get new problems.

J.L.   After the revolution you have the problem of keeping things going, of sorting out all the different views. It's quite natural that revolutionaries should have different solutions, that they should split into different groups and then reform, that's the dialectic, isn't it – but at the same time they need to be united against the enemy, to solidify a new order. I don't know what the answer is; obviously Mao is aware of this problem and keeps the ball moving.

R.B.   *The danger is that once a revolutionary state has been created, a new conservative bureaucracy tends to form around it. This danger tends to increase if the revolution is isolated by imperialism and there is material scarcity.*

J.L.   Once the new power has taken over they have to establish a new status quo just to keep the factories and trains running.

R.B.   *Yes, but a repressive bureaucracy doesn't necessarily run the factories or trains any better than the workers could under a system of revolutionary democracy.*

J.L.   Yes, but we all have bourgeois instincts within us, we all get tired and feel the need to relax a bit. How do you keep everything going and keep up revolutionary fervour after you've achieved what you set out to achieve? Of course Mao has kept them up to it in China, but what happens after Mao goes? Also he uses a personality cult. Perhaps that's necessary, like I said, everybody seems to need a father figure. But I've been reading *Khrushchev Remembers* – I know he's a bit of a lad himself – but he seemed to think that making a religion out of an individual was bad – that doesn't seem to be part of the basic communist idea. Still, people are people, that's the difficulty. If we took over Britain, then we'd have the job of cleaning up the bourgeoisie and keeping people in a revolutionary state of mind.

T.A. *A personality cult is totally alien to Marxism, which is about ideas . . . Marx, Lenin and Trotsky were always against it and so was Mao to begin with but then he found it politically useful to use it to break the grip of the Liu Shao Chi group on the Party. I was in China briefly last year and it was obvious that the cult of Mao had got out of hand. Of course Mao is quite different from Stalin – Mao led a revolution while Stalin betrayed one. But that doesn't mean that there aren't serious weaknesses in the Chinese Revolution. During the Cultural Revolution some very interesting criticisms were developed by Red Guard groups in Shanghai and elsewhere – they insisted on discussing the real issues much more openly than they were being encouraged to . . .*

J.L. The Cultural Revolution seems to have been instigated by Mao himself, wasn't it? There was no national feeling 'Well, there are too many opportunists and too much apathy.'

T.A. *A revolutionary leadership is necessary and one that trusts the masses, but in China the leadership stopped the Cultural Revolution as well as starting it.*

R.B. *Clearly the Cultural Revolution was a very bold step despite the limits set on it. Mao felt in a position to take it partly because the popular participation in the Chinese Revolution, built up over twenty years of people's war, was much deeper than it could be in Russia where the old order almost collapsed of itself under the tremendous strain of the First World War. Mao couldn't have instigated the masses against the Party bureaucracy unless he was confident of their support. But of course the decisive thing is to build popular power right into the heart of the new revolutionary state. In Britain unless we can create a new popular power – and here that would basically mean workers' power – really controlled by, and answerable to, the masses, then we couldn't make the revolution in the first place. Only a really deep-rooted workers' power could destroy the bourgeois state.*

Yoko   That's why it will be different when the younger generation takes over.

J.L.   I think it wouldn't take much to get the youth here really going. You'd have to give them free rein to attack the local councils or to destroy the school authorities, like the students who break up the repression in the universities. It's already happening, though people have got to get together more. And the women are very important too, we can't have a revolution that doesn't involve and liberate women. It's so subtle the way you're taught male superiority. It took me quite a long time to realise that my maleness was cutting off certain areas for Yoko. She's a red-hot liberationist and was quick to show me where I was going wrong, even though it seemed to me that I was just acting naturally. That's why I'm always interested to know how people who claim to be radical treat women.

R.B.   *There's always been at least as much male chauvinism on the left as anywhere else – though the rise of women's liberation is helping to sort that out.*

J.L.   It's ridiculous. How can you talk about power to the people unless you realize the people is both sexes.

Yoko   You can't love someone unless you are in an equal position with them. A lot of women have to cling to men out of fear or insecurity, and that's not love – basically that's why women hate men . . .

J.L.   . . . and vice versa . . .

Yoko   So if you have a slave around the house, how can you expect to make a revolution outside it? The problem for women is that if we try to be free, then we naturally become lonely, because so many women are willing to become slaves, and men usually prefer that. So you always have to take the chance 'Am I going to lose my man?' It's very sad.

J.L.   Of course Yoko was well into liberation before I met her. She'd had to fight her way through a man's world – the art world is completely dominated by men – so she was full of revolutionary zeal when we met. There was never any question about it: we had to have a fifty–fifty relationship or there was no relationship, I was quick to learn. She did an article about women in *Nova* more than two years back in which she said 'Woman is the nigger of the world'.

R.B.   *Of course we all live in an imperialist country that is exploiting the Third World, and even our culture is involved in this. There was a time when Beatle music was plugged on Voice of America . . .*

J.L.   The Russians put it out that we were capitalist robots which we were I suppose . . .

R.B.   *They were pretty stupid not to see it was something different.*

Yoko   Let's face it Beatles was twentieth-century folksong in the framework of capitalism, they couldn't do anything different if they wanted to communicate within that framework.

R.B.   *I was working in Cuba when* Sergeant Pepper *was released and that's when they first started playing rock music on the radio.*

J.L.   Well I hope they see that Rock and Roll is not the same as Coca Cola. As we get beyond the dream this should be easier, that's why I'm putting out more heavy statements now and trying to shake off the teeny-bopper image. I want to get through to the right people, and I want to make what I have to say very simple and direct.

R.B.   *Your latest album sounds very simple to begin with, but the lyrics, tempo and melody build up into a complexity one only gradually becomes aware of. Like the track* Mummie's Dead *echoes the nursery song 'Three Blind Mice' and it's about a childhood trauma.*

J.L.   The tune does, it was that sort of feeling almost like a Haiku poem. I just recently got into Haiku in Japan and I just think it's fantastic. Obviously, when you get rid of a whole section of illusion in your mind you're left with great precision. Yoko was showing me some of these Haiku in the original. The difference between them and Longfellow is immense. Instead of a long flowery poem the Haiku would say '*Yellow flower in white bowl on wooden table*' which gives you the whole picture, really.

T.A.   *How did you find Japan?*

J.L.   I think it's ripe for communism, I mean the workers have terrible conditions there and many unions are just run by the big companies They're building factories coast to coast and the smog is dreadful, it chokes you. It's all bullshit about them doing so well in Japan. The workers in different countries have got to get together. What's your position on the Common Market? The *Morning Star* is against it but I'm not sure at all. The feeling I have is that it would be a conglomeration of capitalist Europe but that the movement of workers throughout Europe would bring them together so that it could consolidate communism as well as capitalism I think.

T.A.   *We should work for a united workers' Europe, a Socialist United States of Europe, a Red Europe . . .*

J.L.   It is fantastic to think of the power workers could have with the Italians and Germans together and all that gear.

T.A.   *How do you think we can destroy the capitalist system here in Britain John?*

J.L.   I think only by making the workers aware of the really unhappy position they are in, breaking the dream they are surrounded by. They think they are in a wonderful free-speaking country, they've got cars and tellies and they don't want to think there's anything more to life, they are prepared to let the bosses run them, to see their children fucked up in school. They're dreaming someone else's dream, it's not even their own. They should realize that the blacks and the Irish are being harassed and repressed and that they will be next. As soon as they start being aware of all that, we can really begin to do something. The workers can start to take over. Like Marx said, 'To each according to his need' – I think that would work well here. But we'd also have to infiltrate the army too, because they are well trained to kill us all. We've got to start all this from where we ourselves are oppressed. I think it's false, shallow, to be giving to others when your own need is great. The idea is not to comfort people, not to make them feel better but to make them feel worse, to constantly put before them the degradations and humiliations they go through to get what they call a living wage.

Index